Litigating Transnational Human Rights Obligations

Human rights have traditionally been framed in a vertical perspective with the duties of States confined to their own citizens or residents. Obligations beyond this territorial space have been viewed as either being absent or minimalistic at best. However, the territorial paradigm has now been seriously challenged in recent years in part because of the increasing awareness of the ability of States and other actors to impact human rights far from home both positively and negatively. In response to this awareness various legal principles have come into existence setting out some transnational human rights obligations of varying degrees. However, notwithstanding these initiatives, judicial institutions and adjudicating bodies continue to show an enormous hesitancy in moving beyond a territorial reading of international human rights law.

This book addresses the issue in an innovative and challenging way by crafting legally sound hypothetical "judgments" from a number of adjudicatory fora. The judgments are based on real world situations where extraterritorial or transnational issues have emerged, and draw on existing international human rights law, albeit a progressive interpretation of this law. The book shows that there are a number of judicial and quasi-judicial systems where transnational human rights claims can, and should be enforced. These include: the World Trade Organization; the International Court of Justice; the regional human rights monitoring bodies; domestic courts; and the UN treaty bodies. Each hypothetical judgment is accompanied by detailed commentary placing it in context in order to show how international human rights law can address issues of a transnational character.

The book will be of interest to human rights scholars and lawyers, practitioners, activists and aid officials.

Mark Gibney is the Belk Distinguished Professor at University of North Carolina Asheville. Since 1984, Gibney has directed the Political Terror Scale (PTS), which measures levels of physical integrity violations in more than 185 countries (politicalterrorscale.org).

Wouter Vandenhole holds the UNICEF Chair in Children's Rights at the Faculty of Law of the University of Antwerp (Belgium) and is the Co-Director of the Law and Development Research Group.

Routledge Research in Human Rights Law

Available titles in this series include:

The Right to Development in International Law
The Case of Pakistan
Khurshid Iqbal

Global Health and Human Rights
Legal and Philosophical Perspectives
John Harrington and Maria Stuttaford

The Right to Religious Freedom in International Law
Between Group Rights and Individual Rights
Anat Scolnicov

Emerging Areas of Human Rights in the 21st Century
The Role of the Universal Declaration of Human Rights
Marco Odello and Sofia Cavandoli

The Human Right to Water and its Application in the Occupied Palestinian Territories
Amanda Cahill

International Human Rights Law and Domestic Violence
The Effectiveness of International Human Rights Law
Ronagh McQuigg

Human Rights in the Asia-Pacific Region
Towards Institution Building
Hitoshi Nasu and Ben Saul

Human Rights Monitoring Mechanisms of the Council of Europe
Gauthier de Beco

The Positive Obligations of the State under the European Convention of Human Rights
Dimitris Xenos

Vindicating Socio-Economic Rights
International Standards and Comparative Experiences
Paul O'Connell

The EU as a 'Global Player' in Human Rights?
Jan Wetzel

Regulating Corporate Human Rights Violations
Humanizing Business
Surya Deva

The UN Committee on Economic, Social and Cultural Rights
The Law, Process and Practice
Marco Odello and Francesco Seatzu

State Security Regimes and the Right to Freedom of Religion and Belief
Changes in Europe Since 2001
Karen Murphy

The European Court of Human Rights in the Post-Cold War Era
Universality in Transition
James A. Sweeney

The United Nations Human Rights Council
A Critique and Early Assessment
Rosa Freedman

Children and International Human Rights Law
The Right of the Child to be Heard
Aisling Parkes

Litigating Transnational Human Rights Obligations
Alternative Judgments
Mark Gibney and Wouter Vandenhole

Forthcoming titles in this series include:

Jurisdiction, Immunity and Transnational Human Rights Litigation
Xiaodong Yang

Litigating Transnational Human Rights Obligations

Alternative Judgments

Edited by Mark Gibney and Wouter Vandenhole

The European Science Foundation (ESF) provides a platform for its Member Organisations to advance science and explore new directions for research at the European level. Established in 1974 as an independent non-governmental organisation, the ESF currently serves 78 Member Organisations across 30 countries.

LONDON AND NEW YORK

First published 2014
by Routledge
2 Park Square, Milton Park, Abingdon, Oxfordshire OX14 4RN

and by Routledge
711 Third Avenue, New York, NY 10017

Routledge is an imprint of the Taylor and Francis Group, an informa business

First issued in paperback 2015

© 2014 Mark Gibney and Wouter Vandenhole

The right of Mark Gibney and Wouter Vandenhole to be identified as editors of this work has been asserted by them in accordance with sections 77 and 78 of the Copyright, Designs and Patents Act 1988.

All rights reserved. No part of this book may be reprinted or reproduced or utilised in any form or by any electronic, mechanical, or other means, now known or hereafter invented, including photocopying and recording, or in any information storage or retrieval system, without permission in writing from the publishers.

Trademark notice: Product or corporate names may be trademarks or registered trademarks, and are used only for identification and explanation without intent to infringe.

British Library Cataloguing in Publication Data
A catalogue record for this book is available from the British Library

Library of Congress Cataloging-in-Publication Data
Litigating transnational human rights obligations : alternative judgements / Mark Gibney and Wouter Vandenhole.
pages cm. – (Routledge Research in Human Rights Law)
Includes bibliographical references and index.
ISBN 978-0-415-85811-3 (hbk) – ISBN 978-0-203-79747-1 (ebk) 1. Human rights.
I. Vandenhole, Wouter. II. Title.
K3240.G533 2014
342.08'5–dc23
2013020572

ISBN 978-0-415-85811-3 (hbk)
ISBN 978-1-138-63950-8 (pbk)
ISBN 978-0-203-79747-1 (ebk)

Typeset in ITC New Baskerville
by Cenveo Publisher Services

Contents

Preface		xi
List of Contributors		xiii

1 Introduction: Transnational Human Rights Obligations   1
WOUTER VANDENHOLE AND MARK GIBNEY

PART I
International Economic Governance Bodies   **11**

2 U.S. Trade Sanctions (World Trade Organization, Panel Report)   13
CLAIRE BUGGENHOUDT

3 Biofuels and the Right to Food (World Trade Organization, Panel Report)   31
ALEXIA HERWIG

4 Land Grabbing and Gender Issues (International Finance Corporation, Compliance Advisor Ombudsman)   49
JOSS SAUNDERS

PART II
Global (Human Rights) Monitoring Bodies   **61**

5 Putting an End to Victims Without Borders: Child Pornography (Committee on the Rights of the Child)   63
GAMZE ERDEM TÜRKELLI

6 Shared Responsibility for the Right to Health (Committee on Economic, Social and Cultural Rights)   79
RACHEL HAMMONDS AND GORIK OOMS

viii *Contents*

7 Economic, Social and Cultural Rights of the Purak Peoples
(Committee on Economic, Social and Cultural Rights)   99
JERNEJ LETNAR ČERNIČ

8 "Only the Little People Pay Taxes": Tax Evasion and
Switzerland's Extraterritorial Obligations to Zambia
(Committee on Economic, Social and Cultural Rights)   116
NICHOLAS J. LUSIANI

9 Labour Rights in a Transnational Perspective
(Committee on Economic, Social and Cultural Rights)   135
ARNE VANDENBOGAERDE

10 Climate Change (Human Rights Committee,
Ad Hoc Conciliation Commission)   155
MARGREET WEWERINKE

11 Development Assistance to Education for Children
with Disabilities (Committee on the Rights of
Persons with Disabilities)   172
WOUTER VANDENHOLE

12 Land Grabbing in Uganda by a Multinational Corporation
(World Court of Human Rights)   186
CHRISTOPHER MBAZIRA

13 Structural Adjustment and Farmers' Suicides in India
(International Court of Justice)   202
AMITA PUNJ

14 (Economic) Crimes Against Humanity
(International Criminal Court, Appeals Chamber)   221
MICHAEL WABWILE

PART III
Regional Human Rights Monitoring Bodies   237

15 Public Duties for Private Wrongs: Regulation of
Multinationals (African Commission on
Human and Peoples' Rights)   239
TAKELE SOBOKA BULTO

16 Forced Evictions in Zimbabwe (African Commission
on Human and Peoples' Rights)   261
KHULEKANI MOYO

Contents ix

17 **Land Grabbing in South America (Inter-American Human Rights Commission)** 283

ANA MARÍA SUÁREZ-FRANCO

18 **Enforcing Extraterritorial Social Rights in the Eurozone Crisis (European Committee of Social Rights)** 302

MATTHIAS SANT'ANA

19 **Military Interventions in Non-European States (European Court of Human Rights)** 325

NICO MOONS

PART IV
Domestic Courts 339

20 **Extraordinary Rendition (U.S. Supreme Court)** 341

MARK GIBNEY

Index 358

Preface

This edited volume has a long history. The first time the idea of writing an "Alternative Judgments" book on transnational human rights obligations came up was during a conference call in preparation for the 2008 Heidelberg meeting of the ETO Consortium – in full: the Extra-Territorial Obligations Consortium – which is a unique mixture of academics and members of non-governmental organizations (NGOs) who challenge the exclusively territorial basis of human rights. One of the things that the ETO Consortium has had to work against, and which was discussed, is that the territorial approach has been so dominant that finding counter-examples where human rights have been given a universal application has not been easy.

Both of us have written extensively on the spatial aspect of human rights and in much of this work we have sought to show how a strictly territorial approach to "universal" human rights leaves many vulnerable people without human rights protection. Both of us will certainly continue with this work, but we also wanted to offer something different. Above all, what we want to do is to show with various adjudicatory bodies that deal with human rights issues – the UN human rights treaty bodies, the International Court of Justice, the European Court of Human Rights, the Inter-American Court of Human Rights, the African Commission on Human and Peoples' Rights, the International Criminal Court, the World Trade Organization, domestic courts, and so on – how issues of extraterritoriality arise, but also the manner in which they could be addressed.

Each time we met after that, we reconfirmed our commitment to this idea. But it was at the May 2011 GLOTHRO conference in Antwerp, Belgium, that we actually launched the book project. The GLOTHRO stock-taking conference, held in conjunction with the 2011 ETO Consortium meeting, was organized by the Research Networking Programme 'Beyond Territoriality: Globalization and Transnational Human Rights Obligations' (GLOTHRO), and brought together scholars working on extraterritorial human rights obligations and on human rights obligations of actors other than the state. GLOTHRO receives financial support from the European xii *Preface*

Science Foundation, the European University Institute and the University of Antwerp.

The wealth of expertise at these two conferences made us confident about the viability of the current project, and soon thereafter we approached scholars about contributing to this volume. In May 2012, we had a meeting of the authors in Venice, Italy, which was hosted by the European Inter-University Centre for Human Rights and Democratization, and co-funded by GLOTHRO. At that time, there was an extensive analysis and critique of earlier drafts. We all benefited tremendously from the expert comments that we received on our draft legal opinions, and thoroughly enjoyed the rich and provocative discussions.

It should be clear that the issue of transnational/extraterritorial human rights obligations is relatively new in international human rights law. However, it is a topic that has already attracted a lot of attention, particularly among younger scholars who are not so wedded to the dominant territorial approach as well as those from the Global South. Both groups are well represented here.

The basic message conveyed by the present volume is that there is no reason to be fearful of such issues. What the "alternative judgments" in this book show is what a progressive interpretation of (existing) international human rights law could (and, we think, should) look like. However, the real question is whether those entrusted with protecting human rights undertake this vital task more systematically and more universally than they have to date.

Mark Gibney
Wouter Vandenhole

List of Contributors

Claire Buggenhoudt received a Master's in Law, magna cum laude, from the University of Antwerp (Belgium) in 2009. She is currently employed as a PhD student and teaching assistant in public international law at the University of Antwerp. Her doctoral thesis examines the approach of international judicial bodies to public interest concerns in litigation on natural resource exploitation. Her research interests include international adjudication, human rights, environmental protection and transnational obligations.

Takele Soboka Bulto is Assistant Professor of Law and International Studies at the University of Canberra and a Visiting Fellow of the Centre for International Governance and Justice in the Regulatory Institutions Network (RegNet) of the Australian National University. Previously, he was a Judge of the Supreme Court of Oromia State in Ethiopia. He has also practiced before the African Commission on Human and Peoples' Rights where he served as Legal Counsel for and represented victims of human rights violations from many African states, including Angola, Ethiopia, Kenya, and Zimbabwe. He has widely published on various national, regional and global human rights topics. He is the winner of multiple research awards, including *The Harold Luntz Prize for Best PhD Research in Law* (2011) at the Melbourne Law School, and *The Chancellor's Prize for Excellence in the PhD Thesis*, University of Melbourne. He is author of a forthcoming book (2013): *Extraterritorial Application of the Human Right to Water in Africa* (Cambridge University Press).

Gamze Erdem Türkelli is currently a PhD candidate at University of Antwerp's Faculty of Law, conducting research on children's rights responsibilities of non-state economic actors. She received her Bachelor's degree from Bogazici University's (Istanbul, Turkey) Department of Political Science and International Relations and Master's degrees from Université Paris 1-Pantheon Sorbonne (Paris, France) and Yale University (New Haven, CT, USA), where she specialized in public international law, children's rights and development as a Fulbright Fellow. She has also worked in different capacities for NGOs focusing on children's

xiv *List of Contributors*

education and welfare as well as in the private sector prior to commencing her doctoral studies.

Mark Gibney is the Belk Distinguished Professor at UNC-Asheville. His most recent book projects include: *The Handbook of Human Rights* (edited volume with Anja Mihr) (Sage Publications, forthcoming); *Watching Human Rights: The 101 Best Films* (Paradigm Publishers, 2013); *The Politics of Human Rights: The Quest for Dignity* (with Sabine Carey and Steven Poe) (Cambridge University Press, 2010); *Universal Human Rights and Extraterritorial Obligations* (edited volume with Sigrun Skogly) (University of Pennsylvania Press, 2010); and *The Global Refugee Crisis* (ABC-CLIO, 2010). Since 1984, Gibney has directed the Political Terror Scale (PTS), which measures levels of physical integrity violations in more than 185 countries (www.politicalterrorscale.org).

Rachel Hammonds, JD, is a Researcher in the Public Health Department at the Institute of Tropical Medicine (Antwerp, Belgium) and a member of the Law and Development Research Group at the Law Faculty of the University of Antwerp. She studied law at the University of Ottawa and Edinburgh University and is a NY State licensed attorney. Her work focuses on the intersection of development policy, health and human rights.

Alexia Herwig is an Assistant Professor in the area of subsidiarity and multi-level governance at the Faculty of Law of the University of Antwerp with research interests in international economic law and particularly WTO law. She holds a JSD and LLM from NYU School of Law and a BSc from the London School of Economics. Prior to joining the University of Antwerp, Alexia has held post-doctoral research positions at the Fonds Wettenschappelijk Onderzoek Vlaanderen and the University of Bremen's Centre for Transformations of the State. Alexia practiced law as an attorney with a Brussels law firm in 2002 and 2003 and worked as an intern in the Legal Affairs Division of the WTO.

Jernej Letnar Černič is Assistant Professor of Human Rights Law at the School of Government and European Studies, where he also acts as Vice-Dean. He graduated from the University of Ljubljana with the France Prešeren award and obtained an LLM in Human Rights Law at the Raoul Wallenberg Institute for Human Rights Law and Humanitarian Law, University of Lund, Sweden. He completed his PhD in Law at the School of Law, University of Aberdeen, Scotland. He is a member of the International Human Rights Committee and Feminism and International Law Committee of the International Law Association and of the Institut International des Droits de l'Homme. He has written extensively on human rights law and international law.

Nicholas J. Lusiani is Senior Researcher at the Center for Economic and Social Rights, New York, focused on developing alternative human rights-centred economic and development policies. Lusiani also has experience in the fields of international humanitarian relief, youth imprisonment, indigenous rights, and human rights in the natural resource sector. He has worked in the United States, Mexico, Syria and Ecuador. He received a Master's degree in International Affairs from the School of International and Public Affairs at Columbia University, where he specialized in international human rights law and economics. His recent publications include *Economic and Social Rights in the 'Great Recession': Towards a Human Rights-Centered Economic Policy in Times of Crisis* (Oxford University Press, forthcoming), and *Rationalizing the Right to Health: Is Spain's Austere Response to the Economic Crisis Impermissible under International Human Rights Law?* (Cambridge University Press, forthcoming).

Christopher Mbazira is an Associate Professor at the School of Law, Makerere University, Uganda, attached to the Human Rights and Peace Centre. He is also the Coordinator of the recently established Public Interest Law Clinic (PILAC) and Visiting Associate Professor at the School of Law, University of Witwatersrand. Mbazira teaches public international law and international human rights law at both undergraduate and graduate levels. He has published widely on the subject of economic, social and cultural rights, focusing particularly on the judicial enforcement of these rights. His publications include a book entitled *Litigating Economic and Social Rights in South Africa: A Choice Between Corrective and Distributive Justice* (Pretoria University Law Press, 2009).

Nico Moons received a Master's in Law (specializing in international and European Law) from the University of Antwerp in 2011. His Master's thesis, "Extraterritorial jurisdiction: the possible interpretations of the Al-Skeini case and its desirability", explored the obligations of member states to the ECHR in regard to military activities abroad. He has interned at the Permanent Representation of Belgium to the UN in Geneva and worked at the Belgian Council for Alien Law Litigation. He is currently a PhD student at the law faculty of the University of Antwerp, where he conducts research on the effectiveness of socio-economic rights and the right to housing in particular.

Khulekani Moyo is a Senior Lecturer at the Nelson R Mandela School of Law, University of Fort Hare, South Africa. He received his PhD from Stellenbosch University on privatization and the human right to water under international human rights law. Khulekani obtained his LLB (Hons) from the University of Zimbabwe and an LLM in Public International Law from the University of Oslo, Norway. He also holds two diplomas in the international protection of human rights and justiciability of economic, social and cultural rights from Abo Akademi University in Finland. Khulekani was admitted to practice law in

xvi *List of Contributors*

Zimbabwe in 2003 as legal practitioner, conveyancer and notary public. He has practiced law in Zimbabwe, worked in Namibia as legal advisor to an insurance company and has worked for the Norwegian Centre for Human Rights at the University of Oslo. His other areas of interest include international criminal law and regional integration law.

Gorik Ooms is a Researcher in public health at the Institute of Tropical Medicine (Antwerp, Belgium), and Adjunct Professor of Law at Georgetown University (Washington DC, USA). Trained as a lawyer with special interest in human rights, Dr Ooms worked with Médecins Sans Frontières (Doctors Without Borders) Belgium for many years, and as executive director from 2004 to 2008. He was appointed Global Justice Fellow at Yale University for the 2009–2010 academic year. His work draws on human rights law, public health, philosophy and macroeconomics, but most importantly on the real life struggle for essential social rights for all.

Amita Punj is an Assistant Professor of Law at the National Law University, Delhi. She has also taught at Guru Gobind Singh Indraprastha University, Delhi. After completing her undergraduate degree in law she worked with national and international NGOs on the issues of human rights and social justice. On completion of her postgraduate study in law from the University of Delhi, India she pursued a specialization in Law in Development from the University of Warwick, UK and has been a British Chevening scholar. She has been engaged in research and creation of easily understandable learning material on women's rights, prisoners' rights and Human Rights Commissions in India. She is currently engaged in research on the legal dimensions of economic globalization especially with respect to their impact on the marginalized in India.

Matthias Sant'Ana holds a law degree from the University of Brasília, Brazil, and Master's degrees in International and European Law (DES, DEA), and in Human Rights Law (DES) from Université Catholique de Louvain. He is currently a teaching assistant at the Charles de Visscher Centre for International and European Law (CeDIE/UCLouvain) and preparing his doctoral dissertation, entitled *Human Rights and Economic Globalization: A Reinterpretation of International Responsibility* (under the supervision of Olivier De Schutter), at the Centre for the Philosophy of Law (CPDR/ UCLouvain). He has previously worked for the Inter-American Commission on Human Rights (Washington, DC) and the Marangopoulos Foundation for Human Rights (Athens, Greece).

Joss Saunders has been the General Counsel of Oxfam GB, the international development charity, since 1998. Before then he was a commercial litigation lawyer in the City of London, a lecturer in law in Warsaw University, Poland, and a partner in Blake Lapthorn, the English law firm, a role he maintains on a part-time basis. He has worked in the UK,

France, Germany, Poland and Uganda, and carried out assignments in many more countries. He is a regular speaker on international legal issues, and is a frequent writer on international law and intellectual property, as well as speaking at numerous legal conferences on climate change, litigation, and the role of lawyers in development. He was a founder of Advocates for International Development and of the Legal Response Initiative (www.legalresponseinitiative.org), which advises the Least Developed Countries on international law aspects of climate change.

Ana María Suárez Franco holds degrees in law from the Universidad Javeriana (Bogotá), as well as in public policies from the Universidad de los Andes (Bogotá). Originally from Colombia, she moved to Germany in 1999, where she has received the titles LLM. from the University of Heidelberg and Doctor *Juris* from the University of Mannheim. She developed her main research as a guest of the Max Plank Institute for Comparative International Law and International Public Law, being a member of the "*Coloquio Iberoamericano*" of this Institution. Her main topics of research have been the Justiciability of Economic, Social and Cultural Rights and the monitoring of public policies related to the Human Right to Food. Moreover she is a regularly invited Lecturer at the Faculty of Law of the University of Mannheim, the Department on Gender and Nutrition of the University of Hohenheim, The European Master's on Human Rights at the EIUC and the Graduate Institute of International and Development Studies, as well as at some Latin American Universities. As a practitioner, Suárez Franco has been responsible for justiciability, country and case work at FIAN International (FoodFirst Information and Action Network), and currently she is the Permanent Representative of this organization at the UN Human Rights System, in Geneva.

Arne Vandenbogaerde is the programme coordinator of the Research Networking Programme Beyond Territoriality: Globalisation and Transnational Human Rights Obligations (GLOTHRO) and a doctoral candidate at the Law and Development research group at the Faculty of Law of the University of Antwerp. He holds an MA degree in International Relations (University of Ghent) and obtained an LLM in International Human Rights Law from the Irish Centre for Human Rights (Galway, Ireland). His doctoral research specifically focuses on the issue of accountability in international human rights law. Previous to his current research at the University of Antwerp he worked in numerous NGOs and inter-governmental organizations such as the FAO Right to Food Unit.

Wouter Vandenhole holds the UNICEF Chair in Children's Rights at the Faculty of Law of the University of Antwerp (Belgium) and is the

xviii *List of Contributors*

Spokesperson of the Law and Development Research Group. His research interests include economic, social and cultural rights, children's rights, and the relationship between human rights law and development, including the issue of transnational obligations. He chairs the Research Networking Programme Beyond Territoriality: Globalization and Transnational Human Rights Obligations (GLOTHRO). He is a founding member of the editorial board of *Human Rights & International Legal Discourse*. He has published extensively on human rights and his recent books include *Global Justice, State Duties. Extraterritorial Human Rights Obligations in the Area of Economic, Social and Cultural Rights*, edited with M. Langford, M. Scheinin and W. van Genugten (Cambridge University Press, 2013) and *Human Rights and Development in the New Millennium: Towards a Theory of Change*, edited with P. Gready (Routledge, 2014).

Michael Wabwile is Head of the Department of Private Law, Moi University, Kenya. He has been Commonwealth Scholar at Fitzwilliam College in the University of Cambridge and post-doctoral Commonwealth Academic Fellow at De Montfort University, Leicester. His research interests are in international protection of human rights; economic, social and cultural rights; States' diagonal/extraterritorial human rights responsibility; children's rights; human rights and governance in the developing world; environmental law (human rights aspects); and comparative private law. His studies in human rights include *Legal Protection of Social and Economic Rights of Children in the Developing World: Reassessing International Cooperation and Responsibility* (Intersentia, Antwerp 2010).

Margreet Wewerinke holds a European Master's Degree in Human Rights and Democratisation (EMA) and a Graduate Diploma in Law from Nottingham Law School (United Kingdom). She is currently a Visiting Scholar at the Lauterpacht Centre for International Law at the University of Cambridge and a PhD Researcher at the Law Department of the European University Institute in Florence (Italy). Her doctoral research focuses on responsibility of States for the adverse effects of climate change from an international human rights law perspective. She is a co-founder of International-Lawyers.Org, an international NGO based in Geneva, and has advised governments and civil society organizations from all regions on legal issues related to climate change and human rights.

1 Introduction
Transnational Human Rights Obligations

Wouter Vandenhole and Mark Gibney

Human rights have traditionally been framed in a vertical perspective, with the duties of States confined to their own citizens or residents. Obligations beyond this 'territorial space' have been viewed as either being non-existent or minimalistic at best. This territorial paradigm has achieved particular prominence in political philosophy, but also in the interpretation of international human rights conventions, although there is language in many of these treaties that would indicate a much broader scope of application. For example, the International Covenant on Economic, Social and Cultural Rights (ICESCR) makes no mention of either 'territory' or 'jurisdiction'. Furthermore, this treaty, along with the Convention on the Rights of the Child (CRC) and the Convention on the Rights of Persons with Disabilities (CRPD), explicitly references international assistance and cooperation. Yet, it has been common, reflexive even, to limit a state party's human rights obligations to its own territorial borders.

Much has changed and the exclusively territorial basis of international human rights law is now being challenged, and it is envisioned that the present volume will add much to our rethinking and conceptualization of human rights. For one thing, the ability of States and other actors to impact human rights far from home – both positively and negatively – has never been clearer. Moreover, globalization has highlighted and arguably heightened socio-economic disparities across the world. The result is that global social inequality is not only expressed in terms of inter-State justice, but as implicating human rights obligations as well.[1]

State-of-the-art

There is now a growing body of legal scholarship to rethink human rights doctrine in light of these challenges. Most of it is dedicated to the human rights obligations of States other than the territorial State (usually coined

---

1 T. Pogge, *World Poverty and Human Rights: Cosmopolitan Responsibilities and Reforms,* Cambridge: Polity Press, 2002.

2 Introduction: Transnational Human Rights Obligations

extraterritorial or transnational obligations).[2] Much of the earlier scholarship raised these issues by analyzing how human rights law fails to respond to the new realities.[3] Some have focused on civil and political rights and the key issue here is the meaning of the term 'jurisdiction'.[4] Others have analyzed socio-economic rights of children,[5] or taken a right-by-right approach,[6] or else, they have zoomed in on the more conceptual questions of attribution and causation.[7] Other issues with a decidedly extraterritorial dimension

---

2 For an overview article, see W. Vandenhole, 'Extraterritorial Human Rights Obligations: Taking Stock, Looking Forward', *European Journal of Human Rights*, forthcoming.

3 See inter alia M. Gibney, C. Tomaševksi, and J. Vedsted-Hansen, 'Transnational State Responsibility for Violations of Human Rights', *Harvard Human Rights Journal* 12, 1999, 267–96; S. Skogly and M. Gibney, 'Transnational Human Rights Obligations', *Human Rights Quarterly* 24, 2002, 781–98; M.E. Salomon, A. Tostensen and W. Vandenhole (eds), *Casting the Net Wider: Human Rights, Development and New Duty-Bearers*, Antwerp: Intersentia, 2007.

4 F. Coomans and M.T. Kamminga, *Extraterritorial Application of Human Rights Treaties*, Antwerp: Intersentia, 2004; V. Mantouvalou, 'Extending Judicial Control in International Law: Human Rights Treaties and Extraterritoriality', *International Journal of Human Rights* 9, 2005, 147–63; D. Kamchibekova, 'State Responsibility for Extraterritorial Human Rights Obligations', *Buffalo Human Rights Law Review* 13, 2007, 87–149; K.M. Larsen, 'Attribution of Conduct in Peace Operations: The "Ultimate Authority and Control" Test', *The European Journal of International Law* 19, 2008, 509–31; R. Wilde, 'Triggering State Obligations Extraterritorially: The Spatial Test in Certain Human Rights Treaties', in R. Arnold and N. Quénivet (eds), *International Humanitarian Law and Human Rights Law. Towards a New Merger in International Law*, Leiden/Boston: Martinus Nijhoff, 2008, 133–53; M. Gondek, *The Reach of Human Rights in a Globalising World: Extraterritorial Application of Human Rights Treaties*, Antwerp: Intersentia, 2009; M. Milanovic, *Extraterritorial Application of Human Rights Treaties. Law, Principles, and Policy*, Oxford: Oxford University Press, 2011; S. Besson, 'The Extraterritoriality of the European Convention on Human Rights: Why Human Rights Depend on Jurisdiction and What Jurisdiction Amounts to', *Leiden Journal of International Law* 25, 2012, 857–84.

5 W. Vandenhole, 'Economic, Social and Cultural Rights in the CRC: Is There a Legal Obligation to Cooperate for Development?', *International Journal of Children's Rights* 17, 2009, 23–63; M. Wabwile, *Legal Protection of Social and Economic Rights of Children in Developing Countries. Reassessing International Cooperation and Responsibility*, Antwerp: Intersentia, 2010.

6 M. Mustaniemi-Laakso, 'The Right to Education: Instrumental Right Par Excellence', in Salomon, Tostensen and Vandenhole *supra* note 3, 331–52; M. Gibney and S. Skogly, *Universal Human Rights and Extraterritorial Obligations*, University of Pennsylvania Press, 2010; B.S. Takele, 'Towards Rights-Duties Congruence: Extraterritorial Application of the Human Right to Water in the African Human Rights System', *Netherlands Quarterly of Human Rights* 29, 2011, 491–523; R. Hammonds, G. Ooms and W. Vandenhole, 'Under the (Legal) Radar Screen: Global Health Initiatives and International Human Rights Obligations', *BMC International Health and Human Rights* 12, 2012, article 31 (met) http://www.biomedcentral.com/bmcinthealthhumrights/

7 S. Skogly, *Beyond National Borders: States Human Rights Obligations in International Cooperation*, Antwerp: Intersentia, 2006; Y. Dahan, H. Lerner and F. Milman-Sivan, 'Global Justice, Labor Standards and Responsibility', *Theoretical Inquiries in Law* 12, 2011, 439–64; M. Langford, W. Vandenhole, M. Scheinin and W. van Genugten (eds), *Global Justice, State Duties. Extraterritorial Human Rights Obligations in the Area of Economic, Social and Cultural Rights*, Cambridge: Cambridge University Press, 2013.

Litigating Transnational Human Rights Obligations 3

involve development cooperation between North-South,[8] international migration[9] and armed conflict.[10] And finally, at least some attention has also been given to the issue of the amenability of extraterritorial obligations to litigation.[11]

Beyond the scholarship on the duties of foreign states, important work has also been done on the direct human rights obligations of international

---

8 R. Hennessy, 'Defining States' International Legal Obligations to Cooperate for the Achievement of Human Development: One Aspect of Operationalising a Human Rights-Based Approach to Development', in M. Scheinin and M. Suksi (eds), *Human Rights in Development Yearbook 2002. Empowerment, Participation, Accountability and Non-Discrimination: Operationalising a Human Rights-Based Approach to Development*, Leiden/Boston: Martinus Nijhoff Publishers, 2005, 71–98; M.E. Salomon, *Global Responsibility for Human Rights. World Poverty and the Development of International Law*, Oxford: Oxford University Press, 2007; M.E. Salomon, 'Is there a Legal Duty to Address World Poverty?', *RSCAS Policy Paper* 2012/03, http://cadmus.eui.eu/bitstream/handle/1814/22197/RSCAS_PP_2012_03. pdf?sequence=1; Salomon, Tostensen & Vandenhole, *supra* note 3; W. Vandenhole, 'Third State Obligations under the ICESCR: A Case Study of EU Sugar Policy', *Nordic Journal of International Law* 76, 2007, 73–10; W. Vandenhole, 'EU and Development: Extraterritorial Obligations under the International Covenant on Economic, Social and Cultural Rights', in Salomon, Tostensen and Vandenhole *supra* note 3, 85–106; Wabwile *supra* note 5; W. Vandenhole and W. Benedek, 'Extraterritorial Human Rights Obligations and the North-South Divide', in Langford, Vandenhole, Scheinin and van Genugten, *supra* note 7, 332–63.
9 T. Gammeltoft-Hansen, *Access to Asylum: International Refugee Law and the Globalisation of Migration Control*, Cambridge: Cambridge University Press, 2011; M. den Heijer, *Europe and Extraterritorial Asylum*, Oxford: Hart Publishing, 2012.
10 M. Dennis, 'Application of Human Rights Treaties Extraterritorially in Times of Armed Conflict and Military Occupation', *The American Journal of International Law* 99, 2005, 119–41; Larsen, *supra* note 4; N.K. Modirzadeh, 'The Dark Sides of Convergence: A Pro-Civilian Critique of the Extraterritorial Application of Human Rights Law in Armed Conflict', *Int'l L. Stud. Ser. US Naval War Col.* 86, 2010, 349–410; R.K. Goldman, 'Extraterritorial Application of the Human Rights to Life and Personal Liberty, Including *habeas corpus*, During Situations of Armed Conflict', in R. Kolb and G. Gaggioli (eds), *Research Handbook on Human Rights and Humanitarian Law*, Cheltenham: Edward Elgar, 2013, pp. 104–24.
11 M. Sepúlveda, 'Obligations of "International Assistance and Cooperation" in an Optional Protocol to the International Covenant on Economic, Social and Cultural, Rights', *Netherlands Quarterly of Human Rights* 24, 2006, 271–303; C. Courtis and M. Sepúlveda, 'Are Extra-Territorial Obligations Reviewable under the Optional Protocol to the ICESCR?', *Nordic Journal of Human Rights* 27, 2009, 54–63; A. Khalfan, 'Accountability Mechanisms', in Langford, Vandenhole, Scheinin and van Genugten, *supra* note 7, 391–416; M.E. Salomon, 'Deprivation, Causation and the Law of International Cooperation', in Langford, Vandenhole, Scheinin and van Genugten, *supra* note 7, 2013.

4   Introduction: Transnational Human Rights Obligations

financial institutions (IFIs),[12] corporations,[13] and non-State actors more generally.[14] The human rights obligations of all actors other than the domestic State are here referred to as transnational human rights obligations, hence the title 'litigating transnational human rights obligations'.[15]

In addition to this scholarship, the Extraterritorial Obligations (ETO) Consortium was created in 2007 and it now has upwards of 100 members, either academics or individuals who work for NGOs including Amnesty International, Human Rights Watch, Oxfam, Greenpeace, FIAN and ESCR-Net. Two of the founding members of the ETO Consortium, Coomans and Künnemann published in 2012 an annotated collection of factual case studies that were developed through the work of the Consortium.[16]

Furthermore, a European Research Networking Programme on transnational human rights obligations has also been established: *Beyond Territoriality – Globalisation and Transnational Human Rights Obligations* (GLOTHRO). GLOTHRO has a dual objective: it seeks to deepen and broaden the understanding of transnational human rights obligations, and it aims at consolidating a research community on the topic. The ETO Consortium has also

---

12 S. Skogly, *The Human Rights Obligations of the World Bank and IMF*, London: Cavendish, 2001; W. van Genugten, P. Hunt and S. Mathews (eds), *World Bank, IMF and Human Rights*, Nijmegen: Wolf Legal Publishers, 2002; M. Darrow, *Between Light and Shadow: The World Bank, the International Monetary Fund and International Human Rights Law*, Oxford: Portland, 2003; D.D. Bradlow and D.B. Hunter (eds), *International Financial Institutions & International Law*, Alphen aan den Rijn: Kluwer Law International, 2010; A. McBeth, *International Economic Actors and Human Rights*, London: Routledge, 2010.

13 M. Kamminga and Zia-Zarifi, *Liability of Multinational Corporations under International Law*, The Hague: Kluwer International Law, 2000; S.R. Ratner, 'Corporations and Human Rights: A Theory of Legal Responsibility', *The Yale Law Journal* 111, 2001, 443–545; N. Jägers, Corporate Human Rights Obligations: In Search Of Accountability, Antwerp: Intersentia, 2002; D. Weissbrodt, 'Business and Human Rights', *University of Cincinnati Law Review* 74, 2005, 55–73; D. Kinley and R. Chambers, 'The UN Human Rights Norms for Corporations: The Private Implications of Public International Law', *Human Rights Law Review* 6, 2006, 447–97; O. De Schutter (ed.), *Transnational Companies and Human Rights*, Oxford: Portland, 2006; McBeth, *supra* note 12; D. Bilchitz, 'The Ruggie Framework: An Adequate Rubric for Corporate Human Rights Obligations?', *SUR International Journal on Human Rights* 7, 2010, 199–229; R. Raffaelli and B. Wray, 'False Extraterritoriality? Municipal and Multinational Jurisdiction over Transnational Corporations', *Human Rights & International Legal Discourse* 6, 2012, 108–30.

14 P. Alston (ed.), *Non-State Actors and Human Rights*, Oxford: Oxford University Press, 2005; A. Clapham, *Human Rights Obligations of Non-State Actors*, Oxford: Oxford University Press, 2006.

15 This is to be distinguished from transnational human rights litigation as coined in American literature, where it refers to the reliance on (traditional) international human rights law before domestic courts (W.J. Aceves, 'Liberalism and International Legal Scholarship: The Pinochet Case and the Move Toward a Universal System of Transnational Law Litigation', *Harvard International Law Review* 41, 2000, 129–84). In our approach, transnational refers to duty-bearers other than the domestic state.

16 F. Coomans and R. Künneman, *Cases and Concepts on Extraterritorial Obligations in the Area of Economic, Social and Cultural Rights*, Cambridge: Intersentia, 2012.

paved the way for the elaboration and adoption of the Maastricht Principles on Extraterritorial Obligations in the Area of Economic, Social and Cultural Rights, which were adopted by a group of international lawyers in September 2011.[17]

Responding to the mismatch between the traditional human rights doctrine with its territorial focus and current realities, which are often characterised by their extra- and transnational dimensions, various sets of legal principles have also come into existence. The 2002 *Tilburg Guiding Principles on the World Bank, IMF and Human Rights* (the Tilburg Guiding Principles)[18] address the obligations of member States of international organizations (the international financial institutions in particular) and of these organizations themselves as direct duty-bearers. The 2003 *Norms on the Responsibilities of Transnational Corporations and Other Business Enterprises with Regard to Human Rights* (the Norms) and the 2011 *UN Guiding Principles on Business and Human Rights* (the UN Guiding Principles) address the obligations of home States and of transnational companies as direct duty-bearers.[19] Finally, while the previously mentioned Maastricht Principles on Extraterritorial Obligations focus on economic, social and cultural rights, these same principles are equally applicable to every aspect of human rights.[20] All four sets of principles have their strengths and limitations, and represent in varying degrees an attempt to move beyond a territorial, State-centric understanding of human rights law.[21]

Notwithstanding these doctrinal developments and standard-setting initiatives, judicial institutions and monitoring bodies (including those within the United Nations) continue to show an enormous hesitancy in moving beyond a territorial reading of international human rights law. This book will show that this hesitancy is no longer warranted, and it achieves this by

---

17 The Maastricht Principles have been published in the *Netherlands Quarterly of Human Rights* 29, 2011, 578–90.

18 Tilburg Guiding Principles on the World Bank, IMF and Human Rights (2002) http://papers.ssrn.com/sol3/papers.cfm?abstract_id=957195&

19 For a scholarly commentary, see R. Mares (ed.), *The UN Guiding Principles on Business and Human Rights – Foundations and Implementation*, Leiden: Martinus Nijhoff Publishers, 2012.

20 First scholarly comments include: W. Vandenhole, 'Beyond Territoriality: the Maastricht Principles on Extra-Territorial Obligations in the Area of Economic, Social and Cultural Rights', *Netherlands Quarterly of Human Rights* 29, 2011, 429–33; M.E. Salomon and I. Seiderman, 'Human Rights Norms for a Globalized World: The Maastricht Principles on the Extraterritorial Obligations of States in the Area of Economic, Social and Cultural Rights', *Global Policy* 3, 2012, 458–62; O. De Schutter, A. Eide, A. Khalfan, M. Orellana, M. Salomon and I. Seiderman, 'Commentary on the Maastricht Principles on Extraterritorial Obligations of States in the area of Economic, Social and Cultural Rights', *Human Rights Quarterly* 34, 2012, 1084–1169.

21 W. Vandenhole, 'Emerging Normative Frameworks on Transnational Human Rights Obligations', *EUI Working Papers RSCAS 2012/17*, http://cadmus.eui.eu/bitstream/handle/1814/21874/RSCAS_2012_17.pdf?sequence=1

6   Introduction: Transnational Human Rights Obligations

crafting legally sound 'judgments' on extra- and transnational human rights issues from a number of adjudicatory fora. To be clear, the 'judgments' are hypothetical. However, all are based on real world situations where extraterritorial or transnational issues have emerged, and all are based on existing international human rights law, albeit a progressive interpretation of this law. The focus of the judgments is really on the challenging aspects of extra- and transnational dimensions of the cases. Where authors also include unresolved issues under more mainstream human rights scholarship (e.g. the meaning of the prohibition of retrogressive measures, and its relationship with the respect obligation), they were asked not to elaborate on these pending doctrinal questions.

We have organized the volume along the logic of the adjudicatory bodies concerned. While this grouping mechanism will allow these bodies and others to easily trace the chapters that they are interested in from an institutional point of view, the substantive commonalities and findings across adjudicatory bodies must not be overlooked. The 'judgments' truly do span geographic categorization and include an impressive array of issues: climate change (Wewerinke); international corruption and tax evasion (Lusiani;Wabwile); land grabbing (Mbazira; Suárez; Saunders); extraordinary rendition (Gibney); international governance issues like structural adjustment (Punj) and financial and economic crises (Hammonds and Ooms, Sant'Ana and Vandenhole), weak governance zone (Černič); child pornography on the internet (Erdem); labour practices (Vandenbogaerde); resource exploitation (Černič; Moyo); and development cooperation (Hammonds and Ooms; Vandenhole). In what follows, we will flag up some of these.

Some findings

What is borne out by the hypothetical judgments in this volume? Few will question that enforcement represents the weakest link in terms of the protection of human rights, and yet one of the things shown in this book is that there are a number of judicial and quasi-judicial systems where transnational human rights claims can – and should – be pressed. These include human rights bodies like regional human commissions and courts and the UN treaty bodies, but also the International Court of Justice, the International Criminal Court, the dispute settlement system of the World Trade Organization, the Compliance Advisor Ombudsman with the International Finance Corporation of the World Bank Group, and domestic courts as well. In its own way, each 'judgment' shows that there are no insurmountable legal obstacles concerning admissibility or a decision on the merits on issues that deal with transnational human rights claims. What is needed is a progressive interpretation of the law that presently exists, but also the political will to make use of existing mechanisms. Thus, although several international conventions contain an inter-State complaint mechanism, there has never been a single case, at least under the UN system, where one State has filed such a complaint against another.

Unlike the 'real world,' several of the contributions in this volume do make use (at least for theoretical purposes) of the inter-State complaint system – and all address important human rights issues that have transnational dimensions. This, of course, is not to underestimate or to downplay the courage it may take, legally and politically, to move beyond the mainstream interpretation, but what this should help achieve is to dispel the idea – the myth, really – that transnational human rights issues are too complex to address.

What this volume demonstrates is that these issues can be taken up and that this can be done without a major overhaul of legal rules or procedures – or of the law itself. As indicated earlier, the issue of 'jurisdiction' has dominated much of the debate on extraterritorial obligations, particularly in the area of civil and political rights. Several 'judgments' in this volume (Černič; Moons; Suárez; Vandenbogaerde; Vandenhole; Wewerinke) demonstrate that this does not need to be a controversial issue (any more). In terms of some of the other human rights bodies, a major challenge may be how to bring transnational human rights issues within their mandate. The 'public morals' exception is such an entry point to the dispute settlement mechanism of the World Trade Organization (Buggenhoudt), while Wabwile presents the idea of bringing a claim before the International Criminal Court based on 'economic crimes against humanity' as a way of addressing the economic devastation brought on by 'kleptocracies' – but also those who aid and assist such practices.

Both structural issues affecting large sections of the population and issues affecting identified or identifiable individuals have been taken up. Under the former category, cases range from the detrimental effects of climate change (Wewerinke), tax evasion (Lusiani), biofuels (Herwig), land grabbing (Mbazira; Suárez; Saunders) and structural adjustment policies (Punj) to withdrawal of development assistance (Vandenhole) on the enjoyment of human rights. Under the latter category, issues of land eviction (Mbazira), labour rights (Vandenbogaerde) and extraordinary rendition (Gibney), amongst others, have been addressed.

Much of the political debate on extraterritorial human rights obligations can be narrowed down to the question of whether there is an obligation of international assistance and cooperation, although some scholarship has convincingly shown that the debate is much broader.[22] However, questions of international assistance and cooperation should not be completely side-lined either. In this volume, Hammonds and Ooms, Lusiani, and Vandenhole flesh out what the concrete meaning of such an obligation can be in the

---

22 e.g., Vandenhole, *supra* note 5.

8 *Introduction: Transnational Human Rights Obligations*

areas as disparate as health rights (access to treatment for HIV/AIDS), the prevention of tax evasion and disability rights.

Many issues are indeed complex – but more on the surface than in reality. Rather, what these 'judgments' show is that we have readily come to accept a rather simple (and simplistic) model of the causes and consequences of human rights violations. If, however, we take a few steps backward and look more broadly what we see is that determining rights and responsibilities is anything but difficult. To be sure, these judgments invariably deal with more than one State (and in many instances could be extended to cover a multitude of States). In addition, most involve abstract legal questions: causation; the relationship between different branches of international law (in particular human rights law and the law on State responsibility for internationally wrongful acts); joint or shared responsibility for human rights violations (of territorial and third states; non-State actors, and individuals); and sovereignty. However, what they also show is that if one wants to get at the root causes of violations of human rights it will be essential to expand our scope and our thinking of what this means.

The 'judgments' in this volume seem to suggest, at least implicitly, that it is more likely at this stage to litigate extraterritorial obligations of third states than transnational obligations of non-state actors (some 'judgments' explicitly engage with this issue, see, e.g., Moyo). There may be several reasons for that. One is that at least from the human rights monitoring bodies, it would require a major leap forward to also address the human rights obligations of non-State actors. In seeking the middle way between progressive interpretation and legal soundness, most authors seem to have judged that the time is not yet ripe to litigate the human rights obligations of non-state actors. This cautious approach may also have been informed by the fact that the substantive discussions on the human rights obligations of non-State actors are not yet so advanced as those of third States. By and large, the discussion on non-State actors is still very much about the question *whether* they have human rights obligations, rather than on their precise scope. Both sets of principles for international financial institutions (Tilburg Principles 2002)[23] and for companies (UN Guiding Principles 2011) reflect the early state of the debate, notwithstanding the work that has been done over the past decades. This shows an urgent need to develop a thicker understanding of the transnational obligations of non-State actors in order to increase the likelihood of future litigation that involves them. At the same time, several contributions to this volume bear out how at least the obligations of companies can be addressed indirectly, by holding the State

---

23 In the context of GLOTHRO, the Tilburg Principles are currently undergoing revision, precisely to move beyond making the point that international financial institutions have human rights obligations, and to elaborate more substantive guidance on which obligations they have.

of incorporation accountable (see Černič; Mbazira; Moyo; Suarez; Takele). One judgment deals specifically with a supranational organization, the European Union (Herwig); three others with international financial institutions (Punj; Sant'Ana; Saunders).

The volume also demonstrates that the Maastricht Principles on Extraterritorial Obligations in the Area of Economic, Social and Cultural Rights are a useful tool for the adjudication of extraterritorial issues. The Maastricht Principles have been used in this volume to address questions of admissibility, in particular on the thorny question of jurisdiction (see e.g. Černič; Vandenbogaerde; Vandenhole), as well as to take decisions on the merits (on, e.g., foreseeability, see Punj). Use has been made of these principles in order to flesh out the meaning of the obligation to protect (position to regulate) (see Lusiani; Mbazira; Moyo; Suarez); the obligation to fulfil (international assistance and cooperation) (see Lusiani; Vandenhole); and remedies (see Černič). A point the Maastricht Principles remain largely silent on, and for which they have been criticized,[24] is the apportioning of responsibility.

Attribution and apportioning of responsibility will certainly be on the (research) agenda for the coming decade. Key reference points to elaborate a coherent theory on the apportioning of responsibility have been identified, but need further elaboration.[25] This collection of alternative judgments offers a promising start.[26]

---

24 Vandenhole, *supra* note 21.

25 A. Khalfan, 'Division of Responsibility among States', in Langford, Vandenhole, Scheinin and van Genugten, *supra* note 7, pp. 299–331; Salomon, *supra* note 11; W. Vandenhole, G.E. Türkelli and R. Hammonds, 'New Human Rights Duty-Bearers: Towards a Re-conceptualisation of the Human Rights Duty-Bearer Dimension', in A. Mihr and M. Gibney (eds), *Handbook of Human Rights*, London: Sage, forthcoming.

26 In this volume, for example, Herwig deploys a *de minimis* contribution causation standard that may be transplanted to other contexts than the WTO.

Part I

International Economic Governance Bodies

2 U.S. Trade Sanctions (World Trade Organization, Panel Report)

Claire Buggenhoudt

Abstract

In 2008, the United States enacted the JADE Act (Block Burmese Junta's Anti-Democratic Efforts) with the aim of promoting human rights and democracy in Myanmar. One of the provisions of this act prohibits the import into the United States of jewellery containing rubies and jadeite mined or extracted in Myanmar. Because the ban also applies to stones that are transformed in a third country, the measure has a significant impact on the Thai jewellery industry. In an effort to protect its industry, Thailand hypothetically brings the ban before the WTO Dispute Settlement Body, claiming that the United States' measure constitutes a quantitative import restriction, which is prohibited by Article XI:1 GATT. While the WTO Panel agrees with this claim, it considers the import ban to be justified under the exception of Article XX (a) GATT (exception to protect public morals). Taking account of the importance of the protected values, the lack of less restrictive alternatives and the exceptional position of Myanmar in the international community, the Panel concludes that the ban is necessary to protect public morals and does not constitute an arbitrary or unjustifiable discrimination, or a disguised restriction on international trade.

Introductory note[1]

From the late 1980s until 2011, a military junta that titled itself the 'State Peace and Development Council' (SPDC) ruled the South Asian state of Myanmar. The junta was known for violently suppressing anti-governmental actions and has repeatedly, but to little avail, been encouraged to improve its human rights record by the international community.[2] This chapter explores the approach of the United States, which imposed significant

---

1 Disclaimer: While this case is based on true facts, no account was taken of recent developments and significant changes have been made. The discussed complaint and subsequent findings are completely fictional.

2 For example, on the issue of forced labour, the ILO General Conference adopted the 2000 *Resolution concerning the measures recommended by the Governing Body under article 33 of the ILO Constitution on the subject of Myanmar, adopted at its 88th session.*

14 *U.S. Trade Sanctions*

trade sanctions on the country, and the compatibility of that approach with the WTO law.

In 2003, the United States enacted the Burmese Freedom and Democracy Act (BFDA) with the aim of ending human rights violations and implementing a democratic government in Myanmar.[3] The BFDA introduced unilateral trade sanctions against the regime, including an asset freeze, a ban on the export of financial services to Myanmar and a ban on the import of goods originating from Myanmar. However, Myanmar's regime was partly evading the ban on the import of its goods by selling raw gemstones to third countries, such as Thailand, where the gems were 'substantially transformed' to (semi) finished products. Under the WTO Rules of Origin, this transformation changed the origin of the gemstones to that of the third country, thereby exempting them from the BFDA ban.[4]

After the junta's forceful suppression of peaceful protest in September 2007, the United States strengthened its sanctions regime against Myanmar through the enactment of the Tom Lantos Block Burmese JADE (Junta's Anti-Democratic Efforts) Act.[5] One section of the JADE Act modifies the BFDA to prohibit the import into the United States of (jewellery containing) rubies and jadeite mined or extracted in Myanmar, regardless of whether they were substantially transformed in a third country.[6] Because of the significant economic consequences of this provision on the Thai gemstone trade, Thailand hypothetically challenged the measure at the WTO.

The World Trade Organization has a compulsory dispute settlement system that resolves disputes between WTO member States, such as the U.S. and Thailand, concerning the conformity of domestic measures with the series of multilateral treaties and agreements that constitute WTO law. The hypothetical decision below is a first ruling made by a Panel which can be appealed on points of law to the Appellate Body. The Dispute Settlement Body (the member States) can only reject the final conclusion of the Panel or the Appellate Body by consensus.[7]

The most challenging issue that the Panel has to deal with concerns the extraterritorial dimensions of the measure. Trade sanctions are prohibited under WTO law[8] and can only be justified in specific circumstances, for

---

3 Burmese Freedom and Democracy Act of 2003, *Pub. L.* 108–61, ss. 1–9, 117 *Stat.* 864, 864–71 (2003). The Act will be lifted once sufficient progress has been made towards the realisation of core human rights.

4 Article III (b) WTO Agreement on Rules of Origin, as implemented by the U.S. in domestic legislation.

5 Tom Lantos Block Burmese JADE (Junta's Anti-Democratic Efforts) Act of 2008, *Pub. L.* 110–286, ss. 6, 122 *Stat.* 2632, 2638 (2008).

6 Section 6 JADE Act of 2008.

7 For an overview of the system see World Trade Organization, *Understanding the WTO*, 2011, available at www.wto.org.

8 See, in particular, Article XI GATT.

Litigating Transnational Human Rights Obligations 15

example, if they are necessary for the protection of public morals.[9] At first glance, this exception seems limited to allowing for the protection of the human rights of the inhabitants of the State that issues the measure.

However, the hypothetical decision will argue that the disputed measure can be justified under the public morals exception because the promotion of human rights and democracy is in line with the public values that are widely embodied in the law, regulation and policy of the United States. Concerning the necessity of the measure, the decision will show that a material contribution to the protection of public morals that are vital may outweigh the restrictive effect of a measure on international trade.

The Panel decision is limited to the consideration of the exception on public moral grounds for reasons of efficiency. If this were a real WTO decision, the findings would be more elaborate and other legal provisions would also be discussed. The same limitation applies to the evidence that supports this decision. Throughout the decision reference is made to evidence that is hypothetical (but not unlikely to be found); in a real decision this evidence would be discussed before the findings.

In contrast, it is noteworthy that none of the legal quotes or references to the case law of the Appellate Body are hypothetical. While this would be the first WTO decision that explicitly refers to human rights obligations, the decision will show that many parallels can be drawn with the existing case law of the WTO dispute settlement system. These parallels have been broadly discussed in the academic literature that inspired this Panel decision.[10]

CASE

Facts

On 3 January 2008, the United States adopted the JADE act, which banned the import of rubies and jadeite mined or extracted in Myanmar.[11] The act was explicitly linked to the protection of human rights and democracy in Myanmar. The U.S. Congress established that the human rights violations,

---

9 See Article XX GATT.

10 In writing the findings, the author was particularly inspired by an article of Robert Howse and Jared Genser. R. Howse and J. Genser, 'Are EU Trade Sanctions on Burma Compatible With WTO Law?', *Mich. J. Int'l L.* 2007–2008, 165–96. Other articles on the issue include S. A. Aaronson, 'Seeping in Slowly: How Human Rights Concerns are Penetrating the WTO', *World Trade Review* 2007, 413–49; G. Marceau, 'WTO Dispute Settlement and Human Rights', *European Journal of International Law* 2002, 753–814 and A. Panday, 'The Role of International Human Rights Law in WTO Dispute Settlement', *U.C. Davis Journal of International Law & Policy* 2009, 245–71.

11 Tom Lantos Block Burmese JADE (Junta's Anti-Democratic Efforts) Act of 2008, *Pub. L.* 110–286, ss. 6, 122 *Stat.* 2632, 2638 (2008).

16   *U.S. Trade Sanctions*

undemocratic policies and military activities in Myanmar were partly financed by the import of gemstones to the United States.[12] On the basis of these findings and the lack of effect of previous national and international efforts, it adopted a law to restrict trade in Myanmarese gemstones.

The enactment of the JADE Act had significant effects on the Thai gemstone industry. According to Thai jewellery industry representatives, Thailand's multi-billion dollar jewellery exports to the United States declined by 30 per cent by the end of 2008. Moreover, an estimated 100,000 jobs were lost in the jewellery industry by March 2009.[13] While the global economic recession is partly to blame for these losses, they are largely due to the import ban imposed by the JADE Act. Although the Thai gemstone industry is now making the transition to African rubies, it has lost its competitive advantage of having easily accessible resources and well-established networks with Myanmar's ruby traders.[14]

In an effort to protect its jewellery industry, Thailand took the initiative to start consultations with the United States at the level of the World Trade Organisation with a view to reaching a mutually satisfactory solution. Because these consultations failed to resolve the dispute with regard to the JADE Act, Thailand decided to ask for the establishment of a Panel by the WTO Dispute Settlement Body. Thailand claims that the measure imposes a prohibition on the importation of rubies mined or extracted from Myanmar and articles of jewellery containing rubies mined or extracted in Myanmar into the United States inconsistent with Article XI:1 of GATT 1994.

The United States does not submit arguments in relation to the measure's consistency with Article XI:1. On the contrary, it recognizes that the import prohibition on jadeite and rubies mined or extracted in Myanmar imposed by the United States is a *prima facie* violation of Article XI:1. However, the United States claims that this import prohibition is justified under Article XX (a) of GATT 1994. Article XX (a) provides that nothing in the Agreement shall prevent the adoption of measures necessary for the protection of public morals.

VII. Findings of the Panel

The Panel will first consider Thailand's claim under Article XI:1 and then, as necessary, the parties' arguments on the U.S. defence of its actions under Article XX (a) of GATT 1994.

---

12 Section 2, subsection (6) of the JADE Act.

13 United States Governmental Accountability Office, *Report to Congressional Committees, International Trade,* GAO-09-987, available at www.gao.gov/new.items/d09987.pdf, 10–11 (last accessed 21 June 2012).

14 *Ibid.*

A. VIOLATION OF ARTICLE XI:1 OF GATT 1994

7.1   With regard to Thailand's claim of inconsistency with Article XI:1, we note that the United States 'does not dispute that the prohibition on importation of jadeite and rubies mined or extracted in Burma as included in the JADE Act of 2008 constitutes an import prohibition within the meaning of Article XI:1 of GATT 1994'.[15]

7.2   Even if this declaration does not amount to an admission of a violation of Article XI:1, the Panel considers that the evidence made available enables the Panel to determine that the U.S. prohibition of imports of rubies mined or extracted in Myanmar is inconsistent with Article XI:1.

7.3   Article XI:1 of GATT 1994 provides that

> No prohibitions or restrictions other than duties, taxes or other charges, whether made effective through quotas, import or export licenses or other measures, shall be instituted or maintained by any contracting party on the importation of any product of the territory of any contracting party or on the exportation or sale for export of any product of the territory of any contracting party.

7.4   Both parties identify the Tom Lantos Block Burmese JADE (Junta's Anti-Democratic Efforts) Act of 2008 as the legal basis of an import ban on rubies mined or extracted in Myanmar. Under Section 6 of the JADE Act of 2008, the Burmese Freedom and Democracy Act of 2003 is amended to include the 'prohibition on importation of jadeite and rubies from Burma and articles of jewellery containing jadeite or rubies from Burma'.

7.5   The relevant provisions of the JADE Act of 2008 read as follows

SEC. 3A. PROHIBITION ON IMPORTATION OF JADEITE AND RUBIES FROM BURMA AND ARTICLES OF JEWELLRY CONTAINING JADEITE OR RUBIES FROM BURMA.

(a) Definitions – In this section: (…)
    (2) Burmese covered article – The term 'Burmese covered article' means
        (A) jadeite mined or extracted from Burma;

---

15   United States' reply to Panel question No. 42. This statement is in accordance with Section 6 of the JADE Act, which prescribes in subsection (b)(3)(a) that the President shall seek the 'issuance of a draft waiver decision by the Council for Trade in Goods of the World Trade Organization granting a waiver of the applicable obligations of the United States under the World Trade Organization with respect to the provisions of this section and any measures taken to implement this section'.

18   *U.S. Trade Sanctions*

> (B) rubies mined or extracted from Burma; or
>
> (C) articles of jewellry containing jadeite described in subparagraph (A) or rubies described in subparagraph (B) (...)

(b) Prohibition on Importation of Burmese Covered Articles —

(1) In general — Notwithstanding any other provision of law, until such time as the President determines and certifies to the appropriate congressional committees that Burma has met the conditions described in section 3(a)(3), beginning 60 days after the date of the enactment of the Tom Lantos Block Burmese JADE (Junta's Anti-Democratic Efforts) Act of 2008, the President shall prohibit the importation into the United States of any Burmese covered article.

7.6   Article XI:1 prohibits both 'prohibitions' and 'restrictions' with respect to the importation of any goods from other WTO Members. The exclusion of 'prohibitions' entails that Members cannot forbid the importation of any product of any other Member into their markets. The U.S. statutory provision in question expressly requires the imposition of an import ban on imports from Myanmar.

7.7   The Panel thus finds that the Tom Lantos Block Burmese JADE (Junta's Anti-Democratic Efforts) Act of 2008 is inconsistent with Article XI:1 of GATT 1994.

B. EXCEPTION UNDER ARTICLE XX OF GATT 1994

7.8   The United States submits that, because the measure that has been challenged by Thailand serves an important policy objective, it falls within the scope of Article XX of GATT 1994, in particular Article XX (a). Moreover, the United States argues that the measure is applied in a way that complies with the requirements of the chapeau of Article XX.

7.9   Thailand, on the other hand, considers that, although the JADE Act may perhaps be considered to fall within the scope of the 'protection of public morals' within the meaning of Article XX (a), it is certainly not 'necessary' to attain that public policy goal and constitutes an arbitrary and unjustifiable discrimination.

7.10   Article XX of the GATT 1994 provides in relevant part that

> Subject to the requirement that such measures are not applied in a manner which would constitute a means of arbitrary or unjustifiable discrimination between countries where the same conditions prevail, or a disguised restriction on international trade, nothing in this

Agreement shall be construed to prevent the adoption or enforcement by any contracting party of measures:
(a) necessary to protect public morals; (…)

7.11 Following the Appellate Body's established case law with regard to Article XX of the GATT 1994, a two-tiered analysis must be made.[16] The measure must fall within the scope of one of the recognized exceptions set out in paragraphs (a) to (j) of Article XX and it must meet the requirements of the introductory provisions of Article XX, the so-called 'chapeau'.

7.12 We will first examine whether section 6 of the JADE Act can be provisionally justified under Article XX (a), the provision invoked by the United States. If provisionally justified, we will then consider whether the United States has successfully met the requirements of the chapeau of Article XX with respect to the challenged measure.

1. Provisional justification under Article XX (a)

7.13 Pursuant to the text of Article XX (a), the Member invoking that provision must demonstrate two elements to provisionally justify its measure. First, it has to prove that the challenged measure is designed to protect the public policy goal, namely, the protection of public morals, and secondly, it has to demonstrate that the measure has sufficient nexus with the protected interest. The Panel will now examine these two elements in turn.

<u>a) Measure…to protect public morals</u>

7.14 The United States argues that the challenged measure is designed to protect public morals under Article XX (a) as it is explicitly connected to the promotion of human rights protection and democracy. The United States adds that the flagrant violation of human rights by Myanmar is repugnant to the public values embodied in the legislation, policy and jurisprudence of the United States. Thailand recognizes that the promotion of human rights and democracy may be considered to be an issue of public morals in the United States.

7.15 The Panel will first examine the meaning of 'public morals' in Article XX (a). In the context of Article XX, the Appellate Body has repeatedly stated that 'the content of these concepts for Members can vary in time and

---

16 Appellate Body Report, United States – Standards for Reformulated and Conventional Gasoline, WT/DS2/R, adopted 26 January 1996, 22; Appellate Body Report, United States – Import Prohibition of Certain Shrimp and Shrimp Products, WT/DS58/AB/R, adopted 12 October 1998, paras. 115–19; Appellate Body Report, Korea – Measures Affecting Imports of Fresh, Chilled and Frozen Beef, WT/DS161/169/AB/R, adopted 11 December 2000, para. 156.

20 *U.S. Trade Sanctions*

space, depending upon a range of factors, including prevailing social, cultural, ethical and religious values'[17], nevertheless, the Panel will have to give meaning to the concept of 'public morals' in Article XX (a) in order to apply it to the facts of this case.[18]

7.16 In the case of *China – Publications and Audiovisual Entertainment Products*, the Panel adopted the interpretation given to the concept in the context of Article XIV (a) of the GATS[19] to Article XX (a).[20] Because we see no reason to depart from the interpretation of 'public morals' given in previous jurisprudence, we will adopt the same interpretation for our analysis. Considering the definitions of 'public' and 'moral' in the Shorter Oxford English Dictionary, the Panel finds that public morals are 'standards of right and wrong conduct maintained by or on behalf of a community or nation'.[21]

7.17 Thailand does not specifically contest that the violation of human rights standards and democracy is contrary to public morals in the United States. Nevertheless, we do note that the United States has put forward evidence that shows that the promotion of human rights and democracy is widely embodied in the law, regulation and policy of the State.

7.18 The Panel therefore finds that the purpose of the JADE Act falls within the scope of Article XX (a) and the challenged measure is designed to 'protect public morals'.

b) Measure…necessary to protect public morals

7.19 After establishing that the challenged measure is designed to protect public morals, the Panel will examine whether the measure is 'necessary' to attain this public policy goal. The Panel notes that the standard of 'necessity' is an objective standard. The necessity of a measure is, in the first place, determined by a Member's characterization of a measure's objectives and of the effectiveness of its regulatory approach. However, (contrary) evidence may also be proffered by the structure and operation of the measure or the complaining party.

---

17 Panel Report, Measures Affecting the Cross-Border Supply of Gambling and Betting Services, WT/DS285/R, adopted 10 November 2004, para. 6.461.

18 Appellate Body Report, United States – Import Prohibition of Certain Shrimp and Shrimp Products, WT/DS58/AB/R, adopted 12 October 1998, para. 155.

19 Panel Report, Measures Affecting the Cross-Border Supply of Gambling and Betting Services, WT/DS285/R, adopted 10 November 2004, para. 6.465.

20 Panel Report, China – Measures Affecting Trading Rights and Distribution Services for Certain Publications and Audiovisual Entertainment Products, WT/DS363/R, adopted 12 August 2009.

21 Panel Report, Measures Affecting the Cross-Border Supply of Gambling and Betting Services, WT/DS285/R, adopted 10 November 2004, para. 6.465.

Litigating Transnational Human Rights Obligations 21

7.20 The Panel would like to make two preliminary remarks. First, the Panel wishes to point out that the meaning of 'necessary' measures is closely related, but not limited to, indispensable or inevitable measures. In the case of *Korea – Various Measures on Beef* the Appellate Body found that

> Measures which are indispensable or of absolute necessity or inevitable to secure compliance certainly fulfil the requirements of Article XX (d). But other measures, too, may fall within the ambit of this exception. As used in Article XX (d), the term 'necessary' refers, in our view, to a range of degrees of necessity. At one end of this continuum lies 'necessary' understood as 'indispensable'; at the other end, is 'necessary' taken to mean 'making a contribution to'. We consider that a 'necessary' measure is, in this continuum, located significantly closer to the pole of 'indispensable' than to the opposite pole of simply 'making a contribution to'.[22]

7.21 The Panel is of the view that these statements are equally applicable in the context of Article XX of the GATT, including Article XX (a).

7.22 Secondly, with regard to the burden of proof, the Panel wishes to point out that it is well established that a responding party invoking an exception must demonstrate that the challenged measure satisfies the requirements of that exception. However, if the responding party has *prima facie* established that the measure is necessary, it is not required to counter every possible WTO–consistent measure.[23] For a measure to be considered necessary by the Panel, the responding party must only demonstrate why alternatives proposed by the complaining party are not reasonably available in light of the values pursued and the desired level of protection.

7.23 In the context of Article XX (d) of the GATT 1994, the Appellate Body established that the necessity of a measure should be determined through 'a process of weighing and balancing a series of factors'.[24] Subsequently, the challenged measure should be compared to less restrictive alternatives, taking account of the importance of the interests at issue, to determine whether it is reasonably available.

7.24 On the basis of the articulation of the guiding principles for the 'weighing and balancing' test by the Appellate Body in *Korea – Various*

---

22 Appellate Body Report, Korea – Measures Affecting Imports of Fresh, Chilled and Frozen Beef, WT/DS161/169/AB/R, adopted 11 December 2000, para. 161.

23 Appellate Body Report, United States – Standards for Reformulated and Conventional Gasoline, WT/DS2/R, adopted 26 January 1996, 22–3.

24 Appellate Body Report, Korea – Measures Affecting Imports of Fresh, Chilled and Frozen Beef, WT/DS161/169/AB/R, adopted 11 December 2000, para. 164.

22 *U.S. Trade Sanctions*

Measures on Beef and, subsequently, in *EC – Asbestos*,[25] the following factors should be examined:[26]

- The importance of interests or values that the challenged measure is intended to protect. (With respect to this requirement, the Appellate Body has suggested that, if the value or interest pursued is considered important, it is more likely that the measure is 'necessary'.)[27]
- The extent to which the challenged measure contributes to the realization of the end pursued by that measure. (In relation to this requirement, the Appellate Body has suggested that the greater the extent to which the measure contributes to the end pursued, the more likely that the measure is 'necessary'.)[28]
- The trade impact of the challenged measure. (With regard to this requirement, the Appellate Body has said that, if the measure has a relatively slight trade impact, the more likely that the measure is 'necessary'. The Appellate Body has also indicated that whether a reasonably available WTO-consistent alternative measure exists must be taken into consideration in applying this requirement.)[29]

(1) Importance of the protected values

7.25   The first factor the Panel will consider is the relative importance of the values protected by the challenged measure.[30] In terms of the importance of the values at stake, the United States argues that the protection of human rights and democracy is 'of vital importance' and supports this statement by referring to a large number of domestic as well as international measures it has taken to strengthen the protection of these interests. Thailand does not indicate any disagreement with the United States' assessment on this issue.

---

25 Appellate Body Report, Korea – Measures Affecting Imports of Fresh, Chilled and Frozen Beef, WT/DS161/169/AB/R, adopted 11 December 2000, para. 178; Appellate Body Report, European Communities – Measures Affecting Asbestos and Asbestos-Containing Products, WT/DS135/AB/R, adopted 5 April 2001, para. 172.

26 Panel Report, Measures Affecting the Cross-Border Supply of Gambling and Betting Services, WT/DS285/R, adopted10 November 2004, para. 6.477.

27 Appellate Body Report, Korea – Measures Affecting Imports of Fresh, Chilled and Frozen Beef, WT/DS161/169/AB/R, adopted 11 December 2000, para. 162.

28 *Ibid.*, para. 163.

29 *Ibid.*, paras. 163 and 166.

30 Appellate Body Report, Korea – Measures Affecting Imports of Fresh, Chilled and Frozen Beef, WT/DS161/169/AB/R, adopted 11 December 2000, para. 162; Appellate Body Report, European Communities – Measures Affecting Asbestos and Asbestos-Containing Products, WT/DS135/AB/R, adopted 5 April 2001, para. 172.

7.26   As stated above, the Panel agrees that the values protected by the JADE Act include fundamental human rights and democracy. The Panel finds that these societal interests can be characterized as 'vital and important in the highest degree'.[31]

(2) Contribution to the ends pursued

7.27   A second factor to consider in determining the necessity of the measure at issue is the contribution of the measure to the realization of the ends pursued by it. The United States has provided the Panel with several detailed reports that cite that the gem industry is a significant source of income for the Myanmar regime. Furthermore, the United States provided evidence of the financial implications of the BFDA ban and the subsequent JADE Act for the import of Myanmarese gemstones in the United States. Thailand does not contest these reports but alleges that the effect of the JADE Act on the junta is minimal because most of the Myanmarese rubies are smuggled into Thailand, yielding little revenue to the regime.

7.28   The Panel recalls that the purpose of the contested measure is to protect the public values of human rights and democracy. Given that the JADE Act effectively *prohibits* the import of jadeite and rubies from Myanmar, products that have been associated with the violation of these values, the Panel finds that the Act must to some extent contribute to addressing these concerns.[32]

7.29   The Panel therefore concludes that the JADE Act, at least to some extent, contributes to the ends pursued.

(3) Restrictive impact

7.30   With regard to the restrictive impact of the challenged measure on international commerce, the United States considers that the JADE Act's impact on the trade of Myanmarese gems is significant because of the strict control and sanctions that are applied. According to the United States, the trade restriction on the same products originating from other countries is limited to keeping a record on the transaction of the article, a measure that does not delay the import of the goods to the United States. Thailand agrees that the trade restriction on Myanmarese jadeite and rubies is

---

31 The protection of human life and health against a life-threatening health risk was found 'vital and important in the highest degree' by the Appellate Body in EC-Asbestos. Appellate Body Report, European Communities – Measures Affecting Asbestos and Asbestos-Containing Products, WT/DS135/AB/R, adopted 5 April 2001, para. 933.

32 Cfr. Appellate Body Report, Measures Affecting the Cross-Border Supply of Gambling and Betting Services, WT/DS285/AB/R, adopted 7 April 2005, para.313.

24 *U.S. Trade Sanctions*

significant, but adds that the measure also negatively influences the trade in non-Myanmarese rubies.

7.31   The Panel concurs that the ban on importing jadeite and rubies mined or extracted in Myanmar by its design has a significant restrictive impact on international commerce in general.[33]

(4) Interim conclusion

7.32   Having addressed the relevant factors separately, it remains for us to weigh and balance them with a view to coming to a conclusion whether, overall, the challenged measure is 'necessary' within the meaning of Article XX (a) to protect public morals. We must weigh the fact that the measure in question makes a material contribution to the protection of public morals that are vital and important to the highest degree against the fact that the condition significantly restricts international commerce by applying strict control.

7.33   At the same time, we also need to take account of the fact that the protection of public morals 'ranks among the most important values or interests pursued by Members as a matter of public policy'[34] and that 'Members, in applying different exceptions under Article XX, have the right to determine the level of protection that they consider appropriate'.[35]

7.34   Weighing these factors, we reach the conclusion that, in the absence of reasonably available alternatives, the measure in question is 'necessary' to protect public morals in the United States.

(5) Alternative measures

7.35   The Panel will now compare the measure with possible alternatives, which may be less trade restrictive while providing an equivalent contribution to the achievement of the objective. The Appellate Body has stated that

---

33 An Article XX defence requires examination of how much the ban restricts imports of those same products. The Panel in Brazil – Retreaded Tyres observed in this regard that the import ban before it was 'by design as trade-restrictive as can be' (Panel Report, Brazil – Measures Affecting Imports of Retreaded Tyres, WT/DS332/R, adopted 12 June 2007, para. 7.211).

34 Panel Report, China – Measures Affecting Trading Rights and Distribution Services for Certain Publications and Audiovisual Entertainment Products, WT/DS363/R, adopted 12 August 2009, para. 7.817.

35 Appellate Body Report, Korea – Measures Affecting Imports of Fresh, Chilled and Frozen Beef, WT/DS161/169/AB/R, adopted 11 December 2000, para. 176; Appellate Body Report, European Communities – Measures Affecting Asbestos and Asbestos-Containing Products, WT/DS135/AB/R, adopted 5 April 2001, para. 168.

this comparison should be carried out in the light of the importance of the interests or values at stake. An alternative measure is not considered to be 'reasonably available' when it is merely theoretical or does not achieve the desired level of protection with respect to the objective pursued.

7.36   Thailand presents several alternative measures that would be less restrictive on international trade. However, the United States argues that nothing less than a full ban is sufficient to protect its interest. Any lesser measure would indirectly allow trade in gems with an abusive country and therefore offend its public morals. The United States further refers to the failed efforts that already have been made by the international community and the ineffective less restrictive sanctions it has taken previously.

7.37   The Panel analyzed Thailand's proposed alternatives. The Panel did not, however, consider measures that permit the import of Myanmarese gems to allow the United States to achieve its desired level of protection of public morals. Because of the importance of the interest at stake and the high level of protection adopted, the Panel concludes that Thailand was not able to demonstrate that an alternative was reasonably available.

(6) Conclusion

7.38 In light of the findings above, the Panel concludes that section 6 of the JADE Act is 'necessary' to 'protect public morals' within the meaning of Article XX (a).

2. Chapeau of Article XX GATT 1994

7.39   The chapeau of Article XX provides that measures are subject to the requirement that they are 'not applied in a manner which would constitute a means of arbitrary or unjustifiable discrimination between countries where the same conditions prevail, or a disguised restriction on international trade (...)'

7.40   The chapeau focuses on the application of a measure inconsistent with one of the obligations under the GATT 1994 but provisionally justified under one of the exceptions described in Article XX (a)–(j). The chapeau requires that measures be applied in a manner that does not to constitute 'arbitrary' or 'unjustifiable discrimination', or a 'disguised restriction on trade in services'. The Member seeking the exception has the burden of proving that its measure is consistent with the chapeau.

7.41   The United States argues that while the trade sanctions against Myanmar constitute discrimination, they are neither unjustified nor arbitrary because of the exceptional record of human rights abuses in Myanmar, which has been internationally recognised. According to Thailand, U.S.

26   U.S. Trade Sanctions

trade sanctions discriminate arbitrarily between like States because they single out gemstones extracted or mined in Myanmar without targeting goods extracted or mined in other countries. Secondly, Thailand argues that the measure is an unjustifiable discrimination because it requires other Members to adopt the same policy as the United States.

7.42   Firstly, the Panel would like to emphasize that the chapeau of Article XX recognizes the need to maintain a balance of rights and obligations between the right of a Member to invoke one or another of the exceptions of Article XX, and the substantive rights of the other Members under the GATT 1994, on the other hand.

7.43   In the words of the Appellate Body

> To permit one Member to abuse or misuse its right to invoke an exception would be effectively to allow that Member to degrade its own treaty obligations as well as to devalue the treaty rights of other Members. If the abuse or misuse is sufficiently grave or extensive, the Member, in effect, reduces its treaty obligation to a merely facultative one and dissolves its juridical character, and, in so doing, negates altogether the treaty rights of other Members.[36]

And also

> The chapeau is animated by the principle that while the exceptions of Article XX may be invoked as a matter of legal right, they should not be so applied as to frustrate or defeat the legal obligations of the holder of the right under the substantive rules of the *General Agreement.* If those exceptions are not to be abused or misused, in other words, the measures falling within the particular exceptions must be applied reasonably, with due regard both to the legal duties of the party claiming the exception and the legal rights of the other parties concerned.[37]

7.44   With these general considerations in mind, we now address the issue of whether the *application* of the United States measure, although the measure itself falls within the terms of Article XX (a), nevertheless constitutes 'a means of arbitrary or unjustifiable discrimination between countries where the same conditions prevail' or 'a disguised restriction on international trade'. The Panel will now examine each of the discussed standards contained in the chapeau in turn.

---

36 Appellate Body Report, United States – Import Prohibition of Certain Shrimp and Shrimp Products, WT/DS58/AB/R, adopted 12 October 1998, para. 156.

37 Appellate Body Report, United States – Standards for Reformulated and Conventional Gasoline, WT/DS2/R, adopted 26 January 1996, 22.

a) Unjustifiable discrimination

7.45   We examine first whether the challenged measure has been applied in a manner constituting 'unjustifiable discrimination between countries where the same conditions prevail'.

7.46   The challenged measure is an economic embargo that requires all other exporting Members, if they wish to exercise their GATT right to export to the United States, to adopt the same trade sanction as that applied by the United States. Thailand questions the justifiability of such a measure.

7.47   However, the Appellate Body in *US – Import Prohibition of Certain Shrimp and Shrimp Products* stated that

> It appears to us, however, that conditioning access to a Member's domestic market on whether exporting Members comply with, or adopt, a policy or policies unilaterally prescribed by the importing Member may, to some degree, be a common aspect of measures falling within the scope of one or another of the exceptions (a) to (j) of Article XX. Paragraphs (a) to (j) comprise measures that are recognized as *exceptions to substantive obligations* established in the GATT 1994, because the domestic policies embodied in such measures have been recognized as important and legitimate in character. It is not necessary to assume that requiring from exporting countries compliance with, or adoption of, certain policies (although covered in principle by one or another of the exceptions) prescribed by the importing country, renders a measure *a priori* incapable of justification under Article XX. Such an interpretation renders most, if not all, of the specific exceptions of Article XX inutile, a result abhorrent to the principles of interpretation we are bound to apply.[38]

7.48   An aspect that bears heavily in the appraisal of justifiable or unjustifiable discrimination are the efforts of the United States and the international community as a whole to engage the targeted State in serious negotiations with the objective of ensuring the protection of human rights, before enforcing the import prohibition.

7.49   The Panel notes that an import prohibition is, ordinarily, the heaviest 'weapon' in a Member's armoury of trade measures. The evidence, however, shows that serious efforts were made by the United States to enforce human rights protection through diplomatic measures. The record also shows that the United States attempted to negotiate international trade sanctions before imposing a unilateral import ban. It is thus convincingly

---

38 Appellate Body Report, United States – Import Prohibition of Certain Shrimp and Shrimp Products, WT/DS58/AB/R, adopted 12 October 1998, para. 155.

28   *U.S. Trade Sanctions*

demonstrated that alternative courses of action were no longer reasonably open to the United States for securing the legitimate policy goal of its measure.

7.50   A second aspect that regards the justifiability of discrimination is the fact that the statute permits a degree of discretion or flexibility to other countries in how the trade in the concerned articles is prevented in practice.[39]

7.51   In light of efforts of the United States to pursue the protection of human rights through diplomatic and multilateral actions and the flexibility given to other Members in the prevention and certification of the targeted goods, the Panel finds the application of the challenged measure to be justifiable under the chapeau of Article XX.

b) Arbitrary discrimination

7.52   We now consider whether the import prohibition has been applied in a manner constituting 'arbitrary discrimination between countries where the same conditions prevail'. The complaining Member argues that the measure is arbitrary because it discriminates between different countries where human rights abuses occur by singling out Myanmar. The United States finds the case of Myanmar to be distinguishable from other situations due to the unprecedented international condemnation.

7.53   The Panel notes that selectivity as such does not constitute an arbitrary discrimination under the chapeau of Article XX GATT. If the mere occurrence of discrimination in the measure would make it *a priori* incapable of justification under Article XX, most, if not all, of the specific exceptions of Article XX would be rendered inutile, a result that would be contrary to the principles of interpretation we apply. Therefore, only selectivity that is unreasonable, i.e., arbitrary, is prohibited by the chapeau.

7.54   To determine whether the situation in Myanmar can reasonably be distinguished from the situation in other Member States, the Panel will consider the international action and condemnation that has occurred in the last decade.

7.55   Firstly, the human rights record of Myanmar was scrutinized on the international level in the context of the International Labour Organization. Focusing on the regime's practice of forced labour, the ILO compelled the regime, by way of a resolution, to adhere to its international obligations under the Forced Labour Convention in 2000. This action clearly differentiates the situation in Myanmar from that in other States, as it was the first

---

39   Section 6, subsection (c) of the JADE Act.

time that the ILO adopted such a resolution under Article 33 of its Constitution.

7.56   Secondly, the human rights situation in Myanmar has attracted an unprecedented level of condemnation on the level of the United Nations. The human rights record of Myanmar has been the subject of a vast number of U.N. resolutions. Moreover, since 2006, the situation in Myanmar has also been on the formal agenda of the Security Council of the United Nations, implying *inter alia* that the Members of the Security Council now request regular reports on the situation in Myanmar from the Special Adviser to the Secretary-General for Myanmar.

7.57   Taking account of the international efforts described above and the failure of Myanmar's regime to interact with the international community, the Panel considers the human rights situation in Myanmar to be exceptional. While the human rights record of certain other Members may in some aspects be comparable to that of Myanmar, the lack of other options available to address this specific situation distinguishes it from others.

7.58   The Panel therefore concludes that the unprecedented international action and condemnation of the situation in Myanmar distinguishes it in such a way that discrimination against this Member should not be considered inherently unreasonable or arbitrary.

c) Disguised restriction on international trade

7.59   'Disguised restriction on international trade' comprises not only concealed or unannounced restriction or discrimination in international trade but also restrictions amounting to arbitrary or unjustifiable discrimination in international trade taken under the guise of a measure formally within the terms of an exception listed in Article XX.

7.60   In *US Gasoline* the Appellate Body found that

> the kinds of considerations pertinent in deciding whether the application of a particular measure amounts to 'arbitrary or unjustifiable discrimination', may also be taken into account in determining the presence of a 'disguised restriction' on international trade. The fundamental theme is to be found in the purpose and object of avoiding abuse or illegitimate use of the exceptions to substantive rules available in Article XX.[40]

---

40 Appellate Body Report, United States – Standards for Reformulated and Conventional Gasoline, WT/DS2/R, adopted 26 January 1996, 25.

30 U.S. Trade Sanctions

7.61 Accordingly, a measure is considered to be a disguised restriction if it aims to conceal the pursuit of trade-restrictive objectives. Examining its design, architecture and revealing structure may ascertain the aim of a measure.[41] In these three elements the Panel finds nothing that might lead to the conclusion that the measure has protectionist objectives.

7.62 In practice, the discussed measure may have the effect of favouring the domestic substitute product. Because this is a natural consequence of prohibiting a particular product, it does not automatically lead to the conclusion that a measure has protectionist aims. In this particular case, the evidence does not show any relevant benefit to the domestic industry in comparison with the total of third country industries. Consequently, the panel concludes that the measure does not constitute a disguised restriction.

7.63 In light of the above, the Panel considers the challenged measure to satisfy the conditions of the chapeau of Article XX GATT 1994.

d) Conclusion

7.64 The Panel concludes that the import prohibition on jadeite and rubies mined or extracted in Myanmar, which violates Article XI:1 of the GATT 1994, is justified under Article XX (a).

Overall conclusions

7.65 In the light of the above, the Panel concludes as follows:

(a) On the basis of its findings above, the Panel concludes that the prohibition on import of jadeite and rubies mined or extracted in Myanmar constitutes a prohibition within the meaning of Article XI:1 GATT 1994.
(b) With respect to the measure found to be a prohibition by a contracting party on the importation of a product of the territory of a contracting party, the Panel concludes that the prohibition is incompatible with Article XI:1 of the GATT 1994.
(c) However, on the basis of its findings above, the Panel concludes that the prohibition, insofar as it introduces a treatment of these products that is prohibited under Article XI:1, is justified as such and in its implementation by the provisions of paragraph (a) and the introductory clause of Article XX of the GATT 1994.

---

41 Appellate Body Report, European Communities – Measures Affecting Asbestos and Asbestos-Containing Products, WT/DS135/AB/R, adopted 5 April 2001, para. 8.236.

3 Biofuels and the Right to Food (World Trade Organization, Panel Report)

Alexia Herwig

Abstract

This fictitious WTO panel report shows that the WTO's non-violation remedy can be used to make claims related to the extraterritorial responsibility of WTO Members to protect human rights in their trade relations. The non-violation complaint about hindrances to the attainment of treaty objectives can be invoked if a WTO Member threatens standards of living in another WTO Member through WTO-consistent measures. Conducting trade relations with a view to raising standards of living is mentioned in the preambles of the GATT 1994 and the Agreement Establishing the WTO. The International Covenant on Economic, Social and Cultural Rights creates extraterritorial obligations in respect of the right to an adequate standard of living. The ICESCR is part of the legal context of the WTO and must be used to interpret the preamble, resulting in an interpretation of the preamble that confers extraterritorial responsibility on WTO Members consistently with the international law on State responsibility.

Introductory note

The shift to crop-based biofuel production in developed countries such as the EU and the US is alleged to have led to the diversion of sugar and starchy crops and vegetable oils from food to fuel production.[1] The increase in demand for crops and vegetable oils is associated with food shortages and price increases, worsening food security, particularly in developing countries.[2] While several developing countries have started to produce more in response to demand, the last years have witnessed price increases for several crops and vegetable oils, which were partly caused by the shift to

---

1 Fonseca, M. B. et al. (2010), 'Impacts of the EU Biofuel Target on Agricultural Markets and Land Use. A Comparative Modelling Assessment', Joint Research Centre Institute for Prospective Technological Studies Reference Reports, 10.

2 Ibid., at 20–3, with further references to other studies estimating the price increase for vegetable oils due to biofuel policies to be between 15% to 30%.

32 *Biofuels and the Right to Food*

biofuels.[3] This suggests that demand outstrips supply. While increased demand for crops and vegetable oils benefits some developing countries, such as Indonesia, Malaysia and Nigeria, smallhold farmers, the rural and urban poor or net food importing countries do not benefit.[4]

The issue presented in this hypothetical WTO panel report is whether a non-violation complaint can be used to require a WTO Member to account for negative effects on the right to an adequate standard of living produced through its measure (in essence laws or regulations) instituting a switch to biofuels.[5] The *non-violation remedy* is available to claim that a WTO-consistent measure poses impediments to the attainment of treaty objectives or nullifies or impairs benefits arising from the WTO agreements.[6] The GATT 1994 mentions in its preamble that trade and economic relations should be conducted with a view to raising standards of living. Non-violation *cases* imply that the measure complained of does not violate WTO obligations. A *situation complaint* is available for making the same claims in 'any other situation' in which a measure by a WTO Member is not the subject of the complaint.[7] In case a complaint is successful, a WTO Member is not required to withdraw the measure. Rather, it must make a mutually satisfactory adjustment, which may include compensation.[8] The non-violation and situation complaint mechanisms are available provided the relevant WTO agreement allows for their use.[9] The non-violation remedy applying to measures is governed by the dispute settlement procedure of a violation complaint, subject to a few limited specifications.[10] In the case of a situation complaint, no appeal to the Appellate Body is possible and a panel

---

3 FAO (2011), 'Addressing High Food Prices: A Synthesis Report of FAO Policy Consultations at Regional and Subregional Level', available at http://www.fao.org/fileadmin/user_upload/ISFP/High_food_prices_synthesis_CFS_FINAL.pdf, p. 16. The current food price index is high but still below its 2011 peak. See FAO (2012), 'FAO Food Price Index Holds Steady', available at http://www.fao.org/news/story/en/item/155659/icode/.

4 FAO, IFAD, WPF (2012), 'Joint Statement from FAO, IFAD and WFP on International Food Prices', available at http://www.fao.org/news/story/en/item/155472/icode/.

5 My analysis is partly based on Herwig, A. (2012) 'WTO Non-Violation or Situation Complaints: A Remedy for Extraterritorial Effects on the Human Right to an Adequate Standard of Living' *Global Policy* 3(4), 471–5.

6 Article XXIII :1 (b), GATT 1994.

7 Article XXIII :1 (c), GATT 1994.

8 Marrakesh Agreement Establishing the World Trade Organization, 1867 UNTS 3 (entered into force 1 January 1995), Annex 2, Understanding on the Settlement of Disputes (DSU), Article 26.1(b) and (d).

9 Marrakesh Agreement, n. 2, Annex 2 (Dispute Settlement Understanding) (DSU), Article 26.1 and .2. This is the case for TRIPS. See Böckenförde, M. (2006) 'Article 26 DSU', in R. Wolfrum, P.-T. Stoll and K. Kaiser (eds) *Max Planck Commentaries on World Trade Law: WTO – Institutions and Dispute Settlement*, Leiden, Boston: Martinus Nijhoff, 572–86: 579. GATS has its own non-violation complaint in Article XXIII:3.

10 Article 26.1, DSU.

Litigating Transnational Human Rights Obligations 33

report requires the positive consensus of all WTO Members in order to become adopted.[11]

As of this writing, no human-rights related claims have ever been filed under the non-violation or situation remedy provisions. Complainants have generally used the non-violation remedy to claim that a member has nullified or impaired benefits of increased market access due to tariff reductions. Prior to the development of real disciplines on subsidies, members used the non-violation remedy to complain that domestic subsidies undermined their expectation of increased market access.[12] In *Japan – Film*, the US complained about the Japanese government impeding access to its market for photographic film and paper through certain provisions on rebates and retail restructuring measures that allegedly favoured or tolerated private restraints on competition by Japanese competitors.[13]

GATT and WTO panels have seldom made adverse findings in non-violation cases. According to Böckenförde, only three cases were ever successful and these would today be violation cases because WTO disciplines now exist.[14] The subsequent creation of WTO disciplines addresses concerns that non-violation and situation findings could have little legitimacy because panels decide without detailed rules.[15]

A few commentators have wondered whether the non-violation and situation complaint can be used to advance a human rights agenda in the WTO. Bagwell and Staiger inquire whether a WTO Member lowering its domestic standards of environmental protection or labour rights might nullify or impair the benefits producers in high-standards jurisdictions expected from tariff reductions.[16] This could be the case where the lower environmental or labour standards lower costs of production of the WTO

---

11 Article 26.2, DSU.

12 GATT Panel Report, *EEC – Oilseeds*, BSID 37S/86. A subsidy is defined as a financial contribution or income and price support by the government. The trade concern with subsidies is that they change the competitive playing field to the advantage of the subsidized companies.

13 WTO Panel Report, *Japan – Measures Affecting Photographic Film and Paper*, WT/DS44/R, adopted 22 April 1998.

14 See Böckenförde, M. (2006) 'Article 26 DSU' in R. Wolfrum, P.-T. Stoll and K. Kaiser (eds) *Max Planck Commentaries on World Trade Law: WTO – Institutions and Dispute Settlement*, Leiden, Boston: Martinus Nijhoff, 572–86: 577–8. There has not been a successful situation complaint.

15 See in particular Cho, S. (1998) 'GATT Non-Violation Issues in the WTO Framework: Are They the Achilles' Heel of the Dispute Settlement Process ?, *Harvard International Law Journal* 39 (1), 311–51 and Cottier, T. and Nadakavukaren Schefer, K. (1997) 'NVNI Complaints in WTO/GATT Dispute Settlement: Past, Present and Future', in E.-U. Petersmann (ed.), *International Trade Law and the GATT/WTI Dispute Settlement System, Studies in Transnational Economic Law*, Vol. 11, The Hague: Kluwer Law International, 145–83: 182.

16 Bagwell, K. and Staiger, R.W. (2001) 'The WTO as a Mechanism for Securing Market Access Property Rights: Implications for Global Labor and Environmental Issues', *The Journal of Economic Perspectives* 15(3), 69–88.

34   *Biofuels and the Right to Food*

Member's domestic companies to the detriment of the ability of foreign suppliers to compete because they must comply with high environmental or labour standards in their home jurisdiction. Panizzon has suggested that censorship requirements of illiberal WTO Members may nullify and impair expected market access benefits under the GATS for audiovisual and entertainment services.[17]

In my view, invoking human rights in nullification and impairment of benefits cases encounters hurdles and limitations. First, the lower human rights standards must be a source of competitive advantage, and this may not always be the case. For instance, higher standards of labour protection could also result in higher productivity. Second, panels have added the further requirement that the nullification and impairment must be unforeseen at the time the concession was negotiated.[18] In that way, the worst and most persistent human rights violating WTO Members might well be immune from the non-violation remedy.[19] Third, I doubt that panels would recognize what in effect amounts to a duty to compensate for regulatory change in all but the most extreme cases for fear of being accused of interfering too much with the sovereignty of WTO Members.[20]

The invocation of impediments to the attainment of treaty objectives could be used to articulate the extraterritorial responsibility of WTO Members for foreseeable and deliberate impacts on living standards they create through their governmental measures.[21] It might be available in

---

17 Panizzon, M. (2008) 'How Human Rights Violations Nullify and Impair GATS Commitments', in Panizzon, M., Pohl, N. and Sauvé, P. (eds), *GATS and the Regulation of International Trade in Services*, Cambridge: Cambridge University Press, 534–60.

18 Measures that are also governed by the general exceptions justify the imposition of a stricter burden of proof with regard to their unforeseeability. See Panel Report, *EC – Asbestos*, para. 8.282. For an extensive analysis of the unforeseeability requirement and GATT case law, see Panel Report, *Japan – Film*, paras 10.72–10.81.

19 According to the panel in *EC – Asbestos*, the mere fact that a measure is a continuation of past governmental policy in existence at the time the tariff concession was negotiated is not enough to make the measure foreseeable. See Panel Report, *EC – Asbestos*, para. 8.291.

20 In *EC – Asbestos*, the panel was of the opinion that non-violation remedy was not rendered inapplicable because Article XX also applies. However, the non-violation remedy is particularly exceptional in these circumstances. See Panel Report, *European Communities – Measures Affecting Asbestos and Asbestos-Containing Products*, WT/DS135/R, paras 8.270 and 8.272.

21 The Maastricht Principles on the Extraterritorial Obligations of States in the area of Economic, Social and Cultural Rights consider states to be responsible extraterritorially when a state has effective control over a foreign territory, when a state has brought about foreseeable effects on human rights outside of its territory or when it has decisive influence over the realization of economic, social and cultural rights. Maastricht Principles on Extraterritorial Obligations of States in the Area of Economics, Social and Cultural Rights, Principles 3, 9, 13, 17, 20–7 and De Schutter et al. (2012) 'Commentary to the Maastricht Principles on Extraterritorial Obligations of States in the area of Economic, Social and Cultural Rights', *Human Rights Quarterly* 34(4), 1084–69: 1109–15.

cases where export subsidies displace developing country farmers, and their home government cannot remedy their decline in living standards. Such a situation might also be considered as one where the WTO interferes with the ability of the developing country to protect human rights.[22] If a WTO Member's trade with an illiberal government enables that government to stay in power and the WTO Member has knowledge that the illiberal government does not redistribute the gains from trade to its population so that its living standards rise, a non-violation complaint might also be successful. Under human rights law, the WTO Member might also be responsible for aiding and abetting a foreign government in the commission of human rights violations in these circumstances.[23] Where a WTO Member has knowledge that it is causing irremediable declines in living standards abroad it cannot be considered to be conducting trade relations with a view to raising standards of living.

With non-attainment complaints there should not be a requirement of unforeseeability of the measure because this type of complaint strikes me as regulatory in nature, unlike the nullification and impairment of benefits remedy, which is concerned with safeguarding expectations formed during negotiations and as a result of concessions. My report assumes that the *de minimis* causation standard for nullification and impairment non-violation cases also applies to non-attainment complaints.[24] I also assume that the parties agree that the preamble of the GATT sets forth treaty objectives and that a non-violation complaint can be based solely on the preamble.

The legal issue in this fictitious report is the question of whether the objective of conducting trade and economic relations with a view to raising standards of living refers only to a WTO Member's duty to redistribute gains from trade to its own population or also to the duty of WTO Members to account for impacts on standards of living their trade causes abroad. Another issue of interpretation is whether or not the objective applies only to long-term prospects on living standards of populations in the aggregate. The report next turns to the evaluation of the facts in light of the conditions for a successful non-violation complaint for impediments to the attainment of treaty objectives. It analyzes whether the Renewable Energy Directive caused a foreseeable increase in demand for palm oil and other biofuel crops; whether Benin could correct any negative effects on standards of living of its population; and whether the EU had knowledge of or control over Benin's ability to correct adverse effects on standards of living.

---

22 The Maastricht Principles consider that a state would be extraterritorially responsible for a human rights violation in such a situation. See Principle 21.

23 Ibid.

24 The Panel Report in *Japan – Film* established the causation standard of more than a *de minimis* contribution. See para. 10.84.

36 *Biofuels and the Right to Food*

WTO Panel Report

...

II. Factual aspects

2.1 Palm oil is obtained from the oil palm tree. It is used for cooking and is a key food ingredient in West African cuisine. Palm oil is rich in Vitamin A and E and polyunsaturated fats. Its high content of fatty acids and heat stability also makes it important in the production of oleochemicals and, more recently, of biodiesel.

2.2 Benin produces palm oil but is a net importer of palm oil from other countries. Eighty per cent of Benin's population is active in the agricultural sector. Palm oil is produced mainly in the south of Benin. In the north, farmers produce grain and starchy staples such as cassava. Benin is among the poor but not least developed countries in Africa. Its annual GNP per person is between €700–1200. More than 40 per cent of the population live below the international poverty line of having less than USD 1.25 a day of income.

2.3 The Renewable Energy Directive lays down mandatory shares of energy from renewable sources in transports for the European Member States. By 2020, at least 10 per cent of the final consumption of energy in transport must derive from renewable sources. Renewable sources include biomass.[25] However, renewable energy may only be counted towards the 10 per cent target if the energy production meets certain sustainability criteria laid down in Article 17.

2.4 Biodiesel obtained from palm oil results in a low level of aggregated greenhouse gas emissions from cultivation, production, transport and distribution provided that methane emitted during the pressing of palm oil is captured, compared to other types of fuels obtained from biomass.[26]

...

VII. Findings

7.1 Article XXIII:1(b) is sometimes referred to as a non-violation complaint. We note that it sets out three requirements: There must be (1) a measure, (2) an impediment to the attainment of any objective of the

---

25 Directive 2009/28/EC of the European Parliament and of the Council of 23 April 2009 on the promotion of the use of energy from renewable sources and amending and subsequently repealing Directives 2001/77/EC and 2003/30/EC, *Official Journal of the European Union* L 140 of 5 June 2009, p. 16, Art. 3(4).

26 Directive 2009/28/EC, Annex V.

Litigating Transnational Human Rights Obligations 37

Agreement, and (3) the impediment must be the result of the measure. We also note that there are two types of non-violation complaints: (a) a complaint alleging nullification and impairment of benefits, and (b) a complaint alleging impediments to the attainment of any objective of GATT 1994.

7.3   The present complaint is a case of first impression. No panel before us has dealt with a situation in which the complainant only invokes the existence of impediments to the attainment of an objective of the GATT, without at the same time alleging the nullification and impairment of benefits. We note that panels and the Appellate Body before us have characterized the non-violation remedy as an exceptional remedy to be approached with caution.[27] Such caution seems to us to be warranted. A treaty interpreter should not lightly create burdens additional to the legal obligations a treaty imposes. Nevertheless, the fact that a remedy is exceptional cannot absolve this panel from making findings in this case.

7.4   The panel in *Korea – Government Procurement* has characterized the nullification and impairment non-violation remedy as an emanation from the principle of good faith in the performance of treaty obligations.[28] According to this principle, a State party to a treaty should refrain from acts that would frustrate the object and purpose of a treaty even though they are consistent with treaty provisions.[29] We consider this characterization useful for the present case as well and rely on it in our analysis. A State party to a treaty must be assured that other signatories to the treaty do not threaten the attainment of the objectives of the treaty through actions consistent with the word but not the spirit of a treaty.

7.5   With this in mind, we now turn to the analysis of the legal claims and arguments made by the disputing parties.

Whether the GATT's preambular objective pertains to the extraterritorial effect of trade policies

7.6   Benin argues that the plural possessive pronoun of the GATT's preambular term '*their* relations in the field of trade and economic endeavour' can have meaning only if the responsibility of a WTO Member does not stop at its border. Benin maintains that GATT 1994, other WTO agreements and the ICESCR as context for the interpretation of the

---

27 Appellate Body Report, *European Communities – Measures Affecting Asbestos and Asbestos Containing Products*, WT/DS135/AB/R, para. 186; WTO Panel Report, *Japan – Measures Affecting Photographic Film and Paper*, WT/DS44/R, para. 10.36.

28 Panel Report, *Korea – Government Procurement*, WT/DS163/R, paras 7.94–7.95, 7.102.

29 Ibid., para. 7.94.

38 *Biofuels and the Right to Food*

preambular objective confirm the extraterritorial responsibility of a WTO Member.

7.8   To the European Union, the plural possessive pronoun in the preamble is just a grammatical consequence of the mentioning of the contracting parties in the plural in the GATT's preamble. It merely indicates that each WTO Member is responsible for correcting impacts on standards of living inside its own jurisdiction. Nevertheless, should the panel be of the opinion that WTO Members are responsible for the welfare of foreign populations, the European Union argues that such responsibility applies to all the indicators jointly as mentioned in the preambular heading, namely, standards of living, employment, income and demand.

7.10   Further, the European Union contests that the ICESCR is a relevant rule of international law applicable in the relations between the parties because it does not bind all WTO Members. Moreover, the European Union contests that the ICESCR imposes extraterritorial obligations.

7.11   We begin our analysis with the question of what WTO Members are responsible for before we turn to the issue of the possible extraterritorial nature of such responsibility. The disagreement between the parties centers on whether there is responsibility for the combined effects of all of the items in the preambular heading or for each individual item.

7.12   The text of Article XXIII:1(b) resolves this disagreement clearly. It speaks of 'any objective' in the singular. The ordinary meaning of the text therefore makes clear the injunction to impede the attainment of each one of the items listed in the preamble.

7.13   To analyze the possible extraterritorial scope of the responsibility for standards of living, we begin with the textual meaning of the preambular provision in question. To us, the plural possessive pronoun can sustain Benin's and the European Union's interpretation. We find the term 'in the field of trade and economic endeavour' more instructive because it suggests that the objective is limited to a particular field of application. Merely by joining the WTO, a member does not become responsible for any impact on standards of living produced abroad. It is only responsible if the impact is produced through measures affecting trade.

7.14   We turn next to the disagreement of the parties about whether the text of the GATT 1994 confirms the extraterritorial responsibility of WTO Members for effects it produces abroad.

7.15   To us, several provisions of the GATT indicate that WTO Members are responsible for matters beyond reductions in competitive opportunities. Thus, WTO Members have clearly accepted the responsibility of considering the impact of their policies on developing countries and the promotion of their integration into the world trading system. Under the

Litigating Transnational Human Rights Obligations

Agreement on Subsidies and Countervailing Measures, they have also accepted the responsibility for conduct that produces other undesirable effects on welfare, employment and the viability of enterprises in another WTO Member.

7.16   These provisions indicate that WTO Members bear some responsibility for welfare produced through their trade policies and suggest that the aim of conducting relations in the field of trade and economic endeavours confers extraterritorial responsibility on WTO Members in certain circumstances.

Whether or not the ICESCR is a relevant rule of international law applicable in the relations between the parties

7.17   We now turn to the question of whether or not the ICESCR constitutes relevant context for the interpretation of the preamble of GATT 1994. We note our disagreement with the analysis of the panel in *EC – Biotech*.[30] The definition of the term 'parties' in the VCLT refers to a State which has consented to a treaty and for which the treaty is in force.[31] The reference to the singular to us suggests that other rules of international law applicable in the relations between the parties can refer to rules binding on a subset of WTO Members of a multilateral treaty to be interpreted. Furthermore, we note that the VCLT's indirect purpose is the achievement of cooperation among nations.[32] In our view, this cooperation is better achieved if the term 'parties' in Article 31.3(c) refers to a subset of parties because it allows for the systemic integration of a greater number of rules of international law.

7.18   Our position also finds support in the Appellate Body's decision in *EC – Aircraft*. In para. 845, the Appellate Body noted that the treaty interpreter should be guided by the purpose of treaty interpretation of ascertaining the common intention of the parties, but that account must also be taken of Article 31.3(c) being an expression of the principle of systemic integration of treaty provisions. It then referred to the International Law Commission's characterization of this principle as ensuring an interpretation of treaty provisions by reference to their wider normative environment so as to give coherence and meaningfulness to the process of legal interpretation. The Appellate Body stated that 'when recourse is had to a non-WTO

---

30 WTO Panel Report, European Communities, *Measures Affecting the Approval and Marketing of Biotech Products*, WT/DS291/R, WT/DS292/R, WT/DS293/R, adopted 29 September 2006, paras 7.58ff.

31 Vienna Convention on the Law of Treaties (VCLT), 1155 UNTS 331 (entered into force 27 January 1980), Article 2.1.

32 VCLT, Preamble.

40   *Biofuels and the Right to Food*

rule for the purposes of interpreting provisions of the WTO agreements, a delicate balance must be struck between, on the one hand, taking due account of an individual WTO Member's international obligations and, on the other hand, ensuring a consistent and harmonious approach to the interpretation of WTO law among all WTO Members'.

7.19   We understand the Appellate Body's reference to balancing necessarily to imply that it disagrees with the panel's ruling in *EC – Biotech* that the source of contextual interpretation must bind all WTO Members. To us, the treaty interpreter must look beyond form to the substance in the attempt to ascertain the common but not necessarily identical normative commitments of the parties, otherwise, in an international legal context with a growing number of multilateral treaties, the principle of systemic integration could hardly be given meaning. We thus consider that where WTO Members have recognized a non-WTO rule of international law as binding, albeit in different instruments or with slightly different content or towards different states, such a rule is a 'rule of international law applicable in the relations between the parties' in the sense of Article 31.3(c) of the VCLT and should be taken into account in interpreting provisions of the WTO agreements.

7.20   In this connection, we note the almost universal support the right to an adequate standard of living has achieved. States not bound by the ICESCR have recognized directly or indirectly similar obligations in two specialized human rights instruments: Article 24 and 27 of the Convention on Rights of the Child (CRC) and Article 3 and Article 14.2(h) of the Convention on Elimination of all Forms of Discrimination against Women (CEDW). In Article 4 of the CRC, they commit to international cooperation for the implementation of economic, social and cultural rights of children. In Article 3 of the CEDW, they commit to take all appropriate measures for the purpose of ensuring the non-discriminatory exercise and enjoyment of their protected rights. Inasmuch as international cooperation is an appropriate measure, the parties have bound themselves to it. WTO Members have also expressed their support for this right in Article 25(1) of the Universal Declaration of Human Rights. We note that the CRC has received 193 ratifications and the CEDW has received 187 ratifications, covering all WTO Members with full competences and internationally accepted sovereignty, except the United States of America.

7.21   The United States has committed itself to realizing components of the right to an adequate standard of living and taken on extraterritorial obligations in this respect in regional treaties.

7.22   Article 34 (j) and (h) of the Charter of the Organization of American States commits States to do their utmost to realize proper nutrition and adequate housing. In Article 30, the parties pledge themselves to a united

Litigating Transnational Human Rights Obligations 41

effort to ensure international social justice in their relations. Article 31 affirms that inter-American cooperation for integral development is the common and joint responsibility of the Member States. In Article 45, the parties to the Charter recognize the right to material well-being of all human beings without distinction as to nationality and other factors and the right to work to be performed under conditions of ensuring for the worker and his family a decent standard of living, including during old age. Article 26 of the American Convention on Human Rights commits States to international cooperation for the progressive, full realization of the rights implicit in the economic, social, educational, scientific, and cultural standards set forth in the OAS Charter.

7.23   The United States has ratified the Charter of the OAS and signed but not ratified the American Convention on Human Rights, the ICESCR, and the Conventions on Rights of the Child and on Elimination of all Forms of Discrimination against Women. Through its ratification of the Charter, it has agreed to be bound by obligations pertaining to the right to an adequate standard of living and to international cooperation towards its realization.

7.26   Our analysis shows that all WTO Members with the powers able to do so have bound themselves to observe the right to an adequate standard of living or components thereof, including through international cooperation. Given its recognition by all WTO Members, we consider that the right to an adequate standard of living is a rule of international law applicable in the relations between the WTO Members in the sense of Article 31(3)(c) VCLT and hence a source of contextual interpretation for the preamble of the GATT 1994. Recourse to non-WTO treaties not binding upon all WTO members as a source of contextual interpretation of WTO law does not detract from establishing the common but not necessarily identical intentions of the WTO Members regarding the interpretation of WTO law where they have taken on in substance the same obligation in other legal instruments. Accordingly, we consider that we may properly rely on the ICESCR in interpreting WTO law.

Whether or not there is an extraterritorial obligation to protect, respect and fulfill the right to an adequate standard of living in the ICESCR

7.27   One main point of contention between the parties to this dispute is whether the duty to cooperate in respecting, protecting and fulfilling human rights in the ICESCR is evidence of the territorial scope of human rights obligations.[33] We agree with the European Union that the duty leaves

---

33   International Covenant on Economic, Social and Cultural Rights, 993 UNTS 3 (entered into force 3 January 1976), Articles 2.1 and 11.2.

42   *Biofuels and the Right to Food*

unspecified the aim or scope of the cooperation. However, we consider that this open-endedness may well have been a deliberate choice of the parties to enable an evolutive interpretation of this duty to take account of the contemporary concerns of nations as they emerge to reflect changes in the international legal and political order.

7.28   In our view, the notion of a 'duty' to cooperate in respecting, protecting and fulfilling human rights obligations necessarily implies that human rights obligations of the parties to the ICESCR do not stop at their national borders because a 'duty' is other-regarding and an action or omission owed to someone. Unless the parties bear some responsibility for the human rights situation abroad, the notion of a 'duty' to cooperate does not make sense. At a minimum, it requires a good faith effort at cooperation with a view to respecting, protecting and fulfilling human rights together. As a treaty interpreter must give meaning to all words of the treaty, we cannot ignore use of the word 'duty' rather than 'possibility' or 'may'.

7.29   The text of the ICESCR supports the construction of human rights obligations as extraterritorial. We note that the ICESCR obliges its parties to take steps for the progressive, *full* realization of its human rights obligation and makes clear that nothing in it may be interpreted as implying for *any* state, group or person *any* right to engage in *any* activity or to perform *any* act aimed at the destruction of *any* of its rights.[34] These categorical obligations are relevant as context for the interpretation of the right to an adequate standard of living and the duty of international cooperation. They support the construction of human rights obligations as extraterritorial.

7.30   In addition, Articles 55 and 56 of the UN Charter constitute an obligation to cooperate for the *universal* respect of human rights and higher standards of living.[35] If such respect is to be universal, the obligation of international cooperation must, at a minimum, make a State responsible in accordance with the international law on State responsibility, that is, where a reduction in standards of living or a human rights violation occurs under its control, its coercion or where it aids and assists another State it knows to commit internationally wrongful acts.[36]

7.31   The context of the ICESCR therefore supports construing its obligations as extraterritorial. With this determination in mind, we see no need

---

34 ICESCR, Article 2.1 and 5.1.
35 Charter of the United Nations, entered into force 24 October 1945, Articles 55 and 56.
36 International Law Commission (2001), Articles on Responsibility of States for Internationally Wrongful Acts with Commentaries adopted by the International Law Commission, Report of the International Law Commission on the Work of its 53rd session (23 April to 1 June and 2 July to 10 August 2001), UN Doc. A/56/10, Articles 16–18.

Litigating Transnational Human Rights Obligations 43

to address the further legal argument whether or not the omission of any further jurisdictional clause in the ICESCR is indicative of the scope of human rights obligations.

Conclusion on whether or not the GATT's preambular objective implies the extraterritorial responsibility of WTO Members

7.32   We recall that our analysis of the ordinary meaning of the preambular objective has not settled conclusively that WTO Members are responsible for increases in standards of living beyond their territory. We have determined that the context of the preamble comprises the text of the GATT 1994, other WTO agreements and the right to an adequate standard of living as recognized in the ICESCR. These sources of contextual interpretation confirm that the responsibility of WTO members for the well-being and standard of living extends beyond their territories to foreign populations. For this reason, we find that the preambular objective of conducting trade and economic relations with a view to raising standards of living comprises an extraterritorial responsibility of WTO Members consistent with international law standards of responsibility. We turn to the appraisal of the Renewable Energy Directive and its causal connection to living standards in Benin below.

Whether or not the objective of conducting trade relations with a view to raising standards of living, income and real demand implies a responsibility to raise standards of living across the aggregate of a population or for groups of individuals

7.33   Benin argues that the objective of conducting trade and economic relations with a view to raising standards of living is threatened where the standard of living of a large section of the population is irreversibly worsened. A State impeding the ability of a home State to protect the human rights of its population is responsible for a violation of international law under the international law on state responsibility.

7.35   The European Union maintains that making WTO Members responsible for the welfare of groups of individuals abroad in the conduct of their trade relations is absurd because trade liberalization necessarily implies that the welfare of individuals is worsened as they can lose their employment due to foreign competition.

7.38   We consider that normally the home government of individuals or groups adversely affected by trade does or could exercise direct control to remedy declines in living standards. Such a case must, however, be distinguished from a situation where a home government is unable due to political, technical or economic problems to protect and fulfill human rights effectively and another state is in control over these circumstances. If another State has knowledge of and control over these constraints

44 Biofuels and the Right to Food

faced by the home State and takes actions that threaten human rights in the home State, it must be considered as exercising effective control over the human rights situation in that State and should bear its share of responsibility. To us, this situation is captured by the international ascription of State responsibility in case a State has direction and control over the commission of an internationally wrongful act.[37] The impediment arises because the action of the State produces effects abroad which make the political, technical or economic constraints faced by the other State acute.

7.39   We consider that the international law on State responsibility must inform our interpretation of the preamble of GATT 1994, with the effect that a WTO Member may be considered to fail to conduct trade relations with a view to raising standards of living even if its measure is of net long-term benefit to another WTO Member but it had knowledge of the fact that the other WTO Member would be unable promptly to mitigate short-term declines in living standards arising from the same measure due to severe political, technical or economic constraints.

7.40   Our conclusion is clearly confirmed by the text of the preambular objective of GATT 1994. It refers to conducting relations in the field of trade and economic endeavour '*with a view to* raising standards of living...' [our emphasis]. The term 'with a view to' must be interpreted as referring to the goals or intentions of the WTO Members in the conduct of their trade and economic relations.

7.41   Where a WTO Member has knowledge that another WTO Member is unable to remedy negative effects on standards of living brought about through its measures affecting trade or has control over the ability of the other WTO Member to remedy negative effects on standards of living and it puts in place such measure without amendment, it cannot be considered to be conducting its trade and economic relations with the intention or the goal of raising standards of living.

7.42   Our conclusion is also borne out by the non-violation or situation remedy being an expression of the principle of good faith.[38] Where a WTO Member knowingly makes it impossible to attain the treaty objectives, it cannot be considered to be acting in good faith.

7.43   We turn next to our analysis of the facts and their assessment in light of the standards imposed by Article XXIII:1(b) of GATT 1994.

---

37 International Law Commission (2001), 'Articles on Responsibility of States for Internationally Wrongful Acts', Article 17.
38 Panel Report, *Korea – Government Procurement*, paras. 7.94–7.95, 7.102.

Litigating Transnational Human Rights Obligations 45

Whether or not the Renewable Energy Directive constitutes an impediment to conducting trade and economic relations with a view to raising standards of living[39]

Does the Renewable Energy Directive cause an increase in demand for palm oil?

7.44   Benin argues that the Renewable Energy Directive makes more than a *de minimis* direct contribution to the increase in the price of palm oil and other staple crops and the food shortage because it sets high sustainability targets, which make palm oil effectively the best biofuel option.

7.46   The European Union maintains that there is no direct causal connection between its Renewable Energy Directive and any increases in the price of palm oil.

7.47   Article 3.4 of the Renewable Energy Directive requires that by 2020, at least 10 per cent of the final consumption of energy for transport be derived from renewable sources.[40] According to Article 2, biomass is included in the definition of renewable sources.[41] In order to count towards the 10 per cent threshold, Article 17.1 requires the energy from biofuels or bioliquids to fulfill sustainability criteria set out in paragraphs 2 to 6. Paragraph 2 requires that greenhouse gas emissions savings from biofuels and bioliquids compared to emissions from conventional fuel must amount to 35 per cent now and to 50 per cent by 1 January 2017.[42] In essence, this requirement amounts to a phasing out of biofuels and bioliquids that do not achieve this level of savings in greenhouse gas emissions.

7.48   Table A in Annex V shows that several biofuel options meet the emissions savings target. However, palm oil offers the most favourable mix of crop yield, low price and energy yield when compared to the other biofuel crops. Moreover, biogas is simply not an option for most European consumers who continue to demand diesel cars because of lower fuel prices and higher fuel efficiency.

7.50   After reviewing all facts, we conclude that the Renewable Energy Directive creates significant demand for palm oil biodiesel and hydrogenated

---

39 The fact and figures on which the following sections are based were obtained from 'Small Scale Palm-Oil Processing in Africa', FAO Corporate Document Repository available at E:\2 OIL PALM.mht; [farm structure and yield], European Commission Joint Research Centre, 'Impacts of the EU Biofuel Target on Agricultural Markets and Land Use: A Comparative Modelling Assessment'; the website www.indexmundi.org [commodity prices and import-export data, country information on Benin]; Johnston et. al., 'Resetting Global Expectations from Agricultural Biofuels', *4 Environmental Research Letters (2009)*, 14004 and FAO, 'The State of Food and Agriculture, Biofuels: Prospects, Risks and Opportunities'. [yield, energy equivalent] The conditionality of the EU's debt-forgiveness and Benin's particular problems linked to tax evasion are assumptions. Benin's 2011 corruption score with Transparency International is 3, placing it in the middle of all countries assessed but at 2/3 below the best score.

40 Directive 2009/28/EC at n. 24.

41 Ibid.

42 Ibid.

46 Biofuels and the Right to Food

palm oil because of the sustainability criteria it imposes in conjunction with the favourable yield, commodity price and European fuel prices and consumer demand for diesel cars. This demand must have been foreseeable for the European Union.

Effects of the increase in demand for palm oil in Benin and knowledge of the EC thereof

7.51   According to Benin, the increase in demand for palm oil is reflected in a steady price increase of this staple food in Benin, where palm oil is a key supply of fat and calories in a diet poor in meat. Benin asserts that poor families living below or near the international poverty line can no longer afford palm oil.

7.52   According to international market prices, there has been a 143.30 per cent price increase for palm oil in the last ten years and a 30.56 per cent increase in the last five years. Similar price increases exist for other biofuel staple foods. Benin also presents us with data showing that farmers have switched to the production of crops for biofuels and that one-third of its population lives at or below the international poverty line.

7.53   On the basis of a careful examination of this data, we can conclude that access to food for poor families in Benin has been worsened or made impossible because of their inexistent price elasticity of demand. A price increase of between 30 per cent is prohibitively high for families whose income already goes entirely towards purchasing food. Moreover, international data on development indicates a sharp decline in Benin, compared to a stable situation between 2005 and 2010. Thus, in 2011, Benin dropped from number 134 in the country ranking of the Human Development Index to number 167. We consider that this data is indicative of a decline in living standards in Benin and that Benin has succeeded in showing that there is a direct causal connection between the Renewable Energy Directive's 10 per cent target and sustainability criteria, the price increase for crops and vegetable oils, the production decisions of Benin's farmers and the price increase and food shortage in Benin.

7.54   It is clear to us that the EC's Renewable Energy Directive made more than a *de minimis* contribution to the effects on standards of living in Benin. The European Union constitutes a most important market for biofuels and the biggest worldwide market for biodiesel. According to estimates, 30 per cent of the price increase of biofuel crops is due to the shift to biofuels and with the European Union constituting one of the biggest markets for biofuels, a considerable portion of the 30 per cent are due to the Renewable Energy Directive.

7.55   We also consider that the European Union must have had knowledge of this causal connection between the Renewable Energy Directive

Litigating Transnational Human Rights Obligations 47

and food supply and prices in Benin. While the precise extent of the price increase was not known to the European Union, the fact that a significant price increase of vegetable oils and staple crops used for biofuel production would occur was known to the European Union as was data on poverty and food security in Benin.

Whether or not Benin could counteract the rise in food prices and the European Union had knowledge of and control over Benin's ability to do so

7.56 Benin argues that it was unable to counteract the detrimental effects on the availability of staple foods and their prices through a restraint on exports of palm oil, short-term food aid or transfer payments or taxation measures due to its public debt problem, corruption of tax officials and the long latency of the effectiveness of taxes.

7.57 The European Union does not contest these facts but argues that they show precisely that Benin itself is responsible for any declines in standards of living, employment, income and demand.

7.58 We find ourselves in agreement with Benin's argument that an export restraint would be of limited relief for Benin as a net importer of palm oil. We also consider it inconsistent with the trade liberalization objectives of GATT 1994 to make the non-violation remedy inaccessible in case a WTO Member fails to put in place trade restrictive measures that could deprive it of the long-term possibility of increasing standards of living.

7.59 We are also persuaded by Benin's difficulty in counteracting the food shortage and price increase through debt-based government spending and note in this connection that the European Union, as one of Benin's creditors, had control over Benin's ability to incur further public debt through debt-forgiveness or increased official development assistance.

7.60 Benin's inability to collect taxes effectively is to us clearly within the responsibility of Benin. Nevertheless, the European Union must have had general knowledge about the fact that taxation measures would not be of immediate and effective relief.

Findings and Recommendations

7.61 We have found that the objective of conducting trade and economic relations with a view to raising standards of living of the GATT 1994 calls on WTO Members to avoid foreseeable irreversible negative effects on standards of living caused by their domestic measures in the territory of another WTO Member. We have found that the Renewable Energy Directive is the direct cause of decreases in living standards in Benin and that the European Union had knowledge and partial control over Benin's inability to counteract this decline in living standards. We conclude that the European Union

48   *Biofuels and the Right to Food*

failed to conduct its trade and economic relations with a view to augmenting standards of living through the adoption of the Renewable Energy Directive. We therefore recommend that the European Union makes a mutually satisfactory adjustment as foreseen by Article XXIII:1 (b) of the GATT 1994.

4 Land Grabbing and Gender Issues (International Finance Corporation, Compliance Advisor Ombudsman)

Joss Saunders

Abstract

Independent Accountability Mechanisms (IAMs) such as the International Finance Corporation's Compliance Advisor Ombudsman (CAO) provide a soft law instrument for communities to challenge violations of economic and social rights where there is lending by one of the international finance institutions (IFIs) that have such a mechanism. However, such instruments are far from perfect. For one thing, they aim to assess whether the IFI has met its own declared standards, and these standards themselves only partly reflect economic and social rights. Another reason is that they rely for their enforcement on the internal allocation of rules and responsibilities within the IFI. Nevertheless, they are instructive for the application of the Maastricht ETO Principles because many of the mechanisms will have regard to compliance with national and international law, and because the Maastricht Principles are themselves normative and can be used to improve the IFI's standards.

This chapter considers a fictional case of land-grabbing, which then gives rise to a CAO audit, and in particular assesses the application of the IFC's Performance Standards on community impact and on gender.

Introductory note

Many international financial institutions (IFIs) have created Independent Accountability Mechanisms (IAMs). These include: the African Development Bank, the Asian Development Bank, the European Bank for Reconstruction and Development, the European Investment Bank, the Inter-American Development Bank, the Japan Bank for Regional Cooperation, the Nippon Export and Investment Insurance, and the United States Overseas Private Investment Corporation. The World Bank has established the Inspection Panel and the European Union the European Ombudsman. Such mechanisms are formal bodies established by the relevant institutions, as opposed to civil society organizations fulfilling a watchdog function, although there

50   *Land Grabbing and Gender Issues*

are also a number of civil society mechanisms, e.g. the Bank Information Centre,[1] the Bretton Woods Project,[2] BankWatch.org and ifiwatchnet.org.

The Compliance Advisor Ombudsman (CAO) is the World Bank's Independent Accountability Mechanism for the International Finance Corporation (IFC) and Multilateral Investment Guarantee Agency (MIGA). IFC is the World Bank's private lending arm. Established in 2001, its mission is 'to serve as a fair, trusted, and effective independent recourse mechanism and to improve the social and environmental accountability of IFC and MIGA'. As such, it offers a soft law instrument deserving of analysis in relation to its role as an accountability mechanism, and it is instructive to consider its role in the extraterritorial application of economic and social rights.

Between its establishment in 1999 and 2010, the CAO received 127 complaints and requests, of which 76 met its eligibility criteria. Those 76 complaints related to 48 projects in 28 countries. The CAO's Report *CAO at 10: Annual Report FY 2010 and Review 2000 –2010*[3] provides a very useful overview of these complaints and how they were handled. Eighty per cent of the complaints reveal socio-economic issues, and of these, 61 per cent relate to land.

The CAO has three roles. In its *ombudsman* role it seeks to obtain a mediated solution to complaints. Half of all its complaints in its first ten years were resolved in this way. In its *advisory* role it provides advice to the World Bank on environmental and social policies. The third role is the subject of this hypothetical judgment – namely, its *compliance* role.

The compliance function has a two-stage process. The first stage is triggered by the Ombudsman or a request from the World Bank itself, and is an appraisal to determine whether an audit is merited. Appraisals should be conducted within 45 days. The CAO will move to an audit if it finds either: evidence of future adverse environmental and social outcomes; the IFC's policies have not been applied properly; or if IFC/MIGA provisions have failed to provide adequate protection for communities or the environment at the project level. If there is insufficient evidence to determine this, the audit should proceed.

In the first ten years there were two reviews (before the present audit system was settled) and six audits. The two reviews related to mining in Peru and in Bolivia. The six audits dealt with: oil in Kazakhstan; agribusiness in Brazil; mining in the Democratic Republic of Congo; cellulose in Uruguay; palm oil in Indonesia; and agribusiness in Peru. The 2011 and 2012 Reports[4] show an increased caseload, with four cases in 2011 and seven cases in 2012 being reported to the compliance function, although not all of these will necessarily lead to an audit.

---

1 www.bicusa.org
2 www.brettonwoodsproject.org
3 www.cao-ombudsman.org
4 www.cao-ombudsman.org

A significant constraint is that the audit is not of the private sector body carrying out the challenged acts, but of the IFC's involvement in them. Nevertheless, the audit findings can have a powerful normative effect. On the other hand, the CAO findings are not binding on the IFC. This chapter recognises this limitation, which is one that should be addressed by the World Bank.

The present chapter considers the phenomenon of large scale land acquisitions, many of which are criticised as "land grabs". The term land grab is itself contentious, and self-evidently does not apply to every acquisition of land. We use the term land grab as defined by the International Land Coalition's Tirana declaration:[5]

> acquisitions or concessions that are one or more of the following: (i) in violation of human rights, particularly the equal rights of women; (ii) not based on free, prior and informed consent of the affected land-users; (iii) not based on a thorough assessment, or are in disregard of social, economic and environmental impacts, including the way they are gendered; (iv) not based on transparent contracts that specify clear and binding commitments about activities, employment and benefits sharing; and (v) not based on effective democratic planning, independent oversight and meaningful participation.

The role of international corporations has been the subject of considerable debate,[6] and the IFC has itself received robust criticism for its role in land grabs.[7] The present hypothetical decision focuses on the gendered impacts of land grabs. This particular aspect of land grabs has already received detailed attention in the Center for International Environmental Law's 2007 report *Gender Justice: a Citizen's Guide to Gender Accountability at International Financial Institutions*, and more recently in research papers by Nidhi Tandon[8] and by Jessica Chu,[9] as well as the International Food Policy Research Institute's 2011 paper *The Gender Implications of Large-Scale Land Deals.*[10]

Other chapters of this book address the application of the Maastricht ETO Principles in cases concerning indigenous peoples' rights, and

---

5 www.landcoalition.org/about-us/aom2011/tirana-declaration (last accessed 29 July 2012).

6 e.g. *The Great Food Robbery: How corporations control food, grab land and destroy the climate* (GRAIN and Pambazuka Press, 2012)

7 Oakland Institute's 2010 report *Mis(investment) in Agriculture: the role of the IFC in the global land grab* (www.oaklandinstitute.org).

8 Nidhi Tandon, "New agribusiness investments mean wholesale sell-out for women farmers",(2010) 18 *Gender and Development* 3.

9 Jessica Chu, "Gender and 'Landgrabbing' in Sub-Saharan Africa: women's landrights and customary tenure", (2011) 54 *Development* 40.

10 Julia Behrman, Ruth Meinzen-Dick and Agnes Quisumbing, "The gender implications of large-scale land deals", (2011, IFPRI Discussion Paper 01056)

52 *Land Grabbing and Gender Issues*

climate change. Although these issues could also be analyzed in the present chapter, to avoid duplication this chapter focuses on the responsibilities of lenders and corporations in relation to the gendered aspects of land grabs.

CAO audits focus on the IFC's own Performance Standards. The previous standards, which would have been applicable at the time of the hypothetical decision, were the 2006 standards. These standards were revised in 2012 following concerns that they did not sufficiently address the issue of free prior informed consent, gender, and the fact that investments could continue even after a finding of a violation. IFC Performance Standards are important not only for the World Bank, but also because they set the tone for the Equator Principles' Financial Institutions (67 private banks). Space precludes a detailed analysis of the 2012 standards. It should be noted that they do place an increased emphasis on the central demand of affected communities for free prior informed consent, a concept now widely accepted for indigenous people and increasingly for all affected communities.[11] The 2012 standards now provide for "Informed Consultation and Participation".[12] Previously, the IFC had argued that their old standard was functionally the equivalent of this, but it was oftentimes criticised for equating "consultation" with "consent".[13] It is argued here that the concepts of "consultation" and "consent" require a particular focus on women, especially where women's rights to ownership and access are not codified in law, or where customary law (which is often patriarchal) applies. In such circumstances women may not be in a position to influence. Both legal and traditional practices may be discriminatory and affect a woman's consent. In addition to taking up the issue of Performance Standards, this chapter also considers the Protocol on Rights of Women in Africa.[14] The African Women's Protocol has its own extensive literature, and a future work on hypothetical judgments concerning the Protocol itself would be welcome, perhaps along the lines of *Feminist Judgments: From Theory to Practice.*[15] The hypothetical cases in that book show that gender issues can easily get

---

11 Robert Goodland, "Free, Prior and Informed Consent and the World Bank Group" (2004) 4 *Sustainable Development Law and Policy.*

12 e.g. Performance Standard 1, paragraph 31, available on http://www1.ifc.org/wps/wcm/connect/Topics_Ext_Content/IFC_External_Corporate_Site/IFC+Sustainability/Sustainability+Framework/Sustainability+Framework+-+2012/Performance+Standards+and+Guidance+Notes+2012/ (2 May 2013)

13 e.g. by the World Resources Institute in *"Development without conflict: the business case for community consent"*

14 The Maputo Protocol to the African Union's Charter on Human and People's Rights, July 2003, in force 25 November 2005, available on http://au.int/en/sites/default/files/Protocol%20on%20the%20Rights%20of%20Women.pdf (2 May 2013)

15 Rosemary Hunter, Clare McGlynn and Enrika Rackley (eds) *Feminist Judgments: From Theory to Practice* (Oxford and Oregon, Hart Publishing, 2010). I am particularly indebted to Alison Diduck's chapter, "Commentary on *Royal Bank of Scotland Plc v. Etridge (No 2)*"

Litigating Transnational Human Rights Obligations 53

subsumed, and at times even lost, behind legal formalities. Similarly, in land grab cases the investors, the lenders and the courts often see the legal aspects of the case simply in terms of applying existing contract law and land law, and they fail to see the problem as one faced by women who have lost their homes after suffering discrimination and a violation of their rights under international law, in particular, human rights law designed specifically to protect women. The issue becomes this: How could the lender ensure that its investment is not affected by a failure to consider discrimination and the procedural safeguards intended to address the gendered aspects of lending? The need for a gendered decision is highlighted by gender gaps in previous CAO audits. The hypothetical audit in this chapter seeks to better address this issue in the light of the transnational human rights obligations of the IFC as a lender, both under customary international law and under the African Women's Protocol.

Finally, while the hypothetical decision is a decision of the IFC's own ombudsman, it should be noted that under Principle 15 of the Maastricht Principles the State Members of the World Bank (and indeed members of other international finance institutions) must take all reasonable steps to ensure that the relevant international organization (here the IFC) acts consistently with the international human rights obligations of those States. For an example of how this impacts one such State (Switzerland), see Birgit Zimmerle's recent discussion of land grabbing and the role of development finance institutions.[16]

CAO Compliance audit of IFC

Factual Summary

Agraria is a large island in the Indian Ocean off the coast of Africa. Agraria has signed and ratified the African Women's Protocol. The fertile coastal zone, Cornucopia, is highly populated. The highland zone, Zillia, is more sparsely populated. Although Cornucopia has been very fertile in the past, the country has started to experience water stress, with changes in rainfall patterns viewed by some experts as a result of climate change, although other experts express more uncertainty about the causes for the change. Customary law applies in most parts of Agraria, although there has been sporadic land titling in the coastal zone. Where there are land titles, these are mostly in the hands of men. The government of Agraria does not acknowledge the customary rights of many of the highland community, and describes much of the land in Zilia as "unused" land.

---

16 Birgit Zimmerle, "When development cooperation becomes land grabbing: the role of Development Finance Institutions", Brot fuer Alle and Fastenopfer, October 2012.

54 *Land Grabbing and Gender Issues*

1. *Background to the CAO Compliance Audit* [B]

IFC has undertaken two investments in Big Biofuels Incorporated (BBI), a company registered in the British Virgin Islands. The 2008 investment of $3 million was for contract farming in coastal Cornucopia. The investment funded management costs, lease acquisition costs and irrigation, which reduced water supplies in the surrounding area. The 2009 investment of $5 million was for a 20,000 hectare biofuel plantation in the highland zone. In highland Zillia the land was fenced off, restricting access to water points. Both investments were assessed by the IFC under its 2006 Performance Standards and were approved.

BBI has undertaken a number of community projects, and built schools in both Zillia and Cornucopia for the families of their workers. The government of Agraria granted a 25-year lease to BBI for the communal land in Cornucopia and a 25-year lease for the unused land in Zillia. In Cornucopia, BBI called a meeting of male community leaders and offered them contract farming agreements. A large number of the men agreed to the standard contract offered by the company. The Chief in Zillia signed a document consenting to the lease, as did the District Commissioner. As the land in Zillia was untitled and had been declared unused, no compensation was offered to local residents.

In January 2009, BBI held a meeting with male household heads in Zillia and informed them that in two weeks' time a large area of the land would be fenced in for the biofuel plantation. Despite protests, the plans went ahead. There was no violence, and the area that was fenced off did not include any homes.

In March 2009, non-governmental organizations and community groups in central Agraria filed a complaint with the CAO. The complainants are: (a) Les Femmes Paysannes, a union of women farm workers; (b) Les Enfants de la Terre, an Agrarian NGO working on land rights; and (c) 5 women in Cornucopia, and 6 men and 4 women in Zillia, on their own behalf and as representatives of affected people in those districts. The complainants claimed that BBI's activities in Agraria violated a number of IFC standards and requirements.

In July 2009, the CAO Ombudsman disclosed a preliminary stakeholder assessment and transferred IFC-related allegations to CAO Compliance for a compliance appraisal. In October 2009, CAO Compliance concluded that the issues transferred from the CAO Ombudsman merited an audit.

The overall objective of the compliance audit is to assess the reasonableness of IFC's approach to these investments based on its mission, policies, standards, experience and guidance. This includes an assessment of:

- whether the current procedures and established practices provide sufficient and correct guidance to IFC staff;

Litigating Transnational Human Rights Obligations 55

- how IFC assured itself that these investments would comply with IFC Performance Standards and procedures, and with Agrarian and international law;
- whether the IFC's rationale for not carrying out a gender analysis was appropriate.

Specific complainant concerns

The complainants specified their concerns with respect to alleged violations of IFC Performance Standards in several particular contexts: compliance with applicable national laws, including host country obligations under international law; analysis of social and environmental risks and impacts in a Social and Environmental Assessment, and related actions to address potential impacts; and assessments and actions related to provisions given for land acquisition.

Violations of IFC policies and standards

The complainants claim that:

- IFC Performance Standards 1 and 5 were not upheld;
- the environmental and social impact assessments were inadequate;
- the investments fail to comply with applicable law relating to gender.

The complainants further state that the adverse impacts on the ground include:

- failure to consult with affected communities;
- loss of traditional land, and resulting loss of amenities including access to water, firewood, pasture and medicinal plants;
- failure to mitigate or compensate for these losses.

The female complainants and Les Femmes de la Terre claim that the IFC failed to respect the rights of women community members under general international human rights law and under the African Women's Protocol, to which Agraria is a State party.

2. *IFC Processing of the Investment* [B]

The CAO uses the IFC investment cycle set out in its Annual Report to examine investments. In the case of each investment, IFC had provided a due diligence questionnaire and carried out a site visit. IFC determined that both investments were category B in IFC's categorization, i.e., that there would be limited environmental and social impacts which could be avoided or mitigated by good international practice, including IFC Performance Standards, in particular Performance Standard 5. The IFC required the company to carry out public disclosure and outreach required by Performance Standard 1.

56　*Land Grabbing and Gender Issues*

In Cornucopia, IFC's assessment team interviewed male household heads as part of its due diligence review. It was aware of concerns about the water shortages, and a follow-up environmental assessment was scheduled for 2010.

As well as heads of households, IFC met with community leaders, but this was primarily with male community leaders, and IFC had made no effort to communicate with female community leaders, including Les Femmes Paysannes, and had not carried out a baseline assessment or obtained any gender-disaggregated data.

In Zillia, IFC's assessment team visited the District Commissioner and the Chief and were assured that the area to be leased was unoccupied. BBI's local staff took them on a drive across the designated area, and the team made note that there was no housing there.

3. CAO Analysis, Findings and Conclusions [B]

3.1 *Compliance of investment with IFC Policies, Procedures and Performance Standards*

3.1.1 *Social and Environmental Sustainability*

IFC Performance Standard 1 *Social and environmental assessment and management system*

> underscores the importance of managing social and environmental performance throughout the life of a project. An effective social and environmental management system is a dynamic, continuous process initiated by management and involving communication between the client, its workers, and the local communities directly affected by the project (the affected communities).

Cornucopia: IFC identified the development outcome of the Cornucopia project as including a positive effect on farmers and local businesses. On the environmental side, IFC also identified the water stress in the community, and that its more intensive agricultural inputs would impact on other farmers. It put in place mitigation strategies, including support for irrigation. But IFC did not identify the problem of water collection for domestic use. This had not been highlighted in the consultation. However, the CAO notes that in Agraria most water fetching for domestic use is carried out by women and children, and they had not been consulted. Under customary law, women may not have ownership rights, they may have access rights. IFC had failed to consider this possibility. The project could infringe any such rights.

Zillia: In its assessment of the Zillia project, the IFC did not address the water issues in Zillia. The IFC had concluded that as the land was untitled, it did not need to carry out an extensive consultation with affected communities.

The community in Zillia had complained that the area fenced off included grazing land and traditional watering holes for them and their livestock. It also provided firewood. The land had also been used for the collection of medicinal plants. The result of the enclosures was that the affected communities had to travel further into the mountains to find water for their livestock. The community also complained that waterholes that were outside the enclosed area were drying out and that far less water was available.

The CAO concludes that in relation to the Cornucopia investment, the environmental aspects had been considered in line with IFC procedures, except that the impact of the additional water demands of the project on domestic consumption had not been adequately addressed. It recommends a further study and mitigation measures, including if necessary consideration of a piped water supply to the settlements in the area.

The CAO concludes in relation to the Zillia investment that there had been a serious procedural failure, and that the assessment team had erred in concluding that there were no direct impacts on the community. The assessment team should have undertaken wider consultation and enquired of the central government department as to livelihoods of the upland inhabitants in Zillia. The IFC should have applied lessons from other investments in similar districts in other countries, and from civil society organizations working on land use.

3.1.2 *Policy on land acquisition and involuntary resettlement*

Performance Standard 5 paragraph 1 states that "Involuntary resettlement refers both to physical displacement (relocation or loss of shelter) and to economic displacement (loss of assets or access to assets that leads to loss of income sources or means of livelihood) as a result of project-related land acquisition". Paragraph 14 classifies displaced persons as persons (i) who have formal legal rights to the land they occupy, (ii) who do not have formal legal rights to land, but have a claim to land that is recognized or recognizable under the national law, or (iii) who have no recognizable legal right or claim to the land they occupy. The census will establish the status of the displaced persons.

BBI had offered compensation to the holders of land titles in Cornucopia, but no compensation to any other person. In Zillia, no compensation had been offered or paid.

In relation to the Cornucopia investment, the CAO concludes that, subject to the section below on gendered impacts, Performance Standard 5 has been met. The affected community had received a negotiated compensation. Paragraph 6 of the Standard made clear that it does not apply to resettlement resulting from voluntary land transactions, "i.e., market transactions in which the seller is not obliged to sell and the buyer cannot resort to expropriation or other compulsory procedures if negotiations fail". In such cases, Performance Standard 1 should apply, although paragraph 6 goes on to state that if adverse impacts "become significantly adverse at any stage of the project, the client should consider applying the requirements of Performance Standard 5, even where no initial land acquisition was involved".

58   *Land Grabbing and Gender Issues*

However, the CAO concludes that there had been a procedural failing in only consulting holders of land titles, who were all male, and this could lead to negative effects on women, and be in breach of national and international law. This point is addressed at paragraph 3.1.4 below.

In relation to the Zillia investment, while there had not been physical displacement because the community did not have homes in the leased area, there had been economic displacement as defined in paragraph 1 of the Performance Standard. The land transaction was not voluntary, as the affected community had not been consulted. Paragraph 14 (iii) of Performance Standard 5 applied. The CAO concludes that the IFC should offer compensation for loss of assets and amenities, and a detailed remediation scheme was required.

3.1.3 *Information, compensation and free prior and informed consent*

As noted above, in Zillia BBI notified local community members that the land would be fenced off, giving two weeks' notice. *The CAO finds that there was no attempt to engage in consultation with affected community members, principally because there was an assumption that the plantation would not have negative effects on the community, and that the land was not in use at all, save for transit. This was a breach of Performance Standard 5, paragraph 9. The CAO notes that the consultation provisions will be strengthened in the 2012 edition of the Performance Standards, in particular in paragraph 5 of Performance Standard 5, and with an emphasis on Informed Consultation and Participation, in Performance Standard 1, paragraph 31.*

3.1.4 *Gendered impacts*

The CAO notes that Agraria is a party to the African Women's Protocol. In Cornucopia, BBI granted contracts for farmers, but all of these were made with male household heads, and there was no attempt to target female farmers for contract farming. In Zillia, some employment opportunities were made available for local men from the community, in particular as watchmen and cooks for the plantation management and BBI's premises. However, most of the agricultural workers were brought in from other areas.

In Cornucopia, BBI built a school for the families of contract farmers, as well as converting an old building into a community meeting hall. The CAO notes that this does provide a benefit to both male and female members of the community.

In Zillia, although BBI did not recognize the customary rights of the community to the land, it built a small school for children of its plantation workers, many of whom are from outside Zillia.

In Zillia, the CAO finds that the community services for local people did not include healthcare and education, which are particularly beneficial to women.

The CAO finds that the investment in both areas is likely to exacerbate poor conditions relating to female land access and ownership and limit rural women's opportunities for income generation. In Cornucopia women were denied employment opportunities, as well as being disproportionately affected by the shortage of water exacerbated by the more intensive farming methods introduced by BBI. In addition, the assessment had failed to address the gender disadvantage caused by the fact that only men held land titles in Cornucopia, which is contrary to the principle of non-discrimination. In addition, Article 19 of the African Women's Protocol provides that States have an obligation to "promote women's access to control over productive resources such as land and guarantees their right to property". Although under the Agrarian constitution women as well as men are entitled to hold legal title to land, the CAO finds that this right is not reflected in customary practice. The initial assessment should have taken this into account.

In Zillia, the CAO finds that women suffered adverse impacts by being denied access to the land, as they had used the "idle" land for collecting water, firewood and plants for healing. The loss of this land has had a disproportionate impact on women.

The female complainants and Les Femmes Paysannes submitted that under Article 15 of the African Women's Protocol, the right to food security has not been respected. This provides that State parties will:

(a) provide women with access to clean drinking water, sources of domestic fuel, land, and the means of producing nutritious food;
(b) establish adequate systems of supply and storage to ensure food security.

The CAO finds that even though the 2006 Performance Standards are not very specific on women's rights, the IFC assessment should have reflected the need to have regard to women's access to water and fuel, as required by the African Women's Protocol, and that this right was not fulfilled in Zillia. The CAO further finds that the IFC had not respected the requirement of Article 18 (2) of the African Women's Protocol, namely, to take all appropriate measures to ensure greater participation of women in the planning, management and preservation of the environment and the sustainable use of natural resources at all levels. The CAO notes that the IFC has now reflected the greater weight to be given to gender in its 2012 Performance Standards, in particular in the guidance to paragraphs 10 and 12 of Performance Standard 5.

3.2 Underlying causes for non-compliance identified

The CAO finds that commercial pressures were allowed to prevail and the IFC failed to carry out sufficient analysis and to ensure proper consultation. In Cornucopia there was a higher degree of consultation, but the failure related to gendered impacts. In Zillia, men and women were both affected, noting that women also suffered from lack of opportunity for employment.

The CAO considers that the problems in this case demonstrate that the IFC's policies fail to address adequately the adverse impacts of investment in land. It concludes

60 Land Grabbing and Gender Issues

that the IFC should undertake a review of its processes in relation to land designated as "idle", whether by the IFC itself or by local administrative authorities or the company. Legal information from the appropriate governmental authority that the land in Cornucopia was subject to land titles and that the land in Zillia was not subject to any property rights of the local community was important evidence, but the IFC's due diligence needed to include observation and additional enquiry, in particular as to non-residential usages for community purposes in Zillia.

The IFC failed to consider the obligations on it as a lender and on Agraria as a State party to the African Women's Protocol.

The CAO concludes that it is important for the IFC to develop a gender policy and to embed gender analysis and the collection of gender disaggregated data in all its land use projects. Furthermore, the IFC should ensure respect for the African Women's Protocol, and in all continents the IFC should have regard for the relevant rules of customary international law as well as specific regional instruments concerning the rights of women.

Part II

Global (Human Rights) Monitoring Bodies

5 Putting an End to Victims Without Borders

Child Pornography (Committee on the Rights of the Child)

Gamze Erdem Türkelli

Abstract

As mandated by its new Optional Protocol (OPIC), the Committee on the Rights of the Child has received a communication from a group of children who have been abused in the production of pornographic images and footage. The children are nationals and residents of Country X, where the abuse has also taken place. Authorities in Country X have identified that nationals of Country Z have been involved in the production of these abusive materials. Country X has requested the extradition of these individuals, but Country Z has not responded favourably. Furthermore, Country Z has not initiated any proceedings against these individuals through its own judicial system notwithstanding the serious nature of the allegations. What is more, the images of the abused applicants continue to be disseminated through the World Wide Web from internet sites that are registered to companies in Country Y and are suspected of being run from this country. The applicants have brought a complaint against these three State parties X, Y and Z for a number of different breaches of obligations under the Convention on the Rights of the Child (CRC) and the Optional Protocol to the CRC on the Sale of Children, Child Prostitution and Child Pornography (OPSC).

Introductory note

Child abuse images – better known as child pornography – remain a global problem that is exacerbated because of inadequacies in domestic legislation. The International Centre for Missing & Exploited Children (ICMEC) surveyed 196 countries and found that only 45 countries had sufficient legislation to combat 'child pornography' offenses, whereas 89 had no legislation specifically addressing the problem.[1] Many international

---

1 International Centre for Missing & Exploited Children (ICMEC), Child Pornography: Model Legislation & Global Review, 6th Edition, 2010, iii, available online at: http://icmec.org/en_X1/icmec_publications/English__6th_Edition_FINAL_.pdf [Last accessed 2 April 2013].

64 *Putting an End to Victims Without Borders: Child Pornography*

organizations and agencies, such as the Council of Europe and Interpol, use the term 'child abuse images or materials' in lieu of 'child pornography' and argue that the terminology should be changed accordingly in all legal texts and political debates, as the term 'child pornography' fails to clearly convey the seriousness of sexual abuse that occurs when these offenses are committed.[2]

With the advent of the Internet, the number of these abuse images has increased exponentially. A report of the Council of Europe found that prior to 1995 (considered 'year 0' before the Internet boom) Interpol was aware of a total of 4000 child abuse images,[3] whereas by 2009 the UK Child Exploitation and Online Protection Centre had 850,000 child abuse images in its database.[4] The children abused in the production of these images are of all age groups, but an overwhelming majority of the victims are prepubescent children, and the abuse of younger children and even infants is becoming more common.[5]

Estimates from UNICEF point to the existence of over 4 million Internet sites that feature abuse images of children victims.[6] With developments in cyber technology, perpetrators have started using systems such as 'cloud computing', which allows the storage of data in several countries, or split-images that have to be reassembled by authorized users, thereby preventing their detection.[7] The International Association of Internet Hotlines (INHOPE) processed almost 30,000 reports of child abuse material online during 2011:

---

2 Council of Europe (CoE) Parliamentary Assembly, Doc. 12720 Report by Rapporteur Agustín Conde Bajen, 'Combatting "child abuse images" through committed, transversal and internationally co-ordinated action', 19 September 2011, para. 4, available online at: http://assembly.coe.int/ASP/XRef/X2H-DW-XSL.asp?fileid=13159&lang=en [Last accessed 2 April 2013].

3 CoE Parliamentary Assembly, Doc. 12720 para. 8.

4 Child Exploitation and Online Protection Centre, *The Way Forward:* Presented to Parliament by the Secretary of State for the Home Department by Command of Her Majesty, January 2010, p. 7, available online at: www.official-documents.gov.uk/document/cm77/7785/7785.pdf [Last accessed 2 April 2013].

5 International Association of Internet Hotlines (INHOPE), *2011 Annual Report,* p. 17, available online at: www.inhope.org/. Reports of child abuse material online in 2011 showed that 71% of these victims were prepubescent, 23% pubescent and 6% infants. (The 2009 Report of the UN Special Rapporteur on the sale of children, child prostitution and child pornography, Najat M'jid Maalla cites figures of possession: 83% of individuals who possessed 'child pornography' material had images of children between the ages of 6 and 12, 39% had images of children between 3 and 5, 19% had images of babies and infants under 3 years of age.)

6 UN Human Rights Council, 'Promotion and Protection of All Human Rights, Civil, Political, Economic, Social and Cultural Rights, Including the Right to Development – Report of the Special Rapporteur on the sale of children, prostitution and child pornography, Najat M'jid Maalla', A/HRC/12/23, 13 July 2009, para. 14, available online at: http://www.unhcr.org/refworld/pdfid/4ab0d35a2.pdf [Last accessed 2 April 2013].

7 CoE Parliamentary Assembly, Doc. 12720, para. 9.

18 per cent of the reported sites were commercial, while the remaining 82 per cent of the sites were non-commercial.[8] Although the overwhelming majority of exchange of child abuse materials occurs non-commercially, commercial child abuse image exchange has been estimated to produce revenue between 3 and 20 billion USD annually.[9]

Child pornography is oftentimes transnational in scope. A case in point is Operation Carousel where in 2007 some 76,000 abuse images of children were confiscated and 700 suspects from 35 countries were arrested.[10] As this shows, hundreds of offenders from many different nationalities and jurisdictions may be involved in one network.

For the sake of simplicity, the following hypothetical case involves only three countries: Country X, where the abuse of the children and the production of the sexual abuse materials has taken place; Country Y, where these materials are distributed, disseminated and sold through websites run from its territory; and Country Z, whose nationals have participated in the production of the abusive materials. Obviously, real-life cases are likely to be much more complex and involve a multitude of States and actors within those States.

The hypothetical case is brought as an individual communication before the Committee on the Rights of the Child, which is mandated with the new Optional Protocol on a Communications Procedure (OPIC) to receive individual complaints regarding violations of rights enshrined in the CRC, OPAC and OPSC.[11] Along with individual communications, OPIC allows for an inquiry procedure as well as inter-State complaints. OPIC was adopted by the UNGA on 19 December 2011 and opened for signature in 2012. The new OP has been signed by 35 States and ratified by 3 (as of 2 April 2013).[12] OPIC will come into force three months after being ratified by 10 States (OPIC Art. 19(1)).

---

8 INHOPE, 2011 Annual Report, p. 17.

9 M. Aiken, M. Moran and M.J. Berry, 'Child abuse material and the Internet: Cyberpsychology of online child related sex offending', Paper presented at the 29th Meeting of the INTERPOL Specialist Group on Crimes against Children Lyon, France, 5–7 September 2011, p. 2. (The Council of Europe report (*supra* note 3) puts the figure at 21 billion USD, according to 2006 estimates.)

10 UN HRC, A/HRC/12/23, para. 110.

11 The value of an individual petition mechanism to the Convention on the Rights of the Child as regards child sexual exploitation was underscored even as early as in 1994. (Geraldine Van Bueren, 'Child sexual abuse and exploitation: A suggested human rights approach', *International Journal of Children's Rights* 2: 45–59, 1994.)

12 UN Treaty Collection, 'Optional Protocol to the Convention on the Rights of the Child on a communications procedure – Status as at: 02-04-2013 05:04:20 EDT', available online at: http://treaties.un.org/Pages/ViewDetails.aspx?mtdsg_no=IV-11-d&chapter=4&lang=en [Last accessed 2 April 2013].

66 *Putting an End to Victims Without Borders: Child Pornography*

Case

Background and Description of the Facts

A communication has been brought before the Committee on the Rights of the Child (hereafter, 'the Committee') by a group of 'child pornography' victims as defined in Article 34 CRC and Article 2 OPSC, who are residents and citizens of Country X. X's law enforcement agencies identified the applicants as children who have been abused for the production of pornographic materials such as photography and footage as described in Article 2(c) OPSC. X is a medium-income country ranking consistently low on human development indicators, and tourism is its major source of revenue. X is described as a locus for the production of child abuse materials and is regarded as a destination for child sex tourism and child prostitution. It is widely known that many foreign nationals entering X as tourists are involved in sexually soliciting local children and producing sexual abuse materials. Local NGOs note an upsurge in recent years in the number of children who are filmed and abused in this manner, with the Internet serving as the primary medium for the distribution/dissemination of such materials.

The alleged victims have brought complaints in their country of origin, X, which has resulted in criminal proceedings being brought against a number of domestic nationals for producing and assisting in the production of said materials. Although these nationals have been convicted of numerous offenses, foreign nationals who are suspected of organizing the production and distribution of these materials have escaped criminal prosecution. It is believed that these foreign nationals recruited locals to procure children and assisted in producing said materials. X has not been able to prosecute these alleged foreign offenders because the said persons returned to their country of origin (Country Z)pending the investigation. No prosecutions have been instigated against these foreign nationals in Country Z, although Z has been notified by X's authorities of these allegations. X has attempted to extradite these individuals but Z has refused to cooperate.

Interpol (in coordination with several NGOs) has identified several websites containing materials in which the victims are shown, and it has notified X's law enforcement agencies. The website domain names end with extensions that point to State X (including '.com.x', '.net.x', '.org.x', 'biz.x') but are registered to companies in Country Y and are available for viewing worldwide, thereby perpetuating the abuse of these victims. It has not been possible for X to fully address the victims' grievances because although it has blocked these websites domestically, they remain accessible in other countries. X's law enforcement authorities have also taken steps to notify authorities in Y about the websites. There are alleged links between those producing these abuse materials and those distributing them, indicating the existence of a transnational criminal network. While Y has domestic legislation that criminalizes the production, distribution/dissemination of

Litigating Transnational Human Rights Obligations 67

child abuse materials, there is no criminal legislation for simple possession and computer-facilitated offenses.

The communication has been brought against Countries X, Y and Z for not complying with their obligations under the CRC and OPSC. The applicants are considered minors in all three countries. X, Y and Z are all party to the CRC and the OPSC as well as the OPIC establishing a communications procedure for violations of children's rights. The Committee has been provided evidence by X's law enforcement agencies, Interpol, and the UN Special Rapporteur on the Sale of Children, Child Prostitution and Child Pornography.

Views of the Committee on the Rights of the Child under the Optional Protocol to the Convention on the Rights of the Child on a Communications Procedure

<u>Submitted by</u>: The communication is submitted by counsels, Mr A and Ms B, acting as legal representatives of the alleged victims, whose names are not disclosed to protect their privacy.

<u>Alleged victims</u>: The names of the alleged victims are not disclosed to protect their privacy.

<u>States parties</u>: State party X, State party Y and State party Z.

The complaint

1.1 The applicants claim that State party X is in violation of Article 4 OPSC. The applicants argue that State party X has failed to take the necessary measures to establish its jurisdiction over the offenses committed in its territory (Article 4.1) by foreign nationals when these foreign nationals were present in its territory and has failed to protect its nationals who are victims of these offenses (Article 4.2(b)). The applicants also contend that State party X is in violation of its obligations under Article 7 and 9 OPSC, requiring X to seize and confiscate abusive materials and revenues generated through these abusive materials and to effectively prohibit their production and dissemination, respectively.

1.2 Applicants contend that abuse images of the alleged victims continue to be disseminated on the Internet through websites registered to companies in State party Y, hosted by servers run from State party Y. The applicants maintain that these websites are accessible to paying subscribers globally, and that their victimization continues as long as this content remains available online. The applicants and their legal representatives have attempted to seek domestic remedies in State party Y, but their requests have been turned down by domestic authorities in State party Y on the grounds of a lack of jurisdiction. Accordingly, the applicants maintain that State party Y is in violation

68 *Putting an End to Victims Without Borders: Child Pornography*

of 4 OPSC for its failure to take the required steps to establish jurisdiction over the offenses enumerated in Article 3(c) OPSC, although fully aware of the existence of these websites that are registered to companies operating in its territory. Applicants argue also that State party Y is in violation of Article 6 OPSC requiring Y to give X the greatest measure of assistance in connection with such investigations.

1.3 The applicants insist that those engaged in the storage, dissemination and distribution of this content are working in a syndicated fashion with producers and facilitators. Thus, the applicants argue that State party Y is in violation of Article 7 for its failure to seize and confiscate this material and to close down the websites, and Article 34 CRC for not having taken all appropriate national, bilateral and multilateral measures to prevent 'child pornography'.

1.4 Applicants draw attention to the fact that simple possession of abuse images/footage of children regardless of intent to distribute is not considered a penal or criminal offense in State party Y, which allows offenders who in fact distribute such images to enjoy impunity by arguing simple possession. Applicants contend that State party Y is thus in violation of Article 3(c) OPSC.

1.5 Finally, the applicants assert that State party Y is in violation of Article 10 OPSC and Article 4 CRC, which call for international cooperation and coordination in the prevention, detection, investigation, prosecution and punishment of perpetrators. The applicants argue that State party Y has failed to cooperate with State party X and other international organizations, and thus failed to discharge its duty under CRC and OPSC.

1.6 The applicants also argue that State party Z, whose nationals have been identified by State party X's authorities as having taken part in the abuse of the applicants, is also in breach of its international obligations under Articles 5 and 6 OPSC for its failure and refusal to cooperate with State party X in the extradition of these persons.

1.7 The applicants separately argue that State party Z is in violation of its obligations under Article 4.2(a) and 4.3 OPSC, as the alleged offenders are nationals of State party Z and are currently present in its territory, but State party Z has not only refused to extradite these alleged offenders but also refused to instigate proceedings against them under its domestic legal system.

The State parties' submissions on the admissibility and merits of the communication

2.1 State party X contests the admissibility and the merits of the communication and claims that the applicants have failed to exhaust all

Litigating Transnational Human Rights Obligations 69

domestic remedies. State party X holds that the investigation into possible international links of the offenses is ongoing and argues that the communication should be deemed inadmissible until it is clearly demonstrable that no effective remedy has been provided at the end of the ongoing investigation. State party X argues that it has prosecuted perpetrators who are its nationals and has demanded the extradition of foreign nationals from State party Z. State party X states that it has fulfilled its obligation to inform relevant domestic authorities in State party Y of allegations of websites containing child abuse images/footage being run from, and registered to, companies in State party Y. Furthermore, State party X claims that it has blocked these websites domestically, and that it has therefore to the best of its available resources and capability fulfilled its legal obligations under CRC and OPSC.

2.2 State party Y contests both the admissibility and the merits of the communication submitted by the applicants. State party Y claims that it has no jurisdiction in the matter of offenses committed in a third country, involving third country nationals (both victims and perpetrators). State party Y argues that Article 5 OPIC does not allow for the nationals of a State party to bring a communication against another State party. State party Y contends that while it sympathizes with the applicants' desire to seek remedies, the responsibility of providing such remedies rests with State party X since the alleged victims are its nationals and the alleged offenses occurred in its territory. Therefore, State party Y claims that the applicants' claims against State party Y should be dismissed.

2.3 State party Z contests both the admissibility and the merits of the communication. State party Z argues that it has no jurisdiction over this matter, as applicants are not its nationals and the alleged acts in question have been committed outside its territory. State party Z further argues that because there is no extradition treaty between itself and State party X, it cannot lawfully extradite its nationals to State party X to stand trial.

Consideration of admissibility

3.1 Before considering the merits of any claims contained in a communication, the Committee must decide whether or not the communication is admissible.

3.2 As regards the applicants' claims against State party X, State party X does not contest that the victims are its nationals and that the events in question occurred in its territory. In response to the argument of State party X that the ongoing investigation into these offenses should

70 *Putting an End to Victims Without Borders: Child Pornography*

result in the dismissal of the claim for failure to exhaust domestic remedies, the Committee holds that the applicants have exhausted all available domestic remedies in State party X. The Committee further considers that the pending investigation is unlikely to bring effective relief for the grievances of the applicants given the transnational nature of the alleged violations as well as the involvement of several jurisdictions. Thus, it cannot be said that State party X's investigation will necessarily result in the seizure and confiscation of abuse materials or the closure of offending websites. OPIC, from which the Committee derives its mandate, reiterates the need for the best interest of children to be of the primary consideration in pursuing remedies. The Committee deems that postponing remedies for applicants pending an investigation would jeopardize the applicants' best interest. The Committee thus finds that the communication with regard to State party X is admissible.

3.3 As regards the applicants' claims against State parties Y and Z, the Committee is guided not only by the text of the OPIC but also the texts of the CRC and its other two OPs.

3.4 In response to State party Y's argument that the nationals of State party X are not allowed to bring a communication against it, the Committee notes that there is nothing in the text of the OPIC that would prevent individuals who are nationals or habitual residents of one State party from bringing a communication to the Committee against another State party and refers to the previous decisions of other UN human rights bodies (particularly the Human Rights Committee, CAT and CERD). The applicants are allowed to bring a communication against State party Y provided that the conditions enumerated in Article 5 OPIC are fulfilled. Firstly, the 'other' State party must have signed and ratified the OPIC on which the communication is based as well as the CRC (1989) and/or OPSC (2000) and OPAC (2000). Secondly, the said State party's jurisdiction should extend to cover the alleged victims.

3.5 In the present case, State parties Y and Z have signed and ratified all three instruments and are bound by the obligations therein. Therefore, the first requirement has been fulfilled. On the issue of jurisdiction as relates to State parties Y and Z, the Committee is guided by relevant articles of the OPSC in addition to Article 5 OPIC.

3.6 As regards claims against State party Y: According to Article 3 OPSC, the 'produc[tion], distributi[on], disseminati[on], import, export, offer, s[ale] or possess[ion] for the a[forementioned] purposes of child pornography' must be covered, at a minimum, under a State party's penal or criminal law 'whether such offenses are committed domestically or transnationally or on an individual or organized basis'.

The fact that the alleged abuse and production has occurred in State party X involving the nationals of State Party X as victims, and nationals of State parties X and Z as perpetrators, does not discharge State party Y from its obligation (under Article 4.1 OPSC) to establish its jurisdiction over the offenses of dissemination and distribution involving the territory of State party Y. Article 4.2(a) OPSC also makes a case for jurisdiction of State party Y over the offenses 'when the alleged offender is a national of that State or a person who has his habitual residence in its territory'. In the present case, it is clear that alleged offenders in possession of child abuse materials who are distributing, disseminating and selling the materials through websites are present in State party Y's territory and are likely to be its nationals or habitual residents.

3.7 Therefore, in response to State party Y's argument for the lack of jurisdictional basis for the claim, the Committee finds that the requisite basis for jurisdiction has been established in case of offenses described in Article 34 CRC and Article 2 OPSC. The Committee thus finds that the communication with regard to State party Y is admissible.

3.8 As regards claims against State party Z: the Committee restates that the transnational nature of the offense does not preclude the State party's exercise of jurisdiction over it. As regards State party Z's argument that the alleged acts in question have been committed outside of its jurisdiction, the Committee notes Article 4 OPSC explicitly requires State party Z to 'establish its jurisdiction over the offenses' given that the alleged offenders are its nationals (Article 4.2(a)), that they are present in its territory and it has not extradited these persons to State party X (Article 4.3 OPSC). The Committee thus declares the communication with regard to State Party Z admissible.

3.9 To answer if the State parties X, Y and Z are in fact in violation of their obligations under the CRC and its OPs, we now turn to the merits of this present communication.

Consideration of the merits

4.1 Given the fact that the present communication is directed towards three States parties, the Committee will assess whether each of these States parties are in violation of children's rights obligations set forth in CRC and OPSC incumbent upon them.

4.2 The Committee considers that State party X has the primary responsibility for protecting its own nationals, for sanctioning offenses committed in its territory regardless of the nationality of offenders, and preventing the recurrence of the victims' abuse by stopping the production and distribution of child sexual abuse materials.

72 *Putting an End to Victims Without Borders: Child Pornography*

4.3 As regards the responsibility of State party X in relation to the present communication, Article 4 OPSC states that State parties shall take such measures as may be necessary to establish their jurisdiction over such offenses that are committed in its territory. In its General Comment No. 13, the Committee has elucidated the meaning of the term 'shall take' as 'a term which leaves no leeway for the discretion of States parties'. Consequently, it was incumbent upon State party X to investigate allegations not only against its own nationals but also against foreign nationals and to have apprehended, if required by law, these foreign nationals to be tried in State party X, especially after it had become clear that these individuals would effectively be escaping prosecution if permitted to leave the country and that it would not be possible to extradite them. Although State party X is in compliance with its obligations under Article 3 OPSC by covering the offenses under its criminal law, it has failed to establish jurisdiction over all offenders concerned for the offenses in question on its territory with its nationals as their victims. The Committee considers that this amounts to a violation of State party X's obligations under Article 4 OPSC.

4.4 Regarding the applicants' claim that State party X is in violation of Articles 7 and 9 OPSC for failing to ensure the complete suppression of the production and dissemination of the abuse images/footage featuring the victims, the Committee observes that State party X has prosecuted offenders who are its nationals to prevent their production in line with its obligations under Article 9 OPSC and has confiscated the materials apprehended as a part of the investigation into the offenses, thereby acting in line with Article 7 OPSC. State party X has banned the websites in question to prevent the domestic dissemination of the abusive images featuring the victims and has also taken steps to notify authorities in State party Y in order to achieve the necessary cross-border cooperation to completely remove these materials from the Internet. For this reason, the Committee believes that State party X has taken all measures at its disposal aiming at closing premises used to commit such offenses in line with Article 7(c) OPSC and prohibiting their production and dissemination in line with Article 9.5 OPSC and is thus not in violation of the said provisions of the OPSC.

4.5 The Committee reiterates the findings from the Report of the UN Special Rapporteur on the Sale of Children, Child Prostitution and Child Pornography (A/HRC/12/23, 13 July 2009) regarding the need for 'increased international cooperation because [of] the absence of borders between countries on the Internet'. Accordingly, the Committee finds that even if State party X were to take all possible measures to carry out its obligations to the fullest and manage to prohibit the production and circulation of abusive material featuring children in its territory, the said State party alone would not be able to

Litigating Transnational Human Rights Obligations 73

provide an effective remedy to the victims as abuse materials featuring the victims could remain accessible in other countries and even in State party X by using proxy servers, rendering any domestic action ineffectual.

4.6 As regards the applicants' allegation that State party Y is in violation of Article 4 OPSC, the Committee observes the following: The fact that the offenses of abuse and production did not take place in its territory does not preclude State party Y from nevertheless exercising its jurisdictional responsibility for the offenses of distribution, dissemination, offer and sale of the abuse images/footage, as elucidated in the Admissibility part of this decision. The Committee notes here, in addition to the above observation, that State party Y is also a party to the CoE Convention on the Protection of Children against Sexual Exploitation and Sexual Abuse (2007). Under Article 25 CoE Convention, the State party has jurisdiction over offenses not only when they take place in its territory or when victims are its nationals, but also when they are perpetrated by 'one of its nationals' (Article 25(d)) or 'by a person who has his or her habitual residence in its territory' (Article 25(e)). The Committee is of the opinion that State party Y's inaction in the face of the allegations despite being party to two separate treaties requiring it to do so amounts to a violation of Article 4 OPSC.

4.7 The Committee notes that State party Y, despite having been notified of the existence of these commercial websites and their content by authorities of State party X as well as Interpol, has not taken any measures to either execute State party X's request for the closure of these websites by the seizure and confiscation of the related servers or to initiate its own prosecutorial efforts against the alleged offenders. The Committee therefore concludes that State party Y is in violation of its responsibilities under Article 7 OPSC. Even in the absence of such a request from State party X, State party Y would still be under an obligation under Article 4 OPSC to investigate the allegations after the attempts by applicants and their legal representatives to seek domestic remedies in State party Y.

4.8 The Committee notes that violations of a transnational nature, which involve multiple States and multiple jurisdictions such as the present one, require concurrent human rights responsibilities for the States involved. Here, the Committee underlines that the responsibility for measures outlined by Article 7 OPSC, such as seizure, confiscation and closure and the measures for effectively prohibiting dissemination (Article 9.5), is attributable not only to State party X where the initial offense took place, but also to State party Y where the subsequent offenses of storage, dissemination and distribution are being

74 *Putting an End to Victims Without Borders: Child Pornography*

committed. Thus, State parties X and Y have concurrent responsibility in ensuring the complete removal of these exploitative materials from cyberspace and the prohibition of their distribution. It is simply impossible for State party X to achieve this objective individually or through unilateral action. Without the willingness of State party Y to cooperate with State party X and take action, the violation of the rights of the victims will continue. While State party Y is not taking action that harms the alleged victims, its inaction, notwithstanding the serious allegations involved, serves to perpetuate these violations. For this reason, the Committee considers that State party Y has failed to carry out its responsibilities under Article 9.5 OPSC.

4.9 By State Party Y's own admission, its domestic legal system does not allow for third State nationals to bring complaints on the grounds that the 'abuse' (i.e., production of the materials) has occurred outside the territory of State party Y. The Committee considers that the current situation is in contravention of Article 3 OPSC, which creates an obligation for parties to cover the offenses under its legal system regardless of whether they have been committed domestically or transnationally. The result is that there is no recourse for victims in third states to seek justice for continued offenses of abuse and exploitation occurring from the territory of State party Y through the dissemination, distribution and sale of these materials on the Internet. The resulting *lacuna* is ready to be exploited by offenders. The Committee notes with concern that inadequacies in the domestic legal system have not been remedied despite the ratification of the OPSC, which under Article 9 requires States parties to 'adopt or strengthen, implement and disseminate laws, administrative measures or social policies and programmes to prevent the offenses referred to in the Protocol'. The Committee has clarified in its General Comment 5 that a 'comprehensive review of all domestic legislation and related administrative guidance to ensure full compliance with the Convention' is a legal obligation incumbent upon States parties. This means that States parties to CRC and its OPs cannot shield themselves from accountability by claiming that their domestic legal systems are not compatible with their international legal obligations. State party Y is thus found by the Committee to be in violation of its obligations under Articles 3 and 9 OPSC.

4.10 The Committee also notes that while 'simple possession' does not *strictu sensu* figure in Article 3 OPSC, the Committee has previously encouraged its prohibition (Consideration of Reports submitted by States Parties under the OPSC, Concluding Observations on Costa Rica (CRC/C/OPSC/CRI/CO/1, 2 May 2007, paras 14–15, 24–5 and on Chile (CRC/C/OPSC/CHL/CO/1, 18 February 2008, paras 23–4)). The Committee recalls here that State party Y as a party to the

Litigating Transnational Human Rights Obligations 75

CoE Convention is nonetheless under an obligation to criminalize simple possession under Article 20.1(e) of that Convention.

4.11 Having established the above points, the Committee now turns to the applicants' claim that State party Y is in violation of Article 10 OPSC. From the root causes to its effects, the problem of child pornography has strong transnational bearings. Because 'demand' is an important reason for the perpetuation of the problem globally – to recall the assessment of the UN Special Rapporteur (E/CN.4/2006/67) – the eradication of 'child pornography' requires a comprehensive and transnational approach. There is no solely national solution to address the problem of 'child pornography' as there is no possibility of dealing with the question of demand nationally, when such demand is external – unless international cooperation in law enforcement and internal action by third States are achieved. In the absence of measures to tackle the dissemination and distribution of abuse images/footage using children, demand will not be curbed. As long as the dissemination and distribution networks are not effectively disrupted globally, production will simply move where the legal systems are not sufficiently developed to protect vulnerable children. Hence, State party Y is under an obligation under Article 10 to cooperate with State party X and intergovernmental organizations such as Interpol to investigate, prosecute and punish perpetrators to contribute to the longer-term prevention of these offenses against children by deterrence. The Committee observes that despite being informed of the offenses and being approached by State party X and Interpol concerning the present case, State party Y has not taken any measures to cooperate with either. Hence, the Committee finds that State party Y is in breach of Article 10 OPSC.

4.12 As regards the applicants' claim that State party Z is in violation of its obligations under Article 4.2 and Article 4.3 OPSC, the Committee makes the following observations: It is incumbent upon a State party to take the necessary measures to establish its jurisdiction over the alleged offenses when the alleged offenders are present in its territory, especially when this State party does not extradite these alleged offenders to another State party (as per Article 4.3). In addition, the said State party 'may' move to establish its jurisdiction over the alleged offenses when the offenders are its nationals or habitual residents (Article 4.2(a)). In this particular case, the Committee considers that Articles 4.2 and 4.3 should be read as requiring State party Z to establish its jurisdiction over the offenses given that alleged offenders are its nationals and are present in its territory.

4.13 The Committee now turns its attention to whether violations of Articles 5 and 6 OPSC by State Party Z have occurred as claimed by the

76 *Putting an End to Victims Without Borders: Child Pornography*

applicants. Article 5 OPSC unequivocally defines the offenses subject to the communication as extraditable offenses. As regards State party Z's claim that it is not able to extradite these alleged offenders for lack of an extradition treaty between itself and State party X, the Committee considers that Article 5.2 provides sufficient grounds for the extradition, even in the absence of such extradition treaty and domestic legislation. Upon becoming a party to the OPSC, State party Z has accepted the protocol 'as a legal basis for extradition in respect of such offenses' (Article 5.2).

4.14 The Committee further reminds State Party Z that Article 5.5 OPSC requires a State party that decides to decline extradition requests by another to submit the allegations to competent domestic authorities for investigation and prosecution. However, State party Z continues to disregard this obligation even after having denied the extradition requests from State party X.

4.15 Having taken account of the overall situation, the Committee considers that State party Z is in violation of Articles 4 and 5 OPSC for its failure to extradite the alleged offenders and for its failure to prosecute the offenses after the decision not to extradite had been taken. Moreover, the Committee considers that these breaches have amounted to a violation of Article 6 OPSC, which obliges States parties to afford one another the greatest measure of assistance in investigations or criminal or extradition proceedings.

4.16 Having identified a number of distinct violations on the part of all three States parties, the Committee now turns its attention to the issue of responsibility and remedies, and will address questions about how responsibility should be attributed to the States parties as regards the different violations and how that responsibility should be distributed among the three States parties.

Remedy Proposed

5.1 As the Committee has previously stated in its General Comment 5, 'where rights are found to have been breached, there should be appropriate reparation, including compensation, and, where needed, measures to promote physical and psychological recovery, rehabilitation and reintegration, as required by article 39' of the Convention.

5.2 The Committee believes that there are several layers of responsibility concerning the provision of remedies. The Committee considers that the first layer of responsibility lies with State Party X. State party X has the core responsibility for providing remedies to the victims in terms of services to facilitate their recovery, rehabilitation and reintegration as it is in a better position to assess the needs of the victims within the

Litigating Transnational Human Rights Obligations 77

society. Therefore, the Committee calls on State party X to make available any services needed by the victims to ensure their recovery, rehabilitation and reintegration.

5.3 The Committee considers that the prosecution of the offenses that are the subject of this communication and the process of bringing offenders to justice are also an integral part of the process of providing remedies to the victims. Therefore, State party X should ensure that child victims are able to seek damages or compensation from those legally responsible, as permitted by national and international law. At this juncture, the Committee notes that State party Z has concurrent responsibility alongside State party X to enable child victims to seek justice as well as damages or compensation where appropriate. Without the assistance of State party Z, either through extradition or through the prosecution of the alleged offenses domestically, victims will be denied an effective remedy. In response to State party Z's statements on the lack of a bilateral extradition treaty between itself and State party X, the Committee underscores that the legal basis for the extradition of the alleged offenders is found in Article 5.2 OPSC, and therefore that an additional bilateral extradition treaty between State parties X and Z is not needed. The Committee urges State party Z to re-evaluate the extradition request on the basis of this notice. The Committee therefore calls on State party Z, in line with the principle of *aut dedere aut judicare*, to either accept extradition requests for the alleged offenders from State party X, or if it does not extradite the alleged offenders on the basis that they are its nationals, to commence without delay prosecutorial action against the alleged offenders under its domestic judicial system (as required by Articles 4.3 and 5.5). In case State party Z chooses to instigate proceedings under its domestic legal system, the Committee further asks State party Z to cooperate with State party X during the investigation and proceedings including 'assistance in obtaining evidence at [its] disposal necessary for the proceedings' (Article 6.1 OPSC).

5.4 The second layer of responsibility for providing remedies to the victims falls upon State party Y, in particular with respect to remedying the existing situation whereby the abuse images of the victims continue to be globally disseminated and distributed online. The Committee thus calls upon State party Y to initiate required legislative and administrative changes to establish its jurisdiction over the offenses and to swiftly initiate domestic investigations into the allegations in cooperation with State party X and other interested IGOs (such as Interpol) or NGOs in gathering evidence and facts. The Committee also underlines that if allegations are substantiated, State party Y should take all measures necessary to prosecute offenders, to seize and confiscate any media used for distributing the abusive

78 *Putting an End to Victims Without Borders: Child Pornography*

materials, and move for the permanent closure of any operations involved in the storage, distribution or dissemination. The Committee urges State party Y to investigate thoroughly the allegations that the websites are of a commercial nature and to confiscate all proceeds generated illicitly by use of child abuse materials.

5.5 Bearing in mind that by becoming a party to the OPIC the States parties have recognized the competence of the Committee to determine whether there have been violations of obligations under the CRC, OPSC and OPAC, the Committee wishes to receive from the States parties, within 180 days in accordance with Article 11 OPIC, information about the measures taken to give effect to the Committee's Views. The States parties are also requested to publish the Committee's Views.

6 Shared Responsibility for the Right to Health (Committee on Economic, Social and Cultural Rights)

Rachel Hammonds and Gorik Ooms

Abstract

This chapter explores a hypothetical case involving the national and extraterritorial obligations stemming from Article 12 of the International Covenant on Economic, Social and Cultural Rights (the Covenant), the right to the highest attainable standard of physical and mental health. The Committee on Economic, Social and Cultural Rights (the Committee) delivers its response to a Communication brought under the Optional Protocol to the Covenant (Optional Protocol). The case highlights the need to identify and/or create global mechanisms to ensure that all people's rights are guaranteed, which implies accepting shared global responsibility for rights. It highlights how and why an exclusive focus on the human rights obligations of the domestic state is increasingly untenable, and explores some of the implications of interpreting the right to health as a shared responsibility both among States and non-State actors, including international financial institutions, like the World Bank. The Committee explores the contours of the right to health, including the boundaries of a State's obligations to its citizens under the Covenant, the concept of maximum available resources and the importance of ensuring that development cooperation agreements do not discriminate against marginalized and vulnerable people. The Maastricht Principles on Extraterritorial Obligations guide the Committee's assessment of the scope of obligations of international assistance and cooperation pertaining to third States in a position to assist. Its conclusion that international agreements must comply with the international human rights obligations of State parties suggests the potential of the Optional Protocol for enhancing accountability and respect for human rights globally.

Introductory note

That 20 per cent of the world now consumes 86 per cent of its goods and the poorest 20 per cent consume 1 per cent or less is stark evidence of the scale of global inequality.[1] A consequence of this inequitable distribution

---

1 Royal Government of Bhutan, Time for a sustainable economic paradigm, Input com/downloads/Bhutan's%20input%20to%20Rio+20.pdf

80 *Shared Responsibility for the Right to Health*

is massive injustice, human rights violations and widespread preventable death and suffering.[2] Global inequity is reflected in the fact that the highest rates of child mortality are in sub-Saharan Africa – where 1 in 8 children dies before age 5, more than 20 times the average for industrialized countries (1 in 167) – and South Asia (1 in 15).[3] The majority of these deaths have causes for which there are highly effective interventions. What, if any, role is there for international human rights law in countering this inequity?

The international human rights legal system is based on 60-year-old foundations and reflects the prevailing view of that era, namely, the concept of a powerful nation state that has obligations to those on its territory enshrined in various covenants and conventions. The drafters of the International Covenant on Economic, Social and Cultural Rights (the Covenant)[4] recognized that enormous global inequalities would continue to persist without the inclusion of obligations of international assistance and cooperation. However, even today the precise scope of these obligations remains ill-defined and accountability mechanisms notoriously weak. One consequence being that many states in a position to assist and cooperate so as to strengthen rights protections fail to do so adequately.

Much work is required to translate legal concepts of global responsibility for realizing socio and economic rights into workable legal obligations. In the following hypothetical case we focus on one such area, delineating national versus international obligations in a particular area of health rights: access to anti-retroviral (ARV) treatment for HIV/AIDS.

We aim to highlight how and why an exclusive focus on the human rights obligations of the domestic State is increasingly untenable. The role of the international community and States in a position to assist has been clarified to some extent by soft law instruments including, General Comment 14 on the right to health, issued by the Committee on Economic Social and Cultural Rights (the Committee). It situates the related obligations within the international legal framework related to international cooperation and health noting: "In the spirit of Article 56 of the Charter of the United Nations, the specific provision of the Covenant (arts. 12, 2.1, 22 and 23) and the Alma-Ata Declaration on primary health care, States parties should recognize the essential role of international cooperation and comply with their commitment to take joint and separate action to achieve the full realization of the right to health" (para 38).

These lofty pronouncements have proved very difficult to translate into practical legal obligations for either national or international actors.

---

2 Thomas Pogge, 'World Poverty and Human Rights', 19 *Ethics and International Affairs* 1, (2005) 1, at 1.

3 UNICEF, available at: http://www.childinfo.org/mortality.html

4 International Covenant on Economic, Social and Cultural Rights (1976) G.A. Res. 2200A (XXI), U.N. Doc.A/6316.

Litigating Transnational Human Rights Obligations 81

Further, many issues related to the international legal obligation to cooperate and provide assistance to realize, among others, the right to health remain unclear including its parameters and when it is triggered. In simple terms, one key question is what do people in wealthier States owe to people in poorer States?[5] In answering this question some scholars, like Margot Salomon, focus on structural obstacles to realizing rights highlighting the inequitable nature of the current international economic and political systems arguing that this fundamentally undermines the ability of the domestic state to realize rights.[6] A different, complementary approach is being pursued by health activists and scholars engaged in the Joint Action and Learning Initiative on National and Global Responsibilities for Health who are exploring questions related to the parameters of the right to health including the responsibilities of States for the health of people beyond their borders and ensuring accountability of all actors for global health.[7]

Our hypothetical case draws on the impact of the global financial crisis that began in 2008 on international development assistance for health. Not only has the development pie shrunk, as the traditional contributors to development assistance see their budgets reduced, they have also backtracked on commitments to move towards achieving the 0.7 per cent of GDP goal.[8] In the health field, the financial crisis coupled with flagging donor commitment has led to HIV/AIDS funding crises in sub-Saharan Africa and the eastern European/central Asia region, leading to longer waiting times for access to treatment, interruption of treatment and the threat of the discontinuation of treatment.[9] It is worth noting that there are over 34 million people living with HIV, the vast majority in low income

---

5 For many reasons the traditional donor/recipient discourse is no longer appropriate, and more importantly, global statistics on poverty show that most of the world's poor people now live in middle income countries. Dev Kar and Devon Cartwright-Smith, "Illicit Financial Flows from Africa, Hidden Resource for Development" Global Financial Integrity, 2010. Available at: http://www.revenuewatch.org/sites/default/files/GFI_AfricaReport%20 %283%29.pdf Andy Sumner, *The New Bottom Billion; What if Most of the World's Poor Live in Middle Income Countries?* Available at: http://www.cgdev.org/content/publications/ detail/1424922/

6 Salomon, M., *Global Responsibility for Human Rights: World Poverty and the Development of International Law* (Oxford: Oxford University Press, 2007).

7 The JALI recently launched a global campaign for a Framework Convention on Global Health. Available at: http://www.jalihealth.org/documents/FCGHandpost-2015incorporation8-13-12.pdf

8 OECD, Development Assistance Committee, Aid to developing countries falls because of global recession, Available at: http://www.oecd.org/document/3/0,3746, en_2649_37413_50058883_1_1_1_37413,00.html

9 Médecins Sans Frontières, "Getting Ahead of the Next Wave: Lessons for the next decade of the AIDS response" (2011). Available at: http://www.msfaccess.org/sites/default/files/ AIDS_report_GettingAheadWave_ENG_2011.pdf

82 *Shared Responsibility for the Right to Health*

settings and without access to treatment.[10] World leaders have committed to achieving universal access to ARVs, with a target of 15 million on treatment by 2015.[11]

In our hypothetical judgment the Committee is guided by its own General Comments and the recently adopted Maastricht Principles on the Extraterritorial Obligations of States in the area of Economic, Social and Cultural Rights, which provide some assistance in addressing issues of shared responsibility for realizing rights, but are limited in their scope as they focus on State actors.[12] Given the ongoing impact of the policies and programmes of the International Financial Institutions on human rights practices in many countries, we urge an authoritative legal body, for example the International Law Commission,[13] to assess the scope of obligations and responsibility of international organizations under international human rights law to ascertain whether or not the norms contained in the Covenant and other international human rights treaties have acquired the status of customary law or general principles of international law.

In this case, we interpret the accountability function of the Committee as moving beyond naming and shaming in the hope that such procedures can enhance international cooperation to realize rights. We do not seek to provide answers to the issue of multiple attribution of responsibility. Instead we intend to demonstrate that the practice of applying such a concept is not as complex as feared.

It is clear that in a globalized world realizing the right to health for all requires both national and global action and an international system that enhances, not undermines, equity. Our case aims to increase understanding of how and why improving the knowledge base and conceptual underpinnings of shared responsibility for rights is one step towards realizing human rights globally.

---

10 UNAIDS, *Global HIV/AIDS Response – Progress Report 2011*. Available at: http://www.unaids. org/en/media/unaids/contentassets/documents/unaidspublication/2011/20111130_ UA_Report_en.pdf

11 *Political Declaration on HIV/AIDS*, 2011, Available at: http://www.unaids.org/ en/aboutunaids/unitednationsdeclarationsandgoals/2011highlevelmeetingonaids/

12 Available at: http://www.icj.org/dwn/database/Maastricht%20ETO%20Principles%20-%20FINAL.pdf

13 For example the International Law Commission could expand on articles 16 and 60 of the draft Articles on the Responsibility of International Organizations, International Law Commission, *Draft Articles on the Responsibility of International Organizations*, Report of the sixty-first session, 2009 (UN GAOR A/64/10).

Case

Summary of the facts

(1)   The African low-income country of Molea is heavily reliant on external assistance to fund its health and education systems. Molea is a State party to the International Covenant on Economic, Social and Cultural Rights (the Covenant). Asana, a high-income country and a leading OECD member, is also a State party to the Covenant and one of Molea's long-standing international assistance partners.

(2)   In June 2010, the Molean government approved the purchase of 50 fighter planes resulting in most international funders suspending cooperation and assistance programmes. The Asanan government stated it too would end all international assistance unless the Molean government obtains an agreement from the World Bank (Bank) and IMF regarding its poverty reduction strategy programme (PRSP). In August 2010, the Bank proposed a new PRSP including a term specifying that recurrent health sector expenditure cannot exceed 10 per cent of government revenue (defined as the total amount raised through taxes and development assistance) and requiring a balanced budget. On the basis of the new PRSP guidelines, Molea entered into two assistance and cooperation agreements in October 2010, one bilateral between Molea and Asana and one multilateral between the Bank and Molea.

(3)   In accordance with the PRSP guidelines, in January 2011 the Molean government passed a balanced budget with the required health sector spending constraints and new health financing legislation requiring that everyone pay a minimum of 15 per cent of the real costs of health care services. The HIV prevalence rate in Molea is 15 per cent and 100 per cent of those on anti-retroviral (ARV treatment) receive it through a government programme. Under the new health financing legislation, HIV positive people requiring ARVs must make a USD 150 down-payment, or approximately 15 per cent of the cost of five years of ARV treatment.

(4)   In February 2011, Mrs A, a Molean citizen, learned she is HIV positive and requires ARVs. Mrs A went to enroll in the treatment programme and was informed that if she did not pay USD 150 she could only have a place on the treatment waiting list. She decided to contact On the List, a civil society group, which lobbies for HIV positive people's rights, including universal access to ARVs. On the List (the Petitioner) filed a petition in Molean court claiming that the Molean government has failed to comply with its national and international obligations under Article 12 of the Covenant, the right to highest attainable standard of physical and mental health.

84 *Shared Responsibility for the Right to Health*

1. The Petition

(5)   First, the Petitioner claims that by adopting a budget and health financing law limiting health funding, the Molean government has violated Article 12 of the Covenant by limiting access to health care in a manner that discriminates against two marginalized and vulnerable groups, thus violating the obligations to respect, protect and fulfil the right to health.

(6)   Second, the Petitioner challenges the international cooperation agreements with Asana and the Bank alleging a violation of the obligation to respect and protect the right to health stemming from Molea's failure to prioritize its right to health-based legal obligations when entering into these cooperation agreements. The Petitioner further requests that donors, including Asana and the Bank, comply with their obligations of international assistance and cooperation, as required under Article 56 of the UN Charter and Article 2.1 of the Covenant.

(7)   The Petitioner has also filed claims in Molea against Asana, the Bank and Bank Members that are also States parties to the Covenant (including Asana) (WBSP) claiming that they have violated their extraterritorial obligations under Article 2.1 of the Covenant.

(8)   The Molean Supreme Court has denied the Petitioner's claims against Molea and dismissed the claims against Asana, the Bank and WBSP on the grounds that the Molean courts lack jurisdiction.

(9)   Having exhausted all national remedies, the Petitioner has filed a Communication under the Optional Protocol (the Protocol) to the Covenant that is identical to the Petition.

Issues and proceedings before the Committee

2. Consideration of the Competence of the Committee

(10)   The Committee first assessed its competence to receive and consider the Communication under Article 1 of the Protocol. The Committee is satisfied that as specified under Article 1(2) it may consider the application with respect to both the territorial obligations of Molea and the extraterritorial obligations of Asana as they are both States parties and parties to the Protocol.

(11)   As regards the competence of the Committee to consider the part of the Communication related to the Bank, the Committee notes that the Bank is not a State party to the Covenant or the Protocol, as non-States cannot be parties. In the past, this fact has been used as a bar to considering the nature of the Bank's human rights obligations and responsibilities and the Committee awaits authoritative guidance on this issue.

(12)   The Committee next assessed its competence to address the obligations and responsibility of States parties to the Covenant and Protocol, including Asana, for their actions as members of decision making bodies of international institutions, including in this case, the Bank. In General Comment 14 on the right to health (E/C.12/2000/4), the Committee noted that "States Parties have an obligation to ensure that their actions as members of international organizations take due account of the right to health" (para 39). The Committee reaffirmed this logic in para 36 of General Comment 15 on the right to water. The Committee further notes that authoritative guidance on the status of international law is provided by the Maastricht Principles on Extraterritorial Obligations of States in the area of Economic, Social and Cultural Rights (Maastricht Principles). While the Maastricht Principles' primary aim is to clarify the content of extraterritorial State obligations, they also touch on the obligations of States acting as members of international organizations. Maastricht Principle 15 addresses the issue of States committing a wrongful act as part of an organization declaring that "as a member of an international organization, the state remains responsible for its own conduct in relation to its human rights obligations within its territory and extraterritorially". Basing its decision on its logic in General Comments 14 and 15 and on Maastricht Principle 15, the Committee finds that it is competent to address the obligations and responsibilities of Bank Members that are States parties, including Asana, that are the subject of the Communication.

3. Admissibility of the Communication

(13)   In accordance with Article 3(1), the Committee finds that all available domestic remedies have been exhausted. Further, it is not aware of any grounds on which to deem the Communication inadmissible under Article 3(2).

Consideration of the Communication

4. Molea's National Obligations

Assessment of whether Molea has complied with its Covenant obligations

(14)   The Petitioner, *inter alia*, claims that Molea has failed to adequately fund its National Health Policy with domestic resources, arguing the government has: inappropriately devoted large amounts of public funds to military spending, e.g. on fighter jets; passed a budget limiting expenditure on health to 10 per cent of government revenue; and approved a financing law requiring a downpayment for accessing ARV treatment. The Petitioner claims these measures limit access to ARVs for low-income people, a vulnerable group. Second, the Petitioner challenges the international cooperation agreements with Asana and the Bank alleging a violation of the

86 *Shared Responsibility for the Right to Health*

obligation to respect and protect the right to health stemming from Molea's failure to prioritize its right to health-based legal obligations when entering into these cooperation agreements. Molea claims that, as required under Article 2.1 of the Covenant, it expends the maximum of available resources and has engaged in international cooperation with Asana and the Bank to supplement domestic expenditure.

(15)   Under international human rights law, the state of Molea is the primary duty bearer and carries the primary obligation to respect, protect and fulfil the Covenant rights of those residing on Molean territory. The obligations flowing from Article 12 are to be read in conjunction with Article 2.1, which states, "Each State party to the present Covenant undertakes to take steps, individually and through international assistance and co-operation, especially economic and technical; to the maximum of its available resources, with a view to achieving progressively the full realization of the rights." The Committee also notes that in General Comment 3, it made clear that there is a core obligation to prioritize the "minimum essential levels of economic, social and cultural rights" (para 10), and further clarifying this in General Comment 14.

(16)   As specified under Covenant Article 2.1, the Committee must assess whether the Molean government has undertaken measures to the maximum of available resources to safeguard the Article 12 rights of Molean citizens. In doing so, this Committee is required to ascertain whether the Molean government is unwilling or unable to comply with its Article 12 obligations, which also entails an assessment of whether the government has taken "all appropriate means, including particularly the adoption of legislative measures" (General Comment 3).

Maximum of available resources

(17)   In General Comment 14 this Committee noted that the obligation to fulfil the right to health requires that States parties take all necessary steps to realize the right to health, *inter alia*: "to give sufficient recognitions to the right to health in the national political and legal systems, preferably by way of legislative implementation, and to adopt a national health policy with a detailed plan for realizing the right to health" (para 36). Under its obligation to fulfil the right to health, Molea is required, *inter alia*, to adopt policies and laws that provide access on a non-discriminatory basis to health facilities and essential drugs, including ARVs. The Committee finds that in adopting a National Health Plan that is based on fulfilling its core obligations under the Covenant, including providing universal access to ARVs, Molea has complied with one element of its fulfil obligations, as specified in para 36.

(18)   Violations of the obligation to fulfil the right to health stem, *inter alia*, from insufficient domestic expenditure or misallocation of public

resources. The Committee finds no evidence to suggest that the one-off expenditure on fighter jets is a misallocation of public resources. The Committee notes that the fighter jet purchase resulted in many potential development partners refusing to renew cooperation agreements with Molea and encourages all development partners to be flexible and to prioritize human rights commitments in decision-making, noting that defence spending is not incompatible with human rights commitments.

(19) Establishing whether a State party has expended the maximum of available resources with respect to a particular right, as required under Article 2.1 of the Covenant, is a complex process requiring the balancing of many variables. This Committee notes that the burden of proving that the maximum of available resources has been expended rests on the State party (Statement on the obligations of States parties regarding the corporate sector and economic, social and cultural rights, para 9).

(20) The Committee recalls its statement in General Comment 3 "that even where the available resources are demonstrably inadequate, the obligation remains for a State party to strive to ensure the widest possible enjoyment of the relevant rights under the prevailing circumstances". The Committee notes that the Molean budget limits health spending to 10 per cent of domestic government revenue. Molea acknowledges that it did not perform a right to health impact assessment of this level of health sector funding. The 10 per cent of domestic government revenue is a level deemed acceptable under the PRSP that Molea agreed with the Bank and IMF, which is based on financial sustainability criteria, and was a prerequisite for the international assistance and cooperation agreements with Asana and the Bank.

(21) This Committee has held that every State party has a margin of discretion in assessing which measures are most suitable to meet its specific circumstances (E/C.12/2007/1). However, in this case Molea has agreed to cap health sector spending at 10 per cent of government revenue to satisfy the terms of the PRSP without due consideration of the impact on its Covenant obligations and in particular on vulnerable and marginalized groups. In General Comment 3 this Committee stated emphatically that "the obligations to monitor the extent of the realization, or more especially of the non-realization, of economic, social and cultural rights, and to devise strategies and programmes for their promotion, are not in any way eliminated as a result of resource constraints".

(22) The Committee also notes that Molea, like other states in the region, has committed to achieving the Abuja target of 15 per cent of government expenditure on the health sector. All other States in the region have met or exceeded the target. Molea has not met the Abuja target and the current budget ceiling of 10 per cent makes it impossible to do so. Other States in the region have a similar HIV prevalence rate, have higher ARV coverage rates than Molea and have not entered into agreements with the Bank or

88 *Shared Responsibility for the Right to Health*

third States that dictate the level of health sector funding. Most of them have entered into cooperation agreements that require them to fulfil their Abuja commitment in exchange for social sector cooperation and assistance. The Committee finds that Molea has not demonstrated that it has expended the maximum of available resources in pursuing its Covenant obligation to fulfil the right to health.

Assessment of legislative measures including cooperation agreements

(23)   The Committee accepts the Government of Molea's argument that even if it expended the maximum level of resources, Molea would be unable to fulfil its core right to health obligations, due *inter alia* to the high cost of ARVs. The Committee notes that the responsibility of countries in a position to assist to help those unable to realize the right to health with domestic resources alone does not relieve the latter of their human rights obligations. Thus, under Article 2.1 of the Covenant it is obliged to seek international support to supplement its domestic spending so as to fulfil its human rights obligations. The Committee reiterated this view in its 2007 Statement (E/C.12/2007/1).

(24)   The Petitioner claims the budget and related health financing law undermine an essential element of the right to health, namely, access to health care in a non-discriminatory manner, as provided for in Article 12 of the Covenant. The Molean government acknowledges that the budget and health financing law do not allow it to fund access to ARV treatment on a non-discriminatory basis. However, it notes this legislation simply recognizes the unavailability of domestic resources for ARV treatment and seeks to ration them according to financial sustainability principles, as required under the PRSP that forms the basis of the agreements.

(25)   In General Comment 14, para 50, this Committee specified what acts or omissions may amount to a violation of the obligation to respect the right to health. Under its obligation to respect the right to health, Molea is required, *inter alia*, not to enact laws, policies or enter into bilateral or multilateral agreements laws that contravene the standards set out in Article 12 of the Covenant. In General Comment 14, para 12, the Committee offered guidance on these standards noting, *inter alia*, that the right to health requires that health facilities goods and services be available, accessible, acceptable and of high quality. In ensuing accessibility, States must ensure that programmes do not discriminate and that goods and services are financially accessible. This Committee has emphasized that "Equity demands that poorer households should not be disproportionately burdened with health expenses as compared to richer households" (para 12b).

(26)   The Committee finds that the financing legislation enacted by the Molean government disproportionately burdens poorer households with

health-related expenses. As such, the financing legislation fails to respect the right to health of Molean citizens in a non-discriminatory manner, thus breaching Molea's Covenant obligations.

(27)   The Committee notes that in seeking international assistance to supplement its domestic expenditure, Molea failed to prioritize its obligation to fulfil the right to health. The cooperation agreements with Asana and the Bank are based on PRSP requirements that fail to prioritize rights, including the right to health. The Committee acknowledges that resource constraints required Molea to enter into international agreements, but notes that these agreements led to the budget and health financing laws that discriminate against people in low-income households.

Conclusions and Recommendations

(28)   The Committee concludes that Molea has breached its obligations to protect and fulfil the right to health by failing to expend the maximum of available resources due to health sector expenditure budget limitations and by enacting a health financing law that results in discrimination against vulnerable groups. Second, the Committee finds that by entering into international agreements that prioritize financial sustainability over human rights concerns, Molea has violated its fulfil obligation related to seeking international assistance as required under Article 2.1 of the Covenant because these agreements have a negative impact on the right to health of the Petitioner's members, a vulnerable group.

(29)   The Committee requests that Molea review its national legislation and cooperation agreements in light of the Committee's views and submit a follow-up report in six months' time detailing those measures that have been taken.

5. Asana's Extraterritorial Obligations

(30)   The legal basis for international and extraterritorial obligations to cooperate so as to promote human rights can be found in international law, including Article 56 of the UN Charter. More recent declarations, including the 1986 Declaration on the Right to Development (GA Res. 41/128,) and the 2000 Millennium Declaration (UN Doc. A/RES/55/2), highlight the individual and shared responsibility of states for global equity, equality and dignity. In General Comment 14, this Committee recognized States' extraterritorial obligations affirming that "States parties have to respect the enjoyment of the right to health in other countries" (para 34). As the Committee noted above, the primary obligation rests with Molea, but Asana has complementary obligations relating to securing the rights of those on Molea territory. Under Article 2.1 of the Covenant, Asana, as a State party in a position to assist, has the obligation to assist

90 *Shared Responsibility for the Right to Health*

those unable to fulfil their obligations, both through cooperation and assistance. In assessing the actions of Asana with respect to its extraterritorial obligations towards Molean citizens, the Committee applied the tripartite typology framework elaborated in the Maastricht Principles (Articles III, IV, and V).

Obligation to Respect the Right to Health of People in Third Countries

Direct Interference

(31)   Asana is legally obliged to ensure that the conditions of all development cooperation agreements it enters into respect both Parties' Covenant commitments. Maastricht Principle 20 specifies that Asana must refrain from conduct which nullifies or impairs the enjoyment and exercise of the right to health of Molean citizens. Asana claims it engages in bilateral assistance to help Molea fulfil its core obligations pertaining to the right to health, as required under General Comment 3 and General Comment 14 para 39.

(32)   Asana must ensure that all entities subject to its control respect the right to health in Molea. Principle 12(a) asserts that "State responsibility extends to acts and omissions of non-State actors acting on the instructions or under the direction or control of the State". Asana agrees that this Principle applies to Asana-based corporations or State agencies under its control. It is uncontested that the health budget spending ceilings required by the PRSP, which were a prerequisite for the cooperation agreement, have contributed to the ARV treatment waiting lists and the denial of access to treatment for those who cannot afford the downpayment. Asana argues that Bank and IMF economists determined these ceilings help ensure that Molea develops a financially sustainable social sector. Further, Asana argues that its bilateral agreement with Molea complies with PRSP rules.

Core Obligations

(33) In General Comment 14, this Committee emphasized that core obligations include providing access on a non-discriminatory basis to certain medications and that these obligations are not subject to progressive realization. Further, this provision must be read in conjunction with para 45, which states, "For the avoidance of any doubt, the Committee wishes to emphasize that it is particularly incumbent on States parties and other actors in a position to assist to provide 'international assistance and cooperation; especially economic and technical' which enable developing countries to fulfil their core and other obligations indicated in paragraphs 43 and 44 above."

(34)   This Committee reiterated that core obligations related to a particular right are of immediate effect and impose obligations on States parties in a position to assist in paragraphs 37 and 38 of General Comment 15 and

Litigating Transnational Human Rights Obligations 91

paragraphs 39 and 40 of General Comment 17 (UN Doc. E/C.12/GC/17/2005). Maastricht Principle 32 highlights that to discharge its Covenant obligations a State party should prioritize core obligations in cooperation activities.

(35) The Committee holds that by pursuing development policies and programmes that are based on financial sustainability criteria, as provided for in the PRSP, and not respect for right to health core obligations, Asana has engaged in conduct which impairs respect for the right to health in Molea and it has breached its Covenant obligations.

Non-discrimination

(36) In General Comment 14 the Committee noted that the right to health contains interrelated essential elements, specifically that public health care services and goods have to be available, accessible, acceptable and of good quality. Elaborating on the non-discrimination dimension of accessibility, this Committee clarified "Health facilities, goods and services must be accessible to all, especially the most vulnerable or marginalized sections of the population, in law and in fact, without discrimination on any of the prohibited grounds" (para 12b). The financing laws have a *de facto* impact on the economic accessibility of health facilities and services for vulnerable groups, including poor people and HIV positive people. Thus, vulnerable groups face *de facto* and *de jure* discrimination because in the absence of a government programme providing universal access to ARV treatment they face immense financial barriers to access their right to health.

(37) With respect to economic accessibility, this Committee stated "Payment for health-care services... has to be based on the principle of equity, ensuring that these services, whether privately or publicly provided, are affordable for all, including socially disadvantaged groups" (para 12b). Asana's Covenant obligations require it refrains from imposing cooperation conditions that will have a discriminatory impact on vulnerable or marginalized groups. The Committee notes that Maastricht Principle 32 affirms the importance of prioritizing the rights of disadvantaged, marginalized and vulnerable groups. The Committee finds that in formulating and concluding bilateral agreements with Molea based on financial sustainability concerns rather than respect for right to health obligations, Asana advocates and supports policies that exclude Molea's most vulnerable people from health services.

Indirect Interference

(38) Maastricht Principle 21 holds that States must refrain from conduct which aids, assists, directs, controls or coerces another State to breach its international ESC rights obligations, where the former States do so with the

92   *Shared Responsibility for the Right to Health*

knowledge of the circumstances of the act. The Committee must assess whether the conduct of Asana aided, assisted directed, controlled or coerced Molea's Government to violate its right to health obligations as alleged by the Petitioner.

(39)   To enjoy the benefit of Asanan assistance and cooperation, including the transfer of agricultural know-how and favourable trade conditions, Molea was required to impose ceilings or limits on its social sector budget, including health. To engage in cooperation with Asana, Molea had to make human rights considerations secondary. Asana was aware it was in a strong position as Molea had no other potential partners at this time, due to the jet purchase. Engaging in international cooperation that breaches another State's international obligations is an indirect violation of the obligation to respect the right to health in third countries.

(40)   The Committee finds that by predicating international assistance and cooperation with Molea on financial sustainability criteria, Asana indirectly impaired the government of Molea's ability to comply with its right to health obligations.

The Obligation to Protect the Right to Health of People in Third Countries

(41)   The Communication alleges that Asana failed to influence Bank policy and that the PRSP's financial sustainability requirements impacted negatively on the right to health of low-income people in Molea through the budget limits and health financing law. Such a failure would constitute a violation of the obligation to protect the right to health under Maastricht Principle 26. The Petitioner also alleges a violation of Maastricht Principle 27, namely that Asana failed to cooperate to ensure the Bank did not impair the enjoyment of the right to health of the Petitioner's members.

(42)   The World Health Organization's *World Health Report 2006* and the 2006 UNAIDS report, *Scaling Up Access to HIV Prevention, Treatment, Care and Support: The Next Steps* document the negative effect of public health expenditure limits, and consequently the right to health. The latter notes the "burden of sustainability should not fall on the World's poorest countries" (p. 25). Asanan development policy supported the Molean financing law requiring a downpayment for access to ARVs. In doing so, Asana has supported a policy that denies low-income HIV positive people, a vulnerable group, access to life-saving ARVs. Asana acknowledges that it failed to push the Bank to prioritize the protection of human rights over financial sustainability, and that it fully supported the PRSP and encouraged other Bank Members to support the cooperation agreement. The volume of Asana's contributions to the Bank means it has significant but not decisive voting powers.

(43)   The Committee holds that Asana breached its obligation to protect the right to health of people in a third country by supporting Bank policy

that impairs the right to health of Molean citizens. Asana has also failed to comply with Maastricht Principle 13, which imposes an obligation to avoid causing harm.

The Obligation to Fulfil the Right to Health of People in Third Countries

(44)   Under the Maastricht Principles, the obligation to fulfil entails many separate obligations. Generally, as specified in the Covenant, all States must take action separately and jointly through international cooperation to fulfil the right to health of those on their territory and extraterritorially (Principle 28). Neither the Petitioner nor Asana dispute that Asana provides international assistance as required in Principle 33 and under Article 2.1 of the Covenant. The Petitioner claims that the terms of this international assistance undermine Molean citizens' health rights by funding policies that discriminate against vulnerable groups.

Obligation to create an international enabling environment (Principle 29)

(44)   Fulfilling economic, social and cultural rights extraterritorially should guide the international actions of Asana including in trade, international taxation and development cooperation. In this case, Asana prioritized financial sustainability concerns in its cooperation agreement with Molea, which is incompatible with Asana's obligations under the Covenant. As General Comment 14 para 39 notes, "In relation to the conclusion of other international agreements, States parties should take steps to ensure that these instruments do not adversely impact on the right to health". The grounds on which Asana reviews multilateral and bilateral cooperation are flawed.

(46)   To comply with the obligation to create an international enabling environment, Asana should ensure that all human rights, including the right to health, are fully integrated into all aspects of its policy and programming, including development and trade policy. Further, it should ensure that human rights review procedures are in place so that all government programmes and policies, including multilateral agencies it cooperates with, are scrutinized to ensure consistency with its obligation to fulfil human rights in third States. Asana's reviews do not assess compliance with Covenant obligations, but with financial sustainability criteria. Financial sustainability criteria may, in some cases, assist a third State in respecting its human rights obligations, but they should not form the basis for cooperation. The Committee welcomes Asana's engagement in international cooperation and assistance programmes, but notes that the agreement between Asana and Molea does not help Asana fulfil its extraterritorial obligations.

(47)   The Committee finds that Asana has failed to create an international enabling environment that respects the right to health extraterritorially as provided for under Principle 29 and General Comment 14 para 42.

94 *Shared Responsibility for the Right to Health*

Principles and priorities in cooperation (Principle 32)

(48)   In General Comment 3, this Committee affirmed that States parties have a core obligation to satisfy, at the very least, minimum levels of Covenant rights. In General Comment 14, this Committee provided guidance on the prioritization of the core obligations and the rights of disadvantaged, marginalized and vulnerable groups in fulfilling ESC rights extraterritorially (para 43, 44 and 45). Principle 32 reaffirms these principles stating that "In fulfilling economic, social and cultural rights extraterritorially States must: a) prioritize the realization of the rights of disadvantaged, marginalized and vulnerable groups; b) prioritize the core obligation to realize minimum essential levels of economic, social and cultural rights and move as expeditiously as possible towards the full realization of economic, social and cultural rights".

(49)   As discussed above, ensuring that access to ARVs is provided in a non-discriminatory manner engages a core obligation under the right to health. The Petitioner represents members of a marginalized and disadvantaged group: HIV positive people with no access to ARV treatment living in a low-income country dependent on international assistance for much of its social sector spending. Asana's international cooperation programme should be, *inter alia*, prioritizing interventions that strengthen Molea's ability to offer universal access to ARVs for vulnerable groups, like the Petitioner's members. Instead, Asana limits this ability by placing financial sustainability concerns over human rights obligations.

(50)   The Committee finds that Asana fails to cooperate internationally in a manner that is consistent with Article 2.1 of the Covenant or Principle 32 and is in breach of Principle 33, thus breaching the obligation to fulfil the right to health of the Petitioners' members.

6. The Transnational Obligations of Bank Members, including Asana

(51)   Asana argues that there is no legal basis for holding it or other Bank Members that are States parties responsible for the consequences of Bank policies. The Committee acknowledges that this may have been the case in the past, but finds the work of the International Law Commission (ILC, UN Doc. A/64/10) on State responsibility and the recent work on the responsibility of international organizations suggest other, albeit contested, avenues. The Maastricht Principles, although focused on States, also provide limited guidance, in particular under Principle 15. Further, in General Comment 14 this Committee held that "States Parties have to … prevent third parties from violating the right in other countries, if they are able to influence these third parties by ways of legal or political means" (para 34).

Obligations of States as members of international organizations (Principle 15)

(52)   There is no legal basis for the contention that membership of an international organization suspends the international human rights obligations of its members. The 2001 Tilburg Principles suggest that the Bank has an international legal obligation to ensure its policies and programmes respect human rights (paras 5, 25). Member States of the Bank and other international institutions carry their legal obligations under the Covenant through the doors of these institutions. The Committee believes the decisions and acts of the Bank that breach these obligations can be attributed to Bank Members, provided Principle 15 is satisfied.

(53)   Principle 15 states that "As a member of an international organization, the State remains responsible for its own conduct in relation to its human rights obligations within its territory and extraterritorially. A State that transfers competences to, or participates in, an international organization must take all reasonable steps to ensure that the relevant organization acts consistently with the State's human rights obligations". Thus, Bank Members, like Asana, and other States parties, share responsibility for violations of their extraterritorial human rights obligations stemming from Bank policy. With respect to the standard of conduct, the Committee finds the logic underlying Principle 15 convincing as adopting a standard of absolute or strict liability would be counterproductive to creating an international environment conducive to the universal fulfilment of economic, social and cultural rights.

(54)   We shall now consider whether Asana and other Bank Members that are States parties took all reasonable steps to ensure the Bank policies and programmes comply with States parties' human rights obligations. Maastricht Principle 14 provides broad guidance on one reasonable step, namely, impact assessments, noting that "States must conduct prior assessment, with public participation, or the risks and potential extraterritorial impacts of their laws, policies and practices on the enjoyment of economic, social and cultural rights". What would such steps include? First, at a minimum, they would include ensuring that a human rights review procedure is in place to ensure that all programmes and policies are scrutinized for consistency with States parties' human rights obligations in third states. Second, a human rights impact assessment should be an integral part of all monitoring and evaluation exercises. This logic builds on General Comment 2 (UN Doc. E/1990/23) in which the Committee provided "that a 'human rights impact statement' be required to be prepared in connection with all major development cooperation activities" (para 8b). Third, mechanisms that ensure constructive accountability for all policies and programmes should be in place. Such an approach to accountability should move beyond sanctions and naming and shaming, and instead seek to develop an inclusive dialogue around obligations and entitlements that includes all relevant

96 *Shared Responsibility for the Right to Health*

stakeholders. If such human rights safeguards are not in place, then Bank Members that are States parties are not taking all reasonable steps to ensure they act consistently with their human rights obligations.

(55) Asana, like other Bank Members, participates in the funding, decision-making and voting at the Bank. Asana does not dispute that it voted for the agreement that is the subject of this Communication. It also acknowledges that no human rights impact assessment was conducted. The Committee holds that this is *prima facie* evidence of a breach of the required standard of conduct by Asana and other Bank Members who are States parties as they did not take "all reasonable steps" to ensure the agreement in question was consistent with their international human rights obligations.

(56) Further, the Committee believes that taking all reasonable steps would include voting against a particular policy or declining to fund a policy that is inconsistent with a State party's human rights obligations under the Covenant. If such a decision is approved, then a State party should consider suspending funding for the project in question until it is able to receive guarantees that a dialogue on reform will begin. If multiple attempts to enter into a meaningful dialogue about ensuring policy and procedures comply with human rights obligations fail, then a State party should consider suspending cooperation with such an institution. It could then increase cooperation with international institutions that have adopted policies and procedures that prioritize human rights obligations in decision making and have accessible human rights accountability mechanisms in place. Asana has not presented evidence of efforts to begin such a dialogue.

(57) The Committee concludes that in its actions as a Bank Member, Asana, a complementary duty holder, has breached the standard of conduct required of it. This finding holds for other Bank Members that are States parties and raises the issue of multiple attribution of responsibility.

(58) The Maastricht Principles are silent on the issue of multiple attribution of responsibility among states. The ILC Articles on Responsibility of States for Intentionally Wrongful Acts do not provide much clarity when States are acting jointly as members of international organizations. The ILC Articles on the Responsibility of International Organizations also fail to offer sufficient guidance on how to allocate responsibility. The Committee urges the ILC to adopt a clear and progressive rule on multiple attributions that encompass international human rights violations by primary duty bearers and different complementary duty bearers including State and non-State actors.

(59) The Committee notes that the cooperation agreements between the Bank and Molea and that between Asana and Molea have identical conditions. Thus, much of the Committee's analysis of Asana's obligations in part 5 above applies to the obligations of Bank Members that are State parties, including Asana, acting in its capacity as a Bank Member. The Committee

finds that those Bank Members that are States parties and did not openly oppose the Bank cooperation agreement with Molea are jointly and separately responsible for the violations outlined below.

Obligation to Respect the Right to Health of People in Third Countries

Indirect Interference

(60)   The Committee finds that by predicating international assistance and cooperation with Molea on financial sustainability criteria, Asana and other Bank Members that are States parties indirectly impaired the government of Molea's ability to comply with its human rights obligations with respect to the right to health.

The Obligation to Protect the Right to Health of People in Third Countries

(61)   The Committee holds that Asana and other Bank Members that are States Parties breached their obligation to protect the right to health of people in a third country by failing to influence Bank policy that impairs the right to health of Molea citizens.

The Obligation to Fulfil the Right to Health of People in Third Countries

(62)   The Committee finds that Asana and other Bank Members that are States parties failed to cooperate internationally in a manner that creates an international enabling environment as specified under Article 2.1 of the Covenant, thus breaching a key element of their obligation to fulfil the right to health in Molea.

7. Accountability and Remedy

(63)   The Committee welcomes the participation of Molea and Asana, both as a State and as a Bank Member, in these proceedings. It notes that Article 36 of the Maastricht Principles holds that "States must ensure the availability of effective mechanisms to provide for accountability in the discharge of their extraterritorial obligations" and encourages Molea and Asana to enter into a constructive dialogue for the effective implementation of the recommendations in this Communication.

8. Recommendations

(64)   As required under the Covenant, the Committee urges all States parties, including Molea, Asana and Bank Members that are States parties, to ensure that human rights obligations take precedence over financial sustainability issues in all future international cooperation agreements.

98 *Shared Responsibility for the Right to Health*

(65)   In their capacity as Bank members, Asana and Molea should assist the Bank in first implementing a human rights review process to ensure that all international cooperation and assistance programmes and policies are scrutinized for their consistency with States parties' national and transnational human rights obligations. Second, a human rights impact assessment should be an integral part of all monitoring and evaluation exercises. Third, mechanisms that ensure constructive accountability for all policies and programmes should be in place. Such an approach to accountability should move beyond naming, shaming and sanctions and should instead work towards developing an inclusive dialogue around obligations and entitlements that includes all relevant stakeholders.

(66)   The Committee requests that Molea and Asana report on the implementation of the Committee's recommendations within six months of the date of notification.

7 Economic, Social and Cultural Rights of the Purak Peoples (Committee on Economic, Social and Cultural Rights)

Jernej Letnar Černič

Abstract

Country A has been identified in many reports of international organizations and non-governmental organizations as rife with systematic violations of economic and social rights, particularly the right to food, water, education and housing. Country A is rich in natural resources, particularly in oil, natural gas and water resources and in the past two decades, country A has awarded major concessions and foreign investment contracts to three of the world's largest oil corporations: X, Y and Z. Five years ago, these three corporations began to extract oil and gas from several areas across the country. Corporations X and Y are based and incorporated in State B, which is a high-income democracy that generally respects the rule of law and human rights. Both corporations X and Y are under the direct control of State B when operating in weak governance zones. Corporation Z is a public corporation incorporated in and under governmental control in totalitarian country C. Over the course of several decades, B and C have invested in the economy of country A and have repeatedly cooperated with the government of country A notwithstanding constant protests by civil society organizations relating to alleged violations of economic and social rights in the Purak mountains. The author of the present communication before the Committee on Economic, Social and Cultural Rights charges that State party B has failed to properly regulate the behaviour of X and Y corporation and that State party C has failed to properly regulate corporation Z – which has resulted in violations of ESCR.

Introductory note

Context and background

This hypothetical case relates to the situation of an individual who is a member of Nuba peoples, an indigenous ethnic group living in the area of the Nuba mountains in Southern Kordofan in central Sudan. They include a variety of tribes in the Nuba mountains, but what connects them is a common culture and way of life. Salih observes 'the Nuba are indeed the

100 *Economic, Social and Cultural Rights of the Purak Peoples*

indigenous peoples of the Nuba Mountains; they have the strongest ties to their lands and have lived in this region before colonization'.[1] They earn their livelihood through agriculture and raising animals. The Nuba peoples have throughout the centuries been subjected to systematic human rights violations, ethnic cleansing, and superior race policies by different colonial masters ranging from British colonists to Arabs. The Sudanese government's attempts to subdue and demolish them have been ongoing for several decades.

Indigenous land rights derive from several international human rights documents. International law standards provide the lowest common denominator agreed upon and binding on part or all of the international community.[2] Indigenous peoples enjoy the right to property, which derives in particular from the second part of ILO Convention 169 concerning indigenous and tribal peoples in independent countries.[3] Article 13(1) provides that 'Convention governments shall respect the special importance for the cultures and spiritual values of the peoples concerned of their relationship with the lands or territories, or both as applicable, which they occupy or otherwise use, and in particular the collective aspects of this relationship'.[4] Indigenous land rights are inherently connected to individual's enjoyment of economic and social rights.

Economic and social rights have for a long time been considered as secondary. They may be equal in theory with civil and political rights; however, in practice both sets of rights are still not placed on an equal footing. And while an extensive body of case law has come into existence in relation to civil and political rights, courts are still very reluctant to try cases on the basis of economic, social and cultural rights. This refers to the question of the so-called 'justiciability' of economic, social and cultural rights, the question of whether these rights are enforceable before a court of law.[5] Economic, social and cultural rights include rights to housing, food,

---

1 Guma Kunda Komey, The Denied Land Rights of the Indigenous Peoples and Their Endangered Livelihood and Survival: The Case of the Nuba of the Sudan, 31 *Ethnic & Racial Stud.* 991, 991–1008 (2008).

2 *See* S. James Anaya & Robert A. Williams, The Protection of Indigenous Peoples' Rights over Lands and Natural Resources Under the Inter-American Human Rights System, 14 *Harv. Hum. Rts. J.* 33, 36 (2001).

3 Convention Concerning Indigenous and Tribal Peoples in Independent Countries, 72 ILO Official Bull. 59 (entered into force Sept. 5, 1991). So far, only 22 states have ratified this convention. *See NORMLEX,* ILO, http://www.ilo.org/ilolex/cgi-lex/ratifce.pl?C169 (last visited 27 Feb 2013). *See generally* Athanasios Yupsanis, ILO Convention No. 169 Concerning Indigenous and Tribal Peoples in Independent Countries 1989–2009: An Overview, 79 *Nordic J. Int'l L.* 433 (2010)

4 Convention Concerning Indigenous and Tribal Peoples in Independent Countries, art. 13(1).

5 Fons Coomans (ed.), *Justiciability of Economic, Social and Cultural Rights* (Antwerpen – Oxford: Intersentia, 2006).

education, water and health.[6] This set of rights complements the so-called civil and political rights.[7] As Scheinin notes, 'there is no water-tight division between different categories of human rights'.[8] However, despite claims that both sets of rights are of equal importance and interdependent, civil and political rights are more solidly established under international and national law.[9] Economic, social and cultural rights generally have a programmatic nature and are not always directly justiciable to the same extent that civil and political rights are.[10]

Article 26(1) of the UN Declaration on the Rights of Indigenous Peoples states that '[i]ndigenous peoples have the right to the lands, territories and resources which they have traditionally owned, occupied or otherwise used or acquired'.[11] Therefore, occupancy of the territory must be connected with the past, and not necessarily also with the present. In other words, peoples who were forced out of their traditional territories and now live in other areas may also be able to exercise their rights.[12]

In addition, States have obligations to protect the right of peoples to own and possess the land they traditionally use.[13] In this context, Article 2(2)(b) of ILO Convention 169 obliges states to 'promot[e] the full realization of the social, economic and cultural rights of these [indigenous] peoples with respect for their social and cultural identity, their customs and traditions and their institutions'.[14] The African Overview Report emphasizes the importance of this provision, as 'land rights recognised in post-colonial countries often do not give recognition to indigenous peoples' traditions, customs and concepts of ownership'.[15] The strong wording of Article 14 is

---

6   Asbjørn Eide, Economic, Social and Cultural Rights as Human Rights, in *Economic, Social and cultural rights: A textbook* 21, 22 (Asbjørn Eide et al. (eds), 2001); *see also* Amnesty Int'l, *What are Economic, Social and Cultural Rights?*, http://www.amnesty.org/en/economic-and-social-cultural-rights/what-are-escr (last visited 15 Nov. 2012).

7   Martin Scheinin, Human Rights Committee: Not Only a Committee on Civil and Political Rights, in *Social Rights Jurisprudence: Emerging Trends in International and Comparative Law* 540, 540 (Malcom Langford (ed.), 2008).

8   *Ibid.*

9   Martin Scheinin, Economic and Social Rights as Legal Rights, in *Economic, Social and Cultural Rights: A Textbook, supra* note 6, at 41, 53.

10 Eide, *supra* note 6, at 22.

11 United Nations Declaration on the Rights of Indigenous Peoples, *supra* note 12, art. 26(1).

12 *See, e.g.,* S. James Anaya, Maya Aboriginal Land and Resource Rights and the Conflict over Logging in Southern Belize, 1 *Yale Hum.Rts. & Dev. L.J.* 17, 19 (1998)

13 Convention Concerning Indigenous and Tribal Peoples in Independent Countries, *supra* note 4, art. 14.

14 *Ibid.* Art. 2(2)(b).

15 ILO, Overview Report of the Research Project by the International Labour Organization and the African Commission on Human and Peoples' Rights on the Constitutional and Legislative Protection of the Rights of Indigenous Peoples in 24 African Countries 88 (2009), *available at* http://www.ilo.org/wcmsp5/groups/public/—ed_norm/—normes/documents/publication/wcms_115929.pdf.

102 *Economic, Social and Cultural Rights of the Purak Peoples*

somewhat undermined by Article 16, which initially notes that 'the peoples concerned shall not be removed from the lands which they occupy', but '[w]here the relocation of these peoples is considered necessary as an exceptional measure, such relocation shall take place only with their free and informed consent'.[16]

Case

View of the Economic, Social and Cultural Rights Committee under Article 2 of the Optional Protocol to the International Covenant on Economic, Social and Cultural Rights, G.A. res. 63/117 (2008)

Views Communication No. 10/2025
Submitted by: Kari Tayara (represented by counsel)
Alleged victim: The author
State Party: B and C
Date of communication: 10 November 2024 (initial submission)
Date of adoption of Views: 21 July 2025

Background and Description of the Facts

1.   Country A has been identified in many reports of international organizations and of non-governmental organizations as rife with systematic violations of economic and social rights, particularly the right to food, water, education and housing. Country A is rich in natural resources, particularly in oil, natural gas and water resources. It controls the third largest reserves of oil and water in the world. Oil revenues are therefore a major source of the country's gross domestic product. However, high levels of poverty still are prevalent as oil revenues are not distributed equally, but rather, siphoned off by members of the country's ruling party. In the past two decades, country A has awarded major concessions and foreign investment contracts to three of the largest oil corporations in the world: X, Y and Z. Five years ago, these three corporations began to extract oil and gas from fields across the country. X and Y are based in and incorporated in State B, which is a high-income democracy that generally respects the rule of law and human rights. Both X and Y are under the direct control of State B when they operate in weak governance zones. The OECD Risk Awareness Tool for Multinational Enterprises in Weak Governance Zones defines a weak governance zone as 'an investment environment in which governments are unable or unwilling to assume their responsibilities' (OECD, 2006, p. 9). Corporation Z is a public corporation from totalitarian country C. A, B and C are States parties to the International Covenant on Economic, Social and Cultural Rights, and States B and C have

---

16 *Ibid.* Art. 17.

Litigating Transnational Human Rights Obligations 103

also ratified the Optional Protocol to the International Covenant on Economic, Social and Cultural Rights. Over the course of the past few decades, B and C have invested heavily in the economy of country A and have cooperated intensively with the government of country A notwithstanding constant protests by civil society organizations relating to alleged violations of economic and social rights in the Purak Mountains. The author of the present communication has brought an individual communication (complaint) against States parties B and C before the Committee on Economic, Social and Cultural Rights for their failure to regulate and monitor the conduct of corporations X, Y and Z, which resulted in violations of the economic, social and cultural rights of the Purak peoples.

2.   Of particular concern in country A is a mountainous area in the Purak Mountains populated by the indigenous Purak people. These mountains are rich in oil and water resources. Although there are a number of different tribes, what connects them is a common culture and way of life. The Purak people have lived in this area since before colonization by Europeans and they mainly earn their livelihood through agriculture and raising animals. The land is central to the cultural existence, identity and socioeconomic survival of the Purak people. Customary laws have traditionally regulated land tenure in the Purak Mountains. However, State A has seriously disregarded their claim to these ancestral lands. Throughout the centuries, the Purak people have been subjected to systematic human rights violations, ethnic cleansing and superior race policies carried out by various colonial masters. Such attempts have not ceased and the government of A has intensified its efforts to subdue these people after the southern region of the country declared its independence on 15 May 2015.

3.   The government of State A granted concession rights to extract oil to corporations X, Y and Z subject to the several conditions. One of the conditions was that security forces of corporations X, Y and Z would assist governmental forces of State A in shutting down the rebellion of indigenous Puraks who live in this area.

4.   Kai Tayara is the author of the communication, dated 10 November 2019, against countries B and C before the United Nations Committee on Economic, Social and Cultural Rights under the Optional Protocol to the International Covenant on Economic, Social and Cultural Rights. He was born on 7 March 1974, a national of State A living at an unknown location in the Purak Mountains. *The New York Times* reported on 13 July 2019 that the army of country A and security forces of corporations X, Y and Z have been systematically bombing the Purak Mountains with Ukrainian-made bombers. As a result, several hundred civilians, predominantly women and children, have been killed and/or injured. Bombs have been dropped on agricultural fields, schools and water reserves, thereby destroying basic goods needed for the survival of the Purak people. Among others, the

104 *Economic, Social and Cultural Rights of the Purak Peoples*

country's military forces, assisted by the security forces of corporations X, Y and Z, have destroyed the socio-economic livelihood of Mr Kari Tayara.

5.   Mr Tayara brought legal claims against X, Y and Z in domestic courts in B and C for violating his economic and social rights after the courts in State A dismissed his case at pre-trial stage due to the insistence of the government of State A. Therefore, Mr Tayara turned to courts in B and C. However, the national judicial bodies of both of these states dismissed his suit on the grounds that they do not have extraterritorial jurisdiction to ensure that corporations X, Y and Z, which are registered in their jurisdiction, observe economic and social rights extraterritorially. These domestic proceedings in B and C have been already been terminated.

The complaint

6.   Mr Tayara brings the present communication against countries B and C before the United Nations Committee on Economic, Social and Cultural Rights under the Optional Protocol to the International Covenant on Economic, Social and Cultural Rights for violations of his right to an adequate standard of living for himself and his family, including the denial of adequate food, clothing and housing, and to the continuous improvement of living conditions, the enjoyment of the highest attainable standard of physical and mental health, and the right to education, and for not effectively protecting his economic, cultural and social rights before the acts of private and state-owned corporations, which are registered in their jurisdiction.

The author submits that States parties B and C have been in a position to ensure that economic, social and cultural rights are observed extraterritorially in the Purak Mountains, and that they have been aware of the denial of those rights. The author argues that States parties B and C have extraterritorial obligations to ensure that corporations registered in their territory respect, protect and fulfil economic, social and cultural rights extraterritorially. Since the period of decolonialization, States parties B and C have invested heavily in the economy of State A, and in so doing they have contributed to the human rights violations in the Purak Mountains, including those suffered by the author of the present communication. The author also contends that States parties B and C are in a position to exercise decisive influence over their own corporations as well as State A in order to ensure the realization of economic, social and cultural rights in the Purak Mountains.

7.   The author contends that States parties B and C have violated Article 11 (the right of everyone to an adequate standard of living for himself and his family, including adequate food, clothing and housing, and to the continuous improvement of living conditions), Article 12 (the enjoyment of the highest attainable standard of physical and mental health and Article 13 (the right of everyone to education) of the International Covenant on Economic, Social and Cultural Rights by not exercising sufficient due

Litigating Transnational Human Rights Obligations 105

diligence over the conduct of corporations X, Y and Z in the Purak Mountains. The author further claims that States parties B and C failed to provide effective extraterritorial remedies for the violation of these and other human rights. Finally, the author also argues that States parties B and C violated the obligation of international assistance and cooperation (Article 2 of the ICESCR), with a view to achieving progressively the full realization of the rights recognized in the International Covenant on Economic, Social and Cultural Rights.

State party's observations on the admissibility and the merits

8. States parties B and C maintain that the communication is inadmissible. They claim that the author provides no explanation or reasoning to support his allegations of a violation of the Covenant and that he did not exhaust all domestic remedies in relation to the complaints raised. State B and State C assert that proceedings into allegations of violations of economic and social rights are pending. State B argues that it has done all that was possible to control the actions of corporations X and Y. Therefore, State B claims that it has fulfilled its obligations to protect economic, social and cultural rights. State C asserts that it has exercised due diligence and has investigated alleged violations, but it has not found any violations.

9. In addition, States parties B and C submit that they have not exercised effective control over the Purak Mountains, and that their corporations X, Y and Z have only invested in three oil wells in the area and that the jurisdiction over the alleged human rights violations against the author of the present communication has not taken place. States parties B and C argue that the Committee does not have jurisdiction over violations committed in a third country by private actors. States parties B and C acknowledge the suffering of the author of the present communication and of the Purak people. However, both States argue that State A has the primary obligation to protect human rights and to provide an effective remedy for its own nationals when this end has not been achieved.

10. States parties B and C therefore reiterate their request that the Committee declare the communication inadmissible on the grounds that the domestic remedies available in the State party have not been exhausted and that the communication is clearly an abuse of the purpose of the Covenant.

Issues and Proceedings before the Committee

Consideration of admissibility (jurisdiction)

11. Before considering the merits, the Committee must deliver a decision whether this communication is admissible or not. The Committee considers this complaint admissible, as domestic remedies in States parties B and

106 *Economic, Social and Cultural Rights of the Purak Peoples*

C thus far have been either non-effective or the author has in fact exhausted all available remedies. The Committee also notes that ongoing procedures and investigation are not likely to effectively respond to the author's allegations of economic, social and cultural rights violations. The procedures in States parties B and C have already been ongoing for six years; however, no decision has thus far been rendered.

12.   As for the claim that State A would be a preferable jurisdiction, the Committee submits that States parties B and C are the preferable jurisdiction for raising claims relating to alleged economic, social and cultural rights violations of the author of the communication, as country A is either unable or unwilling to effectively protect human rights within its territory. The legal framework in country A is unsatisfactory and it has demonstrated an unwillingness to protect the human rights of the Purak people. The Committee considers that human rights violations go unaddressed in State A mostly due to a lack of effective remedies. Further, the Committee notes that under existing human rights law, states have a responsibility to protect those within their territories from violations of their human rights, which State A has failed to do. The Committee emphasizes that the Inter-American Commission on Human Rights noted in *Saldaño v Argentina* that jurisdiction is not 'limited to or merely coextensive with national territory. Rather, the Commission is of the view that a State party to the American Convention may be responsible under certain circumstances for the acts and omissions of its agents which produce effects or are undertaken outside that State's own territory' (para. 17). The Committee finds that human rights obligations may extend beyond a State's territorial borders. The Committee notes that regional human rights courts and the HRC explicitly distinguish between territory and jurisdiction by advancing that jurisdiction is much broader than territory. The Committee points out that the United Nations Human Rights Committee (HRC) specified in its General Comment 31 that States must 'respect and ensure the rights laid down in the Covenant to anyone within the power or effective control of that State party, even if not situated within the territory of the State party' (para. 2). The Committee also makes note of the fact that the HRC has also employed this approach in its Concluding Observations on several State reports in relation to the application of the treaty. To this end, the Committee notes that the HRC held Israel responsible for implementation of the ICCPR in the Occupied Palestinian Territories since, in its words, there is 'the exercise of effective jurisdiction by Israeli security forces therein' (*Concluding Observations on Israel*, 18 August 1998. UN Doc. CCPR/C/79/Add.93, para. 10). The Committee notes that the HRC noted in its *Concluding Observations on United Kingdom* that ICCPR clearly applies 'to all individuals who are subject to its jurisdiction or control' (*Concluding Observations on United Kingdom of Great Britain and Northern Ireland*, CPR/C/GBR/CO/6, 30 July 2008, para. 14). All in all, the Committee notes that Articles 2 and 3 of the Optional Protocol

to the International Covenant on Economic, Social and Cultural Rights do not impede victims to bring communications against another State party of the Optional Protocol and the International Covenant on Economic, Social and Cultural Rights other than the State party where violations have been committed. States parties B and C have signed and ratified both international instruments. For these reasons, the Committee finds no obstacle in finding the present communication admissible as far jurisdiction of States parties B and C is concerned.

13. As for the claims that States parties B and C do not have jurisdiction over violations committed in a third country by private actors, the Committee notes that States are obliged to respect, protect and fulfil the economic, social and cultural rights of individuals against corporate conduct extraterritorially. They are required to regulate and adjudicate private activities in order to protect against economic, social and cultural rights violations, including corporate acts. The Committee notes that home States are also obliged to ensure that their nationals (natural and legal persons) under their effective control or authority observe economic, social and cultural rights abroad. The Committee finds that home State human rights obligations are not territorially limited and that international human rights bodies have held that States have extraterritorial human rights obligations where they exercise authority or effective control over individuals, or where they exercise effective control over an area of another State's territory. The Committee notes that a home State can be held responsible for corporate conduct if this is carried out under State instructions or if the corporation is *de facto* under the direction or control of the State even when its actions do not constitute the exercise of governmental authority. In such cases, the conduct of a person or group of persons can be considered as the act of a State under international law if the person or group of persons are in fact acting on the instructions, or under the direction or control of, that State. In the present case, the Committee must examine whether corporations X, Y and Z fall under governmental control or the direct control of countries B and C.

14. As for claims against State party B, Article 8 of the International Law Commission Articles on State Responsibility notes that: 'the conduct of a person or group of persons shall be considered an act of a State under international law if the person or group of persons is in fact acting on the instructions of, or under the direction or control of that State in carrying out the conduct'. The Committee observes that Article 8 refers to two situations under which the conduct of private persons or a group of persons becomes attributable to the State (International Law Commission, Draft articles on Responsibility of States for Internationally Wrongful Acts, with commentaries, Article 8, para. 1). First, it refers to situations where the person or group of persons are acting on the instructions of the State (International Law Commission, Draft articles on Responsibility of States

108 *Economic, Social and Cultural Rights of the Purak Peoples*

for Internationally Wrongful Acts, with commentaries, Article 8, para. 1). Second, it covers cases where the person or group of persons are acting under the direction or control of the State (International Law Commission, Draft articles on Responsibility of States for Internationally Wrongful Acts, with commentaries, Article 8, para. 1). In the present case, corporations X and Y have been acting under the direct control of State B as they received its direct instructions and the guidelines. It was identified that State B instructed corporations X and Y to systematically bomb the Purak Mountains with Ukrainian-made bombers. As a consequence, several hundred civilians died. What is more, corporations X and Y directly infringed upon the right to food and water of the author of present communication. What remains open to discussion and analysis is the degree of control State B must exert over corporate actions to trigger international State responsibility for their conduct. In *Military and Paramilitary Activities* the ICJ held that 'for this conduct to give rise to legal responsibility of the United States, it would in principle have to be proved that the State had effective control of the military or paramilitary operations in the course of which the alleged violations were committed' (Merits, para. 115). The Committee notes that the ICJ in the *Bosnian Genocide* case went on to confirm the effective control test formulated in the *Military and Paramilitary Activities* case (paras 402–6). In the present case, the Committee finds out that evidence clearly suggests State B has exercised effective control over corporations X and Y as those corporations were obliged to follow its advice and instruction on which areas of the Purak mountains to bomb. For the above reasons, the Committee finds that the communication with regard to State party B is admissible.

15.   As for claims against State party C, the Committee considers that States can be responsible for the conduct of corporations where the conduct was authorized to exercise elements of governmental authority. In the present case, corporation Z is a State-owned corporation and evidence suggests that since its establishment it has been operating under the authority of State C. Further, the Committee notes that even when corporate conduct of corporation Z does not constitute the exercise of governmental authority, it can still be attributed to the State where the action is either carried out under State instructions or the corporation is *de facto* under the direction or control of a particular State. For the above reasons, the Committee finds that the communication with regard to State party C is admissible.

16.   The Committee notes that the Maastricht Principles on Extraterritorial Obligations of States in the area of Economic, Social and Cultural Rights provide in principle 9 that 'a State has obligations to respect, protect and fulfil economic, social and cultural rights in any of the following: a) situations over which it exercises authority or effective control, whether or not such control is exercised in accordance with international law; b) situations over which State acts or omissions bring about foreseeable effects on the enjoyment of economic, social and cultural rights, whether within or

outside its territory; c) situations in which the State, acting separately or jointly, whether through its executive, legislative or judicial branches, is in a position to exercise decisive influence or to take measures to realize economic, social and cultural rights extraterritorially, in accordance with international law'. In the present case, the Committee submits that States parties B and C have extraterritorial obligations to ensure that corporations X, Y and Z respect, protect and fulfil economic, social and cultural rights of the author of the present communication. The Committee notes that States parties B and C, acting through their executive, legislative and judicial branches, were in a position to exercise decisive influence over corporations X, Y and Z in order to take measures to realize economic, social and cultural rights extraterritorially and not to violate the author's rights.

17.   For the above reasons, the Committee considers that States B and C have extraterritorial jurisdiction to control their corporations relating to economic, social and cultural rights in the Purak Mountains as they exercise extraterritorial effective control and authority as to the enjoyment of economic, social and cultural rights in that territory. Moreover, these States are in a position to exercise decisive influence over corporations X, Y and Z to take measures to realize economic, social and cultural rights extraterritorially. For these reasons, the Committee finds and declares the author's communication relating to States parties B and C as admissible. The Committee now turns to the consideration of the merits of the present communication.

Consideration of merits

18.   The Committee has considered the present communication in the light of all the information made available to it by the parties. The issue before the Committee, as the parties have presented it, is whether States parties B and C have extraterritorial obligations to ensure that private and State-owned corporations respect, protect and fulfil economic, social and cultural rights of the author of communication. The Committee will therefore examine and assess the legal obligations of States parties B and C. The Committee considers that State A has the primary responsibility to ensure economic, social and cultural rights within its territory. However, given that State A is not a State party to the Optional Protocol and is not willing and able to investigate and prosecute alleged human rights violations, the Committee must examine the scope and nature of extraterritorial State obligations of States parties B and C to ensure that corporations X, Y and Z, which have their main headquarters in these jurisdictions, respect economic, social and cultural rights of the author of the present communication.

19.   The Committee makes note of the fact that the basic principle that any signatory State of any human rights treaty is under a legal obligation to

110 *Economic, Social and Cultural Rights of the Purak Peoples*

refrain from violating human rights protections contained within those treaties (obligation to respect), but also to protect individuals from harmful behaviour from third parties, including corporations (see CESCR, Statement on the obligations of States Parties regarding the corporate sector and economic, social and cultural rights Geneva, 2–20 May 2011, E/C.12/2011/1). The Committee considers that faced with allegations concerning the involvement of corporations in relation to extraterritorial human rights violations, the State has to ensure proper monitoring and undertake appropriate investigations. The Committee observes that international human rights treaty bodies require States to i) take steps to prevent and punish economic and social rights violations, ii) properly investigate alleged economic and social rights violations, and iii) prosecute and try perpetrators as well as provide the victims with an effective remedy. This Committee has previously asserted in paragraph 33 of General Comment 15 on the right to water that: 'steps should be taken by States Parties to prevent their own citizens and companies from violating the right to water of individuals and communities in other countries. Where States parties can take steps to influence other third parties to respect the right, through legal or political means, such steps should be taken in accordance with the Charter of the United Nations and applicable international law'. This Committee also noted in its General Comment 12 on the Right to Food that 'the obligation to protect requires measures by the State to ensure that enterprises or individuals do not deprive individuals of their access to adequate food' (para. 15). It further noted that the private sector has 'responsibilities in the realization of the right to adequate food' and that it 'should pursue its activities within the framework of a code of conduct conducive to respect of the right to adequate food, agreed upon jointly with the Government and civil society' (para. 15). The Committee points out that international monitoring bodies require that States ensure investigations, sanctions (judicial, administrative, legislative) and remedies for individuals suffering from economic and social human rights violations at the hands of third parties, including corporations. The Committee emphasizes that these measures are related to the implementation of the right to an effective remedy for economic, social and cultural rights violations. The Committee notes that, for instance, the United Nations Committee on the Elimination of Racial Discrimination (CERD) recommended in its Concluding Observations regarding Suriname, 'the inclusion in agreements with large business ventures ... of language specifying how those ventures will contribute to the promotion of human rights in areas such as education' (CERD, *Concluding Observations on Suriname*, CERD/C/64/CO/9 (2004), para. 19). The Committee observes that CERD also noted that States should 'set up a specific plan of action to combat HIV/AIDS in the interior, where mining and forestry companies operate' (*Ibid.* at para 17). Similarly, the Committee recalls that the CERD's general recommendation 29 asks States to 'take measures against public bodies, private

Litigating Transnational Human Rights Obligations 111

companies and other associations that investigate the descent background of applicants for employment'. Having considered the theoretical underpinnings of State obligations, the Committee now turns to the present case.

20.   As for the obligations of States parties B and C, the Committee notes that State tripartite obligations to respect, protect and fulfil also apply to questions of economic, social and cultural rights in the territory beyond the borders of these States. The Committee finds that States B and C have a legal responsibility to ensure that economic, social and cultural rights are observed extraterritorially in the Purak Mountains, as respect for such rights is critical to the survival and development of the inhabitants of this region. The Committee considers that the lowest common denominator of state obligations is clear. The Outcome Statement of the 2005 World Summit establishes that 'each individual State has the responsibility to protect its populations from genocide, war crimes, ethnic cleansing and crimes against humanity' (UN Doc.A/Res60/L.1, para. 138). The Outcome Statement thus clarifies that 'this responsibility entails the prevention of such crimes, including their incitement, through appropriate and necessary means' (UN Doc. A/Res60/L.1, para. 138). Such a statement could also apply extraterritorially. Having considered the legal basis of obligations of States B and C, the Committee will now turn to the nature of obligations of States B and C to control their corporations extraterritorially. The Committee first turns to obligations of States B and C to ensure respect of economic, social and cultural rights.

21.   The Committee notes that States' obligation to respect economic, social and cultural rights obliges States and other actors to refrain from interfering in the enjoyment of economic, social and cultural rights. The Committee further notes that the security forces of corporations X, Y and Z have participated in bombing missions over the Purak Mountains, which has resulted in the deaths of several hundred civilians, predominantly women and children. The Committee emphasizes that the Maastricht Principles on Extraterritorial Obligations of States in the area of Economic, Social and Cultural Rights specify in Article 13 that: 'States must desist from acts and omissions that create a real risk of nullifying or impairing the enjoyment of economic, social and cultural rights extraterritorially. The responsibility of States is engaged where such nullification or impairment is a foreseeable result of their conduct. Uncertainty about potential impacts does not constitute justification for such conduct.' The Committee therefore considers that the obligation to respect suggests that States must undertake extraterritorial due diligence over corporations on their territory ensuring not only that they comply with human rights obligations concerning economic and social rights, but also that they do everything possible to avoid causing harm. The Committee notes here that the obligation to respect may appear to suggest that States have to undertake extraterritorial due diligence ensuring not only that they comply with human rights

112   *Economic, Social and Cultural Rights of the Purak Peoples*

obligations under the right to food, water, housing and decent standard of living but also that they do everything possible to avoid causing harm. The Committee observes the measures States B and C must adopt to ensure respect for the economic and social rights and indigenous land rights extraterritorially, including: constantly and consistently examining extraterritorial human rights situations where those rights are at stake; effectively monitoring policies that protect economic and social rights; and implementing an effective monitoring system to ensure that human rights policies relating to economic and social rights are being implemented. The Committee therefore finds that such obligations are incumbent upon States B and C. By not fulfilling such obligations, the Committee finds a violation of the Covenant by States parties B and C.

22.   The Committee notes that the obligation of States B and C to protect economic, social and cultural rights is a substantive normative obligation requiring certain conduct of corporations, and that a primary obligation relating to the conduct of third parties such as corporations derives from the ICESCR (see also Maastricht Principle 24). This Committee has previously noted that 'States Parties should also take steps to prevent human rights contraventions abroad by corporations that have their main seat under their jurisdiction, without infringing the sovereignty or diminishing the obligations of host States under the Covenant' (Statement on the obligations of States Parties regarding the corporate sector and economic, social and cultural rights, UN Doc. E/C.12/2011/1 (20 May 2011), para. 5.). The Committee observes that States are also obliged to ensure that private and State-owned corporations will not violate economic, social and cultural rights. The due diligence standard includes an obligation 'to exercise *due diligence* to prevent, punish, investigate or redress the harm caused by such acts by private persons or entities' (HRC, General Comment 31, para. 8.) The Committee notes that in *Velasquez*, the Inter-American Commission on Human Rights held Honduras responsible for failing 'to take reasonable steps to prevent human rights violations and to use the means at its disposal to carry out a serious investigation of violations committed within its jurisdiction, to identify those responsible, to impose the appropriate punishment and to ensure the victim adequate compensation' (para. 147). The Committee therefore notes that States B and C, however, can be held primarily responsible for extraterritorial violations by corporations X, Y and Z, which have their seat in their jurisdiction, if knowledge of States B and C can be established and if those states exercised actual control. To this end, States B and C are required to have a sufficiently adequate administrative and judicial system of preventing and stopping violations as well as a system for providing extraterritorial remedies for victims of violations instigated by the government of State A.

23.   The Committee observes that the third category of extraterritorial obligations of States Parties B and C of the ICESCR concerning economic,

Litigating Transnational Human Rights Obligations 113

social and cultural rights includes the obligation to fulfil, which requires the State to take active measures to ensure the availability, accessibility and affordability of an adequate standard of living for himself and his family, including adequate food, clothing and housing, and to the continuous improvement of living conditions, the enjoyment of the highest attainable standard of physical and mental health, and education. States B and C are and should also be held responsible to fulfil this obligation in A. However, the Committee finds that an extraterritorial State may become the co-holder of an obligation to fulfil economic, social and cultural rights in a failed state relating to corporate actors registered on its territory where there is no efficient governmental control or authority, which would protect indigenous rights as in the Purak Mountains. Corporations X, Y and Z have not provided the indigenous populations in the country, including the complainant, with basic food, water, housing and education services, where the government of State A has refused their provision over several decades. The Committee notes that evidence suggests that those corporations have also actively interfered with the provision of those basic services. By not complying with obligation to fulfil, the Committee finds State parties B and C in violation of their obligation under the ICESCR as they failed to control corporations X, Y and Z and failed to fulfil economic and social rights of the complainant.

24.   Applying these principles to the present case, the Committee considers that States parties B and C have been obliged to take steps to prevent and punish economic, social and cultural rights violations; to properly investigate alleged economic, social and cultural rights violations; and to prosecute and try perpetrators as well as provide the victims with an effective remedy. Such obligations were incumbent on both State parties B and C and derive from the ICESCR. However both parties have failed to comply with them. By not fulfilling such obligations, States parties B and C are in violation of their obligations under Articles 11 (the right of everyone to an adequate standard of living for himself and his family, including adequate food, clothing and housing, and to the continuous improvement of living conditions),12 (the enjoyment of the highest attainable standard of physical and mental health and 13 (the right of everyone to education) of the International Covenant on Economic, Social and Cultural Rights.

25.   As regards the author's allegations that States B and C violated their obligation to cooperate, the Committee makes note of Principle 32 of the Maastricht Principles, which provides: 'all States must take action, separately, and jointly through international cooperation, to protect economic, social and cultural rights of persons within their territories and extraterritorially'. In the present case, States B and C are obliged to ensure that the extraterritorial investment projects of their corporations do not have adverse impacts on economic and social rights of the author of the present

114 *Economic, Social and Cultural Rights of the Purak Peoples*

communication (and others) as such obligations derive from Article 2(1) of the ICESCR.

Remedy Proposed

26.   The Committee considers that the right to a remedy for victims of human rights violations constitutes a basic right. Maastricht Principle 37 provides that 'States must ensure the enjoyment of the right to a prompt, accessible and effective remedy before an independent authority, including, where necessary, recourse to a judicial authority, for violations of economic, social and cultural rights. Where the harm resulting from an alleged violation has occurred on the territory of a State other than a State in which the harmful conduct took place, any State concerned must provide remedies to the victim'.

27.   The Committee notes that the author of the present communication must have the right to an effective remedy if any of the rights as laid down in international human rights treaties have been violated. International human rights treaties also require States to provide effective remedies such as including some form of reparation, which may include compensation, 'restitution, rehabilitation and measures of satisfaction, such as public apologies, public memorials, guarantees of non-repetition and changes in relevant laws and practices, as well as bringing to justice the perpetrators of human rights violations' (HRC, General Comment 31, para. 16). The Committee notes that victims must primarily seek legal redress in the country where a violation occurred. However, State party A has not provided the author of the present communication with an effective remedy as his complaint was dismissed at the pre-trial stage due to the insistence of the government of State A. Thus, the judicial system of State A was not willing to hear the merits of the author's case.

28.   Applying this principle to the present case, the Committee notes that not providing a remedy when being in the position to do so, such as States parties B and C, would certainly not only be a breach of a subsequent positive obligation to protect against private and State-owned corporations abuses, but also a direct breach of a directly imposed positive obligation to provide an effective remedy. Further, the fact that A has not provided the author of the present communication with an effective remedy does not absolve B and C of providing such when their own corporations are the source of harm. Providing an effective remedy would begin by giving victims access to national courts in States parties B and C for extraterritorial violations in state A. Therefore, States parties B and C must grant the author of the present communication the right to an effective remedy in their respective jurisdictions. Finally, the Committee notes that limiting jurisdiction to the State in which the human rights violation itself occurred effectively eliminates the slippery slope argument that opening one's court

systems to any human rights violation victim would lead to an unlimited number of victims claiming the right to an effective remedy in more protective States. The Committee also finds that the States parties B and C must provide the author of the present communication with guarantees of non-repetition and a public apology.

29.   The Economic, Social, and Cultural Rights Committee, acting under article 2 of the Optional Protocol, is of the view that the facts before it disclose a violation of Articles 11, 12 and 13 of the International Covenant on Economic, Social and Cultural Rights. In accordance with Article 2 of the Optional Protocol to Covenant, States parties B and C are under an obligation to provide the author with an effective remedy relating to extraterritorial violations of economic, social and cultural rights, including compensation, guarantees of non-repetition and public apology. The Committee reiterates that States parties B and C should review their legislation to ensure that all persons enjoy both equality before the law and equal protection of the law relating to access to the court, including extraterritorial contexts, such as in the present communication.

8 "Only the Little People Pay Taxes"

Tax Evasion and Switzerland's Extraterritorial Obligations to Zambia (Committee on Economic, Social and Cultural Rights)

Nicholas J. Lusiani

Abstract

Every year, approximately $3 trillion of government revenue is lost to tax evasion around the world. Individuals and business enterprises that evade taxes create an endemic drain on the availability of revenues for the progressive realization of economic and social rights, especially in countries with already high levels of inequality and low levels of tax. Further, tax evasion corrodes the responsiveness, answerability and representative nature and capacity of government institutions, undermining human rights accountability in innumerable ways.

This chapter presents a hypothetical inter-State complaint brought before the UN Committee on Economic, Social and Cultural Rights by the Republic of Zambia against Switzerland – one of the world's leading tax havens – for actively promoting cross-border tax evasion. Tax evaders and those States complicit in tax evasion, it is argued, undermine governments' ability to finance expenditures and conduct non-discriminatory and equitable fiscal policy in accordance with their Covenant obligations. By eroding the State's capacity to exercise its sovereignty in taxing legal and natural persons in its jurisdiction, tax evaders and the countries which allow them to conceal their assets also destabilize the transparency, participation and accountability of public institutions. Switzerland's encouragement and active protection of tax evaders by guaranteeing bank secrecy and tax havens on its territory, the case maintains, undermines Zambia's ability to mobilize the maximum available resources for the progressive realization of the rights as well as protect against third-party infringements on rights under the Covenant. The Committee by extension finds that Swiss conduct in support of tax havens stands in contravention to its solemn duties to international cooperation and assistance in the universal fulfillment of the substantive rights to adequate standard of living, social security, health, and education of all Zambians.

Introductory note

This hypothetical inter-State communications complaint is being brought by Zambia under article 10(1) of the Optional Protocol (OP) to the International Covenant on Economic and Social Rights (ICESCR) against Switzerland for its conduct[1] as it relates to tax evasion and its adverse consequences for Covenant rights in Zambia.

Tax evasion[2] by individuals and business enterprises causes an endemic drain on the availability of revenues for the progressive realization of Covenant rights, especially in countries with already high levels of poverty, inequality and already low tax bases.[3] Governments worldwide reportedly lose $3.1 trillion to tax evasion – about half of the world's total expenditure on healthcare.[4] While high-income countries are among the biggest losers in absolute terms, low- and middle-income countries are particularly vulnerable to these losses. In 2009, almost $1 trillion was reportedly lost in these countries due to illicit financial flows, about 60 per cent of which came from tax evasion.[5] This was more than 10 times official development assistance that year and substantially more than the costs estimated to achieve the Millennium Development Goals.[6]

In addition to providing the revenue base to progressively realize economic, social and cultural rights in non-discriminatory ways in accordance with Covenant duties, tax evasion can also undermine the accountability, responsiveness, and representative nature and capacity of government institutions. Evidence illustrates that governments which are heavily dependent

---

1 Note that this judgment considers Switzerland's obligations under the ICESCR to cooperate internationally to counter tax evasion, which is by definition illegal. This analysis does not assess questions related to the human rights implications of tax avoidance, which is legal but not necessarily legitimate, nor does it consider in depth illicit funds derived from corruption and bribery, with its own distinct set of issues and problems.

2 Tax evasion can be defined as "the illegal non-payment of tax to a government of a jurisdiction to which it is owed by a person, company, trust or other organization who should be a taxpayer", in Richard Murphy, "The Cost of Tax Abuse: A briefing paper on the cost of tax evasion worldwide", Tax Justice Network, November 2011 at http://www.tackletax-havens.com/Cost_of_Tax_Abuse_TJN%20Research_23rd_Nov_2011.pdf.

3 Some studies put the amount lost to illegal capital flight in developing countries at between 6–9% of GDP. By comparison, total tax revenues on average in these countries are only 13% of GDP. See Norwegian Ministry of Foreign Affairs, "Tax Havens and Development: Status, analyses and measures". Report from the Norwegian Government Commission on Capital Flight from Poor Countries, appointed by Royal Decree of 27 June 2008 (hereto after "Norway Commission Report"), at www2.ids.ac.uk/gdr/cfs/TaxNews/NorweigianTaxPolicy.pdf.

4 See Murphy (2011).

5 See Dev Kar and Sarah Freitas, "Illicit Financial Flows from Developing Countries Over the Decade Ending 2009", (December 2011) at http://iffdec2011.gfintegrity.org/

6 See Shantayanan Devarajan, Margaret J. Miller, and Eric V. Swanson, "Development Goals: History, prospects and costs", World Bank Policy Research Working Paper Summary at www.worldbank.org/html/extdr/mdgassessment.pdf

118   *Tax Evasion and Switzerland's Extraterritorial Obligations to Zambia*

on domestic taxes for their revenue have incentives to bargain with their taxpayers, strengthening the overall accountability, democratic and representative decision-making in government, and at the same time supporting the capacity of public institutions.[7] Tax evasion can sever this accountability relationship by generating a revenue escape valve, and in this sense corroding the accountability, responsiveness, and representative nature and capacity of government institutions.[8] For these reasons, tax evasion has been described as the "ugliest chapter in global economic affairs since slavery".[9]

Tax evasion, of course, does not happen in a vacuum, and among the most important external factors is the availability of offshore financial centers, also known as secrecy jurisdictions, or tax havens. While there is no universally accepted definition as yet, tax havens can best be defined as places that "seek to attract money by offering politically stable facilities to help people or entities get around the rules, laws, and regulations of jurisdictions elsewhere".[10] Over half of world trade is estimated to pass through tax havens, 8 per cent of global net financial wealth is held in unrecorded tax havens,[11] and over $10 trillion in private assets are reportedly held in offshore centers to evade and avoid taxes worldwide.[12] While not all assets in tax havens are illegitimate or derived illegally, a number of governments actively help high-net individuals, corporations, criminals and State officials conceal their gains from tax authorities by facilitating and maintaining tax havens, many industrialized countries among them.

Tax havens can also have distributional impacts within societies in that they restrict the ability of governments to tax the wealthiest sectors of the population, which, along with multinational companies, are the largest users of cross-border tax evasion. Tax havens thus likely have the effect of distorting the composition of taxes by reducing capital tax revenue and increasing pressure on other taxes to offset these losses. Those who do not have the wherewithal and mobility to evade taxes are often required to take

---

7 See Mick Moore, "How does Taxation Affect the Quality of Governance?", Centre for the Future State, Institute of Development Studies, April 2007 at www2.ids.ac.uk/gdr/cfs/pdfs/Wp280.pdf;

8 See Michael L. Ross, "Does Taxation Lead to Representation?", B.J.Pol.S. 34, 229–49, 2004, *Cambridge University Press* at http://www.sscnet.ucla.edu/polisci/faculty/ross/taxrep.pdf.

9 See N. Shaxson, Treasure Islands: Uncovering the Damage of Offshore Banking and Tax Havens, *Palgrave Macmillan*, 2011, p. 57

10 See Shaxson (2011), p. 12. This definition is purposefully more comprehensive of possible human rights impacts than the more limited definition related strictly to "offer[ing] businesses and individuals opportunities for tax avoidance", used in R. Griffith, J.R. Hines, and P.B. Sørensen, "International Capital Taxation". In Reforming the Tax System for the 21st Century: The Mirrlees Review, *Institute for Fiscal Studies*, 2008.

11 Gabriel Zucman, "The Missing Wealth of Nations: Evidence From Switzerland, 1914–2010", February 2011, Paris-Jourdan Sciences Economiques Working Paper No. 2011 – 07, 2011 at http://halshs.archives-ouvertes.fr/docs/00/56/52/24/PDF/wp201107.pdf

12 See Financial Secrecy Index at http://www.financialsecrecyindex.com/significance.html.

on the added burden of tax revenue lost to fiscal paradises. Tax authorities, which on their own lack the will or capacity to challenge tax evasion, often have little alternative but to resort to increasing Value-Added Taxes (VAT) and other forms of regressive, discriminatory tax regimes to make up for revenue lost to tax evasion.[13] Either that, or proceed to inequitably slash public budgets in the midst of alternatives, likely leading to retrogressive measures in the realization of Covenant rights.

Tax havens also produce adverse impacts unequally across different types of countries. States with high degrees of wealth inequality are affected disproportionately as a larger proportion of their potential tax base has the access, capacity and motivation to take advantage of tax havens to shield their assets.[14] Declines in tax revenues are of much larger consequence to low- and middle-income countries,[15] and many of these same States suffer from under-resourced public institutions, in particular tax authorities with limited capacities to enforce the law and pursue those who conceal their funds through tax evasion. Research has indicated that tax havens serve to reinforce a vicious cycle "whereby weak institutional capacity facilitates illegal capital flight, and tax evasion and capital flight in the next instance restrict the development of institutions... from the legal system and law enforcement to the civil service and democratic governance in the broad sense".[16] To the extent that tax havens incentivize those in power to weaken accountability and enforcement mechanisms by providing them with significant opportunities to conceal their ill-gotten wealth, tax havens can actually contribute to the deterioration of public institutions specifically designed to combat illicit activity,[17] making it more difficult for civil society to establish democratic and human rights controls on abusive exercise of State power.

Case

Views of the Committee on Economic, Social and Cultural Rights under Article 10(1) of the Optional Protocol of the International Convention on Economic, Social and Cultural Rights (Inter-State Communications)

Author State: Zambia
Respondent State: Switzerland

---

13 See Norway Commission Report, p. 67.
14 See Zucman (2011).
15 See T. Baunsgaard, and M. Keen "Tax Revenue and (or?) Trade Liberalization", IMF Working Paper WP/05/112 (2005),at http://www.imf.org/external/pubs/ft/wp/2005/wp05112.
16 See Norway Commission Report, p. 77
17 See Michael Ross, *Timber Booms and Institutional Breakdown in Southeast Asia*, *Cambridge University Press*, New York, 2001.

120 Tax Evasion and Switzerland's Extraterritorial Obligations to Zambia

Subject matter: Maximum available resources; fiscal policy; tax evasion; extra-territorial human rights obligations

Procedural Issues: Non-exhaustion of remedies; jurisdiction; international cooperation and assistance

Substantive Issues: Right to an adequate standard of living; right to social security; right to health; right to education; right to information; right to property; right to privacy

Articles of the Covenant: 2(1); 9; 11; 12; 13

Articles of the Optional Protocol: 10(1)

The facts as submitted by the author State

Zambia is a land-locked, least-developed country, with almost 60 per cent of its people living in poverty. Zambian citizens expect to live on average 34 years less than Swiss citizens. Inequality in Zambia, already one of the highest levels in sub-Saharan Africa, increased in 2008.[18] Zambia's already stunted tax base suffers from an estimated $1.2 billion loss of revenue every year due to tax evasion. This is almost 9 per cent of GDP, more than total healthcare spending in the country.[19]

Switzerland[20] meanwhile qualifies as one of the world's most significant tax havens, the author State submits. Swiss tax haven banks now house approximately 27 per cent of total global offshore wealth, a larger share than Britain, Ireland and the Channel Islands put together – all significant secrecy jurisdictions in themselves.[21] The President of the Swiss private bankers' association admitted unambiguously: "The large majority of foreign investors with money placed in Switzerland evade taxes."[22] Switzerland not only holds the largest amount of offshore wealth, it is also ranked as the world's most financially secretive jurisdiction, more so than the Cayman Islands and other frequently-cited fiscal paradises.[23]

---

18 See Food Security Research Project, "Factors Affecting Poverty Dynamics in Rural Zambia", July 2011 at http://aec.msu.edu/fs2/zambia/wp55.pdf

19 See Murphy (2011).

20 Please note that this article refers to Swiss conduct on and before the time of writing in April, 2012. No subsequent actions or omissions by the government – positive or negative – are subject to analysis here.

21 See Zucman (2011); see also Tax Justice Network, "Financial Secrecy Index 2011: Focus on Switzerland", October 2011 at http://taxjustice.blogspot.com/2011/10/financial-secrecy-index-2011-focus-on.html.

22 See *The Guardian*, "In the Country where Tax Evasion is no Crime, Swiss Private Banks are Unrepentant about Siphoning off other Governments' Income", February 2009 at http://www.guardian.co.uk/business/2009/feb/05/tax-gap-avoidance-switzerland

23 For more detail on how Switzerland received this bottom ranking, see Tax Justice Network, "Mapping Financial Secrecy: Switzerland", October 2011 at http://www.secrecyjurisdictions.com/PDF/Switzerland.pdf

Given the nature of secrecy and denial of access to information imposed by the Swiss government, no estimates are available on the amount of money currently hidden in Swiss tax havens by Zambian residents (legal and natural persons). Only the Swiss government itself can make these estimates, as the Zambian government is barred from access to information about the taxable holdings of its residents in that country. If the country's copper sector gives any indication, though, the revenue lost in Zambia to cross-border tax evasion in Switzerland is likely to be a substantial amount. Zambia depends to a large degree on copper exports for its revenue base, half of which were consigned to Switzerland in 2008. Much of the copper exports fall prey to trade mispricing, a technique through which multinational companies manipulate export and import prices to shield their substantial tax liabilities in the host country. Had Zambia received the revenue from the prices recorded in Switzerland for its actual exports to that country, the country's GDP would be almost *doubled* in 2008, from US \$14.3bn to US \$25.7bn,[24] an issue prompting investigations in several instances.[25]

The complaint

Considerations of admissibility

As to the admissibility of the communication, the author State maintains that this inter-State communication is admissible under Article 10(1) of the Optional Protocol. The author State notes that there is no territorial or jurisdictional limitations to this clause, allowing the Committee to address substantive violations of the Covenant in light of Article 2(1) regarding international cooperation and assistance.[26] In addition to the rights of individuals under its jurisdiction, Zambia's sovereign interest is also clearly affected by Swiss conduct to encourage and condone cross-border tax evasion, which also gives it every justification to bring the inter-State communications. Further, Zambia confirms that all domestic remedies have been exhausted in the sense that no domestic measures are at all effective in Zambia, nor available in Switzerland, to access the information needed to

---

24 See Christian Aid, "Blowing the Whistle: Time's Up for Financial Secrecy," 2010, p. 23 at http://www.christianaid.org.uk/images/blowing-the-whistle-caweek-report.pdf

25 See Sherpa, Berne Declaration, Centre for Trade Policy and Development, L'Entraide missionaire, Mining Watch, "Specific Instance Regarding Glencore International AG and First Quantum Minerals Ltd. and their Alleged Violations of the OECD Guidelines for Multinational Enterprises via the Activities of Mopani Copper Mines Plc. in Zambia", at oecdwatch.org/cases/Case_208/925/at_download/file

26 See Magdalena Sepulveda and Christian Courtis, "Are Extra-Territorial Obligations Reviewable Under the Optional Protocol to the ICESR?", *Nordisk Tidsskrift For Menneskerettigheter*, Vol. 27, NR 1 (2009), S. 54–63.

122 Tax Evasion and Switzerland's Extraterritorial Obligations to Zambia

properly determine tax liabilities of individuals and corporations shielding their Zambian assets in Swiss tax havens.

Consideration of the merits

Tax evasion, the author State submits, is an endemic drain on the resources available in Zambia to progressively realize, and in some cases meet, the minimum essential levels of Covenant rights. This is particularly the case for the rights to social protection, adequate standard of living, food, housing, health and education, as stipulated in Articles 9, 11, 12 and 13 respectively.

In light of its obligations to international cooperation and assistance under Article 2(1) and 11(1) of the Covenant, the author State contends that Switzerland's promotion and active encouragement of high-net individuals and multinational companies to use their secrecy jurisdiction to evade tax liabilities in Zambia directly interferes, and significantly undermines, Zambia's ability to mobilize the maximum available resources for the progressive realization of Covenant rights. In doing so, Switzerland's support for tax evasion in Zambia has the foreseeable effect of stripping the capacity of the country's already heavily under-resourced social service sector to properly protect against economic crimes by the private sector and to fulfill the rights to education, health care, adequate standard of living, and social security and protection, as both the Covenant and Committee compel Zambia to do. It is therefore Zambia's contention that such conduct contravenes Switzerland's duty to refrain from actions or omissions which impair the enjoyment of Covenant rights (respect) outside their territories.[27] Simultaneously, Zambia argues that Swiss conduct contravenes its duty to protect against abuse by third parties by failing to take measures to ensure that legal and natural persons it is in a position to regulate are not involved in any way in illegal tax evasion or other economic crimes detrimental to the full realization of Covenant rights.[28] Finally, Zambia maintains that Switzerland – by preventing the author State from progressively realizing Covenant rights – is acting unlawfully under its obligations to cooperate and assist in mobilizing the maximum of available resources for the universal fulfillment of the abovementioned Covenant Rights, as is a duty implicit in Article 2(1) of the Covenant and reflected in Article 31 of the Maastricht Principles on Extraterritorial Obligations of States in the area of Economic, Social and Cultural Rights Principles ("Maastricht Principles").

---

27 As reasoned in the Maastricht Principles on Extraterritorial Obligations of States in the area of Economic, Social and Cultural Rights Principles ("Maastricht Principles"), Article 21.

28 As reasoned in the Maastricht Principles, Art. 24.

Litigating Transnational Human Rights Obligations 123

The Republic of Zambia is committed to eliminating poverty, including through a national social protection system and the enhancement of accountability mechanisms to fight corruption as recommended by the UN Special Rapporteur on Extreme Poverty.[29] In order to mobilize the resources necessary in an equitable and just fashion, Zambia considers it a duty to abolish illegal tax evasion internally by upholding the rule of law. Yet, it cannot do so while the Swiss bank secrecy laws motivate and effectively exonerate Zambian tax cheaters from legal liability. The legitimacy and integrity of Zambia's tax system, the author State explains, is under strain when the poor are asked to pay taxes while the rich and corporate elite pay next to none. Swiss secrecy policy provides the access, capacity and motivation for companies to take advantage to shield their assets and outmaneuver the best efforts of the Zambian Revenue Authority, affecting the poorest in Zambia disproportionately.

Despite repeated requests to provide adequate information about Zambian residents shielding their gains in Switzerland, the author State submits, Switzerland refuses to take deliberate, proportional and effective measures to respect Zambia's sovereign right to mobilize available resources to improve economic and social rights enjoyment, and to protect and fulfill Covenant rights through international cooperation and assistance. Switzerland's long-standing conduct to undermine Zambia's tax authority, according to the author State, equates to an historic denial of right to access to and repatriation of stolen or untaxed funds.

Respondent State party's observations

Considerations of admissibility

The respondent State, Switzerland, in its official response declared its recognition of the competence of the Committee to receive and consider inter-State communications regarding its own tax policy, as required in Article 10(1) of the OP. It does not dispute admissibility of the case, in fact stating its welcome of such an inter-State communication to help clarify a misunderstood part of its economic system.

Considerations of the merits

Switzerland asserts that its current tax system is in line with its Covenant obligations on three grounds: 1) overriding principle of State sovereignty; 2) human rights benefits of current tax structure, and 3) existing

---

29 See Magdalena Sepúlveda Carmona, Report of independent expert on the question of human rights and extreme poverty: Mission to Zambia, 11 May 2010, A/HRC/14/31/Add.1 at http://www2.ohchr.org/english/bodies/hrcouncil/docs/14session/A.HRC.14.31.Add1.pdf.

124 *Tax Evasion and Switzerland's Extraterritorial Obligations to Zambia*

contributions toward fulfilling its obligations to international cooperation and assistance.

First, Switzerland argues that policies related to the levying and structuring of taxes and duties, and how government expenditure should be financed, is a fundamental sovereign right under international law. Sovereignty, Switzerland insists, includes the entitlement to implement domestic laws domestically. In the case of bank secrecy laws, Switzerland asserts that under the fundamental principles of territorial sovereignty, sovereign equality and autonomy of its cantons, it has the right to extend its laws and its sovereign protection to all accounts held in its territory to ensure confidentiality and the privacy of account-holders.[30] In line with its own right to sovereignty, Switzerland further stresses, it enjoys the discretion to design its economic development policies in ways which improve the economic outlook of its people through the attraction of trade and capital inflows by minimizing taxes and reducing other restrictions on business operations. While mandatory rules of international law (*jus cogens*) do impose limits on and take precedence over domestic law and Constitutional amendments (Constitution, Article 193, para. 4, and Article 194, para. 2), the respondent State argues, duties under the ICESCR decidedly do not reach the level of peremptory norms under jurisprudence or legal doctrine,[31] and thus cannot trump the overriding principle of State sovereignty.

Second, Switzerland further justifies its support of its financial secrecy laws by arguing that they are beneficial to the realization of economic, social and cultural rights internally in Zambia, and in fact, universally. By promoting tax competition between jurisdictions, the State argues, tax havens can sharpen institutional quality, good governance, lower transaction costs and investor risk. This in turn effectively increases efficiency in the allocation of capital, and thus improves economic growth.[32] In other words, tax havens are a legitimate and economically productive response to an unreasonable surge in taxation and regulation in the postwar era. Furthermore, the State party argues, the very origins of Swiss bank secrecy laws – emerging as they did to protect victims of Nazi Germany during World War II – give evidence to their necessity in upholding the right to

---

30 See Robert Palan, "Tax Havens and the Commercialization of State Sovereignty", *International Organization*, 56, 1, Winter 2002, p. 170 at http://www.unil.ch/webdav/site/iepi/shared/crii/Palan.pdf

31 For more on Switzerland's monist legal system, and the relationship between international and domestic law, see E/C.12/CHE/2–3 Implementation of the International Covenant on Economic, Social and Cultural Rights, Second and third periodic reports of States parties under articles 16 and 17 of the Covenant, Switzerland, 14 May 2008, at http://www2.ohchr.org/english/bodies/cescr/cescrs45.htm

32 See for example, Dhammika Dharmapala, "What Problems and Opportunities are Created by Tax Havens?", Working Papers 0820, 2008, Oxford University Centre for Business Taxation.

property of people under discriminatory duress from their government, especially on the basis of property or socio-economic status.

The offshore financial centers based in Switzerland (and the bank secrecy laws which underpin them), Switzerland further contends, create abundant employment opportunities, not to mention substantial tax revenues for local governments in Switzerland. They are thus essential to discharging Switzerland's obligations to protect and fulfill the right to work under Article 7 of the Covenant, upon which so many other rights depend.[33] In this respect, it is the respondent's contention that its primary obligations under the Covenant are to persons within Switzerland, and where conflict arises with the realization of Covenant rights in other countries, it is perfectly legitimate to prioritize the rights of people within its own territory.

Lastly, Switzerland argues that it has made significant strides in meeting its duties to international cooperation and assistance through its development assistance efforts, including in Zambia. Respect for human rights and the promotion of democracy are one of Switzerland's five foreign policy objectives,[34] and guidelines have been drawn up to incorporate human rights into development cooperation programs. Bilateral and multilateral programs aim to increase attention given to vulnerable and marginalized groups by recipient governments like Zambia, while simultaneously seeking to support the efforts of the authorities to discharge their Covenant obligations, especially in education, water and sanitation, health and the right to property.

Issues and proceedings before the Committee

Review of admissibility

The competence of the Committee in this case is based on Article 10(1) of the Optional Protocol, the main limitation being whether both States in question have submitted themselves to the jurisdiction of the case, to which in this case they have. The Committee finds that Zambia government has the *locus standi* to bring the application as the representative government of the Zambian people with clear connection to Switzerland's conduct under question. Further, Zambia has a legitimate legal interest in having the merits of the application examined. The Committee also affirms Zambia's contention that domestic remedies would be entirely ineffective in this case with cross-border dimensions, so the exhaustion test is irrelevant. The Committee therefore finds no reason why it should decline to exercise jurisdiction in this inter-State complaint.

---

33 See Norway Commission Report, p. 71–2.
34 See "Rapport sur la politique extérieure 2000: Présence et coopération: la sauvegarde des intérêts dans un monde en cours d'intégration" (Foreign policy report 2000: Presence and cooperation: protection of interests in an integrating world), November 2000, FF 2001 237.

126 *Tax Evasion and Switzerland's Extraterritorial Obligations to Zambia*

Consideration of the merits

The Committee will begin its consideration of the merits by reminding Switzerland that the principal obligation for Covenant implementation lies with the federal Government, not sub-national entities. In light of the provisions of Article 28 of the International Covenant on Economic, Social and Cultural Rights, then, any conduct attributed to Swiss cantons that is in breach of Covenant obligations is attributable to, and thus cannot be abdicated by, the State party.

In upholding its solemn duty to respect under the Covenant, no State is permitted to infringe on another State's ability to mobilize the resources necessary for fulfilling Covenant rights, including through fiscal and tax policy.[35] This is a logical correlation of the principle of trans-boundary harm[36] under customary international law, which prohibits States from allowing their own territory to be used in ways which infringe on the enjoyment of Covenant rights elsewhere. Further, the Committee has reiterated in numerous occasions that the duty to protect against human rights abuse by third parties requires State parties to ensure that business enterprises and private individuals operating on their territory respect Covenant rights. Further, State parties to the Covenant have a legal obligation to "take steps, individually and through international assistance and co-operation, especially economic and technical, to the maximum of its available resources, with a view to achieving progressively the full realization of the rights recognized in the present Covenant by all appropriate means".[37] As reasoned in the Maastricht Principles on Extraterritorial Obligations of States in the area of Economic, Social and Cultural Rights ("Maastricht Principles")[38] the obligation of international cooperation and assistance as articulated in Article 2(1) and 11(1) in the Covenant as well as the UN Charter and other international legal sources[39] implies that States must cooperate with – and not undermine – efforts to mobilize the maximum of available resources for the fulfillment of economic, social and cultural rights.

---

35 See R. Balakrishnan, D. Elson, J. Heintz, and N. Lusiani, "Maximum Available Resources & Human Rights: Analytical Report", 2011, Center for Women's Global Leadership, Rutgers University at www.cwgl.rutgers.edu/globalcenter/publications/marreport.pdf
36 See *Trail Smelter Case* (US v. Canada), 2 RIAA 1905, 1941.
37 See Article 2(1), ICESCR.
38 See Maastricht Principles, Article 31, "States must cooperate to mobilize the maximum of available resources for the universal fulfillment of economic, social and cultural rights."
39 On the obligation to international cooperation and assistance, see *inter alia* UN Charter, Article 55 and 56; Convention on the Rights of the Child, Article 4; Declaration on the Right to Development, Articles 3.1, 3.2, 3.3 and 4.2; Vienna Declaration and Programme of Action, Articles 1, 4, 10, and 11.

Litigating Transnational Human Rights Obligations 127

The Committee has stated elsewhere,[40] in concurrence with other treaty bodies[41] and UN Special Procedures,[42] that low and regressive tax collection can have negative impacts on the realization and enjoyment of economic, social and cultural rights. The ESCR Committee, like the Committee on the Rights of the Child,[43] is of the opinion that tax evasion has a similar, if not more adverse, effect. By preventing governments from mobilizing the maximum of available resources for the realization of economic, social and cultural rights and undermining public institutions, such behavior has the ultimate effect of nullifying or impairing the enjoyment and exercise of Covenant rights, particularly those signaled by Zambia under Articles 9, 11, 12 and 13. In light of the significant relationship between effective tax systems and the realization of Covenant rights, then, the Committee asserts that States' duties to international cooperation and assistance include a mutual obligation to cooperate on tax matters, especially to root out cross-border tax evasion, as reasoned in the Maastricht Principles.[44] As summed up unambiguously by the SR on Extreme Poverty, "A human rights approach ... requires States to take steps to eliminate the prevalence of tax evasion, a problem that reduces the resources available for measures to realize human rights".[45] The Committee notes, and concurs, with this legal requirement under the Covenant.

It is the Committee's view as a general matter that tax evaders – as well as those who are complicit in tax evasion – undermine governments' ability to finance expenditures and conduct redistributive fiscal policy in accordance with their Covenant obligations. By eroding the State's capacity to exercise its sovereignty in taxing legal and natural persons in its jurisdiction, tax evaders and the countries which allow them to conceal their assets also destabilize the transparency, participation and accountability of public

---

40 See E/C.12/1/ADD.58 (CESCR, 2001), para. 14
41 Similar conclusions stem from the Committee on the Rights of the Child, in particular in its review of the government of Guatemala, CRC/C/GTM/CO/3-4 (CRC, 2010), paras 25 and 26.
42 See in particular "Report of the Independent Expert on the question of human rights and extreme poverty, Ms. Maria Magdalena Sepúlveda Carmona on the human rights based approach to recovery from the global economic and financial crises, with a focus on those living in poverty" (2011), A/HRC/17/34; Daniel Turk, "The realization of economic, social and cultural rights, Special Rapporteur on Economic and Social Rights," E/CN.4/Sub.2/1992/16; Olivier De Schutter, "Report of the Special Rapporteur on the right to food, Mission to Brazil," 2009, A/HRC/13/33/Add.6, para. 36; Magdalena Sepúlveda, *The Nature of Obligations under the International Covenant on Economic Social and Cultural Rights*, Intersentia, 2003.
43 In its review of Georgia, the CRC impressed upon the State the need to devote its MAR to children by *inter alia* combatting tax evasion: CRC/C/15/ADD.124 (CRC, 2000), paras 18–19; followed up in 2003 CRC/C/15/ADD.222 (CRC, 2003).
44 See also Maastricht Principles, art. 29.
45 See A/HRC/17/34.

128 *Tax Evasion and Switzerland's Extraterritorial Obligations to Zambia*

institutions. As the Committee has noted on several occasions,[46] the extra-territorial duty to protect impels governments to ensure that non-State actors such as these which they are in a position to regulate refrain from nullifying the enjoyment of economic, social and cultural rights, regardless of where non-State actors operate.[47] Therefore, the State duty to protect against infringements on human rights by tax-evading individuals and business enterprises requires governments to prevent such third parties from using their jurisdictions to evade tax liabilities within the countries they operate, and to take steps to ensure effective remedy should such infringements occur.

The Committee will now respond to Switzerland's defense. Switzerland's conduct with regard to international tax cooperation has been previously raised before this Committee.[48] The facts detailed above evidence the substantial adverse impacts tax havens in Switzerland can cause for the enjoyment of Covenant rights in Zambia, and indeed universally. In view of the adverse effects of Swiss conduct, the question before the Committee is whether Swiss bank secrecy laws are essential in reference to other countervailing legal necessities. That is, the Committee will analyze whether Swiss conduct to encourage tax evasion is reasonably calculated to realize the enjoyment of Covenant rights, and can be justified by reference to the totality of the rights provided for in the Covenant.[49]

First, in reference to Switzerland's reliance on the principle of sovereignty, there is no question that a fundamental function and feature of a sovereign State is the right to levy taxes, without which it would be unable to obtain the financial resources to properly engage in its fundamental regulatory and redistributive roles. It is the Committee's view that cross-border tax evasion, as facilitated by secrecy jurisdictions such as the State party's, fundamentally encroach upon, if not erode, the sovereignty of the country of origin to levy and secure its own taxes in non-discriminatory ways for the full realization of Covenant rights. In these circumstances, then, what is at issue is not the sovereignty principle *per se*, but how one might resolve the conflict or competing sovereignties over the right to tax between Zambia and Switzerland. In the words of the Norway Commission report, "the secrecy rules do not, in fact, involve the exercise of domestic sovereignty, since local interests are not involved. The legislation is formulated so that it encroaches deeply on the sovereignty of other States, because the secrecy

---

46 See, for example, General Comment 19 of the CESCR at para. 54.

47 See Maastricht Principles, Articles 23–7.

48 See "Swiss NGO Coalition submission to ICESCR", September 2010 at http://www2.ohchr.org/english/bodies/cescr/docs/ngos/NGOCoalition_Switzerland45.pdf

49 See in particular the CESCR statement, "An Evaluation of the Obligation to Take Steps to the 'Maximum of Available Resources' Under An Optional Protocol to the Covenant", E/C.12/2007/1 at http://www2.ohchr.org/english/bodies/cescr/docs/statements/Obligationtotakesteps-2007.pdf

Litigating Transnational Human Rights Obligations 129

has no purpose other than concealing important information on activities taking place in other States".[50]

While the Committee is not in a position to resolve general conflicts between two competing sovereignties over the right to tax, it reminds both State parties of their duties to cooperate on such matters in ways as to prioritize the enjoyment of Covenant rights. The Committee is of the view that tax policies with extraterritorial effects such as bank secrecy laws which have discriminatory effects, or which undermine a government's ability to meet the minimum essential levels of certain substantive rights, are *prima facie* violations of the Covenant. Considering the substantial sums which are likely to be lost due to tax evasion in Zambia facilitated by Switzerland, and reminding both States of the object and purpose of the Covenant, the Committee suggests that in situations where very little economic activity takes place in the home country itself, the source state principle[51] becomes a standard for resolution of these conflicts. Many of the relevant legal and natural persons domiciled in Switzerland have no intention to actually conduct real activity in that jurisdiction. Yet, their tax liabilities still reside there, and they thus enjoy substantial freedoms from tax laws in Zambia where they functionally operate. In such circumstances, the Committee is of the view that no individual or company should be free from tax on income or wealth for which it is liable in its country of operation, in this case Zambia. Given the enormous gaps in fulfilling the most essential levels of Covenant rights in the author State, ensuring Zambia's sovereign right to tax its legal and natural persons which are not functionally operational in Switzerland should be the primary objective of bilateral tax cooperation between the two countries.

Further, we must consider in this instance how the nature of the rules in Switzerland differ from others, and may put fundamental principles of transparency, accountability and an overriding public interest at risk. Secrecy rules in Switzerland, as pointed out by the official Norwegian Commission on this issue, obstruct the application of normal rules of transparency on accessing information of the public interest in the States where the activities or operations actually take place. The sovereign government of Zambia (let alone rights-holders in this country) is effectively deterred from obtaining the information needed to hold natural and legal persons accountable for their tax liabilities, and thereby properly finance social service and other sectors fundamental to the public interest in its own territory and jurisdiction. Again citing the Norwegian Commission, "...privacy can be abused. No one has the right to use private space to conceal or commit abuse, or to inflict damage or injury on other individuals or the public

---

50 See Norway Commission Report, p. 31.
51 For more on the important distinction between the domiciliary principle and the source state principle, see Norway Commission Report, p. 79.

130 *Tax Evasion and Switzerland's Extraterritorial Obligations to Zambia*

interest. The right to private freedom must therefore be balanced against the right of others to be free from abuse, loss, and damage…the authorities of tax havens emphasize that their policy is to give special protection to the private sector, without taking into account the damage that may be caused to others".[52] Therefore, the Committee is of the view that Switzerland's bank secrecy laws have the effect of denying the Zambian government and the human rights-holders the fundamental right to access information, transparency and accountability which underpin the Covenant.

Second, Switzerland has argued that tax havens are not only legally justifiable they are also instrumental in ensuring the enjoyment of Covenant rights domestically, in Zambia and indeed universally. The Committee is of the view that the human rights benefits of tax havens have been far overstated by Switzerland. Evidence does not support the claim that Swiss bank secrecy laws stem from an interest to protect Holocaust survivors, as suggested, but more from a desire to capitalize on increased taxation in France and other countries designed to finance their social welfare systems after World War II.[53] Furthermore, the Committee reminds Switzerland that the right to property does not exist in the Covenant. While property and socioeconomic status are considered grounds for discrimination according to the Covenant and a recent General Comment,[54] the levying of legitimate taxes on property of those who utilize tax havens – the already superaffluent – can hardly be considered discriminatory in view of the object and purpose of the Covenant. Switzerland's efforts to protect the property of wealthy foreigners are hardly considered best practice in the Committee's view, especially to the extent that they actively undermine the effective enjoyment of rights of low- and middle-income Zambian households, which are much more vulnerable to the adverse human right impacts of tax evasion.

Switzerland also argues that tax havens and tax competition promote economic growth, job creation and thus provide the conditions for the realization of many Covenant rights in both countries concerned. These grounds are even more specious. Recent evidence in fact shows that contrary to the classic neo-liberal model of efficient capital allocation, developing countries actually export much more capital than they import.[55]

---

52 See Norway Commission Report, p. 31.
53 See Zucman (2011), p. 31; see also Sébastien Guex, "The Origins of the Swiss Banking Secrecy Law," 2000, at http://www.jstor.org/pss/3116693
54 See UN CESCR, General Comment 21, "Non-Discrimination in Economic, Social and Cultural Rights (Article 2, para. 2)", 2009.
55 See for example United Nations, "Report of the Commission of Experts of the President of the United Nations General Assembly on Reforms of the International Monetary and Financial System", 2009, at http://www.un.org/ga/econcrisissummit/docs/FinalReport_CoE.pdf

Litigating Transnational Human Rights Obligations 131

The Committee suspects this to be the case in Zambia, with Swiss tax havens contributing to this socially undesirable outcome. Regarding tax competition, furthermore, it is more likely that taxes will be set too low as a result of competition between countries to attract tax objects, as each individual country in practice will care less about the harm they cause other nations than the race to attract investment. The provision of disingenuous domiciliary positions, combined with "zero tax" regimes and secrecy rules in Switzerland, is not legitimate tax competition, as these rules trespass deeply into Zambia's own sovereignty, as mentioned above. It is equally unlikely that secrecy jurisdictions with low-to-no tax rates drive productive investment, as Switzerland has argued, but instead attract unproductive investments, with decreasing – not increasing – potentials for economic growth and the universal realization of Covenant rights.[56]

The Committee would further like to address Switzerland's contention that its primary obligations under the Covenant impel it to consider domestic effects over extraterritorial ones. It is worth reiterating that we are not dealing with a situation of domestic versus external or international obligations. Cross-border tax evasion has by definition an extraterritorial scope, and the support or denial of such a practice inevitably involves regulation with extraterritorial effects. While the efforts of the respondent to secure economic growth and employment domestically are admirable, they are not justified when coming at the expense of other countries' capacity and capability of mobilizing domestic resources, especially those with limited fiscal space and other institutional constraints. The Committee believes that Switzerland's duty to protect implies that it must take measures to ensure that legal and natural persons it is in a position to regulate are not involved in any way in illegal tax evasion or other economic crimes detrimental to the full realization of Covenant rights, no matter their place of operation. For Switzerland to provide such actors protection from tax liabilities in Zambia, while abdicating responsibility to regulate these same actors when discussing their human rights impacts, is insincere and counter to the objects and purposes of the Covenant.

Finally, positive measures to fulfilling Covenant rights in some areas do not create blank checks to abuse them in others. Switzerland's development assistance in Zambia, while laudable, does not exonerate it from its significant influence in supporting tax evasion and the loss of resources which would otherwise be available for ESC rights in that country. The Committee is of the opinion that Switzerland should consider the incoherency, if not hypocrisy, of providing development aid and human rights instruction, on the one hand, while acting in complicity with the siphoning of huge amounts of resources and the erosion of democratic, human rights-supporting institutions in those very recipient countries, on the other.

---

56 For more details, see the Norway Commission Report, p. 68.

132 *Tax Evasion and Switzerland's Extraterritorial Obligations to Zambia*

Holdings and recommendations

In light of Article 2(1) of the Covenant, the Committee holds that Switzerland's current law and policy with regard to bank secrecy effectively undermines Zambia's ability to mobilize the maximum available resources for the progressive realization of the rights as well as protect against third-party infringements on rights under the Covenant. The Committee by extension finds that Swiss conduct stands in contravention to the substantive rights to adequate standard of living, right to social security, right to health, right to education of Zambians.

The Committee would like to address several specific concerns below, and provide recommendations to Switzerland accordingly with a view to finding a friendly solution of the matter on the basis of the respect for the obligations set forth in the Covenant.

The Committee is concerned that the construction of a secrecy jurisdiction by Switzerland effectively encourages individuals and business enterprises in Zambia to shield themselves from their tax and regulatory responsibilities to society by obstructing access to information and transparency by governments and citizens regarding the assets, income, debts and other information of these persons – legal or natural. This unnecessary secrecy has been shown to foreseeably infringe upon the enjoyment of substantive Covenant rights in victim countries – with real impacts on the lives and livelihoods of rights-holders.

The Committee is further deeply concerned with the possible discriminatory effects of tax evasion in Zambia, especially in their effect of displacing tax burdens from the wealthy to poor- and middle-income households.

The Committee draws the attention of Switzerland to its General Comments and most recent statement supporting the extraterritorial obligation to protect against third parties from working in detriment to Covenant right overseas. Accordingly, the Committee would also remind Switzerland of its obligations to prevent and protect against human rights infringements coming as a result of tax evaders it is in a position to regulate, as referenced in the Maastricht Principles.[57]

The Committee recommends that Switzerland comply with its Covenant obligations when negotiating and concluding tax agreements by taking into account the sovereign and equal rights of other countries to levy taxes. Further, the Committee recommends that Switzerland proceed in the elaboration, interpretation, application and regular review of multilateral and bilateral tax treaties to ensure that they effectively combat tax evasion on an equal and transparent ground, no matter their country of origin. In this regard, Switzerland can more effectively ensure coherency between its

---

57 For a description of the circumstances under which the State party is in a position to regulate, see Maastricht Principles, Article 25.

Litigating Transnational Human Rights Obligations 133

development cooperation policies aimed at promoting human rights and democracy, and its international tax cooperation policies which seem to do just the opposite.

The Committee recommends that Switzerland take all appropriate measures to ensure automatic information exchange between tax authorities and country-by-country reporting of multinational enterprise activities to increase the transparency and access to information on tax liabilities, and therefore support other countries to restore the capacity to implement and enforce their tax laws to the benefit of Covenant rights. In discharging the obligation to international cooperation and assistance, multilateral approaches are preferable to bilateral ones on tax cooperation, especially so as to ensure the adequate representation of all countries and rights-holders, in accordance with the fundamental principles of transparency, participation and mutual accountability.

The Committee is equally troubled by the fact that Switzerland's secrecy jurisdiction serves to deny justice to the Zambian government's institutions and individual rights-holders who have been wronged by having enormous sums of resources siphoned away from them. These public and private actors are prevented from even knowing the extent of their losses, and illegally-obtained funds cannot in a consistent manner be recuperated.

The Committee therefore recommends that Switzerland undertake a comprehensive human rights impact assessment to determine the actual and possible consequences of its bank secrecy laws on the enjoyment of economic, social and cultural rights universally, but especially in developing countries like Zambia, with a view toward providing a full assessment of the negative impacts of its bank secrecy laws on the realization of ESCRs.

The Committee is furthermore concerned with Switzerland's refusal to take consistent and coherent measures to account for, and provide effective remedy for, the monies lost to Swiss tax havens over time. The Committee welcomes the recent work of the Norwegian Government Commission on Capital Flight from Poor Countries, in this regard, and agrees strongly with its conclusion of the opportunities provided by treaty bodies such as ours in remedying this historic denial of right to access to and repatriation of stolen or untaxed funds: "Those who suffer a denial of rights, or are denied access, or are denied repatriation because of rigorous secrecy rules, may only have a final answer to what rights they have by lodging complaints against the respective closed jurisdictions in the human rights organs."[58]

In light of the human right to remedy, the Committee recommends that once a comprehensive assessment is completed on the extent of infringements on Covenant rights coming as a result of Swiss bank secrecy laws, Switzerland should engage in cooperation to determine proportional and reasonable measures for remediation of harm done. These should provide

---

58 See Norway Commission Report, p. 64.

effective relief, such as compensation, to victims in proportion to the losses. This may involve, for example, facilitating the payment of back taxes and repatriation of lost funds, especially to victims in countries like Zambia unable to meet their minimum core obligation under the Covenant. Further, remedial action should include guarantees of non-repetition, and the effective dissolution of the circumstances which gave rise to the violation. Remedies should also reflect the disproportionate nature of the harms highlighted and compensate in proportion to harm done, through for example the establishment of funds specifically targeted to strengthen tax systems and mechanisms to combat tax evasion in countries especially lacking in such a regard.

In view of its obligations of international cooperation and assistance, and in complement to its domestic efforts to stamp out tax evasion, the Committee recommends that Switzerland provide substantial support for strengthening the capacity of tax authorities in countries which are vulnerable to tax evasion, in particular those like Zambia with under-resourced or weak enforcement capacities.

In consideration of its own domestic obligations under the Covenant, the Committee also calls on Zambia to take budgetary and fiscal measures to better utilize and mobilize the maximum of its available resources for the realization of Covenant rights, including stepping up its own efforts to combat corruption, tax evasion, as well as tax avoidance internally.

Finally, the Committee requests that both Switzerland and Zambia provide, in its next periodic report, detailed information on the effects of Swiss secrecy jurisdiction on Covenant rights domestically and abroad, and its efforts to meaningfully put an end to tax evasion.

9 Labour Rights in a Transnational Perspective (Committee on Economic, Social and Cultural Rights)

Arne Vandenbogaerde

Abstract

The following chapter considers some of the contentious issues that can arise in an inter-State complaints procedure before the Committee on Economic, Social and Cultural Rights. The case starts with presenting the reader with an unconventional and admittedly idealistic situation where a non-injured State submits a complaint for violations committed outside its territory. Furthermore, the complaint is not only submitted against the domestic or territorial State (the State where the violations took place) but also against a foreign State, which has some involvement in these violations. The chapter deals with whether or not this foreign State can be held accountable for violations committed in the domestic State and how responsibility can be attributed and distributed between these two States. Whereas the domestic State holds the primary responsibility for the violations that have been committed, the foreign State enjoys a parallel responsibility for violations committed in the domestic State. Such parallel responsibility implies that the foreign State's responsibility is independent from i) the fact that the domestic State bears the primary responsibility for the enjoyment of ESC rights, and ii) the fact that this domestic State might be unwilling to control third parties. The obligation of foreign States to refrain from direct or indirect interference with ESC outside their territory as recognized by the Committee in its General Comments is further detailed and applied.

Introductory note

This case deals with an inter-State complaint submitted to the Committee on Economic Social and Cultural Rights (CESCR). The CESCR is the body of independent experts which oversees the implementation of the International Covenant on Economic, Social and Cultural Rights (ICESCR).[1] The CESCR performs various tasks. Its main task is to examine reports by

---

1 International Covenant on Economic, Social and Cultural Rights, G.A. res. 2200A (XXI), 21 U.N.GAOR Supp. (No. 16) at 49, U.N. Doc. A/6316 (1966), 993 U.N.T.S. 3, entered into force January 3, 1976.

136 *Labour Rights in a Transnational Perspective*

State parties on ICESCR implementation. After consideration of a report the CESCR issues a set of concerns and recommendations called 'concluding observations' to the State party. In addition, the CESCR develops General Comments which interpret a particular provision of the ICESCR. These General Comments provide an authoritative interpretation of the rights contained in the ICESCR and help State parties in implementing their obligations under the ICESCR. We will draw on several of these General Comments in the merits section of the case below. Recently, the CESCR has been given the competence to receive complaints about human rights violations. The Optional Protocol to the International Covenant on Economic, Social and Cultural Rights (OP-ICESCR) entered into force on 5 May 2013.[2] The OP-ICESCR establishes three different complaint procedures: an individual communications procedure, an inter-State complaints procedure, and an inquiry procedure. These three mechanisms diverge at the procedural and substantive level and have different advantages for addressing abuses of ESC rights. This chapter illustrates the utility of the inter-State procedure to address violations of ESC rights.

Notwithstanding the fact that States do not enjoy human rights, they can act as 'agents of accountability' and consequently invoke the responsibility of other States when violating their obligations under the relevant human rights treaty. This case discusses such a possibility provided for under Article 10 of the OP-ICESCR.

When confronted with an extraterritorial issue, an inter-State procedure has various advantages over the individual complaints procedures. States that are unable to fulfil their human rights obligations can seek accountability against other States that interfere with their ability to guarantee rights under their jurisdiction. However, a great advantage of the procedure is that States do not necessarily need to be injured in order to invoke the responsibility of another State. This creates an expansive (State) community of accountholders. Considering the fact that economic and political motives restrain States from submitting inter-State complaints, such an expansive community is important. A second advantage is that the substantive scope of the procedure is wider than the individual complaints procedure under the OP-ICESCR as it deals with any failure of a State party to fulfil its *obligations* under the ICESCR. Accordingly, the inter-State procedure can potentially address broad structural issues, which are often inherent in extraterritorial violations of ESC rights. The individual complaints procedure in turn requires and only focuses on a specific *violation* of a human right.

In this fictitious case the domestic State (Zambia) is considered to be unwilling rather than unable to protect its citizens against a foreign State

---

2 Optional Protocol to the International Covenant on Economic, Social and Cultural Rights, G.A. res. 63/117 (2008), entered into force May 5, 2013.

Litigating Transnational Human Rights Obligations 137

company (Sinomin).[3] Consequently, it presents the reader with a scenario where a non-injured State (Belgium) submits a complaint against Zambia as well as a foreign State, the People's Republic of China (PRC). The case demonstrates the various potential hurdles the CESCR might have to take when presented with an extraterritorial case can be overcome.

In this case the PRC argues it bears no obligation for ensuring ESC rights extraterritorially. According to the PRC, such an obligation to secure rights in Zambia would be infringing upon the latter State's sovereignty. Although Article 10 of the OP-ICESCR does not contain a jurisdiction requirement, the case illustrates the inevitable rise of the concept in the admissibility stage. Relying on the recent clarification by the Maastricht Principles on the Extraterritorial Obligations of States the case illustrates that this does not need to be problematic.[4] The case shows how the CESCR can establish that the acts of Sinomin fall under the jurisdiction of the PRC and consequently how the latter's responsibility can be engaged in relation to those acts. A second argument submitted by the foreign State in its defence is that non-injured States cannot submit complaints. The CESCR decides otherwise, relying heavily on the law of State responsibility as interpreted by the ILC.[5]

The main debate in the merits section involves the introduction and discussion of the parallel responsibility of the foreign State and its obligation from interfering with the enjoyment of ESC rights extraterritorially. Such obligation is parallel, as it is independent i) from the primary responsibility of the domestic and State, and ii) the fact that the latter State might be unwilling to secure the rights under its jurisdiction.[6]

The case might also encourage the reader to reflect on some outstanding questions. For example, Belgium regards itself under an obligation to submit a complaint, hereby relying *inter alia* on the General Comments of the CESCR. Although in this case the CESCR considers Belgium not under such obligation, should it do so? And if so, would the Committee need to

---

3 This case is entirely fictional and construed for academic purposes only. However, the facts of the case are in large part based on a report of NGO Human Rights Watch: 'You'll Be Fired if You Refuse – Labor Abuses in Zambia's Chinese State-owned Copper Mines' (US, Human Rights Watch 2011).

4 To consult the ETO Principles see: Olivier De Schutter and others 'Commentary to the Maastricht Principles on Extraterritorial Obligations of States in the area of Economic, Social and Cultural Rights', (2012) 34(4) *Human Rights Quarterly* 1084–169.

5 International Law Commission 'Articles on the Responsibilities of States for Internationally Wrongful Acts, with commentaries' (U.N. Doc. A/56/10).

6 Others have termed this differently and argued that foreign States enjoy a *simultaneous* and *complementary* responsibility with regard to the obligation to respect and protect, see: Wouter Vandenhole and Wolfgang Benedek, 'Extraterritorial Human Rights Obligations and the North-South Divide',in Malcolm Langford, Martin Scheinin, Wouter Vandenhole and Willem van Genugten (eds) *Global Justice, State Duties: The Extra-Territorial Scope of Economic, Social and Cultural Rights in International Law* (Cambridge: Cambridge University Press, 2012), 332–63.

138 *Labour Rights in a Transnational Perspective*

take it up in its assessment of a State's maximum use of available resources? Additionally, if the foreign State (the home State of the company) finds it is unable – after having taken concrete and deliberate steps including through international cooperation – to end human rights abuses under its jurisdiction must it then fully withdraw from operating in the host State? A further issue present in the case is the use of the Ruggie Guiding Principles.[7] The Ruggie Principles consider there is no basis in international human rights law for the establishment of extraterritorial obligations for States. In our case the Committee diverges on this point and interprets international law differently from the Principles. However, considering its universal acceptance by States would it also be able to do so in reality?

An important issue also arises with respect to the use of the inter-State mechanism. Notwithstanding the fact that the inter-State complaints procedure is a promising accountability procedure for violations of a extraterritorial nature, its unlikely use by States demands a focus on the improvement of existing (or the development of new?) accountability procedures at the inter-State level. In particular, attention could be paid to those accountability mechanisms that do not require the formal invocation of responsibility since this appears to be a strong disincentive for States to use the procedure.

Summary of the Facts

1.1   On January 2006, following the privatization of the Zambian mining sector, Sinomin, a Chinese State-owned mining company, bought in an open-bid the Zambesi Copper Mine.

1.2   In Augustus 2008, two months after the start-up, Sinomin was confronted with complaints about unsafe labor conditions and resulting accidents. These conditions include inadequate support for the mining shafts causing rocks to fall free when drilling resulting in the injury of several workers; acid and electrical burns caused by using the chemicals to separate the copper from the rocks; and the provision of inadequate dust masks causing lung diseases and other long-term health consequences such as pneumoconiosis (black lung).

1.3   In September 2009, a general worker protest broke out at the mine due to the failure of Sinomin to improve working conditions. When the workers directed themselves to the Chinese managers of Sinomin, shots were fired and resulted in the wounding of four people. Zambian police allegedly investigated the events but this did not lead to any charges or findings made public.

---

7 See: Guiding Principles on Business and Human Rights: Implementing the United Nations 'Protect, Respect and Remedy' Framework (U.N. Doc. A/HRC/17/31), 21 March 2011.

Litigating Transnational Human Rights Obligations 139

1.4   Workers continued to complain after the events but now increasingly refrained from protests, citing reprisals such as loss of jobs, docked pay, or warnings for insubordination.

1.5   Sinomin employs Zambian safety and health officers, but these officers are not endowed with any decisive authority as the ultimate decision always rests with a Chinese Sinomin manager. However, the Chinese management has generally been unresponsive when safety officers complain about working conditions.

1.6   From the government side, the Zambian Mines Safety Department (within the Ministry of Mining and Mineral Development) is by Zambian law responsible for health and safety in all the Zambian mines and thus for the enforcement of the Mining Safety Rules and Regulations Code. However, the department is understaffed, underfinanced, and reportedly plagued by corruption.

1.7   Zambian unions are barred from accessing the Zambesi mine. Workers can only join the recently established National Union of Miners (NUM). The stronger Mineworkers Union of Zambia (MUZ)cannot be joined by workers of Sinomin since the company has refused to sign a recognition agreement, and the company intimidates or ignores claims of workers when providing the necessary signatures for the establishment of an agreement with MUZ. In December 2008, the court ruled in favor of the workers, but Sinomin still does not recognize MUZ. To date, the Zambian government has yet to enforce this court's decision. Meanwhile, workers have refused to join NUM, as it is considered ineffective and detrimental to the renewal of their contracts.

The complaint

2.1   Belgium claims that the Zambian government is in violation of Article 7 of the ICESCR for failing to ensure safe, healthy and just working conditions in the mine.

2.2   Belgium claims that Zambia is in violation of Article 8 ICESCR for failure to ensure that the miners can join the trade union of their choice and that trade unions can function freely.

2.3   Belgium claims that the Chinese government shares responsibility for these violations since it has refrained from ensuring respect for the provisions under Article 7 and Article 8 ICESCR.

Arguments submitted to the Committee by the different parties

Zambia

3.1   The Zambian government finds that the acts complained of do not give rise to violations of its human rights obligations under the ICESCR.

140 *Labour Rights in a Transnational Perspective*

The Zambian government finds it has discharged its positive obligations under the ICESCR to the maximum of its available resources and capacity.

3.2 According to the Zambian government, Article 2.1 ICESCR obliges States to move as expeditiously as possible towards the full implementation of the rights set forth in the ICESCR. The government maintains that it is progressively realizing these rights – including the rights in question in this complaint – to the maximum of its available financial and technical resources. Notwithstanding its best efforts, the Zambian government considers its lack of resources hinders it in ensuring more adequately the working conditions in the mines. Zambia finds it is thus unable rather than unwilling to secure and ensure the enjoyment of the rights in the ICESCR, and therefore cannot be found in violation of its obligations under articles 7 and 8 of the ICESCR.

People's Republic of China

3.3 The Chinese government finds that since Belgium is a non-injured State party it cannot submit a complaint and/or claim any reparations before the Committee in accordance with the requirements stated in Article 48 of the International Law Commission's Articles on State Responsibility. In addition, the Chinese government submits it has not received any official complaint of the Zambian government over the alleged abuses in the Zambesi mine and therefore considers Sinomin to be operating in accordance with relevant Zambian and international standards.

3.4 The Chinese government further observes that it has no legal responsibility to control the operations of Sinomin abroad as it is not under any obligation to protect the Zambian workers from human rights violations under the ICESCR. It considers the Zambian government to exclusively bear the responsibility to ensure working conditions are safe and adequate in the mines. The PRC reminds the Committee of Principle 2 of the Guiding Principles for the Implementation of the United Nations 'Protect, Respect, and Remedy Framework' wherein it is clearly stated that States are not under any obligation 'to regulate the extraterritorial activities of business domiciled in their territory and/or jurisdiction' (U.N. Doc. A/HRC/17/31, Principle 2). The PRC also reminds the Committee that the Human Rights Council has adopted these Guiding Principles unanimously, which reflects the universal acceptance by the international community of these Principles.

3.5 The Chinese government argues that such absence of obligations is imperative. If found otherwise it would need to enforce the provisions under Article 7 and 8 ICESCR in Zambian territory and thereby be forced to breach the principle of non-intervention and consequently

Litigating Transnational Human Rights Obligations 141

Zambia's sovereignty. This would cause the Chinese government to weaken the effective implementation of the human rights obligations of Zambia and undermine Zambia's obligations as a primary and exclusive duty bearer.

3.6 The PRC thus finds that it does not bear any legal obligation to ensure worker rights in Zambia as this would be manifestly incompatible with Zambia's responsibility to ensure the rights set forth in the ICESCR. As a consequence, the Chinese government submits it cannot be held responsible for any acts or omissions of Zambia.

3.7 Considering the above, the Chinese government can thus only conclude that the complaint constitutes an abuse of the right to submit a communication, as it is clearly politically motivated and solely submitted in an attempt to damage the economic interests of the PRC.

Belgium

3.8 Belgium does not dispute it is a non-injured State but finds itself under the obligation to protect and promote the rights set forth in the Covenant both within and outside its territory. Belgium observes the statement of the Committee that 'where States parties can take steps to influence other third parties to respect the right [in this case right to water], through legal or political means, such steps should be taken in accordance with the Charter of the United Nations and applicable international law' (U.N. Doc. E/C.12/2002/11, para.33). Having failed to reach an adequate solution in Zambia through diplomatic means with both governments, Belgium finds it has been left with no other option but to discharge its (extraterritorial) obligation to ensure respect in accordance with Article 10 of the Optional Protocol to the ICESCR (OP-ICESCR). Belgium notes that Article 10 OP-ICESCR does not contain any provision prohibiting standing for non-injured States. In light of this, Belgium submits that non-injured States are not barred from submitting a complaint under the procedure provided for under Article 10 OP-ICESCR.

3.90 Belgium holds that the complaint submitted does not amount to an abuse of the inter-state procedure. Belgium finds itself under the obligation 'to promote universal respect for, and observance of, human rights and freedoms' (ICESCR, preamble). All State parties to the ICESCR have a collective interest to promote and secure ESC rights for everyone and have committed themselves *vis-à-vis* each other to protect this collective interest. Consequently, any State that violates ESC rights has failed to honor its commitments to the other State parties. Belgium is thus not guided by self-interest, or as the Chinese government argues 'to damage its economic interest', but is rather guided in its actions by a common interest in achieving universal observance of human rights.

142 *Labour Rights in a Transnational Perspective*

Consideration of admissibility

4.1 Prior to the consideration of any claim contained in an inter-state communication, the Committee must decide whether the communication is admissible under the OP-ICESCR.

4.2 As required under Article 10(1) OP-ICESCR, the Committee has ascertained that all the State parties have deposited a declaration recognizing the competence of the Committee to receive and examine inter-state complaints.

4.3 In accordance with Article 10(1c) OP-ICESCR, the Committee observes the nonexistence of domestic remedies for the applicant State, and therefore finds that the requirement for exhaustion of all domestic remedies has been satisfied.

4.4 In order to be able to attribute responsibility for the acts complained of by the applicant, the Committee needs to ascertain whether or not the acts complained of fall under the scope of jurisdiction of the respondent States. The exercise of jurisdiction is a vital condition or requirement for a State party to be able to be held responsible for acts or omissions attributable to it which might give rise to violation of the rights set forth in the ICESCR. However, before turning to this question of jurisdiction, the Committee will first respond to the alleged incompetence of Belgium to submit an inter-state complaint in relation to this case.

- ### Whether Belgium has locus standi *to submit a complaint*

4.5 Article 10 OP-ICESCR dictates no procedural or substantial requirements concerning the submission of an inter-state complaint other than the requirement of a declaration by all parties recognizing the competence of the Committee to receive such complaints and the requirement that the complaint must concern the fulfillment of the obligations under the ICESCR (Article 10(2a)).

4.6 The PRC finds that Belgium cannot submit a complaint by *inter alia* invoking the requirements set forth in Article 48 of the ILC's Articles on State Responsibility. The Committee indeed considers the provisions set forth in Article 48 (Invocation of responsibility by a State other than an injured State) of the ILC's Articles on State Responsibility applicable and to be governing the determination of the right to invoke responsibility before the Committee under Article 10 OP-ICESCR. The Committee observes that the idea behind Article 48 is 'that in case of breaches of specific obligations protecting the collective interests of a group of States or the interests of the international community as a whole, responsibility may be invoked by States which are not themselves injured' (ILC Articles, Article 48). Article 48(1) defines the categories of obligations which give non-injured States the right to invoke responsibility:

Litigating Transnational Human Rights Obligations 143

> 1. *Any State other than an injured State is entitled to invoke the responsibility of another State in accordance with paragraph 2 if:*
> a) *The obligation breached is owed to a group of States including that State, and is established for the protection of a collective interest of the group; or*
> b) *The obligation breached is owed to the international community as a whole.*

4. 7   In accordance with Article 42 (para. 1(a)) two conditions need to be fulfilled in order for a non-injured State to invoke responsibility: the obligation breached must be owed to a group of States (*erga omnes partes*) to which the State invoking responsibility belongs, and secondly, the obligation must have been established for the protection of collective interests of that group.

4.8   Turning to the first requirement, the Committee observes that the ICESCR is a multilateral treaty and Belgium as well as the defendant States – as State parties to the ICESCR – therefore form part of a group of States that have committed themselves *vis-à-vis* each other to ensure the enjoyment of ESC rights under their jurisdiction. If a State party finds – or has reason to believe – that another State party has violated its obligations under the ICESCR, it has the right to bring a complaint before the Committee in accordance with the provision of Article 10 OP-ICESCR as such a State has failed to honor its obligations owed to the other State parties. The Committee therefore deems the first requirement met.

4.9   The second requirement concerns the question whether or not the obligations derived from the ICESCR have been established in a collective interest and thus transcend the traditional bilateralist notion of State responsibility in the sense of a dispute between an injured and wrongdoing State. The Committee finds that 'human rights treaties are plainly (even if not always explicitly) designed to protect a general common interest' (U.N. Doc. A/CN.4/507, para. 92). The Committee reaffirms that States have expressed their collective or common interest – through the UN Charter and Universal Declaration of Human Rights – 'to promote *universal* [emphasis added] respect for, and observance of, human rights and freedoms' (UN Charter (Article 55); UDHR, preamble). The Committee further recalls the 1993 Vienna Declaration where States declared that 'the promotion and protection of all human rights and fundamental freedoms must be considered as a priority objective of the United Nations in accordance with its purposes and principles, in particular the purpose of international cooperation. In the framework of these purposes and principles, the promotion and protection of all human rights is a legitimate concern of the international community' (para. 4). The Committee strongly asserts that by ratifying the ICESCR, State parties have expressed their collective interest to create and ensure universal conditions whereby everyone may enjoy his economic, social and cultural rights. The Committee finds that Belgium is clearly acting out of this collective interest to ensure the enjoyment of ESC

144 *Labour Rights in a Transnational Perspective*

rights for the alleged victims of violations under Article 7 and 8 ICESCR, in this case. In view of the above, the Committee finds the second requirement met and affirms the existence of a right to invoke responsibility for Belgium in accordance with ILC Article 48(1)(a). Consequently, the Committee finds that there exists no abuse of the procedure under Article 10 OP-ICESCR by Belgium.

4.10   The Committee wishes to indicate that Article 10 of the OP-ICESCR gives States a right – not an obligation – to submit an inter-State complaint before the Committee. Article 10 OP-ICESCR cannot be interpreted in such a way to find Belgium under an obligation to submit a complaint in order to fulfill its obligations under the ICESCR. The Committee remarks that the non-injured State thus acts in a secondary or agent-like capacity and is endowed with a 'procedural' right that seeks to ensure that the other State parties comply with their obligations and ensure the enjoyment of ESC rights for victims of human rights violations. The Committee wishes to emphasize that such a dual protection, where not only victims of human rights violations but also State parties to the ICESCR can submit complaints, is vital for the effective protection of ESC rights. The Committee also recalls the statement made by the Human Rights Committee in its General Comment 31: '[T]he contractual dimension of the treaty involves any State Party to a treaty being obligated to every other State Party to comply with its undertakings under the treaty [...] To draw attention to possible breaches of Covenant obligations by other States Parties and to call on them to comply with their Covenant obligations should, far from being regarded as an unfriendly act, be considered as a reflection of legitimate community interest' (U.N. Doc. CCPR/C/21/Rev.1/Add.13, para. 2).

4.11   Having established the right for Belgium to invoke responsibility, the Committee finds it not necessary whether such a right can also be established in accordance with ILC Article 48(1)(b).

- ● **Whether the Relevant Acts Come under the Jurisdiction of Zambia**

4.12   State parties to the ICESCR have the primary obligation to ensure the enjoyment of the rights set forth in the ICESCR for all persons under their jurisdiction.

4.13   The presumption of power of a State to exercise its territorial jurisdiction can only be invalidated in particular circumstances where the State is unable to exercise control or authority over its territory.

4.14   The Committee finds the entire Zambian territory is under the control of the sovereign Zambian government. The Committee concludes that Zambia thus exercises both *de jure* and *de facto* control over its territory. It is therefore not hindered in the exercise of its jurisdiction and consequently is under the obligation to ensure the enjoyment of the rights set forth in

Litigating Transnational Human Rights Obligations 145

the ICESCR. The Committee also notes that the Zambian government does not dispute this finding.

4.15 The facts complained of therefore fall under the jurisdiction of the Zambian government.

- *Whether the Relevant Acts Come under the Jurisdiction of the People's Republic of China*

4.16 The Committee observes that jurisdiction is not exclusively territorial or based on territorial control. In this respect, the Committee stresses that the ICESCR imposes no territorial restrictions on State parties' obligations and asserts that the reach of State parties' obligations is thus not solely determined by territorial control. The Committee warns against a restricted reading of State parties' jurisdiction in sole terms of control over territory.

4.17 A (foreign) State's (extraterritorial) jurisdiction can be established in various situations and thus can co-exist with the jurisdiction of the territorial State (whether or not reduced). Jurisdiction can be established *prima facie* if a foreign State controls the territory of the territorial State. This might happen in cases of military foreign occupation where the occupying State rather than the territorial State exercises effective control (see e.g. the Committee's Concluding Observations on the State of Israel).

4.18 As indicated above in the consideration of Zambian's jurisdiction, the PRC (the foreign State) does not exercise control over Zambian territory and hence its (extraterritorial) jurisdiction cannot be established from this lack of territorial control.

4.19 In addition to control over territory, several other jurisdictional links can and must be discerned and established if relevant. Foreign States can also commit violations without necessarily exercising effective control over the territory of the territorial (domestic) State.

4.20 (Foreign) State parties' jurisdiction (or a jurisdictional link) and consequent obligations to ensure the enjoyment of the ICESCR rights can also be established in the following situations as evidenced by the Maastricht Principles on Extraterritorial Obligations of States in the Area of Economic, Social, and Cultural Rights (ETO Principles), situations over which a State exercises authority or effective control, whether or not such control is exercised in accordance with international law:

- a) situations over which State acts or omissions bring about foreseeable effects on the enjoyment of economic, social and cultural rights, whether within or outside its territory;
- b) situations in which the State, acting separately or jointly, whether through its executive, legislative or judicial branches, is in a position to exercise decisive influence or to take measures to realize

146　*Labour Rights in a Transnational Perspective*

economic, social and cultural rights extraterritorially, in accordance with international law.

4.21　Article 8 of the ILC Articles on State Responsibility states that: 'The conduct of a person or group of persons shall be considered an act of a State under international law if the person or group of persons is in fact acting on the instructions of, or under the direction or control of, that State in carrying out the conduct' (ILC Articles, Article 8). The question before the Committee is thus whether the Chinese government exercised – or found itself in a position to exercise – decisive influence or control on the actions of Sinomin which consequently create *de jure* obligations and responsibilities for the Chinese government under the ICESCR. In order to resolve this question, the factual relation between the Chinese government and Sinomin needs to be analyzed.

4.22　The information submitted to the Committee demonstrates that Sinomin is a State-owned corporation and operates under the wing of the PRC's State-owned Assets Supervision and Administration Commission (SASAC). SASAC supervises and controls Chinese State-owned enterprises and operates under the authority of the government's State Council, which is the highest Chinese executive authority in charge of the State's administration. Senior management of Sinomin consists of State party members and must report directly to SASAC. The Chinese government thus exercises effective authority – or at a minimum can undeniably exercise great influence and oversight – over the daily operations and policies of Sinomin.

4.23　Therefore, the Committee considers it demonstrated that the acts of Sinomin fall within Chinese (extraterritorial) jurisdiction. The acts of Sinomin fall within the jurisdiction of the Chinese government and its responsibility can thus be engaged with regards to the complaint submitted.

4.24　There being no other obstacles to admissibility, the Committee finds the communication admissible and proceeds with the consideration on the merits.

Views of the Committee

5.1　In determining the responsibility of a State party to the ICESCR, the Committee wishes to consider Article 2 of the ILC Articles on State Responsibility, which stipulates that:

There is an internationally wrongful act of a State when conduct consisting of an action or omission:

(a) is attributable to the State under international law; and
(b) constitutes a breach of an international obligation of the State.

According to the Committee, the question of State responsibility can be further detailed and clarified with regard to the ICESCR, as reference can be made to the issue of international cooperation in accordance with Article 2(1) ICESCR. In this respect, the Committee finds that State responsibility is therefore engaged as a result of conduct attributable to a State, acting separately or jointly with other States or entities, which constitutes a breach of its international human rights obligations whether within its territory or extraterritorially (ETO Principles, Principle 11).

a) Whether Zambia discharged its (positive) obligations under the Covenant

5.3 The territorial State has the primary (territorial) responsibility of ensuring the enjoyment of the rights under the Covenant in its territory and cannot be released of such presumption. In highly exceptional circumstances the State can be unable for reasons beyond its control to discharge its obligations and thus ensure the enjoyment of the rights under the Covenant within its jurisdiction. These highly exceptional circumstances theoretically might arise in situations such as those when States have exhausted all possible measures – including through seeking international cooperation and assistance – to attempt to ensure the enjoyment of Covenant rights under its jurisdiction. Yet, this does not signify its primary responsibility has ceased to exist.

5.4 In accordance with Article 2(1) ICESCR, the Committee needs to ascertain whether or not the government of Zambia has undertaken steps to the maximum of its available resources to safeguard persons within its jurisdiction from infringement of the provisions under Article 7 and 8 of the ICESCR. From this flows the requirement for the Committee to make a distinction between the inability and unwillingness of the Zambian government to comply with its obligations under Article 7 and 8 of the ICESCR.

5.5 In this respect the Committee has found in its General Comment 3 that 'the means which should be used in order to satisfy the obligation to take steps are stated in Article 2(1) to be "all appropriate means, including particularly the adoption of legislative measures"' (U.N. Doc. E/1991/23, para.3). The Committee has not given any exhaustive list of appropriate means but finds that 'other measures which may also be considered "appropriate" for the purposes of article 2(1) include, but are not limited to, administrative, financial, educational and social measures'(U.N. Doc. E/1991/23, para.7).

5.6 In its observations, Zambia attributes its failure to take any further steps to ensure the rights of its citizens under Article 7 and 8 ICESCR to a lack of available financial resources. The Committee observes that over the span of three years since the start of the activities of Sinomin the government has not adopted any specific measures to address the abuses in the Zambesi mine. In such circumstances, the Committee has earlier found

148 *Labour Rights in a Transnational Perspective*

'that in case of failure to take any steps [...], the burden of proof rests with the State party to show that such a course of action was based on the most careful consideration and can be justified by reference to the totality of the rights provided for in the Covenant and by the fact that full use was made of available resources' (CESCR, Statement on the obligation of States Parties regarding the corporate sector and economic, social, and cultural rights; para. 9). Thus, Zambia must first and foremost demonstrate that full use was made of its available resources in order to be able to further justify its inaction to progressively realize the rights set forth in the Covenant.

5.7 The Committee emphasizes 'that even where the available resources are demonstrably inadequate, the obligation remains for a State party to strive to ensure the widest possible enjoyment of the relevant rights under the prevailing circumstances' (U.N. Doc. E/1991/23, para.11). The Committee further stresses that 'the obligations to monitor the extent of the realization, or more especially of the non-realization, of economic, social and cultural rights, and to devise strategies and programmes for their promotion, are not in any way eliminated as a result of resource constraints' (U.N. Doc. E/1991/23, para.11). The positive obligation to take certain steps in accordance with Article 2(1) ICESCR is thus an immediate obligation.

5.8 In addition to its complete inaction, the information submitted to the Committee demonstrates that funding for the government's mine safety department has steadily decreased over the course of these three years notwithstanding the reported problems with the Zambesi mines.

5.9 The Committee considers that if a State party uses 'resource constraints' as a reason for any retrogressive measures taken, it must consider the information in the light of objective criteria such as:

(a) the country's level of development;
(b) the severity of the alleged breach, in particular whether the situation concerned the enjoyment of the minimum core content of the Covenant;
(c) the country's current economic situation, in particular whether the country was undergoing a period of economic recession;
(d) the existence of other serious claims on the State party's limited resources; for example, resulting from a recent natural disaster or from recent internal or international armed conflict;
(e) whether the State party had sought to identify low-cost options; and
(f) whether the State party had sought cooperation and assistance or rejected offers of resources from the international community for the purposes of implementing the provisions of the Covenant without sufficient reason. (Statement by the Committee: An evaluation

Litigating Transnational Human Rights Obligations 149

of the obligation to take steps to the 'Maximum of available resources' under an optional protocol to the Covenant; para.10)

5.10   Considering the stable economic situation and absence of conflict or large-scale disasters in Zambia, the government has failed to provide an explanation for the necessity of these retrogressive measures, nor has it identified low-cost alternatives or sought cooperation and assistance to address this alleged lack of resources.

5.11   With regard to the latter point, the Committee would like to reiterate that resources 'refer to both the resources existing within a State and those available from the international community through international cooperation and assistance' (U.N. Doc. E/1991/23, para. 13). What follows is that in this case Zambia is under the obligation to seek international assistance and/or cooperation from other States to address this alleged lack of resources. In this particular case this most certainly could include the request for cooperation by the government of the PRC or requesting the assistance and cooperation of the International Labour Organisation.

5.12   However, the Committee observes that the Zambian authorities have never claimed that the PRC was infringing Zambian and/or international law. The alleged abuses and ensuing protest have not led to an international dispute between the States or any visible deterioration in diplomatic relations between both States. Zambian authorities have not addressed the Chinese government, nor have they lodged any protest or demanded any investigation by the Chinese government.

5.13   For all the above reasons, the Committee consequently finds that the Zambian government did not exhaust all available resources in order to justify such inaction. The Committee finds that in this particular case seeking international cooperation with the PRC in order to address the violations in the Zambesi mine should have been considered.

5.14   Considering the absence of steps to progressively ensure the rights as well as the non-exhaustion of measures available, the Committee rejects the claim of the Zambian government that it has discharged its obligations within the maximum of its available resources as required under the ICESCR.

5.15   Accordingly, the Committee concludes that the Zambian government is unwilling rather than unable to ensure safe and adequate working conditions in the Zambesi mine. As a general principle, the Committee notes that a State party which is unwilling to use the maximum of its available resources for the realization of the rights under the Covenant is in direct violation of its obligations under the ICESCR.

5.16   In relation to the complaint, the Committee recalls it has asserted that 'violations of the obligation to protect follow from the failure of States

150   *Labour Rights in a Transnational Perspective*

parties to take all necessary measures to safeguard persons within their jurisdiction from infringements of the right to work by third parties' (U.N. Doc. E/C.12/GC/18; para. 35).

5.17   Taking into consideration the information received, and having established that the Zambian government has failed to take all necessary measures within their capacity, the Committee finds that Zambian government has failed to regulate, monitor, and ensure compliance of Sinomin with Article 7 and Article 8 of the ICESCR.

5.18   The Committee further concludes that due to the fact that the Zambian government has failed to monitor and enforce compliance with its obligations under Articles 7 and 8 ICESCR, it has left its citizens with no effective remedies to address such abuses when these were brought to the attention of the State party. The Committee is particularly concerned with these facts since Zambia has developed strong mining regulations and labor laws in order to ensure these rights as a result of its long mining history. Zambian laws offer detailed guidance on working conditions such as which equipment must be carried by the workers, the employment of safety officers, and the various safety procedures to be used and implemented in the mines.

5.19   The Committee holds that trade unions play a fundamental role in ensuring respect for the right to adequate work at the local and national levels and in assisting States parties to comply with their obligations under Article 6 ICESCR and consequently the provisions under Articles 7 and 8 ICESCR. The Committee has found that the Zambian government has failed to ensure that workers can join the Mineworkers Union of Zambia (MUZ). The Committee is particularly concerned of this fact since the MUZ is operating in other mining sites without any hindrance.

b) Whether the government of the People's Republic of China's responsibility for the violations is engaged

5.20   In accordance with Article 2 OP-ICESCR, the Committee finds that all States have the obligation to ensure the enjoyment of the rights set forth in the ICESCR under their jurisdiction. Having established the jurisdiction of the PRC, the Committee finds that while Zambia has the primary responsibility for ensuring the enjoyment of ESC rights, the People's Republic of China bears complementary and parallel responsibility for the realization of ESC rights for any acts or omissions occurring under its jurisdiction which impact the enjoyment of ESC rights. The fact that the Committee upholds that the (territorial State) carries the primary responsibility for the enjoyment of the rights set forth in the Covenant does not exclude that in specific circumstances a complementary responsibility can arise for (a) foreign State(s). However, in no case does the primary responsibility of the territorial (domestic) State cease to exist through the existence of another

Litigating Transnational Human Rights Obligations 151

(foreign) State's responsibility. The Committee refers to parallel responsibility as this responsibility is engaged even when the territorial State is unwilling to ensure the rights under the ICESCR, such as is the case in the present complaint. A foreign State party thus cannot escape its international responsibility due to the conduct of the home State.

5.21   Considering the PRC disputes the existence of any obligation to respect and protect workers' rights in the Zambesi mine, the Committee wishes to clarify the scope of obligations of the State party before discussing whether or not it has actually breached its obligations. In relation to the complaint before it, the Committee needs to specifically consider the PRC's international or extraterritorial obligations under Articles 7 and 8 ICESCR.

5.22   The Committee holds that State parties must take all measures necessary in order to refrain from direct and/or indirect interference with the enjoyment of ESC rights outside their territories. The Committee takes note of the PRC's reference to the Guiding Principles on Business and Human Rights, but would like to affirm and stress that these are Guiding Principles which do not represent any legally binding interpretation of the (relevant) provisions in the ICESCR. Having said this, the Committee does find evidence in the Guiding Principles that supports and acknowledges that a State party in certain instances has an obligation to ensure respect for the rights under Articles 7 and 8 ICESCR extraterritorially. Secondly, the Guiding Principles do note that 'where a business enterprise is controlled by the State or where its acts can be attributed otherwise to the State, an abuse of human rights by the business enterprise may entail a violation of the State's own international law obligations' (U.N. Doc. A/HRC/17/31, 9). Having attributed responsibility to the State party for the actions of Sinomin, the Committee thus needs to ascertain whether or not the acts or omissions of Sinomin interfered with the enjoyment of the rights under Article 7 and 8 ICESCR. Some clarification is therefore warranted concerning the notions of direct as opposed to indirect interference.

5.23   ETO Principle 20 (*direct interference*) stipulates that:

> All States have the obligation to refrain from conduct which nullifies or impairs the enjoyment and exercise of economic, social and cultural rights of persons outside their territories.

5.24   ETO Principle 21 (*indirect interference*) holds that:

> States must refrain from any conduct which: a) impairs the ability of another State or international organization to comply with that State's or that international organization's obligations as regards economic, social and cultural rights; or b) aids, assists, directs, controls or coerces another State or international organization to breach that State's or

152 *Labour Rights in a Transnational Perspective*

that international organization's obligations as regards economic, social and cultural rights, where the former States do so with knowledge of the circumstances of the act.

5.25   The Committee considers this obligation to respect (the obligation not to interfere either directly or indirectly) to be a) of an immediate nature and thus not subject to the concept of progressive realization, and b) finds it not only to be a negative obligation but also entailing a positive obligation for a State party to take measures to ensure non-interference with the enjoyment of ESC rights abroad. Mere inaction (refrain) of the State will in most circumstances not allow a State party to claim it has discharged its obligation to respect. With respect to the existence of positive obligations, the Committee notes this obligation might thus better be understood as the obligation to ensure respect, which – depending on the situation – will necessitate positive or negative measures.

5.26   The Committee has asserted such obligations on several occasions. In its General Comment 19 in relation to the right to social security, the Committee held that 'States parties have to respect the enjoyment of the right by refraining from actions that interfere, directly or indirectly, with the enjoyment of the right to social security in other countries' (U.N. Doc. E/C.12/GC/19, para. 53). Likewise in relation to the right to water, the Committee found that: 'International cooperation requires States parties to refrain from actions that interfere, directly or indirectly, with the enjoyment of the right to water in other countries' (U.N. Doc. E/C.12/2002/11, para. 31). However, the Committee has also asserted earlier that positive measures must be taken to ensure respect for the rights in the ICESCR: 'Steps should be taken by States parties to prevent their own citizens and companies from violating the right to water of individuals and communities in other countries' (U.N. Doc. E/C.12/2002/11, para. 33). The Committee believes such obligations applicable to all the rights set forth in the Covenant including Articles 7 and 8 ICESCR.

5.27   As indicated earlier, in order to establish whether a breach of a State party's obligations amounts to a violation of any of the rights set forth in the ICESCR a distinction needs to be made between a State party being unable or unwilling to implement its obligations as the establishment of jurisdiction does not entail a finding of responsibility. This general rule is also found applicable to State parties' extraterritorial conduct. Therefore, while the Committee has established earlier that the conduct of Sinomin is attributable to the PRC as it is found that the PRC effectively controlled Sinomin in the course of the alleged violations (ILC art 8; ETO Principle 12), it must ascertain if the PRC has acted in accordance with Article 2(1) ICESCR to undertake steps to the maximum of its abilities to safeguard persons within their jurisdiction from infringement of the provisions

Litigating Transnational Human Rights Obligations 153

under Articles 7 and 8 of the ICESCR. Considering the fact that the PRC denies the existence of any obligation in this case, and observing the consequent absolute inaction of the State party to ensure respect for the provisions under Articles 7 and 8 ICESCR, the Committee finds it proven the State is unwilling rather than unable to respect the latter rights.

5.28   The Committee observes that the PRC argues that if it would bear such obligations and thus be considered 'able' and required to enforce the provisions under Articles 7 and 8 ICESCR, it would undercut the primary responsibility of Zambia and undermine its sovereignty by interfering in its domestic affairs. The Committee concurs that (foreign) State parties' obligations do not permit an infringement of the sovereignty of the domestic State or any diminishing of its obligations. The Committee also takes note of Article 2(4) of the U.N. Charter, which obliges Member States to 'refrain in their international relations from the threat or use of force against the territorial integrity or political independence of any state, or in any other manner inconsistent with the Purposes of the United Nations' (U.N. Charter, Article 2.4). However, the Committee cannot concur with the Chinese government's reading and reiterates that as a general principle it is irrelevant whether or not a State has a legal title to act. What matters, instead, is whether the relation between an individual affected and the State is satisfactorily close as to establish the obligation of State to ensure that individual's rights. The PRC cannot escape or deflect responsibility as a consequence of the violations of the Zambian government or the risk of undermining its primary human rights responsibilities as the domestic State. As indicated earlier, the obligation to respect international and national standards in Zambian territory is parallel and thus independent from i) the fact that the Zambian government bears the primary responsibility for implementation of Articles 7 and 8 ICESCR, and ii) the fact that it might be unwilling to control third parties such as Sinomin. Although Zambia has been found unwilling to enforce its domestic law and international law obligations under the ICESCR, the PRC cannot benefit or take advantage of such unwillingness.

5.29   The Committee observes that the Chinese government is under an obligation to halt any operations of Sinomin whenever it finds Sinomin cannot operate in accordance with the rights set forth in the Covenant (or the PRC's obligations under the Covenant) due to actions or omissions of the Zambian State.

5.30   In view of the above, the Committee finds that the Chinese government is in direct breach of its obligations under Articles 7 and 8 due to its failure to ensure that Sinomin respects the right of its workers to safe and adequate working conditions in the Zambesi mine and for its failure to ensure that trade unions can operate freely and join the union of their choice.

154 *Labour Rights in a Transnational Perspective*

5.31   The Committee further holds that the PRC is in indirect breach of its obligations under Articles 7 and 8 for undermining the ability of Zambia to comply with its obligation to ensure the enjoyment of the rights under Articles 7 and 8 of the ICESCR.

5.32   In light of the above, the Committee concludes that the PRC is in breach of its obligations under Articles 7 and 8 of the ICESCR.

10 Climate Change (Human Rights Committee, *Ad Hoc* Conciliation Commission)

Margreet Wewerinke

Abstract

This contribution consists of 'Views' of an ad hoc Conciliation Commission established under Article 42 of the International Covenant on Civil and Political Rights (ICCPR) to deal with a fictive complaint submitted by 'Atoll Island State'. The complaint addresses the problem of climate change and its adverse effects on the indigenous inhabitants of the State. These adverse effects allegedly interfere with the inhabitants' rights protected in Articles 1 (right to self-determination), 6(1) (right to life) and 17(1) (right to freedom from interference with private and family life). The international responsibility of a respondent State is invoked based on its historical contributions to climate change and its failure to comply with international obligations to prevent dangerous climate change. It is submitted by Atoll Island State that the Respondent State could have foreseen that its acts and omissions that cause and accelerate climate change would interfere with the rights of people living on low-lying islands. In finding the respondent State responsible for breaches of Articles 1 and 6(1), the Commission refers to an apparent causal link between the respondent State's failure to prevent dangerous climate change and interferences with human rights on the other. It refers to provisions of the Climate Change Convention as "relevant rules of international law applicable in the relations between the parties". In its final remarks, it reiterates that its findings do not absolve Atoll Island State of its legal obligations under the Covenant and calls for international cooperation between the parties.

Introductory note

This fictional case deals with the issue of climate change. It explores a question that is highly debated in academic and intergovernmental discussions on human rights and climate change, namely, whether, and to what extent, the adverse effects of anthropogenic climate change on human beings can be characterized as violations of internationally protected human rights. More specifically, it considers whether a developed State may be held internationally responsible for such violations based on its own contributions to global climate change. According to a study on the relationship between climate change and human rights carried out by the Office of the High

156   *Climate Change*

Commissioner for Human Rights (OHCHR), the answer to this question could be negative due to difficulties related to causation and other scientific uncertainties.[1] However, there are several scholars,[2] non-governmental organisations[3] and some States[4] that have suggested, rightly it is submitted, that these legal obstacles are not necessarily insurmountable. De Schutter has even stated in an opinion piece that "[w]e can overcome the problems of delivering collective action on climate change by treating mining, deforestation, ocean degradation and more as violations of human rights".[5] In the same piece, he argues that international human rights bodies should be "proactive and holistic" in dealing with the matter of climate change.[6]

It may be expected that human rights bodies will provide clearer answers to the "violations question" when confronted with a specific complaint asking it to find one or several States responsible for the impacts of climate change on the enjoyment of specific rights. At the regional level, this strategy has already been pursued by 62 members of Inuit communities from the Arctic regions of Canada and the United States who filed a petition[7] at the Inter-American Commission on Human Rights.[8] The petition claimed that

---

1 *See* Office of the High Commissioner for Human Rights, *Report on the Relationship Between Climate Change and Human Rights* ('OHCHR study'), U.N. Doc. A/HRC/10/61, 15 January 2009,at paras 70 and 96. The study was carried out in accordance with a request made by the U.N. Human Rights Council in U.N. HRC Res. 7/23 of 28 March 2008. For a critical discussions of the report, *see* Knox, J., "Linking Human Rights and Climate Change at the United Nations", 33(1) *Harvard Environmental Law Review* 477, 496 (2009) and Dudai, R., "Climate Change and Human Rights Practice: Observations on and around the Report of the Office of the High Commissioner for Human Rights on the Relationship between Climate Change and Human Rights", 1(2) *Journal of Human Rights Practice* 294, 307 (2009).

2 *See, for example,* Knox, J., *supra,* n. 1, at 488.

3 *See, for example,* Pan African Climate Justice Alliance (PACJA), Petition to the African Commission on Human and Peoples' Rights (17 March 2010), *available at* http://www.pacja.org.

4 *See* Limon, M., "Human Rights Obligations and Accountability in the Face of Climate Change", 38 *Georgia Journal of International and Comparative Law* 543, 563 (2010) (providing an overview of States' positions in the General Debate at the Human Rights Council which discussed the OHCHR study).

5 De Schutter, O., "Climate Change is a Human Rights Issue – and that's how we can solve it", *The Guardian,* Tuesday 24 April 2012.

6 *Id.*

7 Watt-Cloutier, S., *Petition to the Inter American Commission on Human Rights Seeking Relief From Violations Resulting From Global Warming Caused by Acts and Omissions of the United States* (hereinafter *Inuit* petition), availabe at http://www.earthjustice.org (accessed 13 June 2012).

8 The petition triggered a considerable amount of academic interest in the climate change and human rights nexus. *See, for example,* Osofsky, H., "The Inuit Petition as a Bridge? Beyond the Dialectics of Climate Change and Indigenous Peoples' Rights", 31(2) *American Indian Law Review* 675, 698 (2005), Middaugh, M.E., "Linking Global Warming to Inuit Human Rights", 8 *San Diego International Law Journal* 179, 206 (2006–2007) and Aminzadeh, S.C., "A Moral Imperative: The Human Rights Implications of Climate Change", 14 *Australian International Law Journal* 231, 265 (2007).

Litigating Transnational Human Rights Obligations 157

acts and omissions of the United States contributing to the adverse consequences of climate change violated the Inuit's right to the benefits of culture, to property, health, life, to the Inuit's own means of subsistence and self-determination, and to residence and movement. Regrettably,[9] the Commission never formally dealt with the case.[10] Still, the Inter-American Commission invited the petitioners to testify about the effects of climate change on Inuit people before the Commission in March 2007[11] and held another hearing on climate change in March 2011. After the 2011 hearing it issued a press release not only containing clear recognition of the negative impacts of climate change on human rights, but also suggesting that States have legal human rights obligations in the context of international climate negotiations.[12]

At the international level, the U.N. Human Rights Council adopted three resolutions on human rights and climate change. In the first resolution, the Council recognizes that climate change "poses an immediate and far-reaching threat to people and communities around the world and has implications for the full enjoyment of human rights".[13] The second resolution not only reiterates this observation but also lists specific rights that are implicated: "inter alia, the right to life, the right to adequate food, the right to the highest attainable standard of health, the right to adequate housing, the right to self-determination and human rights obligations related to

---

9 *See* Caesens, E. and Rodriguez, M.P., "Climate Change and the Right to Food. A Comprehensive Study", *Heinrich Boll Stiftung Publications Series on Ecology,* 8 (2009) at 92 (calling the Commission's rejection of the petition a "missed opportunity to bridge the gap" between the climate change and human rights regimes, respectively) and International Council for Human Rights Policy (ICHRP), *Climate Change and Human Rights: A Rough Guide* (2008) at 43 (arguing that "[p]ioneering cases such as the Inuit case will play an important part in creating space for innovation, assisted by a widening understanding of the reality of anthropogenic climate change and its potential to injure"). *However, see also* Harrington, J., "Climate Change, Human Rights and the Right to be Cold", 18 *Fordham Environmental Law Review* 513, 535 (2007) at 526 (arguing that "[t]he Commission's decision to reject the [Inuit] Petition on preliminary grounds is admirable, because although there is no doubt that human activities are contributing to global warming, it is not clear that the State bears all responsibility for these activities").

10 The Commission merely wrote a letter to the Petitioners advising them that the Commission "will not be able to process your petition at present... The information provided does not enable us to determine whether the alleged facts would tend to characterize a violation of rights protected by the American Declaration". *See* Revkin, A.C., "World Briefing Americas: Inuit Climate Change Petition Rejected", *New York Times,* 16 December 2006, at 9.

11 *See* Earthjustice Press Release entitled "Inter-American Commission on Human Rights to Hold Hearing on Global Warming", (6 February 2007) available at http://www.earthjustice.org (accessed 1 July 2012).

12 IACHR Press Release entitled "IACHR Concludes Its 141st Regular Session", Press Release No. 28/11 (1 April 2011). Available at http://www.cidh.oas.org/Comunicados/English/2011/28-11eng.htm (accessed 13 July 2011).

13 UN HRC Res. 7/23 (2008), U.N. Doc. A/HRC/7/78 (14 July 2008) at Preambular para.1.

158 *Climate Change*

access to safe drinking water and sanitation..."[14] This resolution was followed by a third one adopted in September 2011, which called for a seminar on addressing the adverse impacts of climate change on the full enjoyment of human rights.[15] The seminar was held on 23–24 February 2012, with the participation of States, academic experts and other stakeholders. One conclusion drawn at the seminar was that capacity must be built within the United Nations to address the impacts of climate change on human rights, including through the integration of climate change and human rights in the work of U.N. treaty bodies.[16]

This contribution builds on the international recognition of the relationship between climate change and human rights. It consists of hypothetical views of the Human Rights Committee ('HRC' or 'Committee'), the body established to monitor compliance with the International Covenant on Civil and Political Rights (ICCPR),[17] and concerns a complaint submitted by a small island State. The ICCPR has 167 State parties, which include all States listed in Annex I to the United Nations Framework Convention on Climate Change (UNFCCC)[18] and dozens of States located in areas where climate change is projected to have serious negative impacts on human life and livelihoods.[19] The Covenant provides for an inter-State complaint procedure under Articles 41 and 42, subject to the States involved having made a declaration recognizing the competency of the Committee to consider inter-State complaints. At the time of writing, only 48 States have made such a declaration[20] and, remarkably, no State has ever resolved

---

14 U.N. HRC Res. 10/4 (2009), U.N. Doc. A/HRC/10/L.11 (12 May 2009) at Preambular para. 7.
15 U.N. HRC Res. 18/26 (2011), U.N. Doc. A/HRC/18/L.26/Rev.1 (28 September 2011) at para. 2.
16 *See* U.N. Human Rights Council, Report of the United High Commissioner for Human Rights on the outcome of the seminar addressing the adverse impacts of climate change on the full enjoyment of human rights, U.N. Doc. A/HRC/20/7 (10 April 2012) at para. 70. The Committee on the Elimination of All Forms of Discrimination Against Women adopted a statement on gender and climate change at its own initiative in 2009. *See* U.N. CEDAW, Statement of the CEDAW Committee on Gender and Climate Change, adopted at the 44th Sess., held in New York, USA, from 20 July to 7 August 2009.
17 International Covenant on Civil and Political Rights (adopted 16 December 1966, entered into force 23 March 1976) 999 U.N.T.S. 171 (ICCPR).
18 United Nations Framework Convention on Climate Change (adopted 9 May 1992, entered into force 19 June 1993) 1771 U.N.T.S. 107 (UNFCCC). The Parties listed in Annex I to this Convention are, roughly speaking, the industrialised States that are historically responsible for climate change. As opposed to non-Annex I Parties, these Parties have specific legal obligations under the UNFCCC related to mitigation, technology transfer and financial assistance to developing countries.
19 For ratification status, *see* http://treaties.un.org/Pages/Treaties.aspx?id=4&subid=A&lang=en (last accessed 14 April 2012).
20 *Id.*

to use the procedure.[21] This situation has led the HRC to underline the "potential value" of the procedure in a recent General Comment.[22] This "potential value" could be very real for some small island States which have, at various occasions, expressed an intention to raise the issue of climate change before the International Court of Justice.[23] Invoking the inter-State procedures established under international human rights treaties instead, or in addition to such legal action, would draw attention to the consequences of climate change suffered by human beings. And although United Nations human rights bodies cannot issue binding judgments, the jurisdictional obstacles inherent in their procedures are much easier to overcome than those of the World Court.[24]

In contrast with the individual complaint procedure established under the Optional Protocol,[25] however, the inter-State procedure is aimed at the amicable settlement of disputes between the State Parties involved. The procedure becomes potentially quasi-judicial only in the second instance, when a so-called "*ad hoc* Conciliation Commission" has been appointed and the State Parties involved fail to reach an amicable solution.[26] At this stage, the Conciliation Commission would produce a report containing its findings on "questions of fact" and "its views on the possibilities of an amicable solution of the matter".[27] This could presumably involve formulating views resembling judicial decisions on the merits, as the HRC has done under Article 5(4) of the Optional Protocol.[28] Our hypothetical *ad hoc* Conciliation Commission indeed interprets its competence under Article 42 broadly and acts like a quasi-judicial body. It also enthusiastically embraces the idea of "systemic interpretation" by taking into account that the fictive respondent State, State X, has been found in non-compliance with its legal obligations under the Kyoto Protocol. It considers the State's

---

21 For a discussion, *see* Nowak, M., *U.N. Covenant on Civil and Political Rights: CCPR Commentary*, (1st edn, N.P. Engel, 1993) at 585. *See also* the Human Rights Committee's General Comment on the Nature of General Obligations, General Comment 31, adopted during the Committee's 80th session in 2004, paragraph 2 (encouraging States to make a declaration under Article 41 and/ or avail themselves of the procedure under that Article).

22 General Comment 31, para. 2.

23 *See* Jacobs, R.E., "Treading Deep Waters: Substantive Law Issues in Tuvalu's Threat to Sue the United States in the International Court of Justice", 14 *Pacific Rim Law & Policy* 103 (2005) and U.N. Press Release, "Palau Seeks UN World Court Opinion on Damage Caused by Greenhouse Gases", 22 September 2011, available at http://www.un.org/apps/news/story.asp?NewsID=39710&Cr=pacific+island&Cr1 (accessed 12 July 2012).

24 For a discussion of these obstacles *see generally* Jacobs, *supra*, n.23.

25 Optional Protocol to the International Covenant on Civil and Political Rights ('Optional Protocol'), G.A. res. 2200A (XXI), 21 U.N. GAOR Supp. (No. 16) at 59, U.N. Doc. A/6316, 999 U.N.T.S. 302, entered into force 23 March 1976.

26 ICCPR, Article 42(1)(a).

27 ICCPR, Article 42(7)(c).

28 *See* Nowak, *supra*, n. 21, at 613.

160   *Climate Change*

obligations under international climate change law as "relevant rules of international law applicable in the relations between the Parties" within the meaning of Article 31(3)(c) of the Vienna Convention on the Law of Treaties.[29]

The views of the Commission are structured in accordance with the general law of State responsibility. The work of the International Law Commission (ILC) on State responsibility does indeed have a visible and increasing influence on the jurisprudence of human rights bodies.[30] One feature of the ILC framework is that it allows for the view that no causal link to a specific damage needs to be proven as a precondition for an allegedly wrongful act attributable to the State.[31] The test for breach of obligation flows from human rights norms viewed in light of their object and purpose. The Commission's consistent use of the term "adverse effects" also creates a normative link with the text of the UNFCCC, which itself implies the existence of a causal link between climate change and "significant deleterious effects", including on "human health and welfare".[32] The result of this approach is that the existence of a causal link between the emission of greenhouse gases and climate change, on the one hand, and between climate change and foreseeable "adverse effects", on the other, becomes a sufficient basis to establish a breach of obligation.[33]

---

29 Fn. 39 and accompanying text.

30 For one of the clearest examples, *see* Inter-American Court of Human Rights, *The Mayagna (Sumo) Awas Tingni Community v Nicaragua* (2001) Series C No. 79, (2003) 10 *International Human Rights Reports* 758, para. 154. For examples in the jurisprudence of the Human Rights Committee *see* McGoldrick, D., *The Human Rights Committee* (Oxford University Press, 1991) at 169. See also Scheinin, M., "Just Another Word? Jurisdiction in the Roadmaps of State Responsibility and Human Rights", in Langford, M., Vandenhole, W., Scheinin, M. and Van Genugten, W. (eds), *Global Justice, State Duties. The Extraterritorial Scope of Economic, Social and Cultural Rights in International Law* (Cambridge University Press, 2012) at 245 (pointing out that the principles of State responsibility are increasingly being used to interpret the rules of admissibility under human rights treaties).

31 *See* International Law Commission, Commentaries on the Report of the International Law Commission, 53rd sess., U.N. GAOR, 56th sess,.Supp. No. 10, U.N. Doc. A/56/10 (supp) (2001) ('ILC Commentaries'), reproduced in Crawford, J. (2002) (discussing causation only in the context of damages and reparations). *See also* Verheyen, R., *Climate Change Damage and International Law. Prevention Duties and State Responsibility* (Leiden, the Netherlands, Martinus Nijhoff, 2005) at 249 and Castellanos-Jankiewicz, L., "Causation and International State Responsibility" (2012) Amsterdam Center for International Law Research Paper 2012-05 (SHARES Series), pp. 11–26.

32 UNFCCC, Article 1(1).

33 On the issue of causation in climate-related litigation, *see, for example,* Boyle, A., "Remedying Harm to International Common Spaces and Resources: Compensation and Other Approaches", in Wetterstein, P. (ed.), *Harm to the Environment* (Oxford, Clarendon Press, 1997) at 89. *See also* Posner, E.A., "Climate Change and International Human Rights Litigation: A Critical Appraisal", 155 *University of Pennsylvania Law Review* 1925 (2006–2007) at 1934.

The legal consequences articulated in this contribution merit explanation, as the case does not result in tangible redress for established violations. The Commission merely recognizes that the established wrongful conduct triggered a duty to cease the violations. These limitations arose by a modest design of the case, namely, as a test case for invoking international responsibility of a State for climate change-induced human rights violations. This design allowed the 'Commission' to stay away from much of the legal and geopolitical complexity of climate change and rely upon the evidence, the provisions of the Covenant and the basic principle that each State is individually responsible for its own conduct. The 'Commission' was also restricted by its own reconciliatory mandate. Legally speaking, however, State X would also have been under an obligation to provide full reparations. The 'Commission' ignores this obligation and thus fails to take account of the victims' right to a remedy. In light of this failure, the following fictive attempt to get to grips with climate change is, at best, imperfect.

Case

Atoll Island State v State X

> Communication No. 774/12 (2017)
> Submitted by: Atoll Island State
> Respondent State Party: State X
> Date of communication: 9 January 2015 (initial submission)
> The ad hoc Conciliation Commission, established under Article 42(1) (a) of the International Covenant on Civil and Political Rights ('the Covenant')
> Meeting on: 18 August 2017
> Having concluded its consideration of communication No. 774/12 submitted by Atoll Island State under Article 41(1) (b) of the Covenant,
> Having taken into account all written information made available to it by the State Parties concerned,
> Adopts the following:

Findings and views under Article 42(7) (c) of the Covenant

1. Atoll Island State has submitted a communication to the U.N. Human Rights Committee claiming that the respondent State is not fulfilling its obligations under the Covenant. They claim that the respondent State, through its acts and omissions, has violated and is still violating Articles 1, 2, 6 and 17 of the International Covenant on Civil and Political Rights.

2. The respondent State is a State Party to the ICCPR and has declared its acceptance of the competence of the Human Rights Committee under Article 41 of the Covenant.

162 *Climate Change*

3.1 At its 114th session, the Human Rights Committee decided to deal with the matter after it found that domestic remedies for the alleged violations of the Covenant were not available.

3.2 The Committee considered the communication in two closed meetings during its 115th and 116th session at which the State Parties concerned were represented. Despite the use of the Committee's good offices by the State Parties, no friendly solution of the matter was found.

3.3. An *ad hoc* Conciliation Commission ('Commission') was established under Article 42 (1) (a) of the Covenant at the 117th session.

3.4 In their initial submissions to the Committee, the complaining State and the respondent State commented extensively on factual and legal issues before the Committee. After the establishment of an *ad hoc* Conciliation Commission, the complaining State submitted additional observations in response to respondent State's submission. The respondent State did not supply any further comments to the Commission.

3.5 No amicable solution was found, and the Commission decided to submit a report to the Chairman of the Committee in accordance with Article 42(7) of the Covenant.

The factual background

4.1 Atoll Island State is an atoll archipelago comprised of seven islands, the highest points of which are located less than one metre above sea level. The inhabitants of the islands are Macronesians whose ancestors are believed to originate from the smallest island in the archipelago, Futafuna. The islanders maintain a distinct culture based on traditional fishing and the processing of coconuts and fruits.

4.2 In the last decade the islanders have observed significant changes in the climatic and weather conditions on the islands. They have noted increased occurrence and intensity of storm surges, droughts, floods and heatwaves. The sea level has risen to an unprecedented high. The storm surges and heatwaves have already claimed the lives of hundreds of islanders, including 78 individuals who died as a result of a particularly destructive storm surge in 2013. Scientific studies show that sea level rise and the increased frequency and intensity of severe weather events, such as the 2013 storm surge, are *very likely*[34] attributable to climate change.

---

34 In the terms used by the Intergovernmental Panel on Climate Change (IPCC) to indicate the assessed likelihood of an outcome, "*very likely*" indicates a >90% probability of occurrence.

Litigating Transnational Human Rights Obligations 163

4.3   In a comprehensive study published in 2014, the World Health Organization (WHO) outlined a range of actual and projected impacts of climate change on human life in Macronesia. It confirmed that extreme high air temperatures, which occur as a result of climate change, contribute directly to deaths from respiratory and cardiovascular disease. The study also highlights the impact of climate change-induced natural disasters in Macronesia, estimating that currently around 1,000 deaths occur annually as a result of such disasters.

4.4   The Commission has received evidence that current climatic changes already affect the islanders' ability to maintain their livelihoods and culture. Coastal erosion and coral mortality have caused freshwater scarcity and decreases in fish stocks, which, according to the WHO, has caused increased prevalence of malnutrition and undernutrition. Extreme weather events have destroyed harvests, homes and essential infrastructure, forcing some of the islanders to relocate to increasingly scarce higher ground within the islands.

4.5   A study commissioned by Atoll Island National University in collaboration with the United Nations Environment Program (UNEP) predicts with an assessed likelihood of 95% that the territory of Atoll Island State would totally submerge if global temperatures were to rise more than 1.5°C. Sea level rise and extreme weather threaten the habitability of the islands even at low rates of warming; however, the study suggests that adaptation measures could mitigate at least some of the impacts on local livelihoods and life-sustaining ecosystems.

Facts related to the conduct of State X

5.1   Atoll Island State submits that the respondent State knew of the impacts of climate change on small island countries. The impacts of the man-made "greenhouse effect" on the Earth's ecosystems and sea levels have been described with increasing detail since the early nineteenth century.[35] The increased concern about the adverse consequences of human-induced global warming led to the creation of an international scientific body, the Intergovernmental Panel on Climate Change (IPCC), in 1988. The IPCC has confirmed in several reports that climate change is *very likely* caused by human beings and has severe consequences for low-lying islands.

5.2   In 1992 the United Nations Framework Convention on Climate Change (UNFCCC) was adopted,[36] which defines climate change as "a change of

---

35   Arrhenius, Svante, "On the influence of carbonic acid in the air upon the temperature of the ground", *Philosophical Magazine and Journal of Science*, V, 41, 251 (1896), pp. 237–76.

36   United Nations Framework Convention on Climate Change (UNFCCC), entered into force 19 June 1993, 31 *I.L.M.* 849, 1771 U.N.T.S. 107.

164   *Climate Change*

climate which is attributed directly or indirectly to human activity that alters the composition of the global atmosphere and which is in addition to natural climate variability observed over comparable time periods".

6.1   Atoll Island State submits that the Respondent State has failed and is still failing to take the necessary measures to reduce and regulate their contributions to global climate change. The Respondent State had emitted more than 157,275 thousand metric tons of carbon by 2008, making it one of the world's largest contributors to historical greenhouse gas (GHG) emissions that have caused the adverse effects of climate change which are experienced at present.[37] Information concerning Policies and Measures to reduce emissions (PaMs) submitted by the Respondent State in accordance with its reporting obligations under the UNFCCC indicate that its GHG emissions have increased each year since it submitted its first National Communication.[38]

6.2   In its Fourth Assessment Report, the IPCC presented evidence suggesting that developed country reductions would need to be within the range of 25–40% below 1990 levels by 2020 in order to limit global temperature rise to 2°C. A temperature rise goal of less than 2°C requires earlier reductions.[39]

7.1   The Respondent State undertook, under Article 3(1) of the Kyoto Protocol,[40] to meet a quantified emission reduction target of 7% reduction in the period 2008–2012 measured against 1990 levels.

7.2   On 12 August 2009, the Prime Minister of the Respondent State announced at a press conference that State X would not comply with its legally binding emission reduction commitment under the Kyoto Protocol. The Prime Minister simultaneously announced the construction of six new mega coal-fired power plants owned by Company Y, which were to become operational by the end of 2011.

7.3   In a declaration made on 5 June 2014, the Kyoto Compliance Committee found that State X had, through a 3% increase in its emissions instead of a 7% reduction, breached its obligations under Article 3(1) of the Kyoto Protocol.

---

37 The data on historic emissions of States are available from the Carbon Dioxide Information Analysis Centre of the Oak Ridge National Laboratory of the U.S. Department of Energy, available at http://cdiac.ornl.gov/trends/emis/tre_coun.html.

38 National communications are available at http://unfccc.int/national_reports/annex_i_natcom/submitted_natcom/items/4903.php.

39 Intergovernmental Panel on Climate Change (IPCC), "Contribution of Working Group I to the Fourth Assessment Report", Chapter 1, available at http://www.ipcc.ch/pdf/assessment-report-ar4-wg1-chapter1.pdf.

40 Kyoto Protocol to the United Nations Framework Convention on Climate Change (Kyoto Protocol), entered into force 16 February 2005, 2303 U.N.T.S. 148.

Litigating Transnational Human Rights Obligations 165

7.4   In September 2014, the President of State X stated at the High-level segment of the Opening of the 68th General Assembly of the United Nations that State X would refrain from taking any measures to ensure a decrease in GHGs emitted by private persons under its jurisdiction until certain developing countries would "lead by example".

The complaint

8.   Atoll Island State claims that anthropogenic climate change, which is for a significant part caused by acts and omissions of the Respondent State, interferes with the Atoll Island people's right to self-determination in violation of Article 1 of the Covenant. The continuation of these acts and omissions, in light of their foreseeable impacts on the territory of the islands and the Atoll Island people's traditional culture, is also claimed to constitute a violation of Article 1.

9.   Atoll Island State further claims a violation by the respondent State of Article 6(1) of the Covenant, since at least dozens of its citizens have died as a result of the 2013 heatwave and other severe weather events that occurred due to dangerous climate change for which the Respondent State is allegedly responsible. The Respondent State's failure to act domestically and internationally to prevent foreseeable deaths due to projected climate-induced natural disasters, diseases and other health impacts is also claimed to violate Article 6(1) of the Covenant.

10.   Atoll Island State further claims a violation of Article 17(1) of the Covenant, since the homes and traditional land of the Atoll Island people are becoming uninhabitable due to sea-level rise, flooding and extreme weather conditions that occur as a result of climate change.

The Respondent State's observations

11.   The Respondent State denies that it has violated international obligations under the Covenant, as it is working through the UNFCCC to develop effective international responses to climate change. The *lex specialis* of this international legal framework is the sole appropriate legal framework to deal with climate change-related matters.

12.   Alternatively, the Respondent State submits that climate change is one of many natural and societal phenomena that may positively or negatively impact on the enjoyment of human rights. It is also a global phenomenon caused by an enormously large and diffuse set of actors. It is therefore legally impossible to find one or several identifiable States responsible for climate change impacts.

13.   The Respondent State furthermore submits that the emission of greenhouse gases is a practice for which not the State, but millions of

166 *Climate Change*

private persons are responsible. In the present case there is thus no act which is attributable to State X under international law.

14. Finally, the Respondent State submits that the State of Atoll Island is solely responsible for respecting and ensuring to all individuals within its territory and subject to its jurisdiction the rights recognized in the Covenant. To construe the Covenant otherwise would undermine the credibility of the Human Rights Committee.

Issues and proceedings before the Commission

15. The Conciliation Commission has considered the present communication in light of all information made available to it by the parties, as provided in Article 42(7) of the Covenant.

16.1 With regard to the applicable rules of interpretation, the Commission recalls that the Covenant must be interpreted in the light of the rules set out in the Vienna Convention on the Law of Treaties.[41] Accordingly, the ordinary meaning of the provisions of the Covenant must be determined in its context and in the light of its object and purpose.[42]

16.2 The Commission must furthermore consider "relevant rules of international law applicable in the relations between the parties".[43] In the present case, these rules include the *lex specialis* of international climate change law. More broadly, the Commission must take into account customary international law, including the relevant rules and principles concerning State responsibility.

17. The Commission wishes to clarify that the existence of relevant *lex specialis* in no way excludes the application of the Covenant, nor does it prohibit the Commission from considering the present communication insofar as it raises issues under the Covenant.

Attribution of acts to State X

18. In order to assess the present communication, the Commission must first consider whether there is legally relevant conduct that is attributable to State X.

19. The Commission has considered the facts related to the historical contributions of State X to global greenhouse gas emissions, as well as the

---

41 Vienna Convention on the Law of Treaties (VCLT), 23 May 1969, 1155 U.N.T.S. 331, entered into force 27 January 1980.
42 Article 31(1) of the VCLT.
43 Article 31(3)(c) of the VCLT. *See also* General Comment No. 12, adopted during the Committee's 21st session in 1984, paragraph 2.

emission patterns which State X has reported to the international community in accordance with its reporting obligations under the UNFCCC and the Kyoto Protocol.

20. In conjunction with these facts, the Commission has considered the scientific evidence produced by the IPCC, which demonstrates a causal link between the emission of anthropogenic greenhouse gases and global climate change.

21. The Commission has furthermore reviewed the evidence submitted by Atoll Island State, which demonstrates a wide range of adverse effects of anthropogenic climate change on the citizens of Atoll Island State, including effects that raise issues under the Covenant.

22. The Commission finds that the Respondent State, through its acts and omissions, has made a material contribution to global climate change and, accordingly, to the adverse effects thereof that are the subject of this communication.

23. The Commission further notes that under general international law, the allocation of international responsibility is based on the principle of independent responsibility of States.

24. It becomes indisputable that the failure of State X to prevent increased emission of greenhouse gases by persons under its jurisdiction from 1990 onwards is an act attributable to State X under international law. State X incurs international responsibility if the act that is attributable to it breaches its legal obligations under the Covenant.

Jurisdiction

25.1 In relation to the facts that allegedly raise issues under Article 1, the Commission finds that an ordinary reading of Article 1 implies that States' obligations to respect and promote the right contained therein extend towards peoples outside their territories. It recalls the Committee's General Comment No. 12, stating that Article 1(3) "imposes specific obligations on State parties, not only in relation to their own peoples but *vis-à-vis* all peoples which have not been able to exercise or have been deprived of the possibility of exercising their right to self-determination".[44]

25.2 The Commission considers, accordingly, that the obligations of State X under Article 1 extend towards the people of Atoll Island State.

26.1 In relation to the facts that allegedly raise issues under Article 6, the Commission has considered whether Article 2(1) of the Covenant excludes

44 General Comment No. 12, adopted during the Committee's 21st session in 1984, paragraph 6.

168   *Climate Change*

an interpretation of Covenant provisions as imposing obligations on State X towards individuals outside its territory.

26.2   The Commission recalls the view of the Human Rights Committee that the provision in Article 2(1) must be read in the light of Article 5(1) of the Covenant, which provides:

> 1. Nothing in the present Covenant may be interpreted as implying for any State, group or person any right to engage in any activity or perform any act aimed at the destruction of any of the rights and freedoms recognized herein or at their limitation to a greater extent than is provided for in the present Covenant.

26.3   It recalls the Committee's finding that in the light of this provision, it would be unconscionable to so interpret the responsibility under Article 2 of the Covenant as to permit a State party to perpetrate violations of the Covenant on the territory of another State, which violations it could not perpetrate on its own territory.[45]

Relevance of international climate change law

27.1   The Commission notes that the respondent State has undertaken an emission reduction target under Article 3(1) of the Kyoto Protocol, and an obligation under Article 4(2)(a) of the UNFCCC to take mitigation measures in accordance with the objective of the Convention.

27.2   The objective of the UNFCCC is to stabilize GHG concentrations in the atmosphere "at a level that would prevent dangerous anthropogenic interference with the climate system". This objective reinforces relevant provisions of the Covenant, which specifically aims to safeguard the fundamental rights of peoples and individuals.

28.   The Commission will proceed to consider whether the acts attributable to State X constitute violations of relevant provisions of the Covenant. As part of this exercise, it must consider whether the facts submitted by Atoll Island State fall within the substantive scope of Articles 1 and 6(1).

Applicability of Article 1 of the Covenant

29.1   The right to self-determination provided in Article 1 implies that a people may determine its political status and social, economic and cultural

---

45   See the Committee's views in case no. 12/52 (*Sergio Euben Lopez Burgos v. Uruguay*), Views adopted on 29 July 1981, CCPR/C/1 3/D/52/1979, paragraph 12.

development free from external interference. The right also contains an economic dimension spelled out in Article 1 (2).[46]

29.2   The Commission notes the evidence demonstrating that the distinct culture of the inhabitants of Atoll Island State is under threat due to climate change. In particular, it notes that some islanders have already been forced to leave their traditional homes located in coastal areas due to dangers associated with sea level rise and extreme weather events. Fragile marine ecosystems that are part of the territory of Atoll Island State no longer provide the islands' people with sufficient means of subsistence.

29.3   The Commission has also considered the evidence that reveals severe threats to the culture and livelihoods of the people of Atoll Island. There is a real threat that the traditional land of the Atoll Island people will disappear completely; a scenario to which the Atoll Island people did not consent. There is no guarantee that the essential conditions for the protection of individual human rights would be fulfilled in such a scenario.

30.   These facts bring the present communication within the ambit of Article 1 of the Covenant.

Applicability of Article 6(1) of the Covenant

31.   Article 6(1) of the Covenant protects the inherent right to life of every human being. It states that this right shall be protected by law, and that no one shall be arbitrarily deprived of his life.

32.   The evidence presented to the Commission indicates that a range of climate impacts, including extreme high air temperatures and associated respiratory and cardiovascular diseases, are already causing loss of human life in Macronesia.

33.   The evidence also suggests that increasing emissions of GHGs will likely trigger loss of human life in the region on a much larger scale. The threat to human life is amplified by increasing freshwater scarcity and decreases in fish stocks, which already has led to malnutrition and undernutrition.

34.   In the view of the Commission, the body of evidence before it brings the present communication within the scope of Article 6(1) of the Covenant.

---

46 General Comment No. 12, adopted during the Committee's 21st session in 1984, paragraph 1.

170   *Climate Change*

State's obligations under the Covenant in relation to Articles 1 and 6(1)

35.1   The Commission refers to Article 2(1) of the Covenant, which defines the scope of the legal obligations, both negative and positive, undertaken by State Parties to the Covenant.[47]

35.2   The positive obligation of States under Article 2(1) entails that a State Party adopts legislative, judicial, administrative, educative and other appropriate measures in order to fulfil their legal obligations.[48] The obligation may be violated as a result of States Parties failing to take appropriate measures or to exercise due diligence to prevent harm caused by private persons or entities.[49]

35.3   In relation to Article 6 of the Covenant, the text of this Article explicates that the right must be protected "by law". The Human Rights Committee has furthermore stated that States must adopt positive measures to comply with their obligations to ensure the right to life.[50]

35.4   In relation to Article 1, the Human Rights Committee has emphasized that all States Parties to the Covenant should take positive action to facilitate realization of and respect for the right of peoples to self-determination.[51] It has also highlighted that the right of self-determination is of particular importance because its realization is an essential condition for the effective guarantee and observance of individual human rights and for the promotion and strengthening of those rights.[52]

35.5   The Commission considers that, in the context of anthropogenic climate change and in accordance with the above, the positive obligations of States under Article 2(1) largely overlap with those under Article 1. These obligations must be viewed in light of the precautionary principle, which is incorporated in international human rights law and in Article 3(3) of the UNFCCC. In accordance with this principle, the phenomenon of climate change triggers an obligation under the Covenant to adopt adequate measures capable of protecting the rights of peoples and individuals, as there is a serious risk that these rights will be interfered with in the absence of such measures.

36.   The Commission's task now consists in reviewing whether the Respondent State has taken all positive measures required by Articles 1 and

---

47 General Comment 31, adopted during the Committee's 80th session in 2004, paragraph 6.
48 General Comment 31, adopted during the Committee's 80th session in 2004, paragraph 7.
49 General Comment 31, adopted during the Committee's 80th session in 2004, paragraph 8.
50 General Comment No. 6, adopted during the Committee's 16th session in 1982, paragraph 5.
51 General Comment No. 12, adopted during the Committee's 21st session in 1984, paragraph 6.
52 General Comment No. 12, adopted during the Committee's 21st session in 1984, paragraph 1.

Litigating Transnational Human Rights Obligations 171

6(1) of the Convention in light of the adverse effects of climate change on the rights protected under those Articles.

Alleged breaches of Covenant obligations

37.1　The Commission notes, first, that the adverse effects of climate change have been well-documented at least since 1990. The reports produced by the IPCC from this time onwards were endorsed by the Respondent State. The Commission also notes that Atoll Island State has been drawing the attention of all States to the impacts of climate change on human beings since 1988.

37.2　On the basis of the above, the Commission concludes that at least from 1990 onwards, the Respondent State knew or should have known that the emission of greenhouse gases for which it is responsible already interferes with, and poses further threats to, the rights to life and self-determination.

37.3　The Commission considers that the Respondent State is responsible for significant historical emissions and thus has significant *de facto* responsibility for the occurrence of climate change at present.

38.　The Commission further observes that the Respondent State has breached its obligations under Article 3(1) of the Kyoto Protocol and that its national emissions are increasing.

39.　The Commission underlines that the Respondent State has not provided the Commission with any information or argument that could justify its conduct. In this light, the Commission cannot but conclude that the Respondent State has failed to comply with its legal obligations under the Covenant related to the right of self-determination and the right to life.

40.　In the circumstances, the Committee does not find it necessary to consider assertions that other provisions of the Covenant were violated.

41.　The Commission, acting under Article 42(7)(c) of the International Covenant on Civil and Political Rights, is of the view that the communication discloses violations of Articles 1 and 6 of the Covenant.

42.　With a view to amicable solutions, the Commission urges the Respondent State to take all necessary measures to ensure compliance with its obligations under the UNFCCC and the Kyoto Protocol and to cooperate internationally to ensure effective global responses to climate change that are fully in accordance with international human rights law.

43.　Finally, the Commission wishes to clarify that its findings on the present communication in no way absolve the Atoll Island State of its legal obligations under the Covenant. In this regard, it calls on the Atoll Island State to continue its adaptation efforts and to cooperate in good faith in international climate negotiations.

11 Development Assistance to Education for Children with Disabilities (Committee on the Rights of Persons with Disabilities)

Wouter Vandenhole

Abstract

European State E decides to disinvest from primary education for children with disabilities in country A, an African state. This disinvestment is in line with State A's own policy choices. It is also a direct consequence of E's suspension of its growth path in development cooperation spending, given the resource constraints it is facing. Following this disinvestment by E in primary education for children with disabilities in A, all inclusive education projects in A come to an abrupt end, and all but one special school for children with disabilities is closed.

In this hypothetical case, the Committee on the Rights of Persons with Disabilities accepts that the claimants are under the jurisdiction of both A and E. It does so after imbuing new meaning to the notion of jurisdiction, building on the Maastricht Principles and the wording of Article 1 Convention on the Rights of Persons with Disabilities (CRPD). On the merits, the Committee defines the scope of the obligation of international cooperation as requiring, at a minimum, disability mainstreaming so as to make international cooperation policies inclusive. The Committee also examines the permissibility of retrogressive measures on the part of donor country E.

Introductory note

This hypothetical case engages with the arguments that tend to be put forward in discussions on the mainstreaming of children's rights in development cooperation. An often-heard argument is that a donor country has to respect the good donor principle of ownership of the recipient country,[1] so that it cannot impose children's rights programmes or projects if the latter is not interested. It thus raises the question whether human rights

---

1 Second High-Level Forum (2005), *Paris Declaration on Aid Effectiveness. Ownership, Harmonisation, Alignment, Results and Mutual Accountability*, para. 15, www.oecd.org: "Donors commit to respect partner country leadership and help strengthen their capacity to exercise it."

Litigating Transnational Human Rights Obligations 173

mainstreaming and good development practice are competing and sometimes contradictory frameworks. Country ownership tends to be invoked quite conveniently against the backdrop of financial and economic crises, which have led many donor countries to suspend their growth path in development cooperation spending, or to cut back development cooperation spending altogether.[2] For example, a commitment entrenched in Belgian law to spend 0.7 per cent of GDP on development cooperation by the end of 2010[3] was politically suspended in the wake of the 2008 financial and economic crisis.[4]

Jurisdiction has been a major obstacle to litigating extraterritorial violations of civil and political rights before the European Court of Human Rights (ECtHR).[5] While this admissibility issue cannot be ignored, the goal of this contribution is to move beyond questions of jurisdiction. An attractive and creative response to the ECtHR's approach to jurisdiction is offered by the Maastricht Principles on Extraterritorial Obligations of States in the area of Economic, Social and Cultural Rights (Maastricht Principles), in that they define the scope of jurisdiction well beyond the traditional situation of authority or effective control, to situations in which foreseeable effects are brought about, as well as situations in which a State is "in a position to exercise decisive influence or to take measures to realize economic, social and cultural rights extraterritorially" (Maastricht Principle 9).

On the merits, the present "alternative judgment" focuses on issues relating to extraterritorial human rights obligations. Thus, the preference for mainstream education for children with disabilities is not fully developed;[6] nor is the question of the legal capacity of children to complain, or even the responsibility of the territorial state. In relation to the latter point, I have deliberately left out the question of the precise apportioning of responsibility in order to show that the absence of a clear doctrine on apportioning responsibility does not exclude *per se* litigation of extraterritorial obligations.

A first question specific to extraterritorial human rights obligations is the legal meaning and scope of the reference to "international cooperation" in Article 32 CRPD, and of similar references to "international assistance and cooperation" in Article 2 International Covenant on Economic,

---

2 See e.g. AidWatch 2012, Aid We Can – Invest More in Global Development, http://aidwatch.concordeurope.org/static/files/assets/3f200cc4/report.pdf

3 Article 458 Programmatic Bill (I), 24 December 2002, *Moniteur Belge*, 31 December 2002.

4 Algemene Beleidsnota Overheidsbedrijven, Wetenschapsbeleid, Ontwikkelings samenwerking en Grootstedenbeleid, *Kamer* 2011–12, doc. 1964/021, p. 25.

5 See e.g. M. Gondek, *The Reach of Human Rights in a Globalising World: Extraterritorial Application of Human Rights Treaties* (Antwerp, Intersentia, 2009); M. Milanovic, *Extraterritorial Application of Human Rights Treaties, Law, Principles, and Policy* (Oxford, Oxford University Press, 2011). See also Moons' contribution in this volume.

6 See Article 24 CRPD.

174 *Development Assistance to Education for Children with Disabilities*

Social and Cultural Rights (ICESCR) and Article 4 Convention on the Rights of the Child (CRC). There is meanwhile a good body of literature on the topic,[7] and the Maastricht Principles shed some light on the question as well (Principles 28–35). I have argued elsewhere that in the CRC Committee's interpretation, there is a shared responsibility for the implementation of the CRC, including specific obligations for development cooperation, such as allocating 0.7 per cent of Gross National Income (GNI) to development assistance and mainstreaming a child rights perspective in all development programmes and projects.[8]

A second question is how to qualify the disinvestment in primary education for disabled children: as a violation of a negative obligation (to respect), as a violation of a positive obligation (to fulfil—provide), or as a violation of the prohibition, at least in principle, of retrogressive measures? Whereas this question of qualification is not unique to extraterritorial obligations, it does merit attention as this question has not yet been resolved satisfactorily in territorial cases either. An additional element that may be taken into consideration when assessing retrogressive measures in light of extraterritorial obligations is whether or not external States have sought to coordinate their actions. In order not to get trapped in the highly politicized discussion on extraterritorial obligations to provide development assistance, I have framed the case in such a way that the *withdrawal* of development assistance becomes the main issue to address.

A major challenge of expanding the duty-bearer dimension of human rights law is the apportioning of obligations and of responsibility for violations of these obligations. The Maastricht Principles remain quite silent on that question, and the literature too has not yet explored the issue in full depth.[9] In order not to unnecessarily complicate the case under consideration, this issue is not fully developed here either. Needless to say, though,

---

7 See e.g. M. Langford, F. Coomans and F. Gómez Isa, "Extraterritorial Duties in International Law", in M. Langford, W. Vandenhole, M. Scheinin and W. van Genugten (eds), *Global Justice, State Duties. Extraterritorial Human Rights Obligations in the Area of Economic, Social and Cultural Rights* (Cambridge, Cambridge University Press, 2013, 51–113); M. Salomon, Is there a Legal Duty to Address World Poverty?, RSCAS Policy Paper 2012/03, http://cadmus.eui.eu/bitstream/handle/1814/22197/RSCAS_PP_2012_03.pdf?sequence=1

8 "Economic, Social and Cultural Rights in the CRC: Is There a Legal Obligation to Cooperate Internationally for Development?", 17 *International Journal of Children's Rights* 2009, (23–63), 61–2.

9 Exceptions include A. Khalfan, "Division of responsibility among States", in M. Langford, W. Vandenhole, M. Scheinin and W. van Genugten (eds), *Global Justice, State Duties. The Extraterritorial Scope of Economic, Social and Cultural Rights in International Law.* Cambridge: Cambridge University Press, 2013, 299–331; W. Vandenhole and W. Benedek, "Extraterritorial Human Rights Obligations and the North-South Divide", in M. Langford, W. Vandenhole, M. Scheinin and W. van Genugten (eds), *Global Justice, State Duties. The Extraterritorial Scope of Economic, Social and Cultural Rights in International Law.* Cambridge: Cambridge University Press, 2013, 332–363.

Litigating Transnational Human Rights Obligations 175

the apportioning of responsibility between the domestic and external State may be an additional challenge in dealing with complaints about extraterritorial obligations.

As of this writing, the CRPD Committee has so far only dealt with one individual complaint and this matter did not address extraterritorial obligations. Given the limited guidance that can be found in the CRPD Committee's own case-law, I have also drawn on the approach adopted by other human rights treaty bodies in dealing with individual complaints.

Case

The Facts

1. European country E, a member of the European Union (EU), suffers from a worldwide economic recession and decides to suspend the implementation of the growth path in its development cooperation towards spending 0.7 per cent of its GNI on development cooperation by 2015. It had politically committed to that growth path in the Monterrey Conference Financing for Development,[10] the European Consensus on Development[11] and other EU policy documents,[12] and domestic legislation.

E became a State Party to the CRPD and its Optional Protocol – which allows for individual complaints – some years ago. Following ratification of the CRPD, it had decided to add disability mainstreaming to the mainstreaming themes in its development cooperation, alongside children's rights and some other themes. These mainstreaming themes have been legally entrenched in its Bill on International Development Cooperation.

2. African country A, one of E's priority partner countries, has just emerged from civil war. Many children were involved in the armed conflict and have been maimed. As a consequence, many face serious physical disabilities. In its discussions with A on the next development programme cycle, the government of E concludes that A is not truly committed any more to education for children with disabilities. Many of these children had participated in the country's armed conflict, and the present government of State A considers them to still be aligned with its former enemy.

---

10 *Outcome of the International Conference on Financing for Development,* United Nations (23 August 2002), UN Doc.A/57/344 (2003), para. 23.

11 *European Consensus on Development,* adopted on 20 December 2005 (*OJ* of 24 February 2006, 2006/C 46).

12 *Millennium Development Goals: EU Contribution to the Review of the MDGs at the UN 2005 High Level Event – Conclusions of the Council and the Representatives of the Governments of the Member States Meeting within the Council,* Doc. 9266/05, para. 4.

176 *Development Assistance to Education for Children with Disabilities*

In line with A's own policy choices, and given the resource constraints following the suspension of its growth path in development cooperation spending, E decides to disinvest from primary education for children with disabilities in A.

3. Following this disinvestment by E in primary education for children with disabilities in A, all inclusive education projects in A come to an abrupt end, and all but one special school for children with disabilities are closed.

Committee on the Rights of Persons with Disabilities

Communication No. 4/2012, X, Y, Z and Inclusive Education Transnational v. E

Views adopted by the Committee at its 10th session

The complaint

4. A complaint is lodged by three disabled children, X, Y, Z who live in A. X is eleven years old, and Y and Z are twelve years old. All three no longer have access to primary education following the end of inclusive education projects and the closure of most special schools. A complaint is also lodged by a non-governmental organization (NGO) *Inclusive Education Transnational*, which focuses on the fate of children with disabilities in the global South. *Inclusive Education Transnational* is based in E and runs primary schools for disabled children in A. The NGO submits the complaint on behalf of all affected children.

The complainants submit that Article 32 (international cooperation) CRPD has been violated, in combination with Articles 16 (freedom from exploitation, violence and abuse) and 24 (right to education) CRPD.

The complaint is directed against E only. The complainants argue that A would have continued education for disabled children had E not suspended its funding for it, and that the lack of access to education for disabled children is therefore attributable to E rather than to A.

State Party E's observations on admissibility and merits

E argues that the complaint must be declared inadmissible, based on the grounds that it does not exercise jurisdiction over X, Y and Z. Even if it was accepted that E did exercise jurisdiction over the children, the complaint should be directed against A only, which is the main and primary duty-holder. E argues that in line with its development policy commitments under the 2005 Paris Declaration on Aid Effectiveness, it fully respects A's ownership. According to E, country A does not prioritize education, and even less so education for disabled children. However, E maintains it cannot force A to do so.

Litigating Transnational Human Rights Obligations 177

Issues and proceedings before the Committee

Consideration of admissibility

5. In accordance with Articles 1 and 2 Optional Protocol to the Convention on the Rights of Persons with Disabilities (OP CRPD) and with Rule 68 of its Rules of Procedure, the Committee on the Rights of Persons with Disabilities (the Committee) shall decide whether the communication is admissible under the OP CRPD.

6. The Committee notes that most admissibility requirements do not pose particular problems, and that in any event E has not raised any inadmissibility arguments except for the one on jurisdiction. As E has argued that it does not exercise jurisdiction over the complainants X, Y and Z, the Committee needs to address the interpretation of the reference "subject to its jurisdiction" in Article 1, paragraph 1 OP CRPD.

Article 1, paragraph 1 OP CRPD reads:

> A State party to the present Protocol ("State Party") recognizes the competence of the Committee on the Rights of Persons with Disabilities ("the Committee") to receive and consider communications from or on behalf of individuals or groups of individuals subject to its jurisdiction who claim to be victims of a violation by that State Party of the provisions of the Convention.

7. While the notion of jurisdiction has been understood as primarily territorial (see e.g. ECtHR 12 December 2001, Bancović v. Belgium and others (adm.)), it also includes authority/power/control over persons outside its own territory. For example, extraterritorial jurisdiction has been accepted in cases in which there was a strong degree of direct and/or physical control over persons, e.g. the arrest or detention of a person (See e.g. ECtHR, *Issa v. Turkey*, no. 31821/96, 16 November 2004, ECtHR (GC), *Öcalan v. Turkey*, no. 46221/99, 12 May 2005; IACHR, *Coard et al. v. the United States*, no. 10.951, 29 September 1999, *Ann. Rep. IACHR* 1999, Report no. 109/99).

However, in the recently adopted 2011 *Maastricht Principles on Extraterritorial Obligations in the Area of Economic, Social and Cultural Rights* (Maastricht Principles), the notion of jurisdiction has been given a broader meaning. Principle 9 on the scope of jurisdiction reads:

> A State has obligations to respect, protect and fulfil economic, social and cultural rights in any of the following:
>
> a)   situations over which it exercises authority or effective control, whether or not such control is exercised in accordance with international law;

178 *Development Assistance to Education for Children with Disabilities*

    b) situations over which State acts or omissions bring about foreseeable effects on the enjoyment of economic, social and cultural rights, whether within or outside its territory;

    c) situations in which the State, acting separately or jointly, whether through its executive, legislative or judicial branches, is in a position to exercise decisive influence or to take measures to realize economic, social and cultural rights extraterritorially, in accordance with international law.

According to this approach, jurisdiction would include not only situations of authority or effective control, but also situations in which acts or omissions bring about foreseeable effects, and situations in which a State is in a position to exercise decisive influence. Employing this standard, the Committee accepts that it was quite foreseeable that E's withdrawal of development funds for primary education for children with disabilities in A would lead to negative effects on the enjoyment of the right to education for children in that country. At a minimum, it cannot be denied that E was in a position to exercise decisive influence or to take measures to realize the right to primary education for disabled children in A.

This broader reading of the notion of jurisdiction in the Maastricht Principles finds support in article 1 CRPD, which defines the purpose of the Convention as the promotion, protection and ensurance of the full and equal enjoyment of all human rights and fundamental freedoms by *all* persons with disabilities, without any territorial or jurisdictional limitation. In Article 4 CRPD, States Parties undertake to ensure and promote the full realization of all human rights and fundamental freedoms for *all* persons with disabilities without discrimination of any kind on the basis of disability. Again, no reference is made to territory or jurisdiction.

The Committee therefore accepts that X, Y and Z fall not only under the jurisdiction of A, but also under that of E as far as the facts of this case are concerned, given the foreseeable effects or, at a minimum, the position to exercise decisive influence or to take measures to realize the right to primary education for disabled children in A. In addition, since E has not challenged the fact that *Inclusive Education Transnational* comes within its jurisdiction, there is no need for the Committee to examine this issue.

8. The fact that the complaint was only lodged against E, while A also exercises jurisdiction, does not prevent the Committee from examining the case before it. However, the Committee will duly consider the obligations of A when assessing whether a violation by E has taken place.

9. The Committee would also like to emphasize that contrary to the wording in the Optional Protocol to the International Covenant on Economic, Social and Cultural Rights (OP ICESCR) and in the Optional Protocol to the Convention on the Rights of the Child on a Communications Procedure (OPCP CRC) under which complaints are only possible concerning violations

of "rights", the OP CRPD allows for complaints concerning violations "of the provisions of the Convention". While not taking any position on the possibility to complain about the lack of international cooperation under the OP ICESCR and the OPCP CRC, it is obvious that complaints about violations of article 32 CRPD on international cooperation are not excluded under the OP CRPD.

10. In accordance with Rule 68(2) of the Rules of Procedures, the legal capacity of the complaining children with disabilities before the Committee has to be decided in light of the criteria set forth in Article 12 CRPD, regardless of whether such capacity is recognized in the State Party against which the communication is directed. While this principle has been developed mainly to address issues of legal capacity of persons with *disabilities*, it applies also to cases like the one under consideration where *children* are concerned. Support for this position can also be found in Article 13 CRPD, which imposes an obligation on States Parties to ensure effective access to justice for persons with disabilities on an equal basis with others, *inter alia*, through the provision of age-appropriate accommodations. Obviously, this principle needs to be extended to access to justice to this Committee.

Consideration of the merits

11. Having established that E exercises jurisdiction over X, Y and Z and over *Inclusive Education Transnational* for the facts of this case, the Committee now needs to assess whether E has violated Article 32 (international cooperation) CRPD alone or in combination with Articles 16 (freedom from exploitation, violence and abuse) and 24 (education) CRPD, by ending its development funding dedicated to primary education for children with disabilities in A. In what follows, the Committee will first define the scope of the obligation incumbent on E under Article 32 CRPD alone and read in conjunction with other provisions in the Convention. Secondly, it will examine whether A has violated those provisions.

a. Scope of the Obligation under Article 32 CRPD

12. Article 32 CRPD on international cooperation reads:

> 1. States Parties recognize the importance of international cooperation and its promotion, in support of national efforts for the realization of the purpose and objectives of the present Convention, and will undertake appropriate and effective measures in this regard, between and among States and, as appropriate, in partnership with relevant international and regional organizations … Such measures could include, *inter alia*:
> > (a) Ensuring that international cooperation, including international development programmes, is inclusive of and accessible to persons with disabilities;

180 *Development Assistance to Education for Children with Disabilities*

(b) Facilitating and supporting capacity-building, including through the exchange and sharing of information, experiences, training programmes and best practices;

(c) ...

(d) Providing, as appropriate, technical and economic assistance, including by facilitating access to and sharing of accessible and assistive technologies, and through the transfer of technologies.

2. The provisions of this article are without prejudice to the obligations of each State Party to fulfil its obligations under the present Convention.

This provision builds on references to international assistance and cooperation in the International Covenant on Economic, Social and Cultural Rights and the Convention on the Rights of the Child (see also CESCR (2000), General Comment No. 14 on the Right to Health, Articles 38–41). The CRPD is, however, the first UN core human rights treaty to contain an autonomous provision on international cooperation.

13. The *travaux préparatoires* of the CRPD show that the issue of international cooperation has featured prominently in the discussions and negotiations on the CRPD. This comes as no surprise, as 66 to 80 per cent of persons with disabilities are believed to be living in developing countries. Although all Parties recognized the importance of international cooperation, the problem was that in the UN context, the term international cooperation has often been code for developmental assistance. During the negotiations on Article 32 CRPD, delegates from North and South emphasized that international cooperation was not a synonym for development assistance and the transfer of resources from North to South. Many other substantive dimensions of international cooperation were evoked, ranging from the transfer of resources and technical assistance and cooperation; to policy advice, the international sharing and exchange of experience, expertise and good practice; to assisting in effective implementation, networking and workshops, training, awareness, cooperation among disabled people's organizations, and development of technologies.

However, while international cooperation cannot be reduced to a mere transfer of resources to developing countries, it cannot be denied that in reality States do find themselves at different levels of development. Therefore, States Parties to the CRPD are to complement national efforts through international cooperation. During the negotiations, a broad consensus emerged on disability mainstreaming in international cooperation for development. Donor countries accepted that in the framework of development cooperation they must at least *refrain* from violating the rights of persons with disabilities in the South. Inclusiveness of development cooperation has expressly been included as one of the measures available (see Article 32, para. 1(a) CRPD).

On the basis of the *travaux préparatoires* and the explicit wording of the text, it can be concluded that Article 32 CRPD requires every State Party to

Litigating Transnational Human Rights Obligations 181

mainstream disability in its policies, including those of international assistance and cooperation for development. Those policies need to be inclusive.

14. A teleological interpretation of the CRPD leads to the same conclusion. The hallmark of the CRPD is inclusiveness and equality, as illustrated in Articles 3 and 4 CRPD, amongst others. This has in particular been confirmed for children in Article 7, paragraphs 1 and 2 CRPD, which read:

> 1. States Parties shall take all necessary measures to ensure the full enjoyment by children with disabilities of all human rights and fundamental freedoms on an equal basis with other children.
> 2. In all actions concerning children with disabilities, the best interests of the child shall be a primary consideration.

15. What disability mainstreaming in development cooperation means in the case under consideration can *inter alia* be found in Articles 16 and 24 CRPD. Article 16, para. 4 CRPD emphasizes the need to protect persons with disabilities from all forms of exploitation, violence and abuse. Persons with disabilities who have become victims of any form of exploitation, violence or abuse are entitled to all appropriate measures to promote the physical, cognitive and psychological recovery, rehabilitation and social reintegration. Quite notably, Article 7 of the Optional Protocol to the CRC on the involvement of children in armed conflict (OPAC) imposes an obligation of international cooperation, "including through technical cooperation and financial assistance", on States Parties in a position to do so, *inter alia*, for the rehabilitation and social reintegration of victims of involvement in armed conflict.

Victims' gender-specific and age-specific needs must be taken into account. Development cooperation therefore has to include recovery, rehabilitation and social reintegration measures for *child* victims of armed conflict, in which their age-specific needs are taken into account. It goes without saying that education is such an age-specific need for 11- and 12-year-old children. That has also been emphasized in Article 26, para. 1 CRPD on rehabilitation and rehabilitation services and programmes, in which explicit reference is made to the area of education.

16. The right to inclusive (primary) education features prominently in the CRPD. The relevant parts of Article 24 CRPD on the right to education read:

> 1. States Parties recognize the right of persons with disabilities to education. With a view to realizing this right without discrimination and on the basis of equal opportunity, States Parties shall ensure an inclusive education system at all levels and lifelong learning directed to ...
> 2. In realizing this right, States Parties shall ensure that:
>   (a) Persons with disabilities are not excluded from the general education system on the basis of disability, and that children with

disabilities are not excluded from free and compulsory primary education ... on the basis of disability;

(b) Persons with disabilities can access an inclusive, quality and free primary education ... on an equal basis with others in the communities in which they live;

(c) Reasonable accommodation of the individual's requirements is provided;

(d) Persons with disabilities receive the support required, within the general education system, to facilitate their effective education;

(e) Effective individualized support measures are provided in environments that maximize academic and social development, consistent with the goal of full inclusion.

Disability mainstreamed development cooperation will therefore need to pay particular attention to inclusive primary education for children with disabilities, on an equal basis with others. Inclusive education not only requires negative measures of abstention, but also positive measures of (individualized) support.

17. In conclusion, Article 32 CRPD requires every State Party, at a minimum, to mainstream disability in its international policies, including those of international assistance and cooperation for development. This is the case with regard to children in particular, and extends to recovery, rehabilitation and social reintegration measures for child victims of armed conflict and to (inclusive) primary education.

Now that the minimal scope of Article 32 CRPD has been defined, the Committee will examine whether that Article, alone or in conjunction with other provisions, has been violated.

b. Whether there has been a violation of Article 32 CRPD

18. In the case under consideration, the Committee is not asked to decide whether a State Party violates Article 32 CRPD if it does not contribute to (primary) education for children with disabilities through its development cooperation. The question that presents itself in the case under consideration is not whether there is an extraterritorial obligation to fulfil, but whether the *withdrawal* of development funding that benefited (primary) education for children with disabilities (who are victims of armed conflict) is in violation with Article 32 *juncto* Articles 16 and 24 CRPD.

19. Article 4 para. 2 CRPD spells out the obligations of States Parties with regard to economic, social and cultural rights in particular. In line with Article 2 para. 1 ICESCR and Article 4 CRC, States Parties are said to be under an obligation to take measures for the realisation of economic, social and cultural rights to the maximum of their available resources with a view to achieving progressively the full realisation of these rights in the Convention.

Litigating Transnational Human Rights Obligations 183

The notion of progressive realisation has been understood by other monitoring bodies, including the Committee on Economic, Social and Cultural Rights (CESCR) and the Committee on the Rights of the Child (CRC Committee), to exclude in principle any *retrogressive* measures. In CESCR's view, "there is a strong presumption of impermissibility of any retrogressive measures taken in relation to the right to education" (CESCR, *General Comment No. 13 (1999) on the right to education*, para. 45). If deliberately retrogressive measures are taken, a State "has the burden of proving that they have been introduced after the most careful consideration of all alternatives and that they are duly justified by reference to the totality of rights provided for in the Covenant in the context of the full use of the State Party's maximum available resources" (*Ibid.*). The CRC Committee has endorsed CESCR's analysis (CRC Committee, *General Comment No. 5 (2003) on general measures of implementation of the CRC*, para. 5).

In its 2007 Statement on available resources, CESCR has clarified how it will assess a State's claim that resource constraints justify retrogressive measures under the OP ICESCR. It will make a country-specific assessment in light of the level of development; the severity of the alleged breach (in particular whether the minimum core content is at stake); the country's economic situation; the existence of other serious claims on the State's resources; whether the State has sought to identify low-cost options; and whether it has sought cooperation and assistance or rejected offers of resources without sufficient reason (CESCR, *Statement: An evaluation of the obligation to take steps to the "maximum of available resources" under an optional protocol to the Covenant*, para. 10). These criteria can *mutatis mutandis* also be applied to extraterritorial States, except for the final one on cooperation and assistance.

The Committee sees no reason to adopt a different view on the issue than the CESCR. The question before the Committee is therefore, on the one hand, what E's economic situation was and which claims were laid on E's resources, and, on the other hand, how serious the alleged breach was. As to the first question, E has clearly been seriously affected by the global economic crisis and recession. While in times of recession and fiscal austerity all kinds of claims for internal purposes are undoubtedly laid on a country's resources, it should be kept in mind that development cooperation represents only a small share of the overall budget. Moreover, no attempt seems to have been made to identify low-cost options or less detrimental savings in the development cooperation budget. These resource considerations need to be balanced against the severity of the alleged breach. To the latter question we will now turn.

20. The withdrawal of E's development cooperation funding concerned primary education for disabled children. Primary education has a special place in the overall scheme of human rights protection in general, and of economic, social and cultural rights in particular. First of all, it has been

184　*Development Assistance to Education for Children with Disabilities*

made clear that the obligation to provide primary education for all is an *immediate* duty, i.e., it is not subject to progressive realization. Likewise, the prohibition against discrimination is subject to neither progressive realization nor the availability of resources (CESCR, *General Comment No. 13 (1999) on the right to education*, para. 51). Article 4, para. 2 CRPD is unique in explicitly acknowledging that some economic, social and cultural rights obligations are *immediately* applicable under international law, and therefore not subject to the general qualification of progressive realisation. Secondly, the prohibition against discrimination in Article 5 CRPD is subject to neither progressive realization nor the availability of resources (CESCR, *General Comment No. 13 (1999) on the right to education, para. 31*). Thirdly, both non-discriminatory access to education and the provision of free primary education are considered to be minimum core obligations (CESCR, *General Comment No. 13 (1999) on the right to education*, para. 57). As CESCR has stated repeatedly (see e.g. CESCR, *General Comment No. 14 (2000) on the right to the highest attainable standard of health*, para. 45), and as reconfirmed by the Maastricht Principles, core obligations and the realization of the rights of disadvantaged and vulnerable groups must be prioritized (Principle 32).

21. Moreover, E does not seem to have considered alternative measures to disinvestment, or a gradual phasing out of development assistance. Nor does it seem to have looked for coordination with other donor countries, e.g. in order to mitigate the consequences of its own disinvestment in primary education for disabled children in A. The retrogressive measures under consideration might therefore also be challenged in light of the doctrine of legitimate expectations[13] and the good donor principle of the predictability of aid.

22. In light of the above, in weighing the resource constraints against the crucial importance of equal access to primary education for children with disabilities and the lack of consideration of alternative measures – including a gradual phasing out and coordination with other donors – the balance clearly tilts towards the importance of the right at stake. Such a balancing exercise does not work out differently in cases of extraterritorial obligations. The Committee therefore concludes that the retrogressive measures taken by E in ending its support for primary education for disabled children in A cannot be justified by invoking resource constraints.

23. The argument that E took these retrogressive measures because A no longer showed a commitment towards primary education for disabled children, in full recognition of A's ownership of its own development, is

---

13 See for the UK, e.g. 9 July 2008 in R (Bhatt Murphy (a firm) and others v Independent Assessor; R (Niazi and others) v Secretary of State for the Home Department [2008] EWCA Civ 755. The European Court of Human Rights has used this doctrine in its interpretation of the right to property.

misconceived. It is debatable whether E's interpretation of ownership corresponds to what was meant in the Paris Declaration. But even assuming that such an ill-conceived meaning was indeed given to the notion of country ownership in the Paris Declaration, it cannot be construed in violation of international human rights obligations. As CESCR has pointed out, when negotiating or concluding international agreements, States must ensure that these agreements do not adversely impact on the right to education (CESCR, *General Comment No. 13 (1999) on the right to education*, para. 56). This has been echoed in Principle 17 Maastricht Principles.

Moreover, Principle 21 of the Maastricht Principles clarifies that States must refrain from conduct that aids or assists another State to breach that State's obligations as regards economic, social and cultural rights, where the former State does so with knowledge of the circumstances of the act. Applied to the case under consideration, E, by giving in to A's policy to exclude disabled children from education because of suspected loyalty to the armed groups to which most of them used to belong, clearly assisted A in breaching its obligations not to discriminate and to provide primary education to disabled children, and did so in full knowledge of the facts, for A has never concealed its motives to E.

24. The Committee therefore concludes that E has violated Article 32 CRPD, read alone and in conjunction with Articles 16 and 24 CRPD. A similar conclusion could have been reached had the Committee been asked to assess E's conduct under the negative obligation to avoid causing harm. Given the foreseeable effects of its disinvestment, E has violated the obligation to avoid causing harm (compare Principle 13 Maastricht Principles).

25. By holding E in violation of the CRPD, the Committee does not exclude that A has (also) committed an internationally wrongful act. In the Committee's view, the CRPD establishes a regime of shared responsibility for the realization of the rights of persons with disabilities. As Article 32, para. 2 CRPD stipulates, the provisions on international cooperation are without prejudice to the obligations of *each* State Party to fulfil its obligations. In particular, A may be under an obligation to mitigate the negative impact of donor disinvestment. However, as the complainants did not lodge a complaint against A, it is not for the Committee to examine *suo moto* A's acts and omissions in light of the CRPD.

At the same time, in the absence of a complaint against one or more States which may bear part of the responsibility for a violation under a regime of shared responsibility, the Committee is not barred from examining the complaint and from holding a State against which a complaint was lodged, responsible for that violation.

12 Land Grabbing in Uganda by a Multinational Corporation (World Court of Human Rights)

Christopher Mbazira

Abstract

Although natural disasters such as floods and landslides have contributed to landlessness, evictions take the biggest share of the blame in many parts of world. Large scale evictions have been carried out to pave way for large scale investment. Many times victims of these usually illegal and forced evictions do not access justice, yet in some cases the State is an accomplice to the evictions. Uganda has not been spared from this trend; the country has witnessed large scale evictions sometimes perpetrated by the State to create room for private capital investment. One such eye-catching case was the 2001 eviction of over 2000 people in Mubende District to create room for the establishment of a large scale coffee firm owned by the German-based Neumann Kaffee Gruppe. It is cases of this nature that motivated the adoption of the Maastricht Principles on Extra-Territorial Obligations of States in the area of Economic, Social and Cultural Rights. This hypothetical judgment, guided by the Mubende *case, is intended to put to hypothetical test the ETO Principles. The failure of the Uganda judicial system to deliver timely remedies for the victims and the failure of the Government of Uganda to address the plight of the victims necessitates the activation of the extra-territorial obligations of Germany to ensure that the victims get justice, Neumann Kaffee Gruppe being a German-based corporation.*

Introductory note

In September 2011, a consortium of experts in international law and human rights convened in the historical city of Maastricht, The Netherlands and adopted the *Maastricht Principles on Extra-Territorial Obligations (ETOs) of States in the area of Economic, Social and Cultural Rights.* The ETO principles affirm the principle that States are under a duty to cooperate and assist each other in ensuring the realization of the economic, social and cultural rights guaranteed under international human rights law. Secondly, the Principles affirm that under international law, a State may be held responsible for human rights violations that may occur outside its territory as a result of its commissions or omissions.

Litigating Transnational Human Rights Obligations 187

One of the cases used as a case-study throughout the processes of developing the ETOs by the experts was the *Mubende* case in Uganda, a case involving the eviction of over 2000 people in 2001 to pave way for the establishment of a large commercial coffee plantation. The plantation is owned by a Ugandan subsidiary of a German company, Neumann Kaffee Gruppe. The evictees were neither adequately and promptly compensated as required by international law nor provided with alternative land, leaving them landless and hopeless. Attempts by the evictees to get justice in Uganda have been futile; their case has been pending in the High Court of Uganda for close to 10 years without a hearing. Attempts to get justice on behalf of the evictees through the Organization for Economic Cooperation and Development (OECD) Guidelines for Multinational Enterprises have also proved futile.

The purpose of this chapter is to use *Mubende* to build a hypothetical case in which the ETO Principles are applied for the benefit of the evictees. The forum used, the International Human Rights Court, is also a hypothetical forum, inspired by the ongoing debates to establish such court. The judgment in this chapter is therefore hypothetical. Nonetheless, in reality, the ETO Principles can be applied in both domestic and international regional fora.

It is important that one contextualizes the hypothetical judgment by understanding the position of international law as regards forced evictions, and particularly those which are induced by large-scale investment. As a matter of fact, one cannot find specific principles of general international law which address the problem of forced evictions induced by investment. However, there are principles that can be located in international human rights law. Human rights law does not stand in the way of development or investment but only requires that development be guided by the human rights-based approach (HRBA). HRBA is intended to translate human rights from rhetoric to reality by entrenching the realization of economic and social rights as part and parcel of development. The approach pays attention to the principle of the indivisibility of rights and provides the tools to operationalize human rights in the economic sphere.[1] It has been argued that the rights-based approach to development is grounded in the acceptance of human rights standards as an important basis for development policy and the recognition that human rights accountability can be used to support development activities.[2] The approach defines the aim of development in a manner which translates the development enterprise into

---

1 Paul Gready, "Rights-Based Approach to Development: What is the Value-Added", (2008) *Development in Practice*, 735–47, at 737.
2 Michael Barutciski, "International Law and Development-induced Displacement and Resettlement", in Chris De Wet *Development-induced Displacement: Problems, Policies and Peoples* (2006) Berghahn Books 72, at 74

188   *Land Grabbing in Uganda by a Multinational Corporation*

claims, duties and mechanisms that can promote and adjudicate the violation of human rights.[3] In this context, it has been argued that "[t]he move from needs to rights, and from charity to duties, also implies an increased focus on accountability".[4]

HRBA has presented itself as a formidable tool to confront some of the shortcomings arising from the global enterprise of economic development and the facilitation of rapid movement of capital across borders, epitomized in the growing power of multinational corporations (MNCs). HRBA serves as an opportunity to reflect more broadly on the power dynamics inherent in the practice of international development.[5] The rapid movement of MNCs' capital from the North to the South has also come with a number of abuses, including serious human rights abuses such as environmental degradation, forced evictions leading to landlessness, and exploitation of labour. Unfortunately, victims of these violations have encountered major obstacles in seeking justice.[6] In most cases, the State in whose jurisdictions the violations take place is either an accomplice to the violations, tolerates them or is unable to regulate the MNCs.

Use of the HRBA will remind the State of its human rights obligations and the need to ensure that people's legitimate human rights claims are respected and accountability promoted. This, however, requires knowledge of the human rights standards to which the States have committed and which define the rights of people and obligations of the State.

As regards evictions, there are a number of applicable human rights standards. The subject of evictions needs to be understood in the context of the economic, social and cultural rights it impacts on. In 1997, the Commission on Human Rights characterized evictions in relation to their impact as follows:

> Forced evictions might not initially be viewed necessarily as an issue of human rights, but rather as a simple side-effect of development, of urban renewal, a consequence of armed conflict, or an aspect of environmental protection or energy generation by, for example, hydroelectric dams. However, to be persistently threatened or actually victimized by the act of forced eviction from one's home or land is surely one of the most supreme injustices any individual, family, household or community can face.[7]

---

3 Peter Uvin, "From the Right to Development to the Rights-Based Approach: How 'Human Rights' entered Development", (2007) 17 *Development Practice*, 597–606, at 602.

4 Id.

5 Andrea Cornwall & Celestin Nyamu-Musembi, "Putting the 'Rights-Based Approach' into Perspective", (2004) 25 *Third World Quarterly*, 1415–37, at 1418.

6 International Federation for Human Rights – FIDH *Corporate Accountability for Human Rights Abuses: A Guide for Victims and NGOs on Recourse Mechanisms* (2012), at 13.

7 Commission on Human Rights, Resolution 1993/77, para 1.

The practice of forced evictions has been defined as the involuntary removal of persons from their homes or land, directly or indirectly attributable to the State. It entails the effective elimination of the possibility of an individual or group living in a particular house, residence or place and sometimes involves irreparable demolition of people's homes.[8] The practice has been described as sharing characteristics with such phenomena as internal displacement of persons, forced removal during armed conflict, ethnic cleansing, mass exodus, and refugee movements.[9]

The UN Committee on Economic, Social and Cultural Rights (UNCESCR) considers instances of forced eviction to be *prima facie* incompatible with the requirements of the Covenant and only justifiable in the most exceptional circumstances, and in accordance with the relevant principles of international law.[10] In addition to violating such economic and social rights as housing, food, health, education and the right to practise one's culture, forced evictions could also violate civil and political rights such as the right to life, the right to security of the person, the right to non-interference with privacy, family and home and the right to the peaceful enjoyment of possessions.[11] The Committee has defined the obligations of the State to include refraining from forced evictions and ensuring that the law is enforced against State agents or third parties who carry out forced evictions.[12] Additionally, it is the duty of States to ensure that prior to carrying out any evictions, and particularly those involving large groups, all feasible alternatives are explored in consultation with the affected persons, with a view to avoiding, or at least minimizing, the need to use force. Legal remedies or procedures should be provided to those who are affected by eviction orders. States parties shall also see to it that all the individuals concerned have a right to adequate compensation forany property, both personal and real, which is affected.[13]

The UNCESCR has also outlined guarantees that must be put in place before and after a forced eviction: (a) an opportunity for genuine consultation with those affected; (b) adequate and reasonable notice for all affected persons prior to the scheduled date of eviction; (c) information on the proposed evictions, and, where applicable, on the alternative purpose for which the land or housing is to be used, to be made available in reasonable

---

8 United Nations Office of the Commissioner for Human Rights, *Fact Sheet No. 25, Forced Evictions and Human Rights.*

9 Id.

10 UN Committee on Economic, Social and Cultural Rights, *General Comment No. 4: The right to adequate housing (Art. 11 (1) of the Covenant)*, E/1992/23 Sixth Session, para 18.

11 UN Committee on Economic, Social and Cultural Rights, *General Comment No. 7: The right to adequate housing (Art. 11 (1) of the Covenant): Forced evictions*, E/1998/22, Sixteenth Session, para 4.

12 Id, para 8.

13 UNESCR, General Comment No. 7, para 13.

190   *Land Grabbing in Uganda by a Multinational Corporation*

time to all those affected; (d) especially where groups of people are involved, government officials or their representatives to be present during an eviction; (e) all persons carrying out the eviction to be properly identified; (f) evictions not to take place in particularly bad weather or at night unless the affected persons consent otherwise; (g) provision of legal remedies; and (h) provision, where possible, of legal aid to persons who are in need of it to seek redress from the courts.[14]

At the national levels, forced evictions are prevalent in all parts of the world and are inducted by the need to create room for international events such as conferences and sports events, development of infrastructure projects, urban development (including beautification of cities), and political conflicts resulting in displacement.[15] In juridical terms, the subject of forced evictions has produced substantial jurisprudence from both international and domestic courts and tribunals. In Europe, the European Court of Human Rights has held that where an individual has an arguable claim that his or her home and possessions have been purposely destroyed by agents of the State, the notion of an "effective remedy" entails, in addition to the payment of compensation where appropriate, a thorough and effective investigation capable of leading to the identification and punishment of those responsible.[16] In the case of *Social and Economic Rights Action Centre & Anor v Nigeria*,[17] the African Commission on Human and Peoples' Rights found that an eviction carried out by the Government of Nigeria to support the investment of Shell violated provisions of the African Charter on Human and Peoples' Rights, including those protecting the rights to development, shelter and food. The African Commission has also condemned Kenya for evicting an indigenous population to create a nature protection area.[18] In South Africa, the Constitutional Court has looked at evictions in the context of the duty to the state to ensure that every person has access to adequate housing and the protection against forced evictions.[19] In India, the Court has stopped evictions that would compromise people's livelihoods thereby infringing their right to life.[20] In Botswana, the Court of

---

14 UNESCR, General Comment No. 7, para 15.

15 See Malcolm Langford and Jean du Plessis, *Dignity in the Rubble? Forced Evictions and Human Rights Law*, available at http://www.escr-net.org/usr_doc/dignity_in_the_rubble_-_forced_evictions_and_human_rights_law_2006.pdf (accessed on 19 April 2013).

16 See *Menteş and Others v. Turkey*, Application No. 23186/94, 28 November 1997, para. 89

17 Communication 155/96.

18 Centre for Minority Rights Development (Kenya) and Minority Rights Group International on behalf of Endorois Welfare Council v. Kenya, 276/2003

19 See, *Government of the Republic of South Africa & Ors v Grootboom & Ors* 2000 (11) BCLR 1169. (CC); *Port Elizabeth Municipality v Various Occupiers* 2004 (12) BCLR 1268 (CC); and *President of the Republic of South Africa and Another v Modderklip Boerdery* (Pty) Ltd 2005 (8) BCLR 786 (CC) (13 May 2005).

20 See *Olga Tellis & Ors v Bombay Municipal Council* [1985] 2 Supp SCR 51; and *Ain o Salish Kendra (ASK) v Government and Bangladesh & Ors* 19 BLD (1999) 488.

Litigating Transnational Human Rights Obligations 191

Appeal ordered the return of the Basarwa people to their ancestral location from which they had been evicted.[21]

The World Court of Human Rights

The hypothetical judgment presented in this chapter is a decision of the hypothetical World Court of Human Rights, a yet to be established court. The use of the World Court of Human Rights by the chapter is not intended to discuss the proposed Court; rather it is intended to illustrate the possibility of the Court, once established, using the ETO principles to adjudicate cases. For this purpose, it is important to briefly discuss the idea of the World Court in order to put the hypothetical judgment in its proper context.

The idea of establishing a World Court of Human Rights dates as far back as 1947 and was indeed one of the first items on the agenda of the United Nations Commission on Human Rights after its inauguration.[22] In the Commission, the proposal was made by a draft resolution brought by Australia, proposing that the Court would have jurisdiction to entertain complaints against State parties to the then envisaged International Covenant on Civil and Political Rights. Later, a Working Group of the Commission supported the idea. However, the idea was torpedoed in the Commission and was superseded with the establishment of treaty monitoring bodies with a certain level of quasi-judicial power. The idea was indeed buried during the time of the Cold War. However, the rejuvenation of human rights in the 1990s resurrected the idea, with the proposal being mooted at the 1993 World Conference on Human Rights, just as it had been at the 1968 World Conference on Human Rights.[23] The idea was resurrected with visible force in 2008 when Switzerland declared that was one of the items of the *Swiss Agenda for Human Rights*.

A number of proposals have been made regarding the structure which the Court should take. The different models proposed include the pyramid model, the ICC model and the sibling model. The pyramid model proposes the establishment of a court which is part of a pyramid that contains the various regional courts and which would have the World Court as the superior court at the top of the pyramid as the ultimate court of appeal.[24] The International Criminal Court (ICC) model envisages a court established by statute like the ICC, with jurisdiction over states that are party to the statute.

---

21 See *Mosetlhanyane and others v. Attorney General of Botswana*, Civil Appeal No. CACLB-074-10.
22 International Commission of Jurists, *Toward a World Court of Human Rights: Questions and Answers*, Supporting Paper to the 2011 Report of the Panel on Human Dignity, available at <http://www.udhr60.ch/docs/World-court-final1211%20.pdf> (accessed on 20 April 2013), at 3.
23 Id, at 4.
24 See Stephan Trechsel, "A World Court for Human Rights", (2004) 1 *Northwestern University Journal of International Law* 3.

192 *Land Grabbing in Uganda by a Multinational Corporation*

Finally, the sibling model would follow the International Court of Justice model and would require an amendment of the Charter of the United Nations.[25] With Swiss support, a Draft Statute for the Court has been drawn. The Draft Statute proposes a permanent court with permanent judges and would enforce all international human rights treaties signed by the respondent State.

The Statute has attracted support, with one of the advocates for the Court being Manfred Nowak, former United Nations Special Rapporteur on Torture, who advanced the following reasons:[26] legal rights without a remedy are empty promises; the UN Human Rights complaint mechanisms still reflect the logic of the Cold War and are no more than non-binding opinions; the UN can learn from regional organizations which have created courts to monitor and enforce the respect of human rights by States; the establishment of the UN Human Rights Council, although a welcome innovation, has shifted its balance towards a state-centred process and it has few tools and mechanisms to protect human rights; the Court will operate under the principle of complementarity, leaving national courts as the first option.

Case

In the World Court of Human Rights

Extra-Territorial Obligations

2000 Mubende residents (Complainants)
vs
Federal Republic of Germany (Respondent)

Judgment of Court

A. Facts of the Case

1. The facts detailed below are found in the petition filed before this Court by the Petitioners. An assessment of all the evidence submitted by the complainants and rebutted by the respondent reveals that the facts as stated here have been established. This conclusion is based on the

---

25 Id.
26 See Tim Siegenbeek Van Heukelom *A World Court of Human Rights?*, available at http://www.lowyinterpreter.org/post/2010/05/28/A-World-Court-of-Human-Rights.aspx (accessed on 20 April 2013). See also Manfred Nowak and Julia Kozma, *A World Court of Human Rights*, available at http://www.eui.eu/Documents/DepartmentsCentres/Academy ofEuropeanLaw/CourseMaterialsHR/HR2009/Scheinin/ScheininClassReading2.pdf (accessed on 20 April 2013).

Litigating Transnational Human Rights Obligations 193

affidavits which were submitted by the complainants and the oral evidence which was presented before the Court. Reports authored by the government of Uganda on the subject have also been considered and found to provide evidence proving the veracity of the allegations as stated by the complainants. One should note from the start that we are dealing with poor, marginalized, vulnerable and illiterate peasant farmers. It is impressive that this community managed to organize their evidence in a coherent manner. The assistance of local and international organizations provided to the complainants also needs to be acknowledged.

2. The case arises from unfortunate events that occurred between 17 and 21 August 2001 in the Naluwondwa Madudu village in the Mubende District in Uganda, where over 390 families, comprising the complainants, were forcefully evicted by the Government of Uganda. The eviction, which affected over 2000 people, was carried out for the purposes of creating room for the establishment of a large coffee plantation owned by the German multinational corporation Neumann Kaffee Gruppe (NKG), through a local Ugandan subsidiary, Kaweri Coffee Plantation Limited. NKG, which was awarded a lease of 99 years on the land totalling approximately 11 sq miles (approx. 2500 hectares of land).

3. The eviction process was brutal and carried out by the military under the directions of the Resident District Commission (RDC) of Mubende District, one Pereze Katamba. People were forcibly removed from their lands at gunpoint, their houses set on fire and property looted. Those who put up resistance were beaten and others detained. Five people actually lost their lives in the process. Six churches and a private clinic were among the properties that were destroyed. A primary school, Kitemba Primary School, was converted into the headquarters of Kaweri Coffee, with school children being confined to a small area of the school land. As a result, many farmers instantly became homeless and lost their sources of livelihood. The community lost access to water, food, shelter, health care and education.

4. In the Affidavit of one of the Complaints, Affidavit C2, this is how the situation of the evictees has been summarized:

> The eviction caused all the people affected to suffer starvation. The evictees took to living in forests and in makeshift shelters and had no food and no clean water as all the boreholes had been left behind in the land from which they were evicted. Many children and the elderly who could not cope with chilly conditions of the forest died in the aftermath of this monstrous catastrophe.

5. Indeed, the precarious situation of the people who were the subject of the eviction has been recorded in an official government report. Immediately after the eviction, the Uganda Ministry of Finance, Planning and Economic Development, through a programme entitled *Uganda Participatory Poverty Assessment Process* (UPPAP), carried out a

194 *Land Grabbing in Uganda by a Multinational Corporation*

fact-finding mission in the area affected by the eviction. UPPAP was initiated as part of the implementation of the Poverty Eradication Action Plan (PEAP), a programme the government of Uganda has adopted as a way of eradicating the high incidence of poverty. The UPPAP was intended as a way of furthering consultation on PEAP and deepening its impact. Kitemba village was selected as one of the sites for a UPPAP study.

6. The UPPAP Report gives this rationale for the case study:

Kitembe village was selected because it represents a case study of people who have been internally displaced due to foreign investment development and as a consequence of the Land Act 1998. Currently, demand for and the price of land have increased and most landlords would like to sell off their [land] as a way of dealing with squatters. It is also government policy to give priority in land allocation to investors, especially to the foreign ones, in order to attract big capital investments that are seen as a springboard to further economic development in Uganda.[27]

7. The eviction took place four days before the President, His Excellency Yoweri Kaguta Museveni, travelled to Mubende to officially commission the coffee plantation on 24 August 2001. In his address, the President praised local government officials for what they had done in acquiring the land.[28]

8. The Ministry of Finance Report describes the eviction as "The great shock";[29] the Report also describes as "strange" the fact that the eviction was carried out by the army and not the police or court bailiffs and observes that "the process of eviction was bedevilled by lack of transparency and poor information flow".[30] Regarding the conduct of the local leaders, the Report observes that lack of commitment by local leaders caused more confusion than it resolved and that the lack of a clear flow of information escalated the crisis.

9. According to the UPPAP Report, there was no preparedness whatsoever: the district did not ensure that the local people duly understood the investment, the lease, and who the *bona fide* tenants were. Yet, people's property was not valued and the squatters were left to the whims of the former landlord and his agents.[31]

10. The UPPAP Report categorizes the consequences of the eviction to include property destruction, loss of food, loss of social services,

---

27 Ministry of Finance, Planning and Economic Development, *Uganda Participatory Poverty Assessment Process (UPPAP), Kitemba Site Report, Madudu Sub-County, Mubende District,* at 3.

28 See Memorandum written by one of the evictees, Baleke Peter Kayiira, addressed to the Speaker of Parliament, dated 17 October 2001.

29 At p. 13.

30 At p. 14.

31 At p. 15.

Litigating Transnational Human Rights Obligations 195

increased morbidity and mortality, loss of status and the break-down of social support systems, overcrowding and increased alcoholic consumption.[32] On morbidity, the Report shows that four children died due to harsh conditions, and during the eviction some people were maimed, the case of a child who broke her leg, which was later amputated, is also referred to. In one case a man who tried to resist the eviction and was beaten by the soldiers died a few days after the eviction.[33] The deaths have also been attributed to the increased level of morbidity, which is attributed to the destruction of clinics and drug shops which occurred during the evictions.[34] At the present time, the evictees live on the border of the coffee plantation on small plots of land which are not enough for them to produce sufficient food and sell the excess to get money for their upkeep and for the payment of such services as health care and education for their children.

B. The Context: Land Tenure and Laws

11. In order to appreciate the human rights violations perpetrated on the complainants in this case, it is important to appreciate Uganda's legal context as it is applicable to land management. The eviction also needs to be understood in the context of the land tenure system as prescribed by the country's land laws. The historical context and how the land laws have developed remain relevant in this regard. This legal exposition shows that Uganda failed to follow its own laws, and as will be seen later, even failed to provide legal remedies to people whose domestically protected rights have been violated. The position of Uganda's law referred to here has been established by this Court by examining domestic legislation. Expert evidence has also been considered as provided at the request of this Court.

12. Before becoming a British colony, the place now called Uganda existed with separate communities in the form of kingdoms and chiefdoms. Generally in these communities, land was governed under a system of customary laws. What was common is that land was communally owned and in some cases only vested in the king or chief as a trustee for the benefit of the community. In some parts of the country, especially the central region, this system was distorted by the colonial government. By the 1900 agreement, the King of Buganda signed off a portion of his kingdom and gave it away to the colonial state as crown land. The remainder of the land came to be known as *mailo* (a local word for the

---

32 At p. 16.
33 See Action Aid Effects of MNCs on Food Security: The Case of Neumann Kaffe Group in Mubende District, Uganda (2008), at p. 26.
34 As above, at p. 30.

196　*Land Grabbing in Uganda by a Multinational Corporation*

distance measure "mile"), which was to be managed under the English equivalent of the Torrens system. Under this system, the government started issuing certificates of title to individuals, who initially were mainly comprised of persons with royal roots or connections, including chiefs. However, most of the land in respect of which titles were issued had squatters, who had initially settled on such land as subjects of the King of Buganda. In return for some form of security, the tenants were legally obliged to pay the landlords annual rent and part of their harvest.

13. In 1975, the government, then under the leadership of Idi Amin, nationalized all land, making the same public land in respect of which only leases would be issued by the state. This system operated until the coming into force of the 1995 Constitution. The 1995 Constitution in Article 26 guarantees the right to property. Article 237(1) provides that land belongs to the people and shall vest in them in accordance with a land tenure system defined by the Constitution. The land tenure system recognized in Article 237(3) of the Constitution includes: customary, freehold, *mailo* and leasehold.

14. To protect the squatters, the Constitution in Article 237(8) provided that upon the coming into force of the Constitution and until Parliament enacts an appropriate law, *lawful* or *bona fide* occupants of *mailo* land, freehold or leasehold land shall enjoy security of occupancy on the land. In 1998, the Land Act was adopted by Parliament to provide for the protection of lawful and *bona fide* occupants. The relevant provision is section 29, which provides:

29. Meaning of "lawful occupant" and "*bona fide* occupant".

(1) "Lawful occupant" means –

    (a) a person occupying land by virtue of the repealed –

        (i)   Busuulu and Envujjo Law of 1928;

        (ii) Toro Landlord and Tenant Law of 1937;

        (iii) Ankole Landlord and Tenant Law of 1937;

    (b) a person who entered the land with the consent of the registered owner, and includes a purchaser; or

    (c) a person who had occupied land as a customary tenant but whose tenancy was not disclosed or compensated for by the registered owner at the time of acquiring the leasehold certificate of title.

(2) "*Bona fide* occupant" means a person who before the coming into force of the Constitution –

    (a) had occupied and utilized or developed any land unchallenged by the registered owner or agent of the registered owner for twelve years or more; or

    (b) had been settled on land by the Government or an agent of the Government, which may include a local authority.

Litigating Transnational Human Rights Obligations 197

15. In the law, both lawful and *bona fide* occupants are collectively referred to as "Tenants by occupancy" and are guaranteed security of tenure. The tenants are legally obliged to pay to the landlord a nominal annual rent determined by government.[35] A 2010 amendment of the Land Act introduced a provision to the effect that a tenant by occupancy can only be evicted for non-payment of rent.[36] Section 35 provides that both tenant and landlord when selling shall give the first option to buy to the tenant or the landlord as the case may be.

C. Justice Denied in the National Courts and Domestic Legal Process

16. The jurisdiction of Court over this matter, as indicated in its founding law, is based on the absence of remedies at the domestic levels. All evidence on record shows that rather than sitting back indolently and suffering hopeless solace, the complainants tried to avail themselves of the domestic political and legal processes. Having suffered failure at the hands of the same political processes that had authorized the eviction in the first place, the complainants decided to take advantage of the judicial process. However, as the exposition below will show, no relief came out of this process.

17. In 2009, FIAN International, a non-governmental organization based in Germany and working on the promotion and protection of the right to food in various parts of the world, tried to get relief for the evictees. FIAN assisted the evictees in filing a formal complaint under the Organization for Economic Cooperation and Development (OECD) Guidelines for Multinational Enterprises. It was argued that the NKG was informed of and benefitted from human rights violations in the form of forced evictions and the accompanying destruction of property without compensation. The complaint was filed through Germany's National Contact Point (NCP) for OECD Guidelines for Multinational Enterprises, which is based in the German Federal Department of Trade and Industry. Unfortunately, no redress came out of this process. The NCP in August 2011 declared closure of the complaint procedure against NKG and did not order any redress.[37]

18. In Uganda, efforts to get domestic remedies started back in 2002 when the evicted community, through representatives, instituted a case against the Attorney General and Kaweri Coffee Plantation in High Court Civil Suit No. 179 of 2002. In the case, the Plaintiffs challenged

---

35 See section 31 of the Land Act.
36 Section 32A.
37 Anton Pieper, *Undermining the Accountability Process – the Mubende-Neumann Case* available at http://www.fian.org/cases/cases2/mubende-uganda-coffee-plant-by-neumann/pdf (accessed on 16 July 2012).

198 *Land Grabbing in Uganda by a Multinational Corporation*

the eviction and demanded compensation and restitution. The legal basis of the suit is that the evictees were *bona fide* occupants entitled to security of tenure and legal protection against the eviction. However, ten years later the case has still not been heard. Initially, the Attorney General and Kaweri Coffee sought to defeat the case by applying for security of costs from the Plaintiffs. Under Ugandan law, a respondent to a case can apply for security for costs if he or she can prove that the plaintiff is unlikely to have the means to pay the costs of the case should he or she lose the matter. Failure to furnish security as ordered by the court results in the suit being dismissed. The plaintiffs were only able to raise the necessary security with the help of civil society.

19. The delay that has been experienced in this case, while symptomatic of the inefficiency of the country's justice system, is also extra-ordinary, as will be shown. Case backlogs have been described as the elephant in Uganda's Justice, Law and Order Sector.[38] One of the causes of case backlogs in Uganda's judicial system has been the lack of adequate numbers of judicial officers. For a very long time, there have been indications of the lack of political will to appoint sufficient numbers of judicial officers. Although the government has reported significant progress in reducing the backlogs, the Mubende case shows that some still fall through the cracks. This case has been adjourned countless times and has repeatedly been transferred between different judges. The situation of the High Court shows a fundamental weakness in the national judicial system and the inability, and perhaps an unwillingness, of the system to address human rights violations of the nature shown in this case.

20. The delay has had a negative impact on the evictees, who have waited for justice for close to ten years. To them, this reminds them of the words of the RDC before the eviction when he said that the evictees are free to sue but they will wait for justice for 30 years, and some of them will be dead even before the case is decided.

D. Application of ETO Principles to the Case

21. The German government has through its legal representative put up a spirited fight, arguing in the main that it is not responsible for violations committed outside of its territory, even when these are committed by its own citizens, in this case NKG. In rebuttal, the complainants have relied on the recently published Maastricht Principles on Extra-Territorial Obligations of States in the Area of Economic, Social and Cultural Rights (ETO principles).

---

38 Paul Gadenya, *The Role of the JLOS Case Backlog Reduction Programme, Achievements and Lessons Learned*, Justice, Law and Order Sector.

Litigating Transnational Human Rights Obligations 199

22. The ETO Principles, adopted by a group of public international law and human rights law experts, have assumed the same status as the Limburg Principles for the Implementation of the International Covenant on Economic, Social and Cultural Rights (1986) and the Maastricht Guidelines on Violations of Economic, Social and Cultural Rights (1997). These principles have recently been given a positive nod by the United Nations.[39] The Court therefore relied on these principles to establish the extraterritorial obligations of Germany to protect human rights outside its territory. These Principles are a progressive and nuanced interpretation of existing international law as reflected in a number of international treaties, including international human rights law treaties.

23. The extraterritorial obligations activated in this case have to be understood against the background of the rights violated. The eviction resulted in the violation of a number of internationally protected human rights, civil and political and economic, social and cultural rights alike. The force used in the eviction violated a number of civil and political rights including: security of the person, freedom from torture, the right to life, among others. In addition, there were a number of violations of economic, social and cultural rights, including the right to: an adequate standard of living, food, water, housing, physical and mental health, economic and social development and cultural rights. In addition, some families lost burial grounds, which are sacred in many Ugandan communities. Both official and unofficial reports indicate that the eviction has escalated poverty in the area of Mubende, arising mainly from the loss of land, a vital means of livelihood in Uganda where many communities survive on subsistence farming.

24. What makes the ETO Principles applicable to this case is the fact that the coffee plantation established on the land from which poor people were evicted is owned by NKG, and yet the evidence shows Neumann's great involvement in the eviction and all attendant violation which has been done through its Ugandan subsidiary, Kaweri Coffee. Thus, when one pierces the corporate veil, Kaweri Coffee is but a direct shadow of NKG. This fact activates the ETOs of Germany, the country in which Neumann Kaffee is registered and has its home. ETO Principle No. 23 requires states to take action, separately and jointly through international cooperation, to protect economic, social and cultural rights of persons within their territories and extraterritorially. With regard to

---

39 See *Analytical Study on the Relationship between Human Rights and the Environment: Report of the United Nations High Commissioner for Human Rights Human Rights Council:* Nineteenth session Agenda items 2 and Annual report of the United Nations High Commissioner for Human Rights and reports of the Office of the High Commissioner and the Secretary-General.

200 *Land Grabbing in Uganda by a Multinational Corporation*

non-State actors, ETO Principle No. 24 imposes on States an obligation to regulate:

> All States must take necessary measures to ensure that non-State actors which they are in a position to regulate, as set out in Principle 25, such as private individuals and organizations, and transnational corporations and other business enterprises, do not nullify or impair the enjoyment of economic, social and cultural rights. These include administrative, legislative, investigative, adjudicatory and other measures. All other States have a duty to refrain from nullifying or impairing the discharge of this obligation to protect.

25. Principle 25 defines the bases of the obligation above by describing the circumstances under which the obligation of the State to take measures is activated. The circumstances include: "where the non-State actor has the nationality of the State concerned"; "as regards business enterprises, where the corporation, or its parent or controlling company, has its centre of activity, is registered or domiciled, or has its main place of business or substantial business activities, in the State concerned"; or "where there is a reasonable link between the State concerned and the conduct it seeks to regulate, including where relevant aspects of a non-State actor's activities are carried out in that State's territory".

26. In this case, all the evidence points to Germany's failure to take timely and meaningful steps to stop NKG from violating the rights of poor and vulnerable people through land grabbing. The evidence points to German's awareness of what was happening in Uganda. Yet, there is no evidence that Germany tried to take any measures against NKG, let alone engage the Ugandan government with a view to prevailing over the latter to undertake corrective remedial measures. The Uganda government should have used its legal framework to stop the eviction, or at the very least to ensure that those affected by the eviction are adequately compensated. Unfortunately, this is not a case where the government simply failed in its protective mandate, but was itself one of the violators. The eviction was carried out in a brutal manner by government forces commanded by the Resident District Commissioner, a direct representative of the President. Yet, the hasty manner of the eviction was intended to pave the way for the President to come and commission the multi-million dollar investment.

It is clear from the evidence from the events before and after the eviction that the evictees were not likely to get remedies in Uganda, where the government was itself the violator. All the events immediately before and after the eviction show that the chances of the evictees getting justice in Uganda were slim. Additionally, the country's legal system is slow to deliver any meaningful and timely remedies. Indeed, the case brought by the complainants has been pending in the courts for over ten years. Yet, throughout the case, Germany has not intervened in accordance with its ETOs as elaborated above, which amounts to a violation.

E. Conclusion and Orders

27. In light of the above, it is the conclusion of this Court that Germany has violated its obligations towards the complainants by failing to regulate the activities of NKG. Indeed, the evidence on record shows that the complainants and several actors tried through the Embassy of Germany in Uganda to bring the violations to the attention of the German government and they sought intervention of the latter. In spite of this, the German government abdicated its responsibilities by not taking any action against NKG and demanding that they indemnify the complainants.
28. As required by principle 25, referenced above, there was a direct link between NKG and the German government. The latter is a corporation registered in Germany and over which the latter should have exercised control to stop the violation or to ensure restitution where the violation had already occurred. The evidence shows that the violations were instigated by the NKG's shadow, Kaweri Coffee, which even provided logistical support to the forces that carried out the eviction. The situation was appropriately brought to the attention of the German government, yet nothing was done.

13 Structural Adjustment and Farmers' Suicides in India (International Court of Justice)

Amita Punj

Abstract

In the past decade and a half, some 250,000 farmers in India have committed suicide. According to social scientists, this is the direct result of factors cumulatively arising out of structural adjustment policies implemented by the IMF and the World Bank. In the following hypothetical opinion, India has been able to pass a resolution in the Economic and Social Council of the United Nations requesting an advisory opinion from the International Court of Justice pursuant to Article 96 paragraph 2 of the Charter of the United Nations. The opinion is sought on the following questions:

1. *Whether the International Bank for Reconstruction and Development (World Bank) and the International Monetary Fund (IMF), two specialized agencies of the UN, are under a legal obligation to respect the right to life while entering into loan agreements with States;*
2. *In the event of an affirmative reply on point 1, whether the suicides by farmers in India constitute a violation of the above stated legal obligation.*

Introductory note

In the past decade and a half, some 250,000 farmers in India have committed suicide.[1] These suicides are most pronounced in certain regions of the country and among farmers growing cash crops. The primary cause for these suicides is the increasing indebtedness of farmers, which in turn is an outcome of a set of policy changes that were introduced in India beginning in 1991.

One of these was trade liberalization, which subjected farmers to market uncertainty. Another policy was a sharp reduction in social spending and public investment, which led to an increase in the input costs of farmers. During the 1990s, controls on fertilizer prices were removed, resulting in

---

1 P. Sainath, "Of Luxury Cars and Lowly Tractors", *The Hindu*, 27 December 2010, available at http://www.thehindu.com/opinion/columns/sainath/article995828.ece?homepage=true

Litigating Transnational Human Rights Obligations 203

greatly escalating costs that negatively affected small-scale farmers. Reforms in the banking system to enhance the efficiency and profitability of that sector had an adverse effect on farmers' access to credit. From 1993 to 2007, 4,750 rural branches of scheduled commercial banks closed down[2] – or the equivalent of one branch every working day, which affected access to credit of nearly three quarters of the population of the country – while the number of banks in urban areas increased exponentially. In addition, credit costs are now vastly more expensive than they had been previously.

These policy changes were part of the structural adjustment programme instituted by the International Monetary Fund (IMF) and the International Bank for Reconstruction and Development (World Bank). What soon followed was this ever-increasing epidemic of farmer suicides. The following questions arise in this context:

1. Whether such suicides constitute a human rights violation.
2. Assuming a positive answer, the second question is who is the violator of the right – the State of India, the IMF or the World Bank? (This broad issue requires an analysis of the state of existing human rights law.)
3. The third question is if there is an international forum where the violation of such rights can be litigated.

The following Advisory Opinion of the International Court of Justice on "Legal Obligations of the IMF and the World Bank to Respect Right to Life of Farmers in India" focuses on these issues.

The International Court of Justice has been chosen in an attempt to emphasize its significance as an alternative forum for litigating extraterritorial human rights obligations, in addition to such institutions as the Human Rights Committee, the Committee on Economic, Social and Cultural Rights, or the Human Rights Council. The International Court of Justice is hypothetically considered to have been approached by the Economic and Social Council. The Economic and Social Council, entrusted with the task of "promoting respect for human rights"[3] and concerned with the "coordination of activities of the specialized agencies"[4] passes a resolution requesting the International Court of Justice to give an advisory opinion pursuant to Article 96 paragraph 2 of the Charter of the United Nations, which provides: "other organs of the United Nations ... may also request advisory opinions of the Court on legal questions arising within the scope of their activities".

---

2 *Handbook of Statistics on the Indian Economy, Reserve Bank of India, 2006–2007*, cited in P. Sainath, "4750 Rural Bank Branches Closed Down in 15 Years", *The Hindu*, 28 March 2008, available at www.thehindu.com/20087/03/28/stories/2008032857540100.htm.
3 The Charter of United Nations Organization, 1945, Article 62(2).
4 *Id.* Article 63(2).

204 *Structural Adjustment and Farmers' Suicides in India*

Furthermore, since the primary focus is on the extraterritorial human rights obligations of States, the opinion does not focus on India's responsibilities, although this certainly should not be interpreted to mean that India has not violated various human rights standards. Through this, the opinion seeks to contribute to the existing state of discourse on extraterritorial human rights obligations of States,[5] especially as members of international financial institutions as well as obligations of the latter as such.[6] Apart from the scholarly discourse, there have been attempts to codify principles existing in international law with respect to the extraterritorial human rights obligations.[7] In addition, the specific context of farmers' suicides viewed in this opinion as violative of the right to life on account of the structural adjustment programme imposed on it by the World Bank and the IMF[8] places extraterritorial obligations at the interface between civil and

---

5 Fons Coomans and Menno Kamminga (eds) (2004) *Extraterritorial Application Of Human Rights Treaties*, Intersentia, Antwerp; W. Vandenhole, M. Salomon and A. Tostensen (eds) (2007) *Casting The Net Wider: Human Rights, Development And New Duty-Bearers*, Intersentia, Antwerp; Mark Gibney and Sigrun Skogly (eds) (2010) *Universal Human Rights And Extraterritorial Obligations*, University of Pennsylvania Press, Philadelphia.

6 D.D. Bradlow and D.B. Hunter (eds) (2010) *International Financial Institutions & International Law*, Alphen aan den Rijn, Kluwer Law International, M. Darrow, "World Bank and International Monetary Fund" in D.P. Forsythe (ed.) (2009) *Encyclopedia Of Human Rights*, Oxford, Oxford University Press, 373–81; M.E. Salomon, "International Economic Governance and Human Rights Accountability", in M.E. Salomon, A. Tostensen and W. Vandenhole (eds) (2007) *Casting The Net Wider: Human Rights, Development And New Duty-Bearers*, Intersentia, Antwerp, 153–83; M. Darrow(2003) *Between Light And Shadow: The World Bank, The International Monetary Fund, And International Human Rights Law*, Oxford, Hart,; S.I. Skogly, "The Human Rights Obligations of the World Bank and the IMF" in W. van Genugten, P. Hunt and S. Mathews (eds) (2003) *World Bank, IMF And Human Rights*, Nijmegen, Wolf Legal Publishers, 45–78; S. Skogly (2001) *The Human Rights Obligations Of The World Bank And The International Monetary Fund*, London, Cavendish; D.D. Bradlow and C. Grossman (1995) "Limited Mandates and Intertwined Problems: A New Challenge for the World Bank and the IMF", 17 *Human Rights Quarterly* 411–42; Sigrun I. Skogly and Mark Gibney (2002) "Transnational Human Rights Obligations", 24 *Human Rights Quarterly* 781–98.

7 Tilburg Guiding Principles on World Bank, IMF and Human Rights, 2002; Maastricht Principles on Extraterritorial Obligations in the Area of Economic, Social and Cultural Rights, 2011.

8 For insight into the literature on the impact of structural adjustment programme on human rights see World Development Report 1990, World Bank; "Adjustment With A Human Face: Protecting the Vulnerable and Promoting Growth," UNICEF, Oxford, 1987; Ravi Kanbur (1990) "Poverty and the Social Dimensions of Structural Adjustment in Côte d'Ivoire" (Social Dimensions of Adjustment in Sub-Saharan Africa, Policy Analysis), World Bank, Washington D.C.; "The Social Dimensions of Adjustment in Africa: A Policy Agenda", African Development Bank, UNDP and the World Bank, 1990; Jolly, Richard, (1988) "Poverty and Adjustment in the 1990s", in *Strengthening The Poor: What Have We Learned?*, Transaction Books, Piscataway, NJ; Malima, Kighoma, "The imperative of reform", in Jill Torrie (ed.) (1983) *Banking On Poverty: The Global Impact Of The IMF And The World Bank*, Between the Lines Press, Toronto.

Litigating Transnational Human Rights Obligations 205

political rights and economic, social rights and thus reinforces the indivisibility and interdependence of both the categories of rights.

The factual situation draws upon a wide range of literature on farmer suicides. These include the 2010 collection *Agrarian Crisis and Farmer Suicides* edited by R.S. Deshpande and Saroj Arora. P. Sainath, a renowned Indian journalist, has been reporting and analyzing the suicide phenomenon for many years.[9] Another source of information has been a field survey prepared by the TATA Institute of Social Sciences regarding farmer suicides in the Jalna District of Maharashtra.[10] The survey of National Sample Survey Organization and reports of the Reserve Bank of India are other highly acclaimed sources used in this work.

The official reports of the World Bank[11] and the statements of its General Counsels[12] have been relied upon to elicit the official position of the World Bank with respect to its human rights obligations.

---

9 "Of Luxury Cars and Lowly Tractors", *The Hindu*, 27 December, 2010, available at http://www.thehindu.com/opinion/columns/sainath/article995828.ece?homepage=true; "Neo-Liberal Terrorism in India: The Largest Wave of Farmer's Suicides in History", *The Hindu*, 12 November 2007; "Oh! What a Lovely Waiver", *The Hindu*, 11 March 2008; "Fertilising Profit, Sowing Misery", *The Hindu*, 16 June 2008; "Soybean Trumps King Cotton in Vidarbha's Regime Change", *The Hindu*, 28 June 2008; "Farming: It's What They Do", *The Hindu*, 24 May 2007; "Farm Suicides Rising, Most Intense in Four States", *The Hindu*, 12 November 2011; "Farm Suicides: A Twelve Year Saga", The Hindu, 3 February 2010.

10 2006 (3) BomCR 867.

11 "Development and Human Rights: The Role of World Bank, 1998", available at http://www-wds.worldbank.org/external/default/WDSContentServer/WDSP/IB/2001/12/01/000094946_01112004010066/Rendered/PDF/multi0page.pdf; "Equity and Development, World Bank, 2006", available at http://www-wds.worldbank.org/external/default/WDSContentServer/WDSP/IB/2005/09/28/000012009_200509281508 47/Rendered/PDF/335910rev0ENGLISH0WDR20060overview.pdf; "Human Rights Indicators in Development: An Introduction, World Bank, 2010"; Statement of General Counsel Ibrahim Shihata, 1993, "The World Bank and Human Rights", A presentation before 1993 UN World Conference on Human Rights, in *World Bank Legal Papers* (2000), Martinus Nijhoff, Leiden, p. 817; Roberto Danino (2006) "The Legal Aspects of the World Bank's Work on Human Rights", in *Development Outreach*, October; World Bank's operational policy on project appraisal (OMS 2.20), available at http://www.bicusa.org/en/Document.101841.pdf; World Bank Inspection Panel, Investigation Report: Honduras: Land Administration Project, available at http://www-wds.worldbank.org/external/default/WDSContentServer/WDSP/IB/2007/06/21/000020439_20070621104 131/Rendered/PDF/399330HN0INSPR200710003.pdf.

12 Statement of General Counsel Ibrahim Shihata, 1993, "The World Bank and Human Rights," A presentation before 1993 UN World Conference on Human Rights, in World Bank Legal Papers, 2000, Martinus Nijhoff, Leiden, p. 817; Roberto Danino (2006) "The Legal Aspects of the World Bank's Work on Human Rights", in *Development Outreach*, October; Ana Palacio (2006) "The Way Forward: Human Rights and the World Bank", in *Development Outreach*, October; Siobhan McInerney-Lankford, Hans-Otto Sano (2010) "Human Rights Indicators in Development", The World Bank, Washington, D.C.

206 *Structural Adjustment and Farmers' Suicides in India*

Case

International Court of Justice

July 15, 2012

Advisory Opinion

Concerning the Legal Obligations of IMF and World Bank to Respect Right to Life of Farmers in India

THE COURT

Gives the following Advisory Opinion:

1. The questions upon which the advisory opinion of the Court has been requested are contained in resolution 2012/12 of the United Nations Economic and Social Council (hereinafter called "the Council"), adopted on 21 January 2012. By a letter dated 1 February 2012, addressed by the Secretary-General of the United Nations to the President of the Court, filed in the Registry on 12 Feb 2012, the Secretary-General formally communicated to the Court the decision by which the Council submitted to the Court a request for an advisory opinion pursuant to Article 96 paragraph 2 of the Charter of the United Nations:

I. Whether the International Bank for Reconstruction and Development (World Bank) and the International Monetary Fund (IMF), specialized agencies of UN, are under a legal obligation to respect right to life while entering into loan agreements with States?

II. In the event of an affirmative reply on point I, whether the suicides by farmers in India constitute violations of the above stated legal obligation?

* * *

2. In seeking to answer the questions put to the Court by the Economic and Social Council, the Court must decide what would be the relevant applicable law.

3. Some of the proponents of the legal obligations of the IMF and the World Bank have argued that the structural adjustment requirements embodied in loan agreements of the two institutions with States are in violation of the human rights obligations of the specialized agencies under the Charter of the United Nations as well as under international human rights law, specially under the International Covenant on Civil and Political Rights (hereinafter ICCPR) and the International Covenant on Economic, Social and Cultural Rights (hereinafter ICESCR).

4. In both their written and oral statements, some States further argued that impairment of the right to life of farmers by the IMF and the World Bank constitute violations of general principles of international law.

Litigating Transnational Human Rights Obligations 207

5. In reply, other States point to the status of the IMF and the World Bank as specialized agencies of the United Nations and their status as international financial institutions, governed by their own articles of agreements, to deny the binding effect of human rights provisions enshrined in the Charter and obligations arising out of international human rights treaties which bind "States Party" to them.

6. Recognizing that the contentions of the States are intimately connected to the merits of the issues before the Court, and at this stage without going into the merits of the claims made by proponents, the Court concludes that the relevant applicable law governing the question is that relating to the human rights obligations of the specialized agencies, if any, emerging from the Charter, the Articles of Agreement of the IMF and the World Bank, and other international human rights norms.

* * *

7. The Court will first address the question of the existence or the absence of human rights obligations on the IMF and the World Bank in general and specific obligation to respect the right to life in the light of the provisions of the UN Charter, the articles of agreement of the two institutions and the specific nature of right to life.

8. One of the purposes of the United Nations, as enshrined in Article 1 paragraph 3 of the Charter, is "to achieve international cooperation in solving international problems of an economic, social or humanitarian character and in promoting and encouraging respect for human rights and for fundamental freedoms for all…" Article 2, paragraph 1 of the Charter recognizes that "the organization is based on the principle of the sovereign equality of all its members". Furthermore, Article 2 paragraph 4 seeks to prevent the members of the United Nations from organizing their international relations in a manner inconsistent with the purposes of the United Nations. Some of the States have argued that from the combined reading of these provisions, it follows that the members of the United Nations are prevented from acting in a manner which violates human rights. On the contrary they emphasize that all "Members" of the United Nations are bound by the pledge "to take joint and separate action" for "promotion of higher standards of living, full employment, and conditions of economic and social progress … universal respect for and observance of human rights and fundamental freedoms for all" (Articles 56, 55).

9. Other States challenge the applicability of these provisions of the Charter with respect to the IMF and the World Bank on the ground that the two are not States members of the United Nations but are specialized agencies of the United Nations. Their association with the United Nations is governed by the agreements entered into by both entities with the United Nations in accordance with Article 63 of the Charter. Moreover, as per the Articles of Agreement of the IMF and the World Bank, their purpose is to promote international

208 *Structural Adjustment and Farmers' Suicides in India*

monetary cooperation, exchange stability and long-range balanced growth of international trade, and to maintain an equilibrium in balance of payments. Article 1 paragraph 2 of the agreement between the United Nations and the IMF recognizes that the fund has "international responsibilities, as defined in its Articles of Agreement, in economic and related fields within the meaning of Article 57 of the Charter of the United Nations". The promotion of human rights being beyond the mandate of these specialized agencies, there can be no obligation on the agencies with respect to the same.

10. Those states that have argued in favour of the legal obligations of the IMF and World Bank point out that the mandates of the IMF and the World Bank are not limited to macroeconomic and financial goals only. Article 1 paragraph (ii) of the Articles of Agreement of the IMF makes reference to the "maintenance of high levels of employment and real income" and the "development of the productive resources of all members as primary objectives of economic policy". Similarly, Article 1 paragraph (iii) of the Articles of Agreement of the World Bank provides for "development of productive resources of members, thereby assisting in raising productivity, the standard of living and conditions of labour in their territory". Perusal of these obligations indicates that in the execution of their macroeconomic and financial mandate, the IMF and the World Bank are under an obligation to realize micro-level outcomes in terms of the maintenance of high levels of employment and real incomes as well as raising standards of living. The complementarity of the respect for human rights and human development in general has been emphasized over and over again by the World Bank in its official reports as well as in the statements made by its general counsels since the early 1990s (*Development and Human Rights: The Role of the World Bank*, 1998; *Equity and Development*, World Bank, 2006; *Human Rights Indicators in Development: An Introduction*, World Bank, 2010; *Statement of General Counsel Ibrahim Shihata*, 1993; Roberto Danino, 2005, 2006). The court specifically notes the World Bank's position in its publication *Development and Human Rights: The Role of the World Bank*, 1998 where it proclaimed:

> The Bank contributes directly to the fulfillment of many human rights articulated in the Universal Declaration. Through its support of primary education, health care and nutrition, sanitation, housing and the environment, the Bank has helped hundreds of millions of people attain crucial economic and social rights... By helping to fight corruption, improve transparency and accountability in governance, strengthening judicial systems and modernizing financial sectors, the Bank contributes to building environments in which people are better able to pursue a broader range of human rights.

Moreover, the World Bank's operational policy on project appraisal (OMS 2.20) requires the Bank to ensure that financed activities are consistent with a borrower's international agreements regarding its environment and the health and well-being of its citizens. This has also been reaffirmed by the Bank's inspection panel (World Bank Inspection Panel, *Investigation Report: Honduras: Land Administration Project*, 2006).

11. The Court notes that maco-level goals such as high levels of employment and raising standards of living that are enunciated in the Articles of Agreements of the IMF and the World Bank are complementary to the purposes of the United Nations i.e., "promoting and encouraging respect for human rights", in particular the "the right of everyone to the opportunity to gain his living by work", ICCPR (Article 6 (1), and the "right to an adequate standard of living", ICESCR (Article 11 (1)). This position is further reinforced by the articulation of its contribution to the fulfillment of human rights by the World Bank.

*

12. Having dealt with Charter provisions and the Articles of Agreement of the IMF and the World Bank with respect to human rights obligations in general, the Court will now examine the nature of the right to life to determine if it binds all the States irrespective of their accession to international human rights treaties.

*

13. In their written and oral pleadings certain States asserted that the right to life not only emanates from specific international human rights treaties but that it now constitutes a general principle of international law. On account of this, the right binds the entire international community and not just States Parties to human rights treaties.

14. On the other hand, some States have argued that the right is only to be found in particular international human rights treaties. These treaties, it is argued, bind only States Parties and because the IMF and the World Bank are entities constituted by representatives of States which may or may not be party to particular international human rights treaties, the right to life is incapable of binding the IMF and the World Bank. Furthermore, the IMF and the World Bank are institutions established for balancing different aspects of the international economic system and since their activities are directed toward the overall financial health of a nation, they are incapable of arbitrarily depriving people of their lives.

15. The Court notes by way of introduction that the right to life is not a narrow one limited to the arbitrary deprivation of life, but rather, encompasses the aim of continuance and the preservation of life. The Human Rights Committee in paragraph 5 of General Comment 6 (1982) has pointed out that "the expression 'inherent right to life' cannot properly be understood in a restrictive manner". This understanding of the right to life read in the light of the primary purpose of the United Nations, which is "to

210   *Structural Adjustment and Farmers' Suicides in India*

maintain international peace and security" (Article 1), reflects an international resolve to preserve life on earth by avoiding wars among nations; prohibiting arbitrary deprivation of life through State action; preventing death through malnutrition, epidemics and so forth; and by taking "positive measures" to preserve life. The preservation of life is sought to be achieved within international human rights law in a number of ways ranging from international to regional and as well as group-specific binding treaties not only prohibiting the arbitrary deprivation of life but also imposing obligations on States to secure continuous enjoyment of the collective as well as individual right to life by not only prohibiting arbitrary deprivation of the means of subsistence, but also by securing them.

16. The Human Rights Committee in paragraph 1 of General Comment 6 (1982) has held the right to life is "the supreme right from which no derogation is permitted even in time of public emergency which threatens the life of the nation". The Committee, referring to all the rights enshrined in ICCPR, has held that "the right to life is the most fundamental of these rights" (Opinion of the Human Rights Committee in A.R.J. v. Australia, Communication No. 692/1996, paragraph 6.8; Chitat Ng v. Canada, Communication No. 469/1991, paragraph 14.1). In explaining the nature of this right the Committee opines that Article 6 states the general rule: "its purpose is to protect life" (Roger Judge v. Canada, HRC, Communication No. 829/1998, paragraph 10.2).

17. The Court notes that the two exceptions to the continuance and preservation of life recognized in international law are: punishment in pursuance of law, and death resulting from lawful acts under Articles 42 or 51 of the Charter of United Nations. Beyond these two exceptions, the embodiment of the right to life in such a large number of international treaties across all civilizations, along with the purpose of the United Nations to secure human life, as well as the domestic laws of all civilized nations prohibiting acts of murder, point to the existence of the right to life that rises to the level of a general principle of law binding not only the States Parties to the abovementioned Covenants but extending beyond them by imposing binding obligations on all non-parties as well.

18. Further, the Court notes that the arbitrary deprivation of life may be caused "through a variety of means", ranging from torture, murder or through "imposition of living conditions calculated to bring about death" (Extraordinary Chambers in the Courts of Cambodia, 26 July 2010, case File/Dossier No. 001/18-07-2007/ECCC/TC). Unlawful deaths include not only those where there is deliberate killing, but also those where perpetrators are aware that "death could occur as a result of their conduct", for instance, the "deprival of access to adequate food and medical care" (Extraordinary Chambers in the Courts of Cambodia, 26 July 2010, case File/Dossier No. 001/18-07-2007/ECCC/TC). The violation of the right

to life can occur in ways other than just the exercise of the police power of the State. This understanding of the right to life is consistent with the interpretation of the right to life made by the Human Rights Committee, as well as the notion of the indivisibility and interdependence of rights. The Inter-American Court of Human Rights has also recognized the inextricable connection between the lack of guarantee of the right to communal property affecting access to traditional means of subsistence and its negative impact on right to a decent life (Case of the YakyeAxa Indigenous Community v. Paraguay, Judgment of June 17, 2005, paragraph 168).

19. In light of the foregoing, the Court points out that the arbitrary deprivation of life is not limited to killing individuals in the exercise of police force but also includes causing death by depriving people of their means of subsistence. Therefore, while pursuing their mandate of maintaining the international financial system by offering loans to States, it cannot be said that the institutions are completely incapable of arbitrarily depriving people of their lives.

**

20. The Court will now assess the scope of obligations with respect to the right to life in terms of the territorial implications this holds.

*

21. Those States that believe that the IMF and World Bank are under a legal obligation to respect the right to life and contend that farmer suicides in India constitute violations of the right to life by the said institutions stress that human rights obligations of States are not limited to the territorial limits of the respective states, but extend beyond them.

22. Extraterritorial obligations are embodied in a number of binding international human rights instruments:

(a) Article 2(1) of ICCPR provides: "Each State Party to the present Covenant undertakes to take steps, individually and through international assistance and cooperation, especially economic and technical, to the maximum of its available resources, with a view to achieving progressively the full realization of the rights recognized in the present Covenant by all appropriate means, including particularly the adoption of legislative measures."

(b) Specifically, related to the context of the question put forth to the Court, Article 11(1) of the ICESCR provides: "The States Parties to the present Covenant recognize the right of everyone to an adequate standard of living for himself and his family, including adequate food, clothing and housing, and to the continuous improvement of living conditions. The States Parties will take appropriate steps to ensure the realization of this right, recognizing

212 *Structural Adjustment and Farmers' Suicides in India*

to this effect the essential importance of international cooperation based on free consent."

(c) Paragraph 10 of General Comment 31 of the Human Rights Committee recognises that: "... State Party must respect and ensure the rights laid down in the Covenant to anyone within the power or effective control of that State Party, even if not situated within the territory of the State Party."

(d) Paragraph 4 of General Comment 12 of the Committee on Economic, Social and Cultural Rights on the right to food recognizes that the indispensability of right to food for the fulfillment of other human rights and its inseparability from social justice requires adoption of policies at "both the national and the international levels, oriented towards the eradication of poverty and the fulfillment of all human rights for all" (also emphasized by General Assembly Resolution 64/159 of 2010, paragraph 32).

23. Apart from binding international treaties, the existence of a large number of non-binding instruments points to the emergence of *opinio juris* with respect to the extraterritorial human rights obligations of States. The following indicate the same:

(a) Article 28 of the UDHR provides: "Everyone is entitled to a social and international order in which the rights and freedoms set forth in this Declaration can be fully realized."

(b) Article 2 of the Proclamation of Tehran (1968) provides: "The Universal Declaration of Human Rights states a common understanding of the peoples of the world concerning the inalienable and inviolable rights of all members of the human family and constitutes an obligation for the members of the international community."

(c) Article 3 of the Declaration on the Right to Development (1986) provides: "States have the primary responsibility for the creation of national and international conditions favourable to the realization of the right to development."

(d) Article 3(3) of the Declaration on the Right to Development (1986) provides: "States have the duty to cooperate with each other in ensuring development and eliminating obstacles to development. States should realize their rights and fulfill their duties in such a manner as to promote a new international economic order based on sovereign equality, interdependence, mutual interest and cooperation among all States, as well as to encourage the observance and realization of human rights."

(e) Article 4(1) of the Declaration on the Right to Development (1986) provides: "States have the duty to take steps, individually and collectively, to formulate international development policies with a view to facilitating the full realization of the right to development."

Litigating Transnational Human Rights Obligations 213

(f) Paragraph 4 of the Vienna Declaration and Programme of Action (1993) provides: "The promotion and protection of all human rights and fundamental freedoms must be considered as a priority objective of the United Nations in accordance with its purposes and principles, in particular the purpose of international cooperation. In the framework of these purposes and principles, the promotion and protection of all human rights is a legitimate concern of the international community..."

(g) Vienna Declaration and Programme of Action (1993) paragraph 1 emphasizes: "... enhancement of international cooperation in the field of human rights is essential for the full achievement of the purposes of the United Nations".

(h) General Assembly Resolution 64/159 of 2010 on the right to food stresses that States should ensure that "their international policies of a political and economic nature ... do not have a negative impact on the right to food in other countries" (paragraph 20).

24. The Maastricht Principles on Extraterritorial Obligations of States in the area of Economic, Social and Cultural Rights, drawn from existing sources of international law and adopted on 28 September, 2011, specifically point out in Principle 4 the extraterritorial obligations of all States to respect, protect and fulfill economic, social and cultural rights, without further excluding the applicability of these principles to civil and political rights in Principle 5.

25. Apart from the extraterritorial obligations of States under the Charter and international conventions, declarations and resolutions, it is now well settled that there are certain obligations which are *erga omnes*. These are the obligations of a State towards the international community as a whole. "The principles and rules concerning the basic rights of the human person" have been recognized as obligations *erga omnes* by this Court (The Barcelona Traction, Light and Power Company, Limited (Belgium v. Spain) *I.C.J. Reports* 1970, p. 3, paragraphs 33, 34). "Elementary considerations of humanity" is a general and well recognized principle giving rise to obligations (United Kingdom of Great Britain and Northern Ireland – Albania, *I.C.J. Reports* 1949, 4, at paragraph 22).

26. Those States which defend the position that there are no legal obligations on the IMF and the World Bank to respect the right to life see a contradiction between the assertions of other States and the express provisions of human rights instruments. They specifically cite Article 2, paragraph 1 of ICCPR which provides: "Each State Party to the present Covenant undertakes to respect and to ensure to all individuals within its territory and subject to its jurisdiction the rights recognized in the present Covenant..." On the basis of this provision it is argued that the obligations under the ICCPR are necessarily limited to the territory of the State and do not in any way

imply extraterritorial human rights obligations. With respect to the obligation "to take steps individually and through international assistance and cooperation" set forth in ICESCR (Article 2(1)), it is contended that the obligation is programmatic in nature aimed at "achieving progressively the full realization of the rights", and the IMF and the World Bank through their structural adjustment loans are assisting the States in the same.

27. The Court notes the use of two separate terms "territory" and "jurisdiction" in Article 2, paragraph 1, ICCPR, which suggests the terms are not coterminous, otherwise one of the terms would be redundant. Further this Court has observed:

"While the jurisdiction of States is primarily territorial, it may sometimes be exercised outside the national territory... in adopting the wording chosen, the drafters of the Covenant did not intend to allow States to escape from their obligations when they exercise jurisdiction outside their national territory" (ICJ, Advisory Opinion on the Legal Consequences of the Construction of a Wall in the Palestinian Territory, paragraph 109). "The Court considers that the International Covenant on Civil and Political Rights is applicable in respect of acts done by a State in the exercise of its jurisdiction outside its own territory" (Advisory Opinion on the Legal Consequences of the Construction of a Wall in the Palestinian Territory, ICJ, paragraph 111). This Court has consistently upheld and applied this interpretation (Democratic Republic of Congo v. Uganda, ICJ, paragraphs 178–80)

28. The existence of extraterritorial obligations of States has been repeatedly affirmed in the views delivered by the Human Rights Committee. The Committee is of the opinion that the expression "to all individuals within its territory and subject to its jurisdiction" "does not imply that the State Party concerned cannot be held accountable for violations of rights under the Covenant which its agents commit upon the territory of another State, whether with the acquiescence of the Government of that State or in opposition to it... In line with this, it would be unconscionable to so interpret the responsibility under Article 2 of the Covenant as to permit a State Party to perpetrate violations of the Covenant on the territory of another State, which it could not perpetrate on its own territory" (Lopez Burgos v. Uruguay, HRC, Communication No. 52/1979, para 12.3).

29. A similar provision in Article 1 of the European Convention for the Protection of Human Rights and Fundamental Freedoms (1950) which also uses the expression "within their jurisdiction" while referring to the obligation of the Contracting Parties to the Convention, has been interpreted in a manner akin to the Human Rights Committee. The European Court of Human Rights has held that a State's jurisdictional competence under Article 1 is primarily territorial, but in certain exceptional circumstances it extends beyond the territorial boundaries of the State (Al Skeini v. United Kingdom, ECHR, Application No. 55721/07, paragraphs 130–42).

Litigating Transnational Human Rights Obligations 215

30. The jurisprudence developed on this issue by the Inter-American Commission of Human Rights further reinforces the existence of extraterritorial human rights obligations. "The Commission does not believe, however, that the term 'jurisdiction' in the sense of Article 1(1) is limited to or merely coextensive with national territory. Rather the Commission is of the view that a State Party to the American Convention may be responsible under certain circumstances for the acts and omissions of its agents which produce effects or are undertaken outside that State's own territory" (Victor Saldano v. Argentina, Inter American Commission, Report No. 38/99, paragraph 17; Coard *et al.* v. United States, Inter American Commission, report No. 109/99, Case No. 10.951, paragraph 37; Armando Alejandre, Jr., *et al.* v. Republic of Cuba, Inter American Commission, Report No. 86/99, Case No. 11,589, paragraph 23).

31. Accordingly, in view of the present state of international law viewed as a whole, as examined above by the Court, the Court is led to observe that the right to life imposes obligations which extend beyond the national territory of a State.

* *

32. Since the question before the Court pertains to the conditionalities imposed by the IMF and the World Bank, the Court will now turn to examine the obligations of States not in their individual capacity, but as members of these two international financial institutions.

*

33. The IMF and the World Bank are institutions created through agreements between States. In furtherance of their mandate these institutions enter into loan agreements with States which also embody conditionalities of structural adjustment. These conditionalities, it is alleged, are imposed in pursuance of their mandate and are therefore completely in accordance with their obligations arising out of the agreements establishing these international financial institutions.

34. Those states that have argued in favour of the legal obligations of the IMF and the World Bank point out that in case of inconsistency between obligations under any international agreement and those under the Charter, the obligations under the latter prevail. They have specifically relied on Article 103 of the UN Charter in this regard:

> In the event of a conflict between the obligations of the Members of the United Nations under the present Charter and their obligations under any other international agreement, their obligations under the present Charter shall prevail.

35. Article 103 pertains to conflicts in obligations of the States under the UN Charter and their "obligations under any other international agreement".

216 *Structural Adjustment and Farmers' Suicides in India*

The World Bank and the IMF have been established through agreements between States and the States are under obligations embodied in those agreements. The Court has already observed the complementarity between the mandate arising from the Articles of Agreement of the IMF and the World Bank and the purposes of the Charter of United Nations, i.e., "promoting and encouraging respect for human rights". Therefore, there is no conflict between the UN Charter and the international agreements establishing the IMF and the World Bank. However, in furtherance of their objectives the World Bank and the IMF, constituted by States, enter into loan agreements, one instance of the same being the loan agreement with India. These loan agreements, also being agreements between two international entities recognized under international law, amount to international agreements within the meaning of Article 103 of the Charter. Thus, the terms of such an agreement also have to be in accordance with the obligations of the states under the UN Charter. Under the UN Charter, all members of the United Nations have pledged to take action for the achievement of the purposes set forth in Article 55 of the Charter (Article 56). The purposes set forth in Article 55 include: promotion of higher standards of living, full employment, conditions of economic and social development and respect for and observance of human rights. Therefore, if conditionalities embodied in the loan agreement between the IMF and any State (in this case India) impair the right to life, a basic human right of farmers, then such an agreement being in violation of the obligations of the Members of the United Nations under Articles 55 and 56 is controlled by the rule laid down in Article 103 of the Charter. In other words, the obligations of the States under the UN Charter prohibit States from entering into any loan agreement which imposes conditions that impair human rights, in this context the right to life of farmers. Secondly, Article 103 read with Articles 55 and 56 also reinforces the extraterritorial human rights obligations of States. The obligation to respect human rights being an obligation undertaken by States under UN Charter and obligations under UN Charter being prioritized over obligations arising from other international agreements (Article 103) the UN Charter requires that the members of UN in their intercourse among each other through other international agreements abide by their obligations under the UN Charter. Therefore no international agreement can be entered between States or entities constituted by members of UN which amounts to violation of the obligation to respect human rights.

36. The Court is therefore of the opinion that the IMF and the World Bank, as specialized agencies of the United Nations and as legal persons, have obligations to respect the right to life. Further, all States in all their actions, whether acting alone or in association with other States under the veil of an international legal personality such as the IMF and the World Bank, possess extraterritorial obligations to respect the right to life.

* * *

Litigating Transnational Human Rights Obligations 217

37. Having determined the nature and scope of the right to life and the extent of obligations in terms of territorial implications, the Court will now apply existing international law to the facts at its disposal in order to examine if the conditionalities embodied in the loan agreements of the IMF and the World Bank with India constitute a violation of the right to life of farmers. Three further questions arise out of this broader question: whether farmers' suicides in India constitute a violation of the right to life; whether the conditionalities in the loan agreement of the IMF and the World Bank with India created a foreseeable risk of the violation of the right to life; and whether the consent of the State of India to the loan conditions absolves the IMF and the World Bank of their responsibility with respect to the right to life.

*

38. Certain States argue that suicide is an individual act attributable to a variety of personal reasons and in no way can it be viewed as violative of the right to life. According to this argument, the right to life protects people against the arbitrary deprivation of life by State action. In addition, the personal act of ending one's own life does not constitute a violation of the right to life. Secondly, the loan conditionalities are in no way connected to these personal acts of suicides by farmers. An entity can be held liable for the violation of the right to life only if an act or omission of that entity arbitrarily deprives human beings of their lives and not otherwise. Thirdly, since the conditionalities were knowingly accepted by the State receiving the loan, the responsibility for the consequences of the terms of the agreement consented to is solely that of the State.

39. On the other hand, other States assert that a number of independent scientific studies have authoritatively established the deep connection between the suicides and loan conditionalities. Suicides are undoubtedly personal acts. However, when an alarmingly high proportion of suicides are committed by a particular class of people in despair because of their miserable economic conditions, these suicides go beyond being individual or personal acts, and can in large part be attributable to economic despair. Secondly, the consent to loan conditionalities is immaterial as far as the responsibility of the IMF and World Bank are concerned.

40. The Court will now assess whether there is a link between farmers' suicides in India and the loan conditionalities set forth by the IMF and the World Bank. By way of introduction, the Court notes that the United Nations in its various reports, research findings, resolutions as well as decision of the Human Rights Council has recognized the effect of structural adjustment policies in generally aggravating the situation of the poor and specifically causing deleterious effects on the full enjoyment of all human rights, particularly economic, social and cultural rights (*Main Research Findings of the System in Major Global Economic and Social Trends, Policies and Emerging Issues, Report of the Secretary General* (E/1990/81), 14 June 1990, pp. 15, 16; *Debt: A Crisis for Development*, Department of Public Information,

218   *Structural Adjustment and Farmers' Suicides in India*

United Nations, March 1990, p.3, resolutions 1989/21, 1998/24 of 17 April 1998, 1999/22 of 23 April 1999, 2000/82 of 26 April 2000, 2004/18 of 16 April 2004 and 2005/19 of 14 April 2005, decision 2/109 of 27 November 2006 of Human Rights Council and resolutions 7/4 of 27 March 2008, 11/5 of 17 June 2009, 14/4 of 17 June 2010 and 17/4 of 6 July 2011). Moreover, with respect to the structural adjustment programmes, the World Bank in 1990 also recognized that well into the 1980s the "evidence of declines in incomes and cutbacks in social services began to mount" (*World Development Report*, 1990, World Bank, p. 103).

41. The facts at the disposal of the Court establish that in 1990 the structural adjustment programme introduced in India as a condition for loans from the international financial institutions required the State to make certain policy changes. These changes required a reduction in social spending and public investment, which resulted in a reduction in State subsidies and support offered to the agriculture sector, which in turn led to an increase in the input costs of farmers. Average expenses per hectare on insecticides that previously had been less than a rupee in the 1970s and just over Rs. 25 in the 1980s increased by 365 per cent in the 1990s and by as much as 1115 per cent in the first half of the present decade. Changes in the banking system to enhance the efficiency and profitability in banking operations resulted in the denial of access to credit to farmers. From 1993 to 2007, 4,750 rural branches of scheduled commercial banks closed down. The direct agricultural lending account of all public sector banks showed a decline from 2.13 crore in 1994 to 1.59 crore in 2000. The share of priority sector advances to the agricultural sector by scheduled commercial banks in gross non-food credit declined from a peak level of 18.4 per cent at the end of March 1987 to 14.8 per cent at the end of March 1991, and further to 12.1 per cent at the end of March 2001. Further, an influx of cheaper products from other countries on account of trade liberalization made the agriculture practised by large numbers of farmers in India economically unviable. These changes dismantled the existing State support that had secured the livelihood of farmers in India. The cumulative effect of all these changes was an impairment of the means of subsistence of farmers, and, in turn, their right to life. The Situation Assessment Survey of Farmers conducted by the National Sample Survey Organisation (NSSO) at the behest of the union ministry of agriculture indicates that given a choice, 40 per cent of the farmers would quit agriculture and take up some other career. A number of other scientifically conducted studies authoritatively establish that the alarming rate of suicides among farmers was a consequence of the policy changes introduced as a result of loan conditionalities.

*

42. In order to answer the question whether farmers' suicides constitute a violation of the right to life by the IMF and the World Bank it is necessary

Litigating Transnational Human Rights Obligations 219

to examine whether the loan conditionalities posed a necessary and fore-seeable risk of violation of the right to life of farmers.

43. The Human Rights Committee has observed that "a State Party may be responsible for extraterritorial violations of the Covenant, if it is a link in the causal chain that would make possible violations in another jurisdiction. Thus the risk of an extraterritorial violation must be a necessary and foreseeable consequence and must be judged on the knowledge the State party had at the time" (Mohammad Munaf v. Romania, HRC Communication No.1539/2006, 21 August 2009, paragraph 14.2; A.R.J. v. Australia, Communication No. 692/1996, HRC, 28 July 1997, paragraphs 6.8, 6.9; Roger Judge v. Canada, HRC Communication No. 829/1998, 28 July 1997, paragraph 10.6, Chitat Ng v. Canada, Communication No. 469/1991, paragraph 15.1).

44. The principle that has thus emerged is the obligation to refrain from acts or omissions that create a real risk of violation of human rights in gen-eral and the right to life in particular. The principle has also been applied by the dispute settlement mechanism of the World Trade Organization, which has opined that avoidance of harm relates to a "real risk in human societies as they actually exist … as against the uncertainty that theoretically always remains…" (Appellate Body, European Communities – Measures Concerning Meat and Meat Products (Hormones), paragraph 187).

45. Principle 13 of the Maastricht Principles on Extraterritorial Obliga-tions of States in the area of Economic, Social and Cultural Rights (2011) provides:

> States must desist from acts and omissions that create a real risk of nul-lifying or impairing the enjoyment of economic, social and cultural rights extraterritorially. The responsibility of States is engaged where such nullification of impairment is a foreseeable result of their con-duct. Uncertainty about potential impacts does not constitute justifica-tion for such conduct.

46. The foreseeability of the risk to Indian farmers is largely influenced by the fact that India is an agrarian society, with 52 per cent of the workforce dependent on agriculture for its livelihood. Of the workforce fully depend-ent on agriculture, fully 80 per cent are small and marginal farmers. Given India's population, any change in the economic strategy affecting agricul-ture was bound to have a deeply adverse impact on large numbers of farm-ers, and given the nature of the Indian economy, this was foreseeable at the time of entering into these loan agreements. Not only did the IMF and the World Bank fail to foresee the result of the conditionalities embodied in the agreement, the loan agreement was not even preceded by a thorough investigation into the likely impact of the conditionalities on the farmers, nor did it provide specific measures with respect to the protection of the

livelihood of vulnerable farmers. Thus, the IMF and the World Bank failed in their responsibility to respect the right to life of farmers in India by exposing them to the foreseeable risk of the impairment of their livelihood.

*

47. The final question before the Court is whether the consent of India with respect to conditionalities in the loan agreement absolves the IMF and the World Bank of their responsibility with respect to right to life of farmers.

48. The policy changes introduced through the conditionalities embodied in the loan agreement, as mentioned earlier, were not made on account of the exercise of free will by the State of India, but can be viewed as being thrust upon the government in a situation of crisis in exchange for the support offered by the IMF and the World Bank. Thus, in this situation it was these international financial institutions that exercised *de facto* "public power normally to be exercised by that Government" (Bankovic v. Belgium, GC Decision No. 52207/99, § 71, ECHR 2001-XII). Further, the breach of extraterritorial obligations is independent of whether the public power is exercised by the transnational entity forcefully or through the "consent, invitation or acquiescence" of the State concerned. Therefore, the consent of the government does not preclude the extraterritorial responsibility of other States and in this case the international financial institutions, the IMF and the World Bank. Thus, in this situation, the IMF and the World Bank remain jointly responsible with the State of India for the policy changes introduced by them through the conditionalities in loan agreement, which then resulted in the massive levels of suicides among farmers in India.

14 (Economic) Crimes Against Humanity (International Criminal Court, Appeals Chamber)

Michael Wabwile

Abstract

The question raised in this hypothetical case is whether the definition of "crimes against humanity" under the Rome Statute can (and should) be extended to cover economic crimes. In this case, a former Head of State is accused of murdering upwards of 80,000 people due to deliberate economic malfeasance. A prosecution such as this would not only underscore the indivisibility of all human rights, but it would also then give licence to the International Criminal Court to take up what is arguably the most pernicious and widespread human rights violations in the world.

Introductory note

In many badly-governed regions of the world, high level corruption by the top political leadership is the major cause of the destruction of the economic foundations of the State and the subversion of the public systems for the realization of economic and social rights. This chain of sabotage pushes the economically disadvantaged sections of the population to subsist in sub-human conditions of extreme deprivation. As a result of this State-enforced conspiracy, thousands of economically vulnerable people in the developing world are dying of corruption.[1] Unlike violations of civil and political rights that have received attention of national and international human rights institutions, there is a tendency to tolerate criminal acts of State agencies that constitute *gross economic crimes*. In a world that still does not have a global human rights court, it is important to explore whether the International Criminal Court can stand guard to uphold human dignity and economic rights in situations where it is demonstrated that the magnitude of economic crimes committed against a society also constitutes (economic) crimes against humanity.

Established by the Rome Statute of the International Criminal Court (hereinafter, the Rome Statute), the International Criminal Court

---

1 Sören Holmberg and Bo Rothstein, 'Dying of Corruption', (2011) 6 *Health Economics, Policy and Law* 529, 540.

222 *(Economic) Crimes against Humanity*

(hereinafter, the ICC) is the first permanent international court vested with global jurisdiction over 'persons for the most serious crimes of international concern'.[2] One category of such crimes is 'crimes against humanity'.[3] As David Laban has argued, the animating idea behind outlawing crimes against humanity is the interest of humankind in preventing and penalizing the atrocities that governments inflict on their own people.[4] The permanent jurisdiction of the ICC enables the UN Security Council, the ICC Prosecutor or a State Party to the Rome Statute to institute enforcement proceedings on behalf of the international community.[5]

It is a basic principle of the Rome Statute that the ICC's jurisdiction is complementary to national criminal jurisdictions.[6] However, in the case of gross (economic) crimes against humanity, national anti-corruption institutions in the affected regions are notoriously inefficient, unable and unwilling to investigate or prosecute cases of high-level corruption involving incumbent leadership.[7] Moreover, even where there is a change of government, the interests of the political class are such that there is no guarantee that the leaders in the previous regimes will be made to account, through national criminal justice systems, for their past abuse of power.[8] In such circumstances, it may become necessary to invoke the complementary jurisdiction of the ICC and engage the international community, to help break the vicious cycle of abuse of power, high level corruption and economic crimes against humanity in the victim communities. The present case gives us the first opportunity to consider whether the mandate conferred on the ICC by the Rome Statute extends and applies to economic crimes against humanity. It also provides occasion to explore if the criminal jurisdiction of the ICC can be applied to confront the impunity of high level corruption and the suffering it inflicts on hapless populations in the affected societies.

---

2 Rome Statute of the International Criminal Court, Preamble, and Article 1.

3 Id, Articles 5, 7.

4 David Laban, 'A Theory of Crimes Against Humanity', (2004) 29 *Yale Journal of International Law* 85, 107.

5 Rome Statute, Article 13.

6 Id, Article 1.

7 See Simon Coldham, 'Legal Responses to State Corruption in Commonwealth Africa', (1995) 39 *Journal of African Law* 115, at 125; William De Maria, 'Whistleblower Protection: is Africa Ready?', (2005) 25 *Public Administration and Development* 217 at 224; Olivier de Sardan, 'A Moral Economy of Corruption in Africa', (1999) 37 *Journal of Modern African Studies* 25 at 30.

8 See Stanley Cohen, 'State Crimes of Previous Regimes: Knowledge, Accountability and the policing of the Past', (1995) 20 *Law and Social Inquiry* 7, suggesting that amnesty, reconciliation and reconstruction etc. may be offered instead of prosecution and punishment under national criminal law.

Case

FHS, SBM and MFS v. Prosecutor

A. THE PARTIES AND ALLEGED MATERIAL FACTS

1. This matter is a criminal prosecution commenced by the Prosecutor of this Court against the three co-defendants. The first defendant, FHS, is a former Head of State of the Republic of Filipina, which ratified the Statute of the International Criminal Court on 28 December 2000. The Second Defendant, SBM, is the Chief Executive Officer and Managing Director of the Universal Banking Synergies, an international banking and financial services corporation which has its head office in the United Kingdom. The Third Defendant, MFS, is the United Kingdom cabinet minister responsible for regulating and exercising State supervision of the financial services sector.

2. It is the prosecution's case that between July 2002 and December 2011, FHS held office as the democratically elected President and Head of State of the Republic of Filipina for two consecutive five-year terms. FHS had won the two elections with landslide majority votes, and as the ruling party Filipina Democratic People's Party's manifestos indicate, FHS's candidacy was based on the promise of economic development, job creation, poverty reduction, financial discipline, political reforms, zero-tolerance to corruption, food security, democratic governance and social rejuvenation. However, these promises were never fulfilled. Instead there was betrayal of public trust, and the people endured two terms of bad governance under FHS.

3. In the second term of FHS's presidency, from 2006 to 2011, very large sums of money were transferred from the public funds of the Filipina government and deposited in various foreign bank accounts. Evidence laid before this court indicates that a sum totalling to ten (10) billion US dollars was deposited in two accounts held at the Universal Banking Synergies in the United Kingdom. The money was deposited in two accounts operated in the names of FHS Holdings (4 billion) and FHS and Son Holdings Ltd (6 billion). Both companies are incorporated in the United Kingdom. It has been shown that these funds were obtained through fraudulent and illegal misappropriation and the stealing of public funds from the government accounts of the Republic of Filipina.

4. The transfer, deposit and safe custody of the stolen funds was orchestrated by the First Defendant through a calculated and well-arranged scheme, under a system designed and facilitated by the senior management of Universal Banking Synergies, then as now under the leadership of the Second Defendant, for their high-value overseas clients. Under this system, the Second Defendant would assign special customer care advisors to personally oversee the opening of the accounts and ensure secrecy regarding

224 *(Economic) Crimes against Humanity*

the First Defendant's accounts. It was submitted by the Prosecution that the schemes of economic crime and sabotage outlined in the facts of this case could not have been successful without the strategic and tactical support, collusion and assistance of the Universal Banking Synergies, and especially the Second Defendant as the Chief Executive Officer of the bank.

5. The Third Defendant is the Cabinet minister responsible for regulating and exercising State supervision of the financial services sector.

6. The case before this Court also raises the issue of legal responsibility of the UK under international law for the loss of resources stolen from Filipina and whether the UK is liable to pay compensation to the victims of the alleged economic crimes. Although the case was brought against the three defendants, the Prosecutor asked the Court to make a determination regarding the responsibility and liability of the UK in these circumstances.

B. THE SPECIFIC CRIMINAL CHARGES

7. The charges against the First Defendant include the murder of 80,000 persons in the Republic of Filipina during the second term of his presidency. Further details of the charges of murder are as follows:

(a) Illegally and fraudulently stealing, misappropriating ten billion (USD) from the public accounts of the Republic of Filipina and transferring, concealing and hiding the same in bank accounts in the UK branch of Universal Banking Synergies.

(b) Planning, devising and implementing a deliberate scheme of fraudulently depriving the complainants and the people of the Republic of Filipina of the use of their public funds and resources as a result of which the country's national systems for health care, water supply, and food security have been totally crippled, leaving the people and the complainants vulnerable and economically exposed.

(c) Due to the crimes indicated in (a) and (b) above, causing the death of 55,500 malaria patients in the public hospitals, including 35,500 children under the age of five years, whose intravenous malaria treatment was discontinued because the hospitals were deprived of the funds previously intended for purchasing anti-malarial drugs and other essential supplies.

(d) As a result of the matters alleged in (a) and (b) above, causing the death of 24,500 people, including 12,000 children under the age of five years, who died of extreme hunger, while the social safety nets of the Republic of Filipina had been totally shredded, and the State was unable to provide emergency food relief to the affected population.

(e) In total, the defendant directed a policy of gross economic sabotage, economic crime and deprivation and the haemorrhaging of the resources of the Republic of Filipina, thereby causing the death of over 80,000 citizens in a period of two years.

Litigating Transnational Human Rights Obligations 225

8. The Charges of murdering 80,000 persons in the Republic of Filipina were filed against the Second Defendant. Further details are as follows:

(a) Designing, crafting and maintaining the business policies, systems and practices at the financial services organization in which he served as the Chief Executive Officer, that enabled the First Defendant to carry out his scheme of economic crime.
(b) Receiving, concealing, hiding and handling stolen funds on behalf of the First Defendant, knowing the same to be stolen property.
(c) Working as chief accomplice, agent and partner of the Defendant in the murder of 80,000 persons in the Republic of Filipina.

9. The case against the Third Defendant is that as the top cabinet minister in charge of regulating and supervising the financial services industry in the State, he knew or ought to have known that economic crimes were being committed within the territory of the State and taken measures to stop the commission of these crimes. The charges are based on the premise that the Third Defendant should bear political responsibility for these crimes alleged to have been committed by the First and Second Defendants within the territory of the United Kingdom. The following Charges were filed against the Third Defendant:

(a) Aiding, permitting, facilitating and suffering the First and Second Defendants to carry on a system of fraudulent and illegal transfers and the concealment of funds stolen from the public accounts of the Republic of Filipina, in the territory of the UK.
(b) Failing to prevent or stop the illegal transfer of funds to the UK or to trace and recover the same when the State machinery within his command could have been applied to do so.
(c) Failing, neglecting and refusing to discharge the extraterritorial obligations to protect the victims of transnational economic crime living in the Republic of Filipina, and failing to exercise proper oversight of the UK financial services industry.

C. SPECIFIC COMPLAINTS

10. This case was brought to the attention of the international community through the campaigns of three civil society organizations: Coalition for Filipina Peoples' Rights (CFPR), Global Action for Transparency (GAT) and Friends of the Filipina Children (FFC). As the campaigns for international intervention intensified, these three were joined by several international civil society organizations, notably the Extraterritorial Obligations Consortium and the University of Antwerp Law School.

11. The specific complaints relate to three categories of claims. First, there are claims brought by survivors of the deceased persons. Secondly, there are claims brought on behalf of 100 individuals whose complaint is that they

226 *(Economic) Crimes against Humanity*

suffered irreparable consequences of malnutrition, when all the programmes for emergency food relief had been discontinued for 'lack of funds'. The third group of complainants have made claims relating to current deprivations alleging that the Second Defendant has continued to offer the same services to successive political leaders in Filipina and other States and should be punished for these offences and stopped. In all these categories of claims, the complainants have asked for compensation and reparations.

D. SUMMARY OF SUBMISSIONS OF PARTIES

12. It is necessary to set out the main arguments presented by the parties to this Court. The First Defendant admitted transferring funds to bank accounts in the UK, but denied the charge that this was the cause of 80,000 deaths in the Republic of Filipina. The First Defendant argued that if there were such deaths as claimed, they were as a result of natural causes. The Defendant also contended that there is no such offence as economic crimes against humanity, and such a concept would be an unlawful addition or extension of the text of the Rome Statute, beyond what was agreed by the parties to this treaty. The Defendant's final argument was that his prosecution in this Court is not proper since the domestic courts of the Republic of Filipina can try the matter and there is no justification for invoking the jurisdiction of this court.

13. The Second Defendant submitted that he carried out the business of a banker as permitted by the applicable UK law and denied all allegations of wrongdoing.

14. The Third Defendant submitted that he was not directly involved in handling bank accounts or funds from the First Defendant. The main argument of the Third Defendant is that in a liberalized economy the private sector-owned banking institutions have the freedom to conduct business. The Third Defendant also disputed the jurisdiction of this Court, arguing that there is no such offence as economic crimes against humanity in international law.

15. The Court also heard submissions on behalf of the Republic of Filipina and the UK on the legal aspects of the case, which are reviewed in the decision.

E. DETERMINATION OF LEGAL ISSUES ON THE MERITS

16. Whether the Rome Statute's application includes *Economic* Crimes against Humanity

The issues of admissibility of the charges and jurisdiction of this Court were contested in the Pre-Trial Chamber and both the Pre-Trial and Trial

Chambers of this Court determined the matter in the affirmative. For the sake of clarity and for the avoidance of any doubts, this Court will make a few observations on the same. As provided in Article 5(1) of the Statute, the jurisdiction of the Court is 'limited to the most serious crimes of concern to the international community as a whole'. The Article indicates that jurisdiction of this Court can be invoked only in the following four categories of criminal offences: (a) the crime of genocide; (b) crimes against humanity; (c) war crimes and (d) the crime of aggression.

In the present case, charges have been brought for 'economic crimes against humanity'. The crux of the common argument of the three defendants is that there is no such category as 'economic' crimes against humanity in Article 7 of the Statute of this Court, and the Statute of the Court does not expressly recognize economic crimes or violations of economic rights in its definition of crimes against humanity. If this contention is upheld, then there would be no valid charge and this Court would not have jurisdiction. This Court is of the considered opinion that the defence argument that there cannot be *economic* crimes against humanity is mistaken and cannot be allowed to stand. The reasons and grounds for this finding are set out in more detail in this section.

17. Definition of Crimes against Humanity in the Rome Statute

Article 7(1)(a) of the Rome Statute states as follows:

> For the purpose of this Statute, 'crime against humanity' means any of the following acts when committed as part of a widespread or systematic attack directed against any civilian population, with knowledge of the attack: (a) murder.

Thus, to constitute a crime against humanity under this Article, the two elements of the crime must be proved: *widespread or systematic attack against a civilian population* i.e., the *actus reus* and (2) the *knowledge of the attack* i.e., the *mens rea.* In Article 7(2) an attack directed against any civilian population is defined as: 'a course of conduct involving the multiple commission of acts referred to in paragraph 1 *against any civilian population, pursuant to or in furtherance of a State or organizational policy to commit such attack'*. There is no requirement that such attacks should be in the context of armed conflict: the Article clearly indicates the practical necessity of this Court to respond to large-scale atrocities committed by governments and political leadership against their own populations in times of peace.[9] Given that human life is very fragile, attacks causing death and murder of human beings can be many and varied and Article 7 of the Rome Statute does not describe these.

---

9 Darryl Robinson, 'Defining "Crimes against Humanity" at the Rome Conference', (1999) 93 *American Journal of International Law* 43–57, at 46.

228 *(Economic) Crimes against Humanity*

In a useful interpretation, the International Criminal Tribunal for Rwanda held that an attack may be defined as an unlawful act of the kind enumerated in the Statute, and this may include unlawful acts or omissions.[10] More significantly, the ICTR held that attacks need not necessarily be violent. Thus:

> attacks may also be non-violent in nature, like imposing a system of apartheid, which is declared a crime against humanity in Article 1 of the Apartheid Convention 1973, or exerting pressure on the population to act in a particular manner, may come under the purview of an attack, if orchestrated on a massive scale or in a systematic manner.[11]

18. From the facts of this case, it is clear that there were concerted attacks of an economic kind, whereby the First Defendant devised, crafted and implemented a policy and practice of large-scale raiding and looting the public funds entrusted to his and his government's trust and custody. These were funds earmarked for financing programmes for health care, emergency food relief, and other social welfare services on which the majority of the country's population relied almost exclusively (over 62 per cent of the Filipina population live on less than 2 USD per day). The requirement that the attacks must have been widespread and systematic has been defined by the ICTR as follows:

> The concept of 'widespread' may be defined as massive, frequent, large scale action, carried out collectively with considerable seriousness and directed against a multiplicity of victims. The concept of 'systematic' may be defined as thoroughly organized and following a regular pattern on the basis of a common policy involving substantial public or private resources. There is no requirement that this policy must be adopted formally as the policy of a State. There must however be some kind of preconceived plan or policy.[12]

19. The Court finds that in the present case, the economic attacks and economic crimes were organized, planned and carried out by the First Defendant and other members of his government as part of a practice and policy of illegal personal gain, unjust-enrichment, and self-aggrandizement. These economic attacks were planned and executed at the expense of the general populace, which relied on the government programmes and public resources to enable them access essential health care services and emergency

---

10 *The Prosecutor v. Jean-Paul Akayesu* (Trial Judgement), ICTR-96-4-T, International Criminal Tribunal for Rwanda (ICTR), 2 September 1998, available at: http://www.unhcr.org/refworld/docid/40278fbb4.html [accessed 4 June 2012]

11 Id, para. 581.

12 Id, par. 580.

relief food. In view of the duration of the acts of the First Defendant, the amounts of money looted over the four-year period, the number of persons who died (over 80,000) and the magnitude of suffering and deprivation, this is a case that clearly constitutes widespread and systematic attacks directed at the civilian population in the Republic of Filipina.

20. The documented death of 24,500 persons as a result of preventable hunger in the State of Filipina is a deeply troubling matter that deserves further consideration. If a government or government leader enforces a policy or practice of prolonging hunger and suffering of famine victims, then such a person is guilty of a crime against humanity, which can be called a *famine crime.* It has been correctly demonstrated that the hunger- and famine-related deaths can be halted and also prevented if governments take the appropriate steps to establish appropriate response systems and mechanisms, thus:

> A person commits a second-degree famine crime by recklessly ignoring evidence that his or her policies are creating, inflicting, or prolonging the starvation of a significant number of persons. A second-degree famine crime is committed by an official recklessly pursuing policies that have already proven their faminogenic tendencies.[13]

20A. It should be noted that whereas the facts of the case reveal massive loss of lives, the law does not require that there should be proof of widespread murder or the like. What is required is the proof of abuse of power, and the commission of a planned, systematic attack directed at a civilian population. In this context, one death resulting from such attack would be enough to establish the offence and sustain a conviction.[14]

21. The basic issue for determination in this matter is whether the economic crimes committed by the First Defendant can fall under the provisions of Article 7(1) and (2) of the Rome Statute. Article 7(2) provides:

> For the purpose of paragraph 1: (a) 'Attack directed against any civilian population' means a course of conduct involving the multiple commission of acts referred to in paragraph 1 *against any civilian population, pursuant to or in furtherance of a State or organizational policy to commit such attack.* (emphasis added)

Academic and judicial authorities interpreting this Article appear to support the proposition that serious economic crimes such as high-level

---

13 David Marcus, 'Famine Crimes in International Law', (2003) 97 *American Journal of International Law* 245–81, at 247.

14 M.Cherif Bassiouni, *Crimes Against Humanity: Historical Evolution and Contemporary Application* (Cambridge University Press, Cambridge, 2011) p. 10.

230   *(Economic) Crimes against Humanity*

corruption committed by government officials can be categorized as crimes against humanity. The critical point is whether the criminal acts complained of were perpetrated pursuant to the official or undeclared State or organizational policy. Schabas has traced the customary international law as well as treaty-text premises of the proposition that it would constitute a crime against humanity if the atrocities complained of were committed by the government officials or other persons acting as agents or on behalf of the State, government or government agency in furtherance of the official or undeclared policy or practice of the government.[15] It is important to note that Schabas distinguishes between purely non-State actors that have no affiliation with the government and State-like agents.[16]

21A. Bassiouni has explained the justification for the requirement that the attacks or atrocities directed against a civilian population must be pursuant to or in furtherance of State or government policy or government practice to commit the attack. He writes:

> The need for international criminalisation of the specific crimes reflected in the various definitions of crimes against humanity is essential, because when such crimes are committed as part of a State's policy, it is likely to produce large-scale victimisation. Thus, the abuse of State power transforms a domestic crime or series of crimes into an international crime. Thus it is not the quantum of the resulting harm that controls, but the potentiality of large-scale harm that could derive from a State's abuse of power…When State actors abuse the power of a State, there is little that can stop them before they carry out their course of conduct against a civilian population that is no longer protected by these actors, but victimised by them.[17]

It is this nexus with the abuse of State power that, according Bassouni's view, not only gives the otherwise domestic criminal acts the international law element, but also recognizes its potential to inflict large scale deprivation and atrocities on civilian populations. However, there is considerable controversy regarding whether there should be any governmental/State policy connection or whether it is sufficient that the crimes complained of were directed by a group, including non-State actors, without any State involvement. Interpreting a similar provision in Article 5 of its Statute, the International Criminal Tribunal for the Former Yugoslavia affirmed the

---

15 William Schabas, 'State Policy as an Element of International Crimes', (2008) 98 *Journal of Criminal Law and Criminology* 953.

16 Ibid., p. 973.

17 M.Cherif Bassiouni *supra* note 14 at 10. For a similar opinion, see M. Cherif Bassiouni, *The Legislative History of the International Criminal Court: Introduction, Analysis, and Integrated Text* (Brill, Leiden, 2005, Vol. I, pp. 151–2),

Litigating Transnational Human Rights Obligations 231

view that there must be some form of governmental, organizational or group policy to commit attacks directed against a civilian population.[18] The International Law Commission has taken the view that the fundamental test of all crimes against humanity is that they must be instigated or directed by a government or by any organization or group.[19]

21B. In the present case, these controversies do not apply because the First Defendant as Head of State and Chief Executive was directly in charge of determining and implementing the State policies and practices which form the basis of the complaints before the Court. In the light of the foregoing, it is possible to recognize the link between the criminal activities and practices of State's political elites led by the First Defendant, and the undeclared policy of the government that they controlled. On this approach, where the top ruling elites execute schemes for subverting and destroying the economic foundations of the State for personal aggrandisement, their chain of criminal acts of high-level corruption has the potential of causing large-scale deprivation, impoverishment, starvation and loss of lives among the disenfranchised masses. These activities and practices can be reconstructed as governmental or organizational policy and practice. It is also important to note that Article 7(2) does not require that such policy should be officially or formally adopted by the State: even undeclared or secret policy, which is evident in the pattern of practices of the government officers, would suffice.[20] Therefore, provided that the foregoing legal requirements of a crime against humanity have been proved, there is nothing in the provisions of customary international law or the Rome Statute that exempts *economic* crimes against humanity from the categories of abuses of State power that the current regime of international criminal law is designed to restrain and punish.

21C. Turning to the issue of knowledge of the acts and consequences of their attacks, it is evident the First Defendant knew his acts had far-reaching consequences on the lives and health of the people of his country. The First Defendant committed the alleged offences during his second term as President and Head of State. To try to visualize the series of events, the crimes committed by the First Defendant can be compared to snatching funds intended for providing baby food and pretending to be unaware of the victims' painful death as the pangs of hunger slowly drain out life from them. By stealing funds intended for financing systems for public health care services, the defendant knew this was like turning off life-support systems, and switching off anti-malarial treatment for hundreds of thousands

---

18 *Prosecutor v. Tadić*, Opinion Judgment No IT-94-1-T par. 652 (7 May 1997).

19 Report of the International Law Commission on the work of its forty-eighth session, UN GAOR 51st Sess. Supp. No. 10: UN Doc. A/51/10 (1996), paras 93–6.

20 Darryl Robinson, 'Defining Crimes Against Humanity at the Rome Conference', (1999) 93 *American Journal of International Law* 43, at 50.

232 *(Economic) Crimes against Humanity*

of patients in the Republic of Filipina who relied on government-provided health care systems.

22. Therefore, the requirements of both the *actus reus* and *mens rea* in respect of the crimes against humanity committed by the First Defendant have been established and sufficiently proven.

23. Regarding the Second Defendant, it has been sufficiently proven that the Second Defendant ran an organization that provided the First Defendant with the financial services and facilities to stash away large sums of looted wealth. Such a grand scheme of theft could not have been attempted without the availability of a willing and supportive partner in economic crime, a role performed with much precision by the Second Defendant. This court therefore affirms and upholds the conviction of the First and Second Defendants by the Trial Chamber.

State responsibility and/or individual responsibility

24. The issue of the Third Defendant's liability has been contested in the appeal before us and counsel tried to demonstrate that the real responsibility, if any, lay not with the individual Cabinet Secretary but with the State of the United Kingdom for permitting economic crimes against humanity to be committed on its territory. It is the duty of all States to ensure good domestic management and housekeeping, such that their territory is properly governed and is not used as a safe haven for foreign looted funds and other resources and all other forms of transnational crime. A useful analogy can be drawn to the concept of State responsibility in international law. In the *Corfu Channel case*[21] the ICJ held that where State authorities knew of the existence of mines laid in its territorial waters, the State was responsible for the harmful consequences resulting from the mines such as the loss of lives and destruction of foreign vessels. Thus, in *Corfu Channel*, the mines were laid by Third parties, with the knowledge and/or acquiescence of Albania because Albanian authorities maintained continued surveillance of their territorial waters. Secondly, although Albanian State authorities knew of the existence of mines in its territorial waters, they failed to act within their powers and competence to prevent the disaster, such as issuing danger alerts to the British warships at least two hours before the latter sailed onto the mines. As the Court observed, these were grave omissions for which the State bore international responsibility.

25. In view of this, it is the considered opinion of this Court that in the present case, the UK is liable in international law for permitting economic crimes against humanity to be committed on its territory by the First and

---

21 *ICJ Reports,* 1949, The Corfu Channel Case (Merits), p. 23.

Second Defendants. However, that is as far as this Court can proceed. The Court's effective powers are limited to exercising jurisdiction over persons for the most serious crimes of international concern defined by the Rome Statute.[22] This means that the Court does not have jurisdiction over States as such, but individuals who bear responsibility for crimes under international criminal law.

The Court is satisfied that the Third Defendant as the Cabinet Secretary responsible for trade and commerce had effective executive powers in the matters concerning regulating the financial services industry, including the power to appoint the State's Financial Services Authority that reported to him. The Financial Services Authority had powers to licence and supervise all service providers in the industry and had powers to access their records and received regular reports regarding cash inflows and outflows in the country's domestic and transnational financial services providers. The Third Defendant is deemed to have had actual and/or constructive knowledge of the economic crimes perpetrated by the First and Second Defendants and bears both political and legal responsibility for the inaction, omission and failure to restrain and stop the economic haemorrhage of the resources of the Republic of Filipina.

Economic crimes against humanity or international human rights: cross-cutting issues

26. In the course of preparing this judgment, we have considered whether in holding as we do that economic crimes against humanity were committed against the affected civilian population of Filipina, for which individuals responsible should be punished, the jurisdiction of this Court might be seen to be applied to protect economic and social rights. One view is that this Court should resist any human-rights activist tendencies and confine itself strictly to its mandate of adjudicating international criminal law, not enforcing international human rights law.[23] However, this view cannot be correct. It is often the case that the 'most serious crimes of international concern' over which this Court should exercise its jurisdiction can also be reanalysed as gross violations of human rights including economic and social rights.

27. It is the considered view of this Court that in all those cases that have been litigated before it, the charges brought against defendants under the Rome Statute have also been either gross violations of internationally recognized human rights or gross violations of international humanitarian law

---

22 Rome Statute 1998, Article 1.
23 Darryl Robinson, 'Defining "Crimes against Humanity" at the Rome Conference', (1999) 93 *American Journal of International Law* 43–57, at 46.

234 *(Economic) Crimes against Humanity*

or, in most instances, both. Four points can be clarified: First, parties and the Court must confine themselves to the concepts and mandate of international criminal law set out in the Rome Statute and the duty of the Court is to interpret and apply the constitutive treaty documents in such manner that would give effect to the objectives and purpose of the treaty.[24] Three of the principal objectives of the Statute of this Court are to: (1) ensure that the most serious crimes of concern to the international community as a whole are being punished, (2) put an end to impunity for the perpetrators of these crimes, and (3) contribute to the prevention of such crimes.[25]

28. Secondly, the ultimate objective of the Rome Statute is to provide international mechanisms and facilities for criminal justice in the most serious crimes, and this is also for the purpose of protecting and providing redress for victims of such crimes. Since the Rome Statute is concerned with jurisdiction over individuals and can provide redress for victims of the most serious crimes, it implies that there is a considerable common ground and overlap between international criminal law and international human rights law. In appropriate cases where there are cross-cutting issues and complaints, the general provisions of the Rome Statute can be extended and applied to mete out criminal sanctions to perpetrators of gross violations of human rights including economic and social rights. The present case is one in which there are overlapping issues and complaints and as the concurring judgments of this Court demonstrate, the Rome Statute can be deployed to redress transnational economic crimes against humanity, which can also be reclassified as gross violations of economic and social rights.

29. Thirdly, it is necessary in this judgment to recognize the connection between gross economic crimes committed by ruling elites in a conspiracy against their national populace and the resultant responsibility of the international community. Here, the international community of States might be requested to provide humanitarian aid/assistance to the deprived victim communities or take steps to protect the affected communities from further deprivation and dehumanization. Thus, mechanisms such as the Rome Statute can and should be regularly deployed to restrain and punish acts of economic crimes against humanity as part of international responsibility to protect the affected communities. If the deprivation and dehumanization of vulnerable persons/communities by their own government elites can be prevented or stopped, then the need for international humanitarian aid assistance would be reduced, if not eliminated.

30. In other words, there is a close link between violations of economic and social rights and enforced economic exclusion and deprivation, on the one

---

24 Vienna Convention of the Law of Treaties 1969, Article 31(1).
25 Rome Statute 1998, Preamble, paras 4, 5.

hand, and the occurrence of civil war, war crimes and other crimes against humanity. The acts of gross economic sabotage, failed political promises and economic crimes against humanity fuel grievances against the State and provide the basis for discontent and dissent by a large section of the national community. When these conditions persist for a long time, such as the presidency of the First Defendant, it provides a perfect setting that triggers civil war. This is because the affected population feels economically deprived, excluded and aggrieved and they have reason to believe that they would be better off if they joined a protest liberation movement, which in turn can morph from civil protests and confrontation with government forces into full-scale civil war. Scholars have demonstrated that 'countries whose citizens enjoy high levels of economic well-being and have access to a more open political system are significantly less likely to experience civil wars than autocratic states with low levels of economic and social individual welfare'.[26]

By including economic crimes into the category of crimes against humanity, this Court is properly discharging its mandate to tackle some of the root causes of civil war, war crimes and related atrocities. This means that all the available tools in the armour of international law and international institutions should be fully applied and mobilized to the cause of protecting internationally recognized human rights and dignity. Therefore, as the only international court with global jurisdiction over persons, this Court should fulfil its role of giving effect to the established regimes of international criminal law in the widest context of extraterritorial human rights responsibility of the international community.

31. Finally, if the criminal jurisdiction of this Court can be deployed to contribute to ending the culture of impunity and preventing the commission of the most serious crimes as defined in international criminal law, it would result in a much safer world for the human family. It would in effect mean that the gross violations of economic and social rights that result in large numbers of hunger-related deaths, oftentimes mistaken or misrepresented as natural deaths, can be stopped or prevented. As this case illustrates, the Rome Statute can be applied to cast the net of criminal responsibility for economic crimes against humanity much wider to include domestic actors and their transnational accomplices. This approach to the Rome Statute is necessitated by the realization that the international community has not established a global human rights court, and yet people everywhere are at risk of gross violation of their human rights. The Rome

---

26 See Patrick Regan and Daniel Norton, 'Greed, Grievances, and Mobilization in Civil Wars', (2005) 49 *Journal of Conflict Resolution* 319, at 322; Barbara F. Walter, 'Does Conflict Beget Conflict: Explaining Recurring Civil War', (2004) 41 *Journal of Peace Research* 371, at 372; Jeffrey Dixon, 'What Causes Civil Wars? Integrating Quantitative Research Findings', (2009) 11 *International Studies Review* 707, at 714.

236 *(Economic) Crimes against Humanity*

Statute provides a very useful ventilation window, whereby in special and appropriate cases, gross violations of human rights can be reconstructed and litigated in this Court as serious crimes against humanity.

F. CONCLUSION

32. In conclusion, it can be seen that the Rome Statute does not expressly mention economic crimes against humanity, but in certain cases the conduct complained of constitutes grievous atrocities which in the judgment of this Court deeply shock the conscience of humanity. The provisions of the Rome Statute can be interpreted in light of emerging jurisprudence as well as the general objectives and purpose of the treaty in such a way as to address these atrocities. It is properly within the duty and mandate of this Court to apply the general provisions of the Statute, in bold and innovative ways in order to bring the perpetrators of such atrocities to justice. The Court therefore upholds the decision of the Trial court convicting the three Defendants and dismisses the appeals of the three defendants for lack of merit.

As the four other members of the Appellate Chamber concur with this decision, this shall be the final determination of this appeal.

Signed

Michael Wabwile
Judge, Appeals Chamber, International Criminal Court, Den Haag

Part III

Regional Human Rights Monitoring Bodies

15 Public Duties for Private Wrongs

Regulation of Multinationals (African Commission on Human and Peoples' Rights)

Takele Soboka Bulto

Abstract

This hypothetical case synthesises the emerging jurisprudence of the African Commission relative to African States' extraterritorial responsibilities for their multinationals operating in other African States. It approaches the reach of a state's extraterritorial duties from the perspective of its responsibility to control, prevent, punish and/or remedy violations of human and peoples' rights abroad when they are caused by multinational corporations incorporated in the implicated state's territory. Since multinational companies cannot be directly brought before the regional human rights body, the main available avenue to prevent, punish and/or remedy human rights violations caused by the (in)actions of multinational companies in foreign States' territories is through their 'home' State's responsibility. This hypothetical decision seeks to provide a model judgment that establishes that the African Charter provides for ample room whereby a multinational company's home State be held responsible for the company's overseas activities that contribute to or constitute violations of human and peoples' rights in third States' territories.

Introductory note

The spatial reach of States' human rights obligations under regional and global human rights treaties has recently become a subject of rumbling academic debate. At the core of the controversy is the question of whether a State owes the quartet layers of duties to 'respect, protect, promote and fulfil' human rights not only to those within its own borders[1] but also to

---

[1] Salomon, for instance, argued that States' human rights obligations were designed to enforce and strengthen the implementation of the rights enshrined therein by the States when they act domestically. See Margot E. Salomon, *Global Responsibility for Human Rights: World Poverty and the Development of International Law* (Oxford University Press, 2007) 190.

240 *Public Duties for Private Wrongs: Regulation of Multinationals*

those beyond its national territory (extraterritorially).[2] It raises the questions: to whom – only to those within or also to those outside a State's territory – are the State's human rights obligations owed; and on whose behalf are the obligations stemming from international human rights law to be fulfilled?[3] In other words, this debate addresses the question of whether State parties to international human rights treaties would be allowed to commit or allow, condone and/or tolerate the commission of violations in another State's territory, which they would be prohibited from committing, condoning or tolerating within their own borders.[4]

The crucial question of the reach of States' human rights duties has been neglected by scholarship on the African human rights system.[5] In contrast, the African Commission on Human and Peoples' Rights has long adjudicated issues involving the extraterritorial reach of States' human rights obligations. Indeed, quasi-judicial scrutiny of the extraterritorial reach of human rights and correlative States' obligations in Africa leapfrogged related academic literature. In fact, complainants attempting to hold States extraterritorially responsible for violations of human rights and freedoms guaranteed under the African Charter started to come before the African Commission almost as soon as the Commission was inaugurated in 1987.[6] Individuals sought to avail themselves of the regional mechanism for redressing violations of their rights

---

2 As Craven observed, 'at least as regards a duty to "respect" or "protect" the enjoyment of ESC [economic, social and cultural] rights on the part of those living in other states – the issue has clearly remained a contentious one'. See Matthew Craven, 'The Violence of Dispossession: Extra-Territoriality and Economic, Social and Cultural Rights' in A. Mashood and Robert McCorquodale Baderin (eds), *Economic, Social and Cultural Rights in Action* (Oxford University Press, 2007) 71, 77.

3 Walter Kalin and Jorg Kunzli, *The Law of International Human Rights Protection* (Oxford University Press, 2009) 93.

4 As Skogly noted, the common perception is that 'whether a state can in any way be held responsible for human rights violations depends not only on the state's actions, but also on where those actions took place, and/or the nationality of the victims of the violations'. Sigrun I. Skogly, 'Extraterritoriality: Universal Human Rights without Universal Obligations?' in Sarah Joseph and Adam McBeth (eds), *Research Handbook on International Human Rights Law* (Edward Elgar, 2010) 71.

5 See Takele Soboka Bulto, *Extraterritorial Application of the Human Right to Water in Africa* (Cambridge University Press, forthcoming, 2013).

6 See, for instance, Communication 7/88, *Committee for the Defence of Political Prisoners v Bahrain*, 7th Annual Activity Report (1993–1994); Communication 38/90, *Wesley Parish v Indonesia*, 7th Annual Activity Report (1993–1994); Communication 2/88, *Iheanyichukwu A.Ihebereme v USA*, 7th Annual Activity Report (1993–1994); Communication 5/88, *Prince J. N.Makoge v USA*, 7th Annual Activity Report (1993–1994); Communication 3/88, *Centre for the Independence of Judges and Lawyers v Yugoslavia*, 7th Annual Activity Report (1993–1994); Communication 37/90, *Georges Eugene v USA and Haiti*, 7th Annual Activity Report (1993–1994). See, for instance, Communication 227/1999, *Democratic Republic of Congo (DRC) v Burundi, Rwanda and Uganda*, 20th Annual Activity Report (2006); Communication 157/96, *Association Pour la Sauvegarde de la Paix au Burundi v Tanzania, Kenya, Uganda, Rwanda, Zaire and Zambia*, 17th Annual Activity Report (2004).

Litigating Transnational Human Rights Obligations 241

by non-territorial actors. This is indicative of the prevalence, if not rampancy, of extraterritorial violations of individuals' and groups' rights in Africa not only by African States but even by non-African countries.

None of these early communications were considered on the merits as the States against whom the communications were lodged were non-African States over which the Commission does not have any jurisdiction. The communications were thus dismissed at their early stages[7]. It is imperative, therefore, to analyze the spatial reach of the Charter in cases where similar violations are committed by State parties to the Charter.

This hypothetical judgment (from the African Commission on Human and Peoples' Rights) addresses the oft-neglected question of whether the main regional human rights instrument, namely, the African Charter on Human and Peoples' Rights ('African Charter' or 'Charter')[8] imposes extraterritorial obligations on its State parties. It specifically addresses the reach of a State's extraterritorial human rights for the (in)actions of non-State actors the headquarters/activities of which are located in the state's territory.

The ensuing judgment draws on comparative case laws and approaches of the European and Inter-American human rights systems on questions of extraterritorial application of human rights in those regional human rights systems. This overview is relevant to the question at hand, due to the African Charter's cross-reference provision which mandates the African Commission to 'draw inspiration' from the jurisprudence of relevant human rights instruments and related case law.[9] After analyzing the Charter's provisions and the African Commission's jurisprudence in comparative context, the judgment concludes that the Charter allows wide latitude for the extraterritorial application of its rights and freedoms and entails the extraterritorial reach of the duties of its State parties, thereby providing a sample (model) judgment for the African Commission to draw upon in its future decisions involving States' extraterritorial responsibility for their multinationals operating in other African States.

CASE

Communication 1000/2012, Justice for All and Rights Without Borders v the Republic of Ormania

Summary of Facts

1. The complaint is jointly filed by two non-governmental human rights organisations ('NGOs'). *Justice for All* is a local NGO registered in

---

7 Ibid.

8 African (Banjul) Charter on Human and Peoples' Rights, Adopted June 27 1981, OAU Doc. CAB/LEG/67/3 Rev. 5, 21 I.L.M. 58 (1982); entered into force 21 October 1986. The African Charter has been ratified by all member states of the African Union, with the then newly emerging Eritrea the last state to accede in January 1999.

9 See Paragraphs 28–29, below.

242   *Public Duties for Private Wrongs: Regulation of Multinationals*

Ogdenia, while *Rights Without Borders* is an NGO based in Geneva, Switzerland. Both have observer status before the African Commission on Human and Peoples' Rights ('Commission' or 'African Commission'.)

2.   This complaint involves two neighbouring African countries of Ormania and Ogdenia. The alleged violations of fundamental rights guaranteed under the African Charter on Human and Peoples' Rights ('Charter' or 'African Charter') mainly arise from the activities of *Transborder Oil Exploration Company* (TOC), a multinational company the headquarters of which is registered in Ormania, with its subsidiaries operating in the Ogdenian State and beyond.

3.   The complaint alleges that TOC has been given licence by the Ogdenian Government to undertake vast oil explorations, mostly in the southern parts of the country that are predominantly inhabited by indigenous Hawas People and other rural groups. TOC, forming a joint venture with *National Oil Company* (NOC), which is owned by the Ogdenian State, began its operations without any consultation with – indeed against the open opposition of – the indigenous Hawas and other rural populations inhabiting the surrounding areas, who were eventually forcibly evicted.

4.   The complaint further alleges that the oil exploration agreement between the TOC and Ogdenian State contains aspects that violate the human rights of TOC-NOC employees who are Ogdenian citizens. The complaint in particular decries a clause in the exploration contract in which Ogdenia's nationals employed in the joint TOC-NOC projects cannot demand salary increments during the first three years of the exploration, a condition that does not apply anywhere else in Ogdenia or to Ormanian nationals working for the TOC-NOC joint venture.

5.   Moreover, the complaint alleges that in one of TOC-NOC's oil extraction fields in Ogdenia leakages of chemicals have polluted the River *Madda*[10] and caused damage of reproductive health and skin cancer to the Hawas indigenous and rural population in the surrounding areas, who depended on the river not only as the sole source of drinking and sanitation water, but also as a source of food (fishing). The *Madda* is now declared a dead river, and signboards are erected warning: 'Do not drink, do not swim, do not fish', leaving the local population with no option but to look for alternative sources of water for drinking and basic sanitation. The primary burden for fetching such water has fallen on women and girls. This has forced Hawas women and girls to travel over three hours every day to find alternative sources of drinking, cooking and sanitation water. Many girls had to drop out of school to help their mothers fetch water. Among those who are also affected by the

---

10 This is a hypothetical river, and to this author's best knowledge there is no river named *Madda* (*Afaan Oromoo*, meaning 'source' or 'wellspring').

Litigating Transnational Human Rights Obligations 243

river's pollution are Ormania's citizens who permanently live in Ogdenia. The *Madda* is an international river and flows into Ormania's territory, and its pollution has affected over 3000 nationals of Ormania at home.

6. Affected nationals of Ormania, including those who returned home from Ogdenia, were given free medical check-ups and treatment and TOC was ordered to pay them compensation. However, nationals of Ogdenia who suffered the same consequences of the pollution and who were attempting to bring a case against TOC in Ormania's courts were denied visas to enter Ormania. A case against TOC is currently pending before the local courts of Ogdenia.

7. The complainants request that the African Commission find Ormania in violation of the rights to equality, health, work, and water of residents of Ogdenia.

I. Ruling on Admissibility

8. Under Article 56(5) of the Charter, communications alleging violations of human rights 'shall be considered if they...are sent after exhausting local remedies, if any, unless it is obvious that this procedure is unduly prolonged'. All complaints alleging violations of Charter-based guarantees must therefore be sent to the Commission only after exhausting local remedies available to the victims in the domestic legal system of the implicated State.

9. This Commission has repeatedly and consistently stressed that the exhaustion of local remedies is one of the crucial preconditions for admissibility of communications that come before it from time to time. This Commission has stressed that resort to international tribunals and remedies are a remedy of last resort.[11] This was made clear in some of its earliest rulings, wherein it stated that the rule of exhaustion of local remedies 'is one of the most important conditions for admissibility of communications, no doubt therefore, in almost all the cases, the first requirement looked at by both the Commission and State concerned is the exhaustion of local remedies'.[12]

10. The present complaint must therefore pass the local remedies test of admissibility. However, the circumstances surrounding the *loci* of the facts of the present case present multiple difficulties for the alleged victims to exhaust local remedies in Ormania. There are simply no local remedies available to the complainants. The history of and

---

11 Communication 299/05, *Anuak Justice Council v Ethiopia*, 20th Annual Activity Report (2006), Para 48.

12 (Joined) Communications 147/95 and 149/96, *Sir Dawada K.Jawara v The Gambia*, 13th Annual Activity Report (2000), Para 30.

244 *Public Duties for Private Wrongs: Regulation of Multinationals*

assumption underlying the local remedies rule is that the complainants are within the country associated with the violations, in which case they are required to access and exhaust local remedies available in the implicated state.

11. In the present case, the complainants are right holders in their home country who seek to have a foreign State, Ormania, be held responsible for its part in the violation of their rights across international boundaries in their own home State of Ogdenia. In this sense, the remedies that may be made available to them from Ormania, strictly speaking, are not local remedies.

12. Additionally, the complainants were denied entry visas to Ormania, hence their access to any remedies within the Ormanian State is effectively curtailed by the immigration procedures of the implicated State. In the instant case, the emerging scenario presents a polar opposite of the *raison d'être* justifying the application of the local remedies rule. The complainants' duty to exhaust local remedies assumes that remedies are available, adequate and effective. In the present case, the complainants have been denied entry visas to the defendant State, and have therefore been effectively denied access to local remedies provided for in Ormania's legal system, if any.

13. It is the established jurisprudence of the Commission that in situations involving serious and massive violations, the complainants are exempted from exhausting local remedies.[13] This Commission reiterated its position in a more recent decision against Sudan, and stated that 'where the violations involve many victims, it becomes neither practical nor desirable for the complainants or the victims to pursue such internal remedies'.[14] This Commission has long ruled that in such instances 'it is impractical or undesirable for the complainant to seize the domestic courts in the case of each violation'.[15] Whether violations are serious and massive depend upon the number of affected people and the gravity of the violations.[16] In the present case, the violations concern almost all of the Hawas people and other indigenous communities living around them as well as all Ogdenian employees of the TOC-NOC. It involves quite a large number of people, and the violations complained of are extremely serious, as they involve complaints about the right to health, including reproductive health and skin cancers, drinking water and the right to work.

---

13 See Joined Communications 25/89, 47/90, 56/91, 100/93, *Free Legal Assistance Group and Others v Zaire*, 9th Annual Activity Report (1995) Para 37.

14 Communication 235/2000, *Dr Curtis Francis Doebbler v Sudan*, 27th Annual Activity Report (2009) Para 117.

15 *Free Legal Assistance Group* Case (n 13 above) Para 37.

16 *Ibid.*

Litigating Transnational Human Rights Obligations

14. One of the reasons justifying the rule of exhaustion of local remedies is the requirement that States must be given adequate notice of the situation giving rise to the complaint so that they might be able to address them through their domestic legal procedures without being called upon to respond to accusations of human rights violations before international or regional tribunals, such as this Commission. The rule of exhaustion of local remedies under Article 56(5) assumes that a State might have prevented or remedied the violations complained of had it been notified of their existence. Thus an attempt by victims or those acting on their behalf to exhaust local remedies may bring the complaint and alleged violations to the attention of the implicated State, whose authorities could have been unaware of the circumstances. The Commission stated that '[t]he exhaustion of domestic remedies requirement should be properly understood as ensuring that the State concerned has ample opportunity to remedy the situation of which applicants complain'.[17]

15. In the present case, Ormania cannot claim not to have any knowledge of the violations TOC caused abroad. Its own nationals who have returned home from Ogdenia have suffered the same violations Ogdenian nationals have complained of in this case. Ormania has indeed provided free medical check-up and treatments for its returning nationals. Additionally, the pollution of the River *Madda*, which crosses from Ogdenia to Ormania, has severely affected the health of some 3,000 Ormanian nationals, a fact that has been widely reported in the local media both in Ormania and Ogdenia. In any event, Ormania cannot claim to have no knowledge of a pollution of this magnitude involving the country's biggest river. Moreover, Ogdenian nationals have informed the Ormanian Embassy in Ogdenia that they have suffered as a result of TOC activities and sought visas to go to Ormania to mount a legal challenge against TOC in Ormania. The Embassy denied them the visas. The combination of all these factors shows that Ormania was aware, or was given adequate notice, of the activities of TOC in Ogdenia that have given rise to the present complaint.

16. For the above reasons, the African Commission declares this communication admissible.

II. Decision on the Merits

2.1 General

17. The instant case presents the Commission with the opportunity to scrutinise novel issues that have seldom been decided on the merits so far.

---

17 Communication 155/96 *The Social and Economic Rights Action Center and the Center for Economic and Social Rights v Nigeria*, 15th Annual Activity Report (2001–2002) Para 38 (hereinafter 'SERAC case').

246 *Public Duties for Private Wrongs: Regulation of Multinationals*

The jurisprudence this Commission has developed has hitherto focused on the domestic State's responsibility to implement the Charter's human and peoples' rights. Only a few complaints involving transboundary violations of rights and freedoms enshrined in the African Charter have been decided on the merits by the African Commission.

18. Rights holders have approached the Commission, seeking redress for the violation of their rights in their home state by foreign States.[18] However, none of these cases could be decided on the merits, as the Commission had to declare them inadmissible simply because the communications were made against non-African states, hence non-parties to the Charter. Thus, the scope of States' human rights obligations for their commissions or omissions that have human rights implications abroad have seldom been decided by the Commission.[19] The present case would thus present the Commission with the opportunity to hand down such a decision.

19. As such, the Commission will rely not only on the text of the African Charter but also on comparative jurisprudence of its global and regional counterparts as mandated by Articles 60–1 of the African Charter.

2.2 The Spatial Scope of State Parties' Obligations

20. Ormania has argued that the African Charter is a territorially minded instrument designed to oblige States to realise the Charter's guarantees for its residents. It argues that the realisation of the human rights of Ogdenian residents is not Ormania's responsibility. This argument is based on the principle that a State is responsible for events, circumstances and persons situated in its own territory. The contention further argues that Ormania cannot interfere in the human rights situations of Ogdenia without violating the latter's sovereignty, a sacrosanct principle of the Charter of the African Union and of the United Nations.

21. The quintessential issue that requires determination in the instant case is whether State parties to the Charter owe obligations to residents of

---

18 See, for instance, Communication 7/88, *Committee for the Defence of Political Prisoners v Bahrain*, 7th Annual Activity Report (1993–1994); Communication 38/90, *Wesley Parish v Indonesia*, 7th Annual Activity Report (1993–1994); Communication 2/88, *Iheanyichukwu A. Ihebereme v USA*, 7th Annual Activity Report (1993–1994);Communication 5/88, *Prince J. N. Makoge v USA*, 7th Annual Activity Report (1993–1994); Communication 3/88, *Centre for the Independence of Judges and Lawyers v Yugoslavia*, 7th Annual Activity Report (1993–1994);Communication 37/90, *Georges Eugene v USA and Haiti*, 7th Annual Activity Report (1993–1994).

19 See, for instance, Communication 227/1999, *Democratic Republic of Congo (DRC) v Burundi, Rwanda and Uganda*, 20th Annual Activity Report (2006); Communication 157/96, *Association Pour la Sauvegarde de la Paix au Burundi v Tanzania, Kenya, Uganda, Rwanda, Zaire and Zambia*, 17th Annual Activity Report (2004).

Litigating Transnational Human Rights Obligations 247

other African States. If this question is answered in the negative, it would not be necessary to go into the analysis of the violations complained of.

22. Unlike its European[20] and Inter-American counterparts,[21] the African Charter does not contain any territoriality or jurisdiction clause, thereby implying the possible extraterritorial reach of the Charter. There is nothing in the African Charter which has the import of 'territoriality' of States' human rights duties. The general obligations clause under Article 1 of the Charter States:

> The Member States of the Organisation of African Unity parties to the present Charter shall recognize the rights, duties and freedoms enshrined in the Charter and shall undertake to adopt legislative or other measures to give effect to them.

23. In addition, the African Charter provides for specific rights that have direct extraterritorial applications. For instance, Article 12(2) of the Charter enshrines every individual's right to return to the country of origin. This right protects an individual who is outside the State of origin. In this sense, the protection afforded to the individual, and the duty of the State to allow the same to return home, applies extraterritorially. Extraterritorial application of human rights therefore can also be seen as an instrument for the protection of individuals and groups abroad from the transboundary violations of their rights by their own state of origin.

24. Similarly, there is another instance of the Charter's explicit extraterritorial application in Article 23 of the Charter, which provides for 'the right to national and international peace and security'. Member States of the Charter are thus enjoined to ensure that 'their territories shall not be used as bases for subversive or terrorist activities against the people of any other State Party to the present Charter'.[22] This is a clear case of a State's duty to protect the right to peace extraterritorially.

25. Moreover, the African Charter has enjoined the African Commission a wide latitude under Articles 60 and 61 to 'draw inspiration' from rules of

---

20 Under the Article 1 of the European Convention on Human Rights: 'The High Contracting Parties shall secure to everyone within their jurisdiction the rights and freedoms defined in Section I of this Convention.'

21 Article 1(1) of the American Convention On Human Rights states:
   The States Parties to this Convention undertake to respect the rights and freedoms recognized herein and to ensure to all persons subject to their jurisdiction the free and full exercise of those rights and freedoms, without any discrimination for reasons of race, color, sex, language, religion, political or other opinion, national or social origin, economic status, birth, or any other social condition.

22 Article 23(2), African (Banjul) Charter on Human and Peoples' Rights, Adopted 27 June 1981, OAU Doc. CAB/LEG/67/3 rev. 5, 21 I.L.M. 58 (1982); entered into force 21 October 1986.

248 *Public Duties for Private Wrongs: Regulation of Multinationals*

international law and international human rights law. Pursuant to these provisions, the Commission has explicitly referred to the case law and treaty provisions of the other regional systems in interpreting the Charter's provisions and rendering decisions on cases that come before it.

26. The pattern of cases with extraterritorial elements in the European human rights system has come in three different forms. The first group arose from violations occurring on territories controlled by the implicated foreign State.[23] The second group of cases involved not control over territory but control over individuals by State agents in third State territories.[24] The third group of cases implicated the responsibility of states extraterritorially as a result of a State's violations of obligations of *non-refoulement,* expulsion or extradition of a person to another State where such might result in the person's torture or cruel, inhuman or degrading treatment or punishment or any other infringement of fundamental rights and freedoms.[25]

27. Similarly, the cases in which the Inter-American Commission held States responsible for the violation of human rights fall into three distinct groups. The first category of cases implicated States' extraterritorial human rights responsibility for extraditing or deporting individuals into foreign territories where their rights were likely to be violated.[26] The second category of cases included those in which States were held liable for violations of human rights in territories under their effective control, even if those territories were not part of the implicated State's territory.[27] The third group of cases included those in which neither the court nor the implicated State questioned the duty to abide by the American Declaration when a State acts outside its own territory.[28]

28. If the African Commission is to draw inspiration from the case law of the Inter-American and European regional counterparts, there have

---

23 See, for instance, *Loizidou v Turkey* (Preliminary Objections) Application No 40/1993/435/514, ECtHR 23 March 1995, Series A, Vol. 310; *Cyprus v Turkey,* Application No. 25781/94, ECtHR 10 May 2001; *Case of Al-Skeini and others v The United Kingdom* (Application No. 55721/07), Judgement of 7 July 2011.

24 *Stocke v Germany,* Case No. 28/1989/188/248, ECtHR 12 October 1989, Series A, Vol. 199; *Cyprus v Turkey,* Applications Nos 6780/74 and 6950/75, ECommHR 26 May 1975, 2 DR (1975); *W.M. v Denmark,* Application No. 17392/90, ECommHR 14 October 1992.

25 See *Soering v The United Kingdom,* Case No. 1/1989/161/217, ECtHR 7 July 1989, Series A, Vol. 161. In this particular scenario, the extraterritorial aspect of state's responsibility is implicated for its contribution to or facilitation of violations of human rights of those that it expels from its territory.

26 *Haitian Centre for Human Rights v the United States ('US Interdiction of Haitians on the High Seas'),* IACHR Report No. 51/96, Case No. 10.675, 13 March 1997.

27 See *Coard and Others v the United States,* Inter-American Human Rights Commission, Report No. 109/1999, Case No. 10.951 (29 September 1999).

28 *Salas and others v the United States ('US Military Intervention in Panama'),* IAHRC Report No. 31/93, Case No. 10.573 (United States), 14 October 1993.

been ample instances in the case law of these human rights systems where States have been held responsible for their roles in human rights violations abroad.

29. Given the lack of a territoriality clause in the Charter, and considering the specific instances where the African Charter has provided for State's extraterritorial obligations, coupled with the examples of the other regional systems which are inspirational sources for the Commission's work, there is firm ground in favour of the extraterritorial application of the African Charter. A contrary interpretation would allow States to violate human rights abroad in ways that they cannot violate at home. This is against the purpose and the object of the Charter, whose aim is to help enhance the realisation of all human and peoples' rights across the continent. Indeed, as the UN Human Rights Committee rightly ruled:

> it would be unconscionable to so interpret the responsibility ...[of a State party to a human rights treaty] as to permit a State party to perpetrate violations of the Covenant on the territory of another State, which violations it could not perpetrate on its own territory.[29]

30. Consequently, Ormania's argument that the Charter is territorially based runs foul of the Charter's provisions, the Charter's object and purpose and comparable international practice from which the Commission is enjoined to draw inspiration. Thus, the African Charter has wide room for extraterritorial application wherein States can be held accountable for the violations of human and peoples' rights abroad through their commissions or omissions.

2.3 Extraterritorial Obligations and the Layer of States' Duties

31. This Commission has developed quartet layers of State obligations that must be cumulatively observed in the domestic implantation of the Charter's guarantees. As explicated in the SERAC decision against Nigeria, these are the duties to respect, protect, promote and fulfill.[30] These duties have both territorial and extraterritorial reach since their scope of application should be congruous with the human and peoples' rights in relation to which they are gauged.

32. States parties have to *respect* the enjoyment of the right in other countries. The extraterritorial duty to respect requires States parties to refrain from actions that interfere, directly or indirectly, with the enjoyment of Charter's rights in other countries. A State is responsible to ensure that any activity, omissions and commissions alike, that is undertaken within its territorial jurisdiction does not deprive

---

29 *Sergio Euben Lopez Burgos v Uruguay*, Communication No. R.12/52 (UN Human Rights Committee), UN Doc. Supp. No. 40 (A/36/40) (1981) Para 12.3.
30 SERAC case (n 17 above) Paras 44–47.

250 *Public Duties for Private Wrongs: Regulation of Multinationals*

another State of the ability to realise the right of persons in its jurisdiction.

33. The State's extraterritorial duty to *protect* requires positive action by way of ensuring that State agents and non-State actors (including multinational companies and individuals within the State's jurisdiction) do not infringe upon the rights and freedoms being enjoyed in other States. At this level, States incur international responsibility for the violation of international human rights law for culpable conduct of non-State actors who, from their location within the territory of one State, engage in conduct that produces extraterritorially prejudicial activities in another State. Among other things, it also requires States to ensure protection of human rights when adopting bilateral and multilateral agreements. A State can thus be held liable for human rights violations in other States for its failure to take into consideration the enjoyment of the rights while taking decisions, sanctions, programmes and policies as a member of international organizations. Arguably, this aspect of States' extraterritorial duty is also an expression of the obligation not to discriminate against those beyond its borders. In other words, States are not allowed to violate the human rights of non-resident, non-nationals, which violations it is prohibited from committing at home. For otherwise, it would violate its duty not to discriminate among Africans on the basis of nationality or place of residence. As the Inter-American Commission on Human Rights stated:

> The fundamental rights of the individual are proclaimed in the Americas on the basis of the principles of equality and non-discrimination – 'without distinction as to race, nationality, creed or sex'. Given that individual rights inhere simply by virtue of a person's humanity, each American State is obliged to uphold the protected rights of any person subject to its jurisdiction. While this most commonly refers to persons within a State's territory, it may, under given circumstances, refer to conduct with an extraterritorial locus where the person concerned is present in the territory of one state, but subject to the control of another State – usually through the acts of the latter's agents abroad. In principle, the inquiry turns not on the presumed victim's nationality or presence within a particular geographic area, but on whether, under the specific circumstances, the State observed the rights of a person subject to its authority and control.[31]

34. The extraterritorial State duty to promote human rights implies that a State must take positive measures aimed at enabling the enjoyment of relevant human rights and freedoms in other States. This includes, for instance, provision of information and transparency regarding

---

31 See *Coard and Others v the United States* (n 27 above) Para 37.

Litigating Transnational Human Rights Obligations 251

impending projects that have repercussions on the realisation of human and peoples' rights in other States.

35. States' extraterritorial duty to 'fulfil' human rights in other States' jurisdictions requires the State to provide material resources to those who cannot afford to pay for those life sustaining resources. In other words, the duty to fulfil is triggered when the donee State is not in a position to provide the bare necessities of life for individuals and groups within its territory and seeks international assistance and cooperation from other States that are in a position to come to its aid. As affirmed in the Maastricht Guidelines, States thus requested 'must consider the request in good faith, and respond in a manner consistent with their obligations to fulfil economic, social and cultural rights extraterritorially'.[32]

36. States must therefore implement their extraterritorial duty to respect, protect, promote and fulfil. A violation of any of these duties leads to a violation of one or more of the Charter's rights and freedoms.

2.4 Private Acts, Public Responsibility

37. Ormania alternatively has argued that, failing the argument on the territoriality of the Charter's scope, its international responsibility is not implicated since no State agent was involved in the violations complained of. It contends that TOC is a non-State entity, whose day-to-day activities abroad are beyond the control and outside the responsibility of Ormania. The State conceded that it would hold the company accountable for similar violations if committed in Ormania in terms of Ormanian law and regulations. However, it maintains that it is the responsibility of Ogdenia to control, monitor and address problems emerging from companies operating in its territory. It thus sought to draw a clear line between State duties for the acts of private actors within its territory, on the one hand, and when these entities operate abroad, on the other. In essence, it argues that it should not be held accountable for acts of private actors abroad.

38. In the SERAC case, the African Commission found Nigeria in violation of its duty to protect the victims' (the Ogoni ethnic group) rights including the right to life, food, water, and shelter which were violated through spoliation of the environment and water resources by the consortium of the Dutch Shell Company and the Nigerian National Petroleum Company.[33] Similarly, in the *Union des Jeunes Avocats v Chad*, the African Commission decided that the State has the duty to protect its citizens

32 See Maastricht Principles on Extraterritorial Obligations of States in the area of Economic, Social and Cultural Rights, Para 35 (hereinafter 'ETOs Guidelines') adopted on 28 September 2011.

33 SERAC (n 17 above) Para 46.

252 *Public Duties for Private Wrongs: Regulation of Multinationals*

through legislative and enforcement measures from the damaging acts that may be perpetrated by third parties in violation of the fundamental rights and freedoms guaranteed under the African Charter.[34] Chad was consequently found to be in violation of its duties under the African Charter because 'the State failed to protect the rights in the Charter from violation by other parties'.[35] The State's duty to protect remains intact in all circumstances and 'even a civil war in Chad cannot be used as an excuse by the State violating or permitting violations of rights in the African Charter'.[36] It is immaterial for the purposes of a State's duty to protect whether the State agents are actively involved in the human rights violations. Rather, this Commission has ruled that:

> [t]he Charter specifies in Article 1 that the States Parties shall not only recognize the rights, duties and freedoms adopted by the Charter, but they should also 'undertake…measures to give effect to them'. In other words, if a State neglects to ensure the rights in the African Charter, this can constitute a violation, even if the State or its agents are not the immediate cause of the violation.[37]

39. We have outlined above that this duty also applies extraterritoriality. Inevitably, there are situations where a multinational company registered in a State might cause harms to human rights abroad without the home State's knowledge. In this scenario, it might be difficult to impute blame on to the State since it cannot control every single activity of its companies abroad. However, no State is allowed under the African Charter to facilitate, allow or condone its companies to violate human rights in another Charter-State's territory, in ways that it cannot at home if the company engages in similar activities.

40. If the violations complained of are well founded, as we will address below, then Ormania will have violated its duty to protect Charter-based human and peoples' rights. Even if the author of the violations is TOC, a non-State company, a State is held responsible for not preventing or remedying the human rights violations committed abroad by private entities incorporated within its jurisdiction provided that the State had knowledge of the said events.

41. Thus, the argument that Ormania has no responsibility regarding the activities of one of its private entities operating abroad, TOC in this case, is untenable. After all, the African Charter has sought to regulate the activities of non-State entities through the duties of States in which they are incorporated. This Commission found Chad in violation of its

---

34 See Communication 74/92, *Commission Nationale des Droits de l'Homme et des Libertes v Chad*, 9th Annual Activity Report (1995–96).

35 Id, Para 18.

36 Id, Para 21.

37 Id, Para 20.

Litigating Transnational Human Rights Obligations 253

duties under the African Charter because 'the State failed to protect the rights in the Charter from violation by other parties'.[38] Similarly, in the SERAC case, this Commission found Nigeria in violation of its duty to protect the victims' (the Ogoni ethnic group) rights to life, food, water and shelter from the operations of the consortium of the Dutch Shell Company and the Nigerian National Petroleum Company.[39] The Charter binds States parties and through them binds non-State entities. A contrary interpretation would allow States to authorise or tolerate blatant violations of human and peoples' rights committed abroad, for which their companies are responsible. This scenario would be an affront to the object and purpose of the African Charter which provides, in its preamble, that 'fundamental human rights stem from the attributes of human beings which justifies their national and international protection'. This Commission concurs with the experts' opinion stated in the Maastricht ETO Guidelines that:

> [a]ll States must take necessary measures to ensure that non-State actors which they are in a position to regulate ... such as private individuals and organizations, and transnational corporations and other business enterprises, do not nullify or impair the enjoyment of economic, social and cultural rights.[40]

2.5. Violations of Specific Rights

Alleged Violation of Article 1

42. Article 1 of the African Charter, which is the general obligations clause, provides that:

> The Member States of the Organization of African Unity parties to the present Charter shall recognize the rights, duties and freedoms enshrined in the Charter and shall undertake to adopt legislative or other measures to give effect to them.

43. The Complainants argue that a violation of any provision of the Charter automatically means a violation of Article 1 of the Charter. The Commission has long ruled that '[i]f a State party to the Charter fails to recognise the provisions of the same, there is no doubt that it is in violation of this Article'.[41] The African Commission is of the view that State parties to the African Charter (including the Respondent State) have the obligation of recognizing the rights, duties and freedoms enshrined in the Charter, as well as the responsibility of providing an environment

---

38 See Communication 74/92, *Commission Nationale des Droits de l'Homme et des Libertés v Chad*, 9th Annual Activity Report (1995–96) Para 18.
39 See SERAC case (n 17 above).
40 ETOs Guidelines (n 32 above) Para 24.
41 Communications 147/95 and 149/96, *Sir Dawda K.Jawara v The Gambia*, Para 46.

254 *Public Duties for Private Wrongs: Regulation of Multinationals*

in which those rights and freedoms can be enjoyed through the adoption of legislative or other measures that give effect to them.[42]

44. This Commission had held that Article 1 of the African Charter proclaims a fundamental principle that not only do the States parties recognize the rights, duties and freedoms enshrined in the Charter, but they also commit themselves to respect them and to take measures to give effect to them.[43] This implies two things. First, if a State party fails to ensure respect of the rights contained in the African Charter, this constitutes a violation of the African Charter on its own even if the State or its agents were not the perpetrators of the violation. Secondly, the State will still be in violation of the Charter where it fails to protect rights holders against violations of their rights by non-State entities (third parties). If the actions or omissions of the Respondent State give rise to a violation of a provision of the Charter, the State will immediately be in violation of the provisions of Article 1 of the African Charter.

Alleged Violation of Articles 3 cum 15

45. The Complainants allege that the policy that prevents Ogdenian nationals from demanding salary increments during the first three years of the TOC-NOC exploration is discriminatory and violates their right to work under equitable conditions as guaranteed under Article 15 of the Charter. This policy has no application elsewhere in Ogdenia nor does it apply to Ormanian nationals working for the TOC-NOC joint venture in Ogdenia.

46. The protection of the fundamental right to equality is a guarantee for the enforcement of other human rights provisions, including the protection and promotion of socio-economic rights in equal and equitable manner. The equality guarantee is therefore a thread that draws together all categories of human rights. The equality guarantee is thus not only a fundamental right in its own right, but it is also a value that underlies the remainder of the human rights *corpus.*

47. Thus, the violation of the right to equality disturbs all the values that inform its content as well as the rights guaranteed through its enforcement. As the African Commission has stressed, '[t]he right to equality is all the more important since it determines the possibility for the individual to enjoy many other rights'.[44]

---

42 Communication 292/2004. *Institute for Human Rights and Development in Africa v Republic of Angola,* Para 82.

43 Communication 231/99, *Avocats Sans Frontieres (on behalf of Gae˜tanBwampamye) v Burundi,* 14th Annual Activity Report (2001) Para. 31.

44 Communication 253/2002, *Antoine Bissangou v Republic of Congo,* 21st Annual Activity Report (2006–2007), Para 68.

Litigating Transnational Human Rights Obligations 255

48. Under Article 3 of the Charter, '[e]very individual shall be equal before the law' and 'shall be entitled to equal protection of the law'. The crucial importance attached to the equality guarantee of the Charter can be discerned from its ordering, as it comes before the right to life (Article 4). Its guarantees in the Charter are extensive, providing for the prohibition of discrimination (Article 2) and equality in and before the law (Article 3). The Charter's provisions on the right to equality have been elaborated by the African Commission:

> Article 3 of the African Charter has two arms, one dealing with equality before the law, that is, Article 3(1), and the other, that is, Article 3(2). The most fundamental meaning of equality before the law or equality under the law is a principle under which each individual is subject to the same laws, with no individual or groups having special legal privileges. On the other hand, equal protection of the law under Article 3(2) relates to the right of all persons to have the same access to the law and courts and to be treated equally by the law and courts both in procedures and in the substance of the law.[45]

49. The right to equality under the Charter applies to all the rights and freedoms guaranteed in the regional instrument and cuts across the traditional civil and political, economic, social and cultural, and group (solidarity) rights that should be enjoyed by every individual and group without discrimination.

50. Article 2 of the Charter sets forth that everyone is 'entitled to the enjoyment of the rights and freedoms recognized and guaranteed in the present Charter without distinction of any kind'. As the Commission has observed, '[e]quality or lack of it affects the capacity of one to enjoy many other rights'.[46]

51. Access to the enjoyment of the Charter's rights and freedoms, such as the right to work, must be available to everyone in equal measure. Thus the violation of a given socio-economic right may trample not just the equality clause but also the specific socio-economic right in the Charter in question. In such instances, the use of the right to equality or, alternatively, proving discrimination, is a valuable instrument as a means of demonstrating violations of socio-economic rights.

52. In the case at hand, while all other employees in Ogdenia can request salary increases and other benefits, those working in the TOC-NOC joint venture have been singled out to be denied this right. Article 2 of the Charter stipulates that '[e]very individual shall be entitled to the

---

45 Communication 293/2004, *Zimbabwe Lawyers for Human Rights and the Institute for Human Rights and Development v Republic Of Zimbabwe*, 24th Annual Activity Report (2007–2008) Para 124.
46 Ibid., Para 125.

256 *Public Duties for Private Wrongs: Regulation of Multinationals*

enjoyment of the rights and freedoms recognized and guaranteed in the present Charter without distinction of any kind'. The differential treatment of Ogdenian nationals employed in the TOC-NOC joint venture is clearly discriminatory, and is in violation of Article 3 of the African Charter. The ground of differentiation used is arbitrary. First, it discriminates against Ogdenian nationals working in the TOC-NOC while all other nationals of Ogdenia working elsewhere do not have limitations on their right to demand or negotiate pay rises. Secondly, it discriminates between employees engaged in the same company in the same project (the TOC-NOC joint venture), and the limitation on the right to negotiate for better pay that has been imposed on Ogdenian nationals does not apply to similarly situated Ormanian nationals working in TOC-NOC. The differentiation that has been made on the basis of nationality is arbitrary, and has no merit.

53. The employees' demand to work under equitable and favorable conditions, as guaranteed under Article 15 of the Charter, should be enforced at all times, irrespective of the nature of the project or of the employer. The fact that TOC is a foreign employer does not detract from employees' right to work. To take away workers' right to negotiate for better pay is to take away the heart of the human right to work and it constitutes a clear infringement of the requirements of Article 15 of the Charter.

54. Ormania's Ministry of Labour and Ministry of Industry have had prior knowledge of this discriminatory practice of TOC since certified copies of all agreements made abroad by companies registered in Ormania must be submitted to the two ministries. Thus, Ormania has failed to live up to its extraterritorial duty to protect Ogdenian nationals' right to equality and right to work under equitable conditions. This is a clear violation of Articles 3 and 15 of the Charter.

Alleged Violations of the Human Right to Water

55. The complaint relating to the violation of the human right to water gives rise to a State's contention that the right does not exist as such. Ormania contends that nowhere in the Charter is the right to water mentioned, and thus, an alleged violation of the same is untenable. Ormania has argued that, in order that the right be respected or protected, it must have normative protection binding upon the State in the first instance and such is not the case under the Charter. The State argues that in the absence of an express provision of a right to water in the Charter it does not owe a legal obligation to realize same even in its own territory, let alone in a foreign State's jurisdiction. Thus, the complaint is nothing more than a violation of an imaginary right, which does have any normative status in the African Charter. It is imperative, therefore, to assess the status of the alleged right under the African Charter.

Litigating Transnational Human Rights Obligations 257

56. It is true that the African Charter does not directly protect the human right to water and sanitation.[47] However, the Commission has ruled that the right to water is implied in protections of the right to life, the right to dignity, the right to work, the right to health, the right to the right to economic, social and cultural development and the right to a satisfactory environment.[48] It entitles everyone to sufficient, safe, acceptable, physically accessible and affordable water for personal and domestic uses.

57. The Commission has long recognized the human right to water as one of those rights that are latently enshrined in the Charter. It derived the right to water from other rights such as the right to dignity (Article 5) the right to health (Article 16) and the right to a healthy environment (Article 24) of the Charter. In *Free Legal Assistance Group and Others v Zaire*, the Commission held that the 'failure of the government to provide basic services such as safe drinking water and electricity and the shortage of medicine...constitutes a violation of Article 16 [right to health]'.[49] Similarly, in the SERAC case, the Commission decided that contamination of sources of drinking water by State or non-State actors is a violation of Article 16 (the right to health) and Article 24 (the right to a satisfactory environment).[50]

58. However, the Commission has affirmed that there is an independent human right to water in the Charter, a stance it explicated in its recent Guidelines on Economic, Social and Cultural Rights of the African Charter.[51]

59. This is a culmination of an earlier guideline that had been developed by the Commission, commonly referred to as the 'Pretoria Statement'. In the 'Pretoria Statement' on socio-economic rights of the Charter, the right to health (Article 16) was taken to entail 'access to basic...sanitation and adequate supply of safe and potable water'.[52]

60. The human right to water therefore entails all layers of State obligations, both territorially and extraterritorially. As outlined above,

---

47 See Principles and Guidelines on Economic, Social and Cultural Rights in the African Charter on Human and Peoples' Rights (2011) Para 71 (hereinafter 'Principles and Guidelines'].

48 Ibid.

49 (Joined) Communications 25/89, 47/90, 56/91, 100/93, *Free Legal Assistance Group and Z Others v Zaire*, 9th Annual Activity Report (1995–1996) Para 47.

50 See Communication 155/96, *The Social and Economic Rights Action Center and the Center for Economic and Social Rights v Nigeria*, 15th Annual Activity Report (2001–2002) Paras 49, 57 and 66 (hereinafter the 'SERAC' case) Paras 50–4.

51 Principles and Guidelines (n 47 above) Paras 71–3.

52 See 'Statement from Seminar on Social, Economic and Cultural Rights in the African Charter' (Adopted in Pretoria, 13–17 September 2004; published in 5 *African Human Rights Law Journal* (2005) 182, 186 (Para 7).

Ormania is aware that TOC activities in Ogdenia have polluted the *Madda* to such an extent that some segments of the river are not usable for drinking, fishing and swimming purposes. The Hawas people's and neighbouring rural communities' access to drinking water within reasonable distances has been severely affected. Women and girls have been forced to travel hours to fetch drinking and sanitation water. This is a clear violation of the human rights of the Hawas and other groups in Ogdenia.

61. Ormania is obligated to ensure that Ogdenian complainants have a legal recourse against TOC. Through its denial of entry visas to the present complainants, and through its failure to hold TOC accountable for the violations it committed in Ogdenia, the Respondent State has violated its duty to protect the human right to water in Ogdenia. As stated above, the violation of the human right to water entails the conjoint violations of numerous human rights such as right to health. Thus the State of Ormania is in violation of the right to health and the right to water.

Alleged Violations of the Human Right to Food

62. The Communication argues that the right to food is implicit in the African Charter in such provisions as the right to life (Article 4), the right to health (Article 16) and the right to economic, social and cultural development (Article 22). By its violation of these rights extraterritorially, the Ormanian government has not only trampled upon explicitly protected rights but also upon the right to food, which is implicitly guaranteed.

63. In its SERAC decision, this Commission has ruled that the right to food is inseparably linked to the dignity of human beings and is therefore essential for the enjoyment and fulfilment of such other rights as health, education, work and political participation. The African Charter and international law require Ormania to ensure that its entities do not destroy food sources of rights holders in other African countries, including Ogdenia. Likewise, it does not allow private parties to destroy or contaminate food sources, and prevent peoples' efforts to feed themselves abroad.

64. The government of Ormania has tolerated and failed to punish and remedy the activities of TOC that destroyed food sources of the Hawas and surrounding areas through the pollution of the river *Madda*, thereby denying them their right to food (by curtailing their access to fishing) since the river is now effectively a dead river. Again, the Ormanian government has fallen short of what is demanded of it as under the provisions of the African Charter and international human rights standards, and hence, is in violation of the right to food of the Hawas and surrounding indigenous people.

Alleged Violations of Article 16

65. Article 16 of the Charter provides:

    (1) Every individual shall have the right to enjoy the best attainable state of physical and mental health.

    (2) State Parties to the present Charter shall take the necessary measures to protect the health of their people and to ensure that they receive medical attention when they are sick.

66. This Commission has developed a consistent jurisprudence that explicates the intricate interplay between contamination of water resources and the right to health. So far, the Commission has mainly interpreted the right to water as a sub-set of the right to dignity (Article 5) the right to health (Article 16) and the right to a healthy environment (Article 24) of the Charter. In *Free Legal Assistance Group and Others v Zaire*, the Commission held that the 'failure of the government to provide basic services such as safe drinking water and electricity and the shortage of medicine...constitutes a violation of Article 16 [right to health]'.[53] Similarly, in a case against Nigeria, this Commission decided that contamination of sources of drinking water by State or non-State actors is a violation of Article 16 (the right to health) and Article 24 (the right to a satisfactory environment).[54] In a case against Sudan, there was a complaint that Sudan was complicit in poisoning wells and denying access to water sources in the Darfur region.[55] Here, too, the Commission ruled that 'the poisoning of water sources, such as wells, exposed the victims to serious health risks and amounts to a violation of Article 16 of the Charter'.[56]

67. In the present case, it is clear that the silence of, or the lack of monitoring and the provision of information by, the Ogdenian and Ormanian governments has meant that the Hawas indigenous group and those living in contiguous areas in Ogdenia have had to drink the excessively polluted *Madda*, to the extent that their reproductive health is seriously damaged while others suffered severe skin problems. Had they been provided with the necessary warning, these health hazards could have easily been averted. Ormania has yet to take any action against TOC to remedy the violations the company committed abroad, although it has

---

53 (Joined) Communications 25/89, 47/90, 56/91, 100/93, *Free Legal Assistance Group and Z Others v Zaire*, 9th Annual Activity Report (1995–1996) Para 47.

54 See Communication 155/96, *The Social and Economic Rights Action Center and the Center for Economic and Social Rights v Nigeria*, 15th Annual Activity Report (2001–2002) Paras 49, 57 and 66 (hereinafter the 'SERAC' case) Paras 50–54.

55 (Joined) Communication 279/03, *Sudan Human Rights Organisation v The Sudan*, and Communication 296/05, *Centre on Housing Rights and Evictions v The Sudan*, 28th Annual Activity Report (2010) Para 207.

56 Id, Para 212.

260 *Public Duties for Private Wrongs: Regulation of Multinationals*

provided medical check-ups and free medical treatment for its own nationals who returned home from Ogdenia and who have suffered from the consequences of TOC's pollution of the *Madda.* Ormania could have averted or mitigated the health hazard that was brought to bear on the Hawas people and others. It should have held TOC to account for the violations it caused abroad, and should have ensured that Ogdenian victims of TOC's pollution had an effective remedy against TOC.

68. Such failure by the Ormanian State constitutes a violation of the Charter. In this regard, this Commission heeds the Maastricht ETO Principles, requiring States to monitor and/or prevent human rights abuses by non-State actors, to hold them to account for any such abuses, and to ensure an effective remedy for those affected.[57]

III. Findings

69. For the reasons stated above, the African Commission finds the Respondent State in violation of Articles **1, 3, 4, 15 and 16**, including the violations of the right to water and the right to food.

70. The African Commission therefore recommends that the Republic of Ogdenia should:

- ensure that TOC pays adequate compensation to the Hawas and other indigenous people groups in Ogdenia who have been affected by the consequences of TOC's pollution of the River *Madda;*

- put in place procedures whereby TOC, in consultation with the Government of Ogdenia, undertakes a comprehensive clean-up of the River *Maddaa;* and

- in consultation with Ogdenian authorities, ensure that the discriminatory clause inserted in the exploration contract signed between Ogdenian authorities and TOC be removed and all employees of the TOC-NOC joint venture be treated the same irrespective of their nationality.

The African Commission further requests that the Republic of Ormania report back to it within six months regarding the measures it has taken to implement the recommendations made in this communication.

---

57 ETOs Guidelines (n 32 above) Para 27 and Paras 36–8.

16 Forced Evictions in Zimbabwe (African Commission on Human and Peoples' Rights)

Khulekani Moyo

Abstract

In the present communication, the complainants allege violations of a wide range of their rights guaranteed under the African Charter by the Respondent State, South Africa (Respondent State). These include Articles 14 (right to property), 16 (right to health), 21 (right to self determination) and 22 (right to development) of the African Charter. The alleged violations occurred in the territory of another State, the Republic of Zimbabwe. The present communication alleges that the violations in question took place when the Marange community was violently forcibly removed from its ancestral communal land by Zimbabwe security forces to make way for diamond mining activities. This legal opinion attempts to address two important legal issues. The first is whether the African Charter imposes any legal obligations on a State Party to observe human rights outside of its territory. The second question is whether the African Charter imposes any obligation on States to ensure that private enterprises registered or domiciled in their territory respect the human rights of those in the territories in which they carry out business activities.

Introductory note

The case which is the subject of the following opinion relates to alleged violations of a host of civil, political, economic and social rights of the Marange community as a result of its forcible removal from its ancestral land by Zimbabwe's security forces to make way for diamond mining activities. The Marange community, represented by Marange Action Centre (Complainant), has filed a complaint at the African Commission on Human and Peoples' Rights (African Commission) against South Africa alleging violation of a wide range of rights of the Marange community in Zimbabwe – in violation of the provisions of the African Charter on Human and Peoples' Rights (African Charter). The Complainant alleges that it has exhausted domestic legal remedies, both under the Zimbabwean and South African courts. The complaint against South Africa is premised on the State's alleged violation of its extraterritorial human rights obligations both under the African Charter as well as under international human rights law by its

262 *Forced Evictions in Zimbabwe*

failure to control the extraterritorial operations of an entity domiciled and registered in its territory.

A key legal issue that arises in the case is whether the African Charter imposes any legal obligations on a State Party to observe human rights outside of its territory. In that regard, the opinion discusses and analyzes the question as to whether South Africa does in fact have any extraterritorial obligations, and if it does, whether those obligations have been met with respect to the Marange community. Furthermore, the opinion will explore the question as to whether the African Charter imposes any obligations on States to ensure that private enterprises registered or domiciled in their territory respect the human rights of those in the territories in which they carry out business activities. Such a question clearly implicates a State's duty to protect individuals and groups outside of its territory from any deleterious activities of its corporations.

If the existence of extraterritorial obligations is recognized under international human rights law, the question arises as to when and how responsibility for compliance with these obligations can be attributed to non-territorial States. This inevitably raises the question of jurisdiction and causation. The biggest challenge is that all international complaint mechanisms for treaties covering socio-economic rights require, as a condition for admissibility of the complaint, that the complainant fall under the jurisdiction of the perpetrator State. Although other treaties such as the European Convention on Human Rights are limited by jurisdiction, some key human rights instruments such as the Universal Declaration on Human Rights have no jurisdictional limitation. The obligations imposed by the later international human rights instruments are framed in universal terms.[1]

Additionally, the existence of extraterritorial obligations brings to the fore the attribution of responsibility between the host State and the foreign State.[2] States are the primary duty bearers for the full range of human rights under the international human rights system hence the primary focus of accountability for the realisation of human rights within their territorial jurisdiction.[3] Significantly, since States are contracting parties to international and regional human rights treaties, they are principally responsible for their implementation. However, territorially confined State duties are bound to leave gaps in the protective regime of international human rights

---

1 See M. Langford et al., "Introduction: An Emerging Field", in: M. Langford et al. (eds) *Global Justice, State Duties: The Extraterritorial Scope of Economic, Social, and Cultural Rights in International Law* (Cambridge University Press 2013) 1.

2 D.M.Chirwa, "Privatisation of Water in Southern Africa: A Human Rights Perspective" (2004) 4 *African Human Rights Law Journal* 218, 232.

3 See J.Oloka-Onyango, "Reinforcing Marginalised Rights in an Age of Globalisation: International Mechanisms, Non State Actors and the Struggle for Peoples' Rights in Africa" (2002–3) 18 *American University International Review* 815, 815.

Litigating Transnational Human Rights Obligations 263

law.[4] The rise in global trade and investment has heightened the capacity of States and non-State actors to negatively and positively impact human rights beyond their borders.[5] It is now accepted in doctrine and jurisprudence that each human right imposes a variety of obligations.[6] The degree of emphasis on any particular duty ultimately depends on the type of rights under consideration. Meaningful enjoyment of rights may require a State to respect, protect, promote or fulfil a given set of rights. The precise nature of the State duty in a given situation would depend on the circumstances of the case.[7]

Some treaty monitoring mechanisms such as the African Commission have previously adjudicated on an inter-State complaint involving the issue of extraterritorial State obligations.[8] The question of States' extraterritorial obligations offers an analytic framework in which States' legal duties beyond their own territorial borders can be understood and complied with. The critical issue, however, is how one may divide responsibilities between domestic and extraterritorial States in light of the accepted international human rights law position that the domestic state is the primary duty-holder.

The Committee on Economic, Social and Cultural Rights has explained with regard to the right to water that States parties to the International Covenant on Economic, Social and Cultural Rights must take steps to prevent their own citizens and companies from violating the right to water of individuals and communities in other countries.[9] It is, however, unclear whether such a pronouncement is an endorsement of States' extraterritorial obligations. Additionally, the CEDAW Committee has elaborated on the Convention on the Elimination of All Forms of Discrimination against Women as imposing an obligation on States to prevent discrimination by private actors regardless of whether the affected persons are in their territory.[10] The above position is further buttressed in Principle 25 of the *Maastricht Principles on Extraterritorial Obligations of States in the Area of Economic, Social and Cultural Rights* which enjoins States to regulate non-State actors interfering with the enjoyment of

---

4 See generally M.Gibney & S.Skogly (eds) *Universal Human Rights and Extraterritorial Obligations* (University of Pennsylvania Press 2010) 2–3.

5 See M. Langford et al. "Introduction: An Emerging Field" in: M. Langford et al. (eds) *Global Justice, State Duties: The Extraterritorial Scope of Economic, Social, and Cultural Rights in International Law* (Cambridge University Press 2013) 1.

6 See *Social and Economic Rights Action Centre (SERAC) and Another v Nigeria* (2001) AHRLR 60 para 44.

7 *SERAC* para 48; M.M. Sepulveda, *Obligations under the International Covenant on Economic, Social and Cultural Rights* (Intersentia 2003) 12.

8 *Democratic Republic of Congo (DRC) v Burundi, Rwanda and Uganda Communication* 227/1999.

9 United Nations Committee on Economic, Social and Cultural Rights, *General Comment 15, The Right to Water* (2002) UN Doc E/C.12/2002/11 para 33.

10 CEDAW Committee General Recommendation No. 28 on the Core Obligations of States Parties under Article 2 of the Convention on the Elimination of All Forms of Discrimination against Women (2010) paras 11–12.

264 *Forced Evictions in Zimbabwe*

economic, social and cultural rights. The African Commission has further elaborated that an act by a private individual or non-State actor, and therefore not directly imputable to a State, can generate responsibility of the State, not because of the act itself, but because of the lack of due diligence on the part of the State to prevent the violation.[11]

The extraterritorial reach of human rights in international human rights law has been explored more in the area of civil and political rights.[12] For example, some treaties such as the Optional Protocol to the Convention on the Rights of the Child on the sale of children, child prostitution and child pornography elaborate on the State's extraterritorial obligations to protect.[13] It must, however, be noted that there has been insignificant extraterritorial litigation in the area of socio-economic rights, hence less attention has been given to the different situations that may involve the extraterritorial responsibility of States.[14] It is against that background that the following opinion examines a claim based on a State's extraterritorial obligations provided for under the African Charter. The opinion further examines the question of the intersection between bilateral investment treaties and human rights, followed by an examination of the right to a remedy and its importance under the African human rights framework.

Case

Communication 274/2012 Marange Action Centre v Republic of South Africa

Summary of Facts

The complaint has been filed by the Marange Action Centre, a representative group of the Marange community of Zimbabwe, which alleges violations of their rights to facilitate diamond mining in the Marange diamond fields as will be elaborated below. The Marange diamond fields are located in the Marange communal area, Manicaland Province in the eastern part of Zimbabwe. The complainants allege that, rather than being a blessing, the immense diamond wealth has turned out to be a bane for the people of Marange from the time (2006) diamond deposits were discovered on their land. The complainants allege that they have been victims of a sinister and vicious security forces operation by the Zimbabwean authorities to get rid of so-called illegal diamond diggers, both from local villages as well as across the country. The complainants allege that some time in 2008 the

---

11 See *Zimbabwe Human Rights NGO Forum/Zimbabwe*, Communication 245/2002.
12 Gibney & Skogly *supra* note 4, 6.
13 UN Doc A/RES/54/263.
14 See Langford *supra* note 5, 6.

Zimbabwean security forces launched Operation "*Hakudzokwi*" or "*You will not return*" designed to secure the diamond fields. This operation resulted in the residents of Marange community being forcibly removed from their lands and the subsequent destruction of their houses and fields. The complainants further allege that the misery of the Marange community has been compounded by their eviction from their traditional lands, the destruction of their homes, the evisceration of their traditional and cultural sites, and the removal of their fields for growing crops for food in order to make way for diamond mining activities and the construction of an airstrip. One of the major companies involved in the mining of diamonds is Mbada Investments, a consortium between the State-owned Zimbabwe Mining Development Corporation (ZMDC) and a South African entity, New Reclamation Group, through its subsidiary, Gladwell Holdings (New Reclamation).

All South African companies and individuals investing in Zimbabwe and *vice-versa* are protected by a Bilateral Investment Promotion and Protection Agreement (BIPPA) signed between Zimbabwe and South Africa on 29 November 2009. South Africa has been extremely aggressive in the past few years in entering in investment protection agreements with various African countries due to concerted pressure from the South African business community concerned about the security of its investments, particularly in volatile African countries.

The Marange Action Centre has attempted to claim compensation on behalf of the evicted Marange villagers within the Zimbabwean courts, but to no avail. Mbada Investments officials have consistently argued that the mining consortium is protected by the BIPPA, hence local courts do not have any jurisdiction over it. According to the BIPPA signed between South Africa and Zimbabwe, any investment-related disputes between the parties are subject to arbitration at the International Centre for the Settlement of Investment Disputes (ICSID) located in Washington, DC. The Zimbabwean courts have thus refused to entertain any claim by the Marange community against Mbada Investments. The Marange Action Centre has also attempted to pursue litigation in South Africa to enjoin the South African government to compel a corporation domiciled and registered in its territory, New Reclamation, a venture partner with the Zimbabwean government in Mbada Investments, to desist from violating the various rights of the Marange community. The South African courts have also rejected the claim, citing jurisdictional issues, pointing out that the South African government has no jurisdiction to legislate extra-territorially. The South African courts further pointed out that the Bill of Rights contained in the South African constitution is territorially limited; hence the claimants should pursue their claim through the Zimbabwean courts. The South African courts have also pointed to the provisions of the BIPPA between Zimbabwe and South Africa, which provide for any

266 *Forced Evictions in Zimbabwe*

disputes pertaining to South African investments in Zimbabwe, and vice-versa, to be subjected to arbitration at ICSID. The Marange Action Centre has also submitted a dossier to the South African government detailing the human rights violations perpetrated on the Marange community. In the dossier, Marange Action Centre alleges that a South African corporation, New Reclamation, is complicit in the violation of the human rights of the community. The complainants claim that despite engaging the South African government at the political level, the latter has been reluctant in putting pressure on a corporation (New Reclamation) domiciled and registered in its territory. The South African government has also argued that the issue was dealt with by the South African Constitutional Court, which ruled that the dispute should be resolved under the provisions of the BIPPA.

As a result of its failure to get any remedy under both the Zimbabwean and South African courts, the Marange Action Centre has filed a complaint at the African Commission on Human and Peoples' Rights (African Commission) against South Africa alleging violation of a wide range of rights of the people of Marange in Zimbabwe – in violation of the various provisions of the African Charter on Human and Peoples' Rights (African Charter). The Marange Action Centre argues that South Africa is in violation of its extraterritorial human rights obligations both under the African Charter as well as under international human rights law by its failure to control the extraterritorial operations of New Reclamation, a corporation domiciled and registered in its territory.

The Marange Action Centre argues that New Reclamation is complicit in the violation of the human rights of the people of Marange as it is benefitting from the violations of the rights of the communities violently forced off their territory by Zimbabwe security officials with the involvement of private guards employed by the mining consortium to make way for diamond mining activities. The complainants further argue that the South African government, apart from not applying pressure on New Reclamation to stop it from being complicit in the violation of human rights abroad, has actually aided and abetted New Reclamation's violation of human rights of the Marange community through the BIPPA.

The African Commission is called upon to make a ruling as to whether South Africa does in fact have any extraterritorial obligations, and if it does, whether those obligations have been met with respect to the Marange community.

In arriving at its conclusion, the Commission will deal with jurisdictional issues, but also questions regarding attribution and responsibility. Furthermore, the Commission will also have to consider the provisions of the BIPPA in light of the human rights protected under the African Charter and determine whether the provisions of the BIPPA superseded the provisions of a multilateral regional human rights treaty.

Litigating Transnational Human Rights Obligations 267

Decision on the Merits

1. The instant communication calls upon the African Commission (Commission) to adjudicate upon a matter that is *sui generis* in that this is the first time the Commission has had to address a matter in which the issue of a State's extraterritorial obligations are expressly raised under the individual/group complaints mechanism provided for under the African Charter.[15]

2. In the present communication, the complainants allege a concerted violation of a wide range of their rights guaranteed under the African Charter by the Respondent State, South Africa (Respondent State). These include Articles 14, 16, 21 and 22 of the African Charter. The applicants have surprisingly not joined Zimbabwe to these proceedings as the territorial State. This issue will be briefly discussed below; suffice to point out that standard judicial procedure dictates that no findings can be made against a party not cited in the proceedings.

3. The alleged violations occurred in the territory of another State, the Republic of Zimbabwe. The present communication alleges that the violations in question took place when the Marange community was violently forcibly removed from its ancestral land by Zimbabwe security forces to make way for diamond mining activities.

Legal Issues

4. Before addressing the alleged violations of the African Charter, the Respondent State has requested the African Commission to decide two issues which are crucial to the determination of this case. The first is whether the African Charter imposes any legal obligations on a State Party to observe human rights outside of its territory. In other words, the facts of this case raise an important question: does the African Charter impose extraterritorial obligations on its member States to observe human rights outside of its territory, i.e., to protect the human rights of those outside their territory? The second crucial question is does the African Charter impose any obligation on States to ensure that private enterprises registered or domiciled in their territory respect the human rights of those in the territories in which they carry out business activities?

5. The Commission finds it useful to address these two key issues before making a determination as to whether the Respondent State is in violation of the African Charter as alleged by the Complainants.

---

15 In the case of *Democratic Republic of Congo v Burundi, Rwanda and Uganda,* the Commission dealt with some aspects of extra-territorial obligations of States within the context of an inter-State complaint. See *Democratic Republic of Congo v Burundi, Rwanda and Uganda,* Communication 227/99.

268 *Forced Evictions in Zimbabwe*

6. The nature of obligations imposed on States by the African Charter

The Commission has previously analyzed the obligations imposed by the African Charter as imposing four levels of State obligations: the duties to respect, protect, promote and fulfil human rights. The African Commission deployed this approach in its decision in *The Social and Economic Rights Action Centre and the Centre for Economic and Social Rights v Nigeria* (SERAC) as an analytic tool to gauge a member State's human rights obligations under the African Charter.[16]

7. Duty to respect

The obligation to respect entails the State's duty to refrain from acts or omissions whose effect is to interfere or deprive individuals' or groups' enjoyment of their right to rights.[17] In other words, the State is enjoined "to respect right-holders, their freedoms, autonomy, resources, and liberty of their actions".[18] The Commission adopted a similar approach in the *SERAC* case, stating that the duty to respect socio-economic rights obliges the State to respect the free use of resources owned or at the disposal of the individual alone or in any form of association with others.[19] The Commission has previously emphasized the importance of respecting resources belonging to collective groups as these communities use them to satisfy their needs.[20] The duty to respect is particularly significant for the purposes of safeguarding the resources of indigenous, nomadic and rural communities. These groups are most vulnerable and often live with the risks of being deprived of their land, food and traditional drinking water sources as was demonstrated by the Commission in the recent case of *Rights Group International on behalf of Endorois Welfare Council v Kenya*.[21] The obligation to refrain from impairing access to a relevant socio-economic right is broad enough to include the adoption of policies that result in denial of access by poor communities to the right, rather than simply prohibiting interference with existing access to the right.[22]

8. Duty to protect

In contrast to the duty to respect, the duty to protect imposes a positive obligation on the State to adopt laws, policies and regulations to protect

---

16 See *The Social and Economic Rights Action Centre and the Centre for Economic and Social Rights v Nigeria* paras 44–8.

17 See W.Screiber, "Realising the Right to Water in International Investment Law: An Interdisciplinary Approach to BIT Obligations" (2008) 48 *National Resources Journal* 431, 445.

18 See *SERAC* para 46. See also Craven who points out that in general terms, this obligation requires the State to refrain from acts which would serve to deprive individuals of their rights protected under the ICESCR. M. Craven, *The International Covenant on Economic Social and Cultural Rights: A Perspective in Its Development* (Clarendon Press, 1995), 110.

19 *SERAC* para 45.

20 *SERAC* para 45.

21 *Rights Group International on behalf of Endorois Welfare Council v Kenya*, Communication 276 / 2003.

22 Craven *supra* note 18, 110.

beneficiaries of rights from interference by non-State actors. This Commission has previously stated in *SERAC* that the duty to protect entails "the creation and maintenance of an atmosphere or framework by an effective interplay of laws and regulations so that individuals will be able to freely realize their rights and freedoms".[23] The State is also enjoined to ensure that remedies are available to victims of violations of human rights and to penalize perpetrators for any interference with the rights which amounts to a violation. In *SERAC*, this Commission explained that the duty to protect beneficiaries of human rights imposes on the State an obligation to adopt the necessary legislation and provision of appropriate remedies in the case of violation.[24] The Commission on Economic, Social and Cultural Rights (CESCR) has also emphasised the State's obligation to protect individual's and groups' interests against third party interferences.[25] The obligation to protect requires State parties to prevent third parties from interfering in any way with the enjoyment of human rights.[26] The duty to protect is a clear recognition that the responsibility of the State goes beyond the actions of itself or its agents, to positive protection of the individual from third party violation.[27] Such measures may be in the form of legislation, policies and judicial decisions.[28]

9. **Duty to fulfil**
   The obligation to fulfil a right enjoins the State to adopt appropriate legislative, administrative, judicial and other measures towards the full realisation of the right in question.[29] The obligation to fulfil is key, particularly towards the realization of socio-economic rights.

10. **Duty to promote**
    The obligation to promote imposes a duty on the State to ensure that there is appropriate education in respect of human rights.[30] In the General Comments of the Committee of Economic, Social and Cultural Rights, this duty is encapsulated under the obligation to fulfil.[31]

---

23 See *SERAC* para 46.
24 *SERAC* para 46.
25 Craven *supra* note 18, 112.
26 CESCR General Comment 15 (2002) para 22.
27 Craven *supra* note 18, 112.
28 Such third parties include individuals, groups, corporations (including private non-State actors operating water supply services) and other entities as well as other agents acting under State authority. See CESCR General Comment No.15 (2002) para 22.
29 See O. de Schutter *International Human Rights: Cases, Materials, Commentary* (Cambridge University Press, 2010) 461.
30 CESCR General Comment No.15 (2002) para 25.
31 See CESCR General Comment No.15 (2002) para 25; CESCR General Comment No. 14 (2000) para 33.

270 *Forced Evictions in Zimbabwe*

11. Does the African Charter impose extraterritorial human rights obligations on States?

The Commission now turns to the question whether the African Charter imposes obligations on States to ensure that corporations registered or domiciled in their territory do not abuse human rights in their extraterritorial business activities. This question implicates a State's duty to protect individuals and groups outside of its territory from any deleterious activities of its corporations.

12. The Commission defines extraterritorial obligations as obligations to respect, protect, promote and fulfil the enjoyment of a human right of a person abroad. Acknowledging States' extraterritorial obligation is not an attempt to jettison the principle that is the domestic State that has the primary responsibility for the realization of its own population's human rights. Rather, the evolution of the concept of extraterritorial obligations is an acknowledgement that territorially-confined State duties invariably leave gaps in the protective regime of international human rights law.[32] The Commission notes that to confine a State's human rights obligations to its territory is also at odds with the effective protection of human rights.

13. The Commission refers to the general obligations clause enshrined under Article 1 of the African Charter which explicitly stipulates that "the Member States of the (African Union) parties to the present Charter shall recognize the rights, duties and freedoms enshrined in the Charter and shall undertake to adopt legislative or other measures to give effect to them". It is therefore noteworthy that the African Charter does not contain any explicit provision that limits State parties' human rights obligations under that instrument to their respective territories only.

14. This Commission has previously adjudicated an inter-State complaint involving the issue of extraterritorial State obligations in the case of *Democratic Republic of Congo (DRC) v Burundi, Rwanda and Uganda (DRC case).*[33] In that case, the Commission invoked the extraterritorial responsibility of Burundi, Rwanda and Uganda for gross violations of the African Charter's rights in the territories of the DRC as a result of the control of Congolese territory by the armed forces of the defendant States and the accompanying human rights violations as a consequence of such occupation.[34]

15. The Commission held the three States to be in violation of various rights protected under the African Charter, including the right to respect for life and the integrity of person (Article 4), the right to

---

32 See generally Gibney & Skogly *supra* note 4, 2–3.

33 *Democratic Republic of Congo (DRC) v Burundi, Rwanda and Uganda Communication* 227/1999.

34 *DRC v Burundi, Rwanda and Uganda,* para 98.

Litigating Transnational Human Rights Obligations 271

dignity (Article 5), the right to freedom of movement (Article 12), the right to property (Article 14), the right to physical and mental health (Article 16), the right to culture (Article 17), the right to unity of a family (Article 18), peoples' right to self determination (Article 19–20), peoples' right to dispose of their wealth and natural resources (Article 21), and peoples' right to economic, social and cultural development (Article 22).

16. It must further be noted that in the *DRC case*, the acts that constituted the violations of the African Charter's provisions were committed entirely within the DRC territory, beyond the territories of any of the defendant States. Nevertheless, this Commission proceeded to attribute responsibility to the defendant States, in the process endorsing the international law position that States are responsible for the violations of human rights they commit abroad.[35] It is particularly noteworthy that none of the States implicated in this case raised any objections contesting the extension by the Commission of their human rights responsibilities to territories beyond their borders.

17. The Commission wishes to state that the reach of States' extraterritorial human rights duties obliges them to abstain from actions that violate the human rights of individuals and groups in third States as well as to prevent third parties located or domiciled in their territory from violating human rights abroad.

18. The Commission notes that although a State's duties to respect, protect, promote and fulfil the human rights of individuals and groups have been developed to bind the States when acting domestically within their territorial jurisdictions,[36] there is nothing in the African Charter to suggest that this obligation is territorially limited.

19. Article 1 of the African Charter enjoins African States to recognize the rights provided for in that instrument and to adopt legislative or other measures to give effect to them.[37] The African Commission is thus fortified in its view that the African Charter imposes extraterritorial obligations on States. The Commission notes that the level of the obligation to respect is the least controversial in terms of its extraterritorial

---

35 In the case of *Loizidou v Turkey*, the European Court of Human Rights ruled that Turkey's obligations under the European Convention on Human Rights applied to its military operations abroad, that is in the so-called Turkish Republic of Northern Cyprus. The court found that Turkey had exercised effective control of an area outside its national territory hence its obligations imposed by article 1 of the ECHR applied to this part of Cyprus. See *Loizidou v Turkey* 40/1993/435/514 para 62.

36 The African Commission on Human and Peoples' Rights has recently adopted this typology of obligations in its landmark socio-economic rights decision in *The Social and Economic Rights Action Centre (SERAC) and the Centre for Economic and Social Rights v Nigeria*, Communication no. 155/96 (2001) AHRLR 51 (ACHPR 2001) paras 44–48.

37 See Article 1 of the African Charter on Human and Peoples' Rights.

272   *Forced Evictions in Zimbabwe*

application. This is because such a duty is mainly negative rather than positive, hence it involves respect for State sovereignty. However, even at this minimal level, a State can interfere with the enjoyment of human rights by people in another State as illustrated in this case.

20. The obligation to protect is also important within the context of extra-territorial obligations. This obligation is very important given that many corporations are now involved in multiple operations in different countries outside the State where such entities are domiciled or regis-tered. The State's duty to protect helps to ensure that these entities do not violate human rights in third States through their business opera-tions or policies.

21. The Commission concedes that the extraterritorial obligation to fulfil has been regarded as the most controversial given its potential inter-pretation as a positive obligation imposed on one State to provide for a third State's population.[38] The Commission points out that such an interpretation of the extraterritorial obligation to fulfil is unrealistic as it undermines the obligation of the territorial State as primarily respon-sible for fulfilling human rights within its territory. The Commission therefore finds that the extraterritorial obligation to fulfil is limited to a duty to facilitate or support the fulfilment of a given human right by the territorial State.[39] The extraterritorial obligation to fulfil thus involves international assistance and cooperation and this is reflected, for example, in the CESCR's General Comment No.15 on the right to water. States are enjoined to recognize "the essential role of interna-tional cooperation and assistance and take joint and separate action to achieve full realization" of human rights.[40]

22. The Commission points out that the application of extraterritorial obli-gations offers an analytic framework in which States' legal duties beyond their own territorial borders can be understood and complied with. Any contrary approach will run counter to the *raison d'être* of the human rights protections in the African Charter and will lead to an untenable situation where a State is liable for human rights violations in its domes-tic territory but free to violate such human rights beyond its borders.

23. The UN Special Rapporteur on the right to food has shown that each of the quartet layers of State human rights duties discussed above could be applicable extraterritorially. He specifically refers to extraterritorial obligation to respect, protect and fulfil in his reports.[41]

---

38 See A. Cahill, "Protecting Rights in the Face of Scarcity: The Right to Water", in Gibney & Skogly *supra* note 4, 194, 198.

39 *Id.*

40 CESCR General Comment 15 (2002) para 30.

41 The reports of the UN Special Rapporteur on right to food are available at:http://www.srfood.org/(accessed 7.06.12).

Litigating Transnational Human Rights Obligations 273

24. If follows that under the African Charter, a State's extraterritorial duty to protect enjoins positive action by way of ensuring that State agents and non-State actors, such as multinational companies, other business enterprises and individuals within a State's jurisdiction, do not infringe or interfere with the rights and freedoms enjoyed by groups or individuals in third States. At this level, the Commission wishes to state that States incur international responsibility for the violation of international human rights law for culpable conduct of non-State actors who, from within the jurisdiction of a State, engage in conduct that produces extraterritorially prejudicial activities.

25. The Commission also notes that under international human rights law, the International Covenant on Economic, Social and Cultural Rights (ICESCR), consistent with the African Charter, does not provide for a territorial restriction of the rights protected in that instrument.

26. The Committee on Economic, Social and Cultural Rights (CESCR) has clearly acknowledged the legal legitimacy of States' extraterritorial obligations, stating that:

    States parties have to respect the enjoyment of the right to health in other countries, and to prevent third parties from violating the right in other countries, if they are able to influence these third parties by way of legal or political means, in accordance with the Charter of the United Nations and applicable international law.[42]

27. This obligation is reiterated in the CESCR's General Comment No. 15 on the right to water, in which the CESCR explicitly states that:

    Steps should be taken by States parties to prevent their own citizens and companies from violating the right to water of individuals and communities in other countries. Where States parties can take steps to influence other third parties to respect the right, through legal or political means, such steps should be taken in accordance with the Charter of the United Nations Charter and applicable international law.[43]

28. Similarly, the Committee on the Elimination of Discrimination of Women (CEDAW Committee) has affirmed that States are obliged to protect against human rights violations, both within their territory and abroad. The CEDAW Committee stated in its General Recommendation No. 28 that the Convention on the Elimination of All Forms of Discrimination against Women "imposes a due diligence obligation on States parties to prevent discrimination by private actors".[44] The CEDAW Committee proceeded to state that "States parties are

---

42 CESCR General Comment No. 14 para 34.
43 CESCR General Comment No. 15 para 33.
44 CEDAW Committee General Recommendation No. 28 para 11

274 *Forced Evictions in Zimbabwe*

responsible for all their actions affecting human rights, regardless of whether the affected persons are in their territory".[45]

29. After an analysis of the concept of extraterritorial obligations, the Commission now turns to the second issue posed by the Respondent State, the question whether the African Charter imposes any obligation on States to ensure that private enterprises registered or domiciled in its territory respect human rights abroad, that is, in the territory in which the corporation carries out business activities.

30. The Respondent State argued that although it has a right to regulate the actions of corporations registered or domiciled in its territory and natural persons, regardless of where their conduct occurs, it is not obliged to do so under the African Charter and extant international law.

31. The Respondent State further argued that it will be in violation of the principle of non-intervention in internal affairs enshrined under article 2(7) of the UN Charter should it promulgate legislation or adopt any administrative or policy measures with an extraterritorial effect.

32. The Respondent State further argued that under the African Charter, States are only responsible for violations that occur within their own territory. The Respondent State further asserted that the territoriality of States' human rights obligations derives from the fact that States are responsible only for actions or events under their control and such an approach is consistent with the principle of State sovereignty.

33. The Respondent State thus argues that a State's extraterritorial responsibility can only be implicated for violations of the African Charter's rights by reasons of an extraterritorial incident or event in cases where the State had a *de facto* control over the incident or event. The Respondent State thus pointed out that this case should be distinguished from the *DRC case*, discussed above, as in that case troops of the defendant States were in physical control over territory in the complainant State.

34. The Respondent State has made reference to the recently adopted UN Guiding Principles on Business and Human Rights: Implementing the United Nations "Protect, Respect and Remedy" Framework (UN Guiding Principles), in particular the commentary to Principle 2, which states that "at present States are not generally required under international human rights law to regulate the extraterritorial activities of businesses domiciled in their territory and/or jurisdiction" to buttress its case.[46]

---

45 CEDAW Committee General Recommendation No. 28 para 12.

46 See Commentary to Principle 2 of the Report of the Special Representative of the Secretary General on the Issue of Human Rights and Transnational Corporations and Other Business Enterprises, John Ruggie: Guiding Principles on Business and Human Rights: Implementing the United Nations "Protect, Respect and Remedy" Framework UN Doc A/HRC/17/3 (21 March 2011).

Litigating Transnational Human Rights Obligations 275

35. The Commission wishes to refer to the recently adopted *Maastricht Principles on Extraterritorial Obligations of States in the Area of Economic, Social and Cultural Rights* which, in the Commission's opinion, is in some respects a restatement of extant international law as well as *lex ferenda*. Principle 25 provides that:

> All States must take necessary measures to ensure that non-State actors which they are in a position to regulate...such as private individuals and organizations, and transnational corporations and other business enterprises, do not nullify or impair the enjoyment of economic, social and cultural rights. These include administrative, legislative, investigative, adjudicatory and other measures.

36. The UN Guiding Principles note that the risk of gross human rights abuses is heightened in conflict-affected areas.[47] According to the UN Guiding Principles, States should help ensure that business enterprises operating in those contexts are not involved with such abuses through:
    (a) Engaging at the earliest stage possible with business enterprises to help them identify, prevent and mitigate the human rights-related risks of their activities and business relationships;
    (c) Denying access to public support and services for a business enterprise that is involved with gross human rights abuses and refuses to cooperate in addressing the situation;
    (d) Ensuring that their current policies, legislation, regulations and enforcement measures are effective in addressing the risk of business involvement in gross human rights abuses.[48]

37. **Alleged violation of Article 14 – the right to property**
    The complainants allege that the Respondent State is in violation of Article 14 of the right to property provided for under the African Charter. Article 14 of the African Charter states: "The right to property shall be guaranteed. It may only be encroached upon in the interest of public need or in the general interest of the community and in accordance with the provisions of appropriate laws."

38. The Complainants argue that the Marange community has a right to property with regard to its ancestral land, the possessions attached to it, including the mineral resources. The Complainants argue that the Marange community's property rights have been violated by the continuing dispossession of its land in the Marange communal area to make way for diamond mining. They further argue that the impact on the community has been disproportionate to any public need or general community interest. They further argue that no compensation has been provided to the complainant as a result of the dispossession from their land.

47 Guiding Principles on Business and Human Rights: Implementing the United Nations "Protect, Respect and Remedy" Framework Principle 7.
48 Principle 7.

276 *Forced Evictions in Zimbabwe*

39. What is unique about this case is that the complainants are not arguing that an organ of the Respondent State, or an entity empowered by the Respondent State, has directly violated their rights. Rather, what the complainants assert is that New Reclamation, a private entity domiciled in the Respondent State and registered under the laws of the Respondent State, is complicit with the Government of Zimbabwe in the violation of their rights, through its venture with the ZMDC in Mbada Investments.

40. The complainants assert that they have brought such abuse of human rights, including violations of its property rights, to the attention of the Respondent State, but to no avail. They therefore argue that the Respondent State has violated its property rights through its failure to exercise due diligence to restrain its corporate citizen, the New Reclamation, from being complicit in the interference of the Marange community's property rights.

41. In the opinion of the African Commission, the Respondent State has an obligation under Article 14 of the African Charter not only to protect against the violation of the right to property by third parties within its territory. The Respondent State also has an extraterritorial obligation to exercise due diligence to protect against the violation of the right abroad by private actors registered or domiciled in its territory.

42. This Commission held in *Zimbabwe Human Rights NGO Forum/Zimbabwe*[49] that an act by a private individual or non-State actor, and therefore not directly imputable to a State, can generate responsibility of the State, not because of the act itself, but because of the lack of due diligence on the part of the State to prevent the violation or for not taking the necessary steps to provide the victims with reparation.

43. The Maastricht Guidelines stipulate several circumstances in which States are enjoined to adopt and enforce measures to protect economic, social and cultural rights from breach by non-State actors. These include where:
    a) the harm or threat of harm originates or occurs on its territory;
    b) where the non-State actor has the nationality of the State concerned;
    c) as regards business enterprises, where the corporation, or its parent or controlling company, has its centre of activity, is registered or domiciled, or has its main place of business or substantial business activities, in the State concerned;
    d) where there is a reasonable link between the State concerned and the conduct it seeks to regulate, including where relevant aspects of a non-State actor's activities are carried out in that State's territory;
    e) where any conduct impairing economic, social and cultural rights constitutes a violation of a peremptory norm of international law.

---

49 *Zimbabwe Human Rights NGO Forum/Zimbabwe*, Communication 245/2002.

Litigating Transnational Human Rights Obligations 277

Where such a violation also constitutes a crime under international law, States must exercise universal jurisdiction over those bearing responsibility or lawfully transfer them to an appropriate jurisdiction.[50]

44. The Commission therefore finds the Respondent State in violation of Article 14 of the African Charter through its failure to exercise due diligence to prevent New Reclamation from violating the property rights of the Marange community, in violation of the African Charter.

45. The complainants further allege a violation of Article 21 of the African Charter by the Respondent State as a consequence of the latter's failure to exercise due diligence to protect the complainants from the injurious acts of New Reclamation.

46. The complainants allege that New Reclamation, along with its Zimbabwean government-owned partner, ZMDC, were and still are involved in the massive exploitation of mineral resources in the Marange communal lands, with no benefits accruing to the Complainants and the Marange people they represent.

47. Furthermore, the complainants allege that in its exploitation of mineral resources in Marange, the diamond mining consortium did not involve the Marange communities in the decisions that affected the development of Marange.

48. The complainants further allege that they made a series of complaints to the Respondent State to restrain New Reclamation from being complicit in the violation of its rights in the Marange communal lands. The complainants therefore allege that by neglecting to protect against its corporate citizen being complicit in the violation of rights abroad, including the looting of the Marange community's natural resources and the lack of material benefits accruing to the local population, the Respondent State is in violation of Article 21 of the African Charter.

Alleged violation of Article 21 of African Charter – right to freely dispose of wealth

49. The relevant provisions of Article 21 provide that:
    1. All peoples shall freely dispose of their wealth and natural resources. This right shall be exercised in the exclusive interest of the people. In no case shall a people be deprived of it.
    2. In case of spoliation the dispossessed people shall have the right to the lawful recovery of its property as well as to an adequate compensation.
    3. The free disposal of wealth and natural resources shall be exercised without prejudice to the obligation of promoting international

---

50 See Maastricht Guidelines para 25.

278 *Forced Evictions in Zimbabwe*

economic cooperation based on mutual respect, equitable exchange and the principles of international law.

50. The Commission noted in the *SERAC case*[51] that the right to natural resources contained within their traditional lands is not limited to indigenous groups, making it clear that a people inhabiting a specific region within a State could also claim under Article 21 of the African Charter.

51. State parties to the African Charter, including the Respondent State, have a duty to protect their citizens, not only through appropriate legislation and effective enforcement but also by protecting them from damaging acts that may be perpetrated by private parties either within their own territory or beyond their borders.

52. The Commission therefore finds the Respondent State in violation of Article 21 of the African Charter by its failure to take due diligence to exercise its protective mandate to protect abuse of the Marange community's rights by New Reclamation.

Alleged violation of the right to adequate housing

53. The complainants also assert that New Reclamation, alongside its consortium partner and the security services in Zimbabwe, have grossly and systematically violated the right to adequate housing of the Marange community as a result of the destruction of the latter's housing and shelter and the accompanying forced eviction to make way for diamond mining in the land previously occupied by the Marange community. The complainants allege that the Respondent State is liable for the violation of the former's rights to housing by the latter's failure to exercise its extraterritorial obligations to protect the Marange community against the injurious activities of New Reclamation.

54. The Commission wishes to state that although the right to housing or shelter is not explicitly provided for under the African Charter, the corollary of the combination of the provisions protecting the right to enjoy the best attainable state of mental and physical health provided under Article 16 of the African Charter, the right to property enshrined under Article 14, and the protection accorded to the family under Article 18(1) of the African Charter proscribes the wanton destruction of shelter because when housing is destroyed, property, health and family life are adversely affected.

55. The Commission therefore makes a finding that the combined effect of Articles 14, 16 and 18(1) reads into the Charter a right to housing.[52]

56. The Commission wishes to state that the Respondent State is obliged to protect the right to housing and must exercise due diligence to prevent

---

51 See *SERAC v Nigeria* paras 56–8.
52 See *SERAC v Nigeria* paras 59–63.

Litigating Transnational Human Rights Obligations 279

its legal or natural persons to desist from violating of any individual or group's right to housing abroad.

57. The Commission finds the Respondent State in violation of the complainants' rights as a consequence of its failure to exercise its protective mandate as alleged by failing to exercise due diligence to make sure that New Reclamation is not complicit in the violation of the complainants' right to housing.

Alleged violation of the right to food

58. The complainants further allege that their fields where they ordinarily grew food crops were destroyed and cleared by the Zimbabwean Government in complicity with New Reclamation to make way for diamond mining. The complainants further allege the Respondent State's responsibility for its failure to prevent New Reclamation from being complicit in the violation of its right to food in violation of the African Charter.

59. The African Commission wishes to point out that although the African Charter does not explicitly provide for a right to food, such a right is implicit in the African Charter, in such provisions as the right to life (Article 4), the right to health (Article 16) and the right to economic, social and cultural development (Article 22).[53]

60. It must also be noted that the right to food is inseparably linked to the dignity of human beings and is therefore essential for the enjoyment and fulfilment of such other rights as health, education, work and political participation.[54] The African Charter obliges member States at a minimum to exercise due diligence to prevent third parties under their control or domiciled in their territory from destroying or contaminating food sources abroad.[55]

61. The Commission therefore finds the Respondent State in violation of the right to food under the African Charter by its failure to exercise due diligence to prevent New Reclamation from being complicit in the destruction of the complainants' fields. In *SERAC v Nigeria*, this Commission observed that "the duty to improve food production and to guarantee access, the minimum core of the right to food requires that the Nigerian

---

53 See *SERAC v Nigeria* paras 64–6.

54 See CESCR General Comment No.12 (2003) on the right to food. The CESCR has stated in para 6 that "the right to adequate food is indivisibly linked to the inherent dignity of the human person and is indispensable for the fulfilment of other human rights enshrined in the International Bill of Human Rights. It is also inseparable from social justice, requiring the adoption of appropriate economic, environmental and social policies, at both the national and international levels, oriented to the eradication of poverty and the fulfilment of all human rights for all". See also *SERAC v Nigeria* ACHPR/COMM/A044/1 para 65.

55 See *SERAC v Nigeria* para 66.

280 *Forced Evictions in Zimbabwe*

Government should not destroy or contaminate food sources. It should not allow private parties to destroy or contaminate food sources, and prevent peoples' efforts to feed themselves".[56] The Commission further iterated the duty of States to protect their citizens, not only through appropriate legislation and effective enforcement, but also by protecting them from damaging acts that may be perpetrated by private parties.[57] This duty was further emphasised by the European Court of Human Rights in *X and Y v Netherlands* where the court ruled that there was an obligation on authorities to take steps to make sure that the enjoyment of the rights is not interfered with by any other private person.[58]

62. The Commission's finding does not in any way exonerate the responsibility of Zimbabwe as the territorial State to respect, protect, promote and fulfil human rights within its territory. The Commission notes, however, that Zimbabwe has not been joined as a party to these proceedings, hence it would violate proper procedure to make any adverse finding against a State that is not party to the proceedings. The Commission takes this opportunity to advise the applicants in this matter and future litigants the desirability of joining the home State as a party in proceedings of this nature. Furthermore, this case also illustrates the desirability of imposing direct human rights obligations on non-State actors such as corporations. It is regrettable that international law in general and international and regional human rights treaties do not impose direct human rights obligations on corporations. This means corporations infringing on human rights abroad can only be addressed through the medium of State responsibility. Such an approach is unsatisfactory. Hence there is an urgent need to develop international human rights law to enable it to directly apply to non-State actors such as corporations.

Right to be heard and to a remedy

63. The complainants argue that their rights guaranteed under Article 7(1) of the African Charter have been violated due to the failure by the Respondent State to investigate and prosecute New Reclamation for its complicity in the abuses of their rights at Marange diamond fields as well as the refusal by the Respondent State's domestic courts to accept the Complainants' petition against New Reclamation.

64. Article 7(1) of the African Charter provides that:
    Every individual shall have the right to have his cause heard. This comprises a) The right to an appeal to competent national organs

56 *SERAC v Nigeria* para 65.
57 *SERAC v Nigeria* para 57.
58 91 ECHR (1985) (Ser. A) 32.

Litigating Transnational Human Rights Obligations 281

against acts of violating his fundamental rights as recognized and guaranteed by conventions, laws, regulations and customs in force.

65. The Respondent State has argued that it was constrained to provide any remedy to the complainant as it was bound by the provisions of the BIPPA it entered with Zimbabwe on 27 November 2009. Article 7 of the BIPPA provides for a dispute settlement mechanism. It provides that any dispute relating to the BIPPA or investments between the two countries shall be settled in terms of Article 7 of the BIPPA. Article 7 of the BIPPA further provides for the referral of such disputes for arbitration at the International Centre for the Settlement of Investment Disputes upon failure to settle any dispute amicably.

66. The Respondent State has thus argued that its domestic courts could not legitimately grant the complainants any remedy as they are precluded from adjudicating on any issue relating to the investments between the two countries as such disputes fall to be resolved exclusively in terms of the BIPPA.

67. The Commission wishes to point out that States have a duty to provide access to a remedy if natural persons or corporations domiciled in their territory violate human rights abroad.

68. The Commission wishes to express its concern at the implications of Article 7 of BIPPA, especially in light of the fact that States are bound under their domestic constitutional and national laws as well as international obligations to respect, protect, promote and fulfil human rights and might find such obligations on a collision course with broad protections conferred on investors in BIPPA as in the instant case.

69. Article 7 of the BIPPA has the effect of impinging on the right to an effective remedy in the appropriate forum enshrined in the African Charter.

70. The Commission wishes to point out that the right to an effective remedy for anyone whose rights have been violated cannot be contracted away by the State nor denied by the operation of inter-governmental institutions, nor provisions of bilateral investment agreements.

71. This Commission has noted in *COHRE v Sudan* that the right to be heard requires that a complainant must have unfettered access to a tribunal of competent jurisdiction to hear her case. Where the authorities put obstacles in the way which prevent victims from accessing the competent tribunals, they would be held liable.[59]

72. In *Zimbabwe Human Rights NGO Forum v Zimbabwe*,[60] the Commission noted that Article 7 protection encompasses the right of every individual to access the relevant judicial bodies competent to have their causes heard and be granted adequate relief.

---

59 *COHRE v Sudan* para 181.
60 Communication 245/2002.

282 *Forced Evictions in Zimbabwe*

73. It is also pertinent to note that Article 8 of the UDHR entitles everyone to an effective remedy by the competent national tribunals for acts violating the fundamental human rights granted him by the constitution and law. Allowing investment or trade tribunals to determine the legality of provisions claimed to have negative effects on the protection and enjoyment of human rights would be in violation of international law as would provisions limiting access by individuals to effective remedies in domestic tribunals for any acts infringing fundamental human rights.

74. The Commission wishes to reiterate the position provided for under Principle 37 of the *Maastricht Principles on Extraterritorial Obligations of States in the Area of Economic, Social and Cultural Rights* that:

> States must ensure the enjoyment of the right to a prompt, accessible and effective remedy before an independent authority, including, where necessary, recourse to a judicial authority, for violations of economic, social and cultural rights. Where the harm resulting from an alleged violation has occurred on the territory of a State other than a State in which the harmful conduct took place, any State concerned must provide remedies to the victim.

75. **Recommendations**

In view of the above findings, the African Commission finds that the Respondent State is in violation of Articles 14, 18, 21 and 22 of the African Charter. The African Commission recommends that the Respondent State:

    (i)   Take measures to prevent New Reclamation from abusing any rights of the Marange community in the Marange communal lands in eastern Zimbabwe, in violation of the African Charter.

    (ii)   Provide adequate compensation to the Marange community for all the loss of land suffered and this should be done in consultation with government of Zimbabwe as the territorial State and Mbada as the consortium to which New Reclamation is a joint-venture partner.

    (iii)   Engage in dialogue with the complainants for the effective implementation of these recommendations.

    (iv)   Report on the implementation of these recommendations within three months from the date of notification.

    (v)   The Commission avails its good offices to assist the parties in the implementation of these recommendations.

Done in Banjul, The Gambia at the 54th Ordinary Session of the African Commission on Human and Peoples' Rights held from 11–25 March 2012.

17 Land Grabbing in South America (Inter-American Human Rights Commission)

Ana María Suárez-Franco

Abstract

In this Merits Report, the Inter-American Human Rights Commission hands down a decision on the international responsibility of State A in a case involving "land grabbing" in State B by corporations from State A, which results in breaches to the rights to life, judicial protection, food, health, water, housing and education of indigenous communities in State B. A is a South American country with a growing economy and strong political influence in the region. The victims allege that State A did not comply with its human rights obligations under the Inter-American Convention on Human Rights and the San Salvador Protocol because it had adopted specific policies and promoted large-scale investments for agro-fuel production in State B, which caused grave harm to vulnerable communities in B. Among the issues addressed by the Commission are the following: Is the Commission competent to decide on violations of the rights of the Convention claimed by victims of violations living outside of State A's territory? Can the Commission pass judgment on purported violations of economic social and cultural rights? And finally, is the responsibility of State A complementary, subsidiary or parallel to the responsibility of State B?

Introductory note

In the current context of climate, energy, food, and financial crises, pressure for control over land and other resources by international investors has increased, opening the space for land grabbing,[1] defined as taking possession of and/or controlling land in another state to produce food, energy, mining, or tourism, which is disproportionate in size in comparison to the

---

1 Borras, Saturnino and Franco, Jennifer, *Towards a Broader View of the Politics of Global Land Grab: Rethinking Land Issues, Reframing Resistance* (Amsterdam, 2010), p.4. Report of the Special Rapporteur on the Right to Food, Olivier de Schutter, UN Doc.A/HRC/13/ 33/ Add.2, 28 December 2009, p. 3, 12.

284 *Land Grabbing in South America*

average land holding in the region.[2] This phenomenon has been identified as a cause of human rights violations around the world.[3]

According to the High Level Panel of Experts of the Committee on World Food Security,[4] around 70 million hectares of land have been negotiated in low- and middle-income countries by international investors looking to rent or buy such lands. Studies analyzing the impact of such large scale land transactions have concluded that such actions negatively impact food security, incomes, livelihoods and the environment of local peoples.[5] UN authorities and civil society organizations have also highlighted how land grabbing is affecting the realization of both ESCR[6] and CP[7] rights. It mainly affects those living in rural areas.[8]

In Latin America and the Caribbean, the negative impact of land grabbing is of deep concern, although there has been some difficulty in measuring

2 FIAN, Land Grabbing in Kenya and Mozambique. A report on two research missions – and a human rights analysis of land grabbing, Heidelberg, April 2010, S. 8; Dakar appeal against land grabbing, at http://www.fian.org/news/press-releases/dakar-appeal-against-the-land-grab/pdf. See also: Mahon, Claire, "The right to food a right for everyone", in *Food Systems Failure: The Global Food Crisis and the Future of Agriculture*, Rosin, Christopher, Stock, Paul and Campbell, Hugh (eds) (Oxford, 2011), p. 10.

3 See: Cotula, Lorenzo, "The international political economy of the global land rush: A critical appraisal of trends, scale, geography and drivers", *Journal of Peasant Studies*, 1–32 (2012); De Schutter, Olivier, "How not to think of land-grabbing: three critiques of large-scale investments in farmland", *Journal of Peasant Studies*, 38: 24979 (2011).

4 Toulmin, Camila et al., "Land tenure and international investments in agriculture, A report of the High Level Panel of Experts on Food Security and Nutrition". Committee on World Food Security, July 2011.

5 Cotula *supra* note 3, 249–79; Report of the Special Rapporteur on the Right to Food to the Human Rights Council, UN Doc. A/HRC/13/33/Add.2, 28 December 2009.

6 On impacts on the right to food see, Report of the Special Rapporteur on the Right to Food, Olivier de Schutter, UN Doc. A/HRC/13/33/Add.2, 28 December 2009, para.3; Statement in the context of the Rio + 20 Conference (June 2012) on "The Green Economy in the Context of Sustainable Development and Poverty Eradication", 48th Session, E/C.12/2012/1.para. 6. (d)

7 On the impact on civil and political rights see: "The criminalization of human rights defenders in Latin America – An assessment from international organisations and European networks" (2012), at http://www.fian.org/news/news/the-criminalization-of-human-rights-defenders-in-latin-america recommedations-for-eu/pdf.

8 Monsalve Suarez, "Land Not For Sale!, Right to Food and Nutrition Watch – Land Grabbing and Nutrition, Challenges for Global Governance", Brot für die Welt, Icco, FIAN, Heidelberg (2010), p. 33–4; On human rights violations of peoples living in rural areas and the need to close gaps of protection see: UN Doc.A/HRC/19/75, para 63. Dakar appeal against land grabbing, at http://www.fian.org/news/press-releases/dakar-appeal-against-the-land-grab/pdf; Nyeleni Declaration: http://www.tni.org/article/conference-declaration-stop-land-grabbing-now.

the number of hectares and households affected.[9] Four types of land grabbers have been identified in the region: international, (Trans)Latina, domestic/national, and "undetermined".[10] When land grabbers are foreign States or companies based in their territory, it can violate both territorial and extraterritorial human rights obligations.[11]

As illustrated in the hypothetical case below, extraterritorial human rights violations resulting from land grabbing can be qualified under the internationally recognized three categories of human rights obligations: to respect, protect and fulfil.[12] At the UN level, the CESCR[13] and the UN Special Rapporteur on the Right to Food have set standards on extraterritorial obligations in reference to the tripartite category that should be applied to land grabbing activities.[14] Another applicable standard is the Maastricht Principles on Extraterritorial Obligations of States in the area of Economic, Social and Cultural Rights.

Legal questions on ETOs and land grabbing at the Inter-American Human Rights System

The inter-American human rights system was created by the Organization of American States to promote and protect human rights. Its main institutions are the Inter-American Human Rights Commission and the Inter-American Human Rights Court.[15] The system's main legal instruments

---

9 For detailed description of a study in 17 countries see: Borras, Saturnino, Franco Jennifer, Key, Cristobal, and Spoor, Max, "Land Grabbing in Latin America and the Caribbean, Viewed from Broader International Perspectives". Version 14 November 2011, p. 5. Buenos Aires, Declaration of Buenos Aires, III Especial Conference for food sovereignty, March 2012, at http://www.grain.org/article/entries/4498-acaparamiento-de-tierras-en-america-latina-si-hay-acaparamiento-de-tierras.

10 Report of the Special Rapporteur on the Right to Food, *supra* note 6, p. 6, para. 11, p. 7, para. 16.

11 On the extraterritorial effects of land grabbing see Mahon, *supra* note 2, at 5–6.

12 For a description of the extraterritorial dimension of the obligations to respect, protect and fulfil see: Maastricht Principles on Extraterritorial Obligations of States in the area of Economic, Social and Cultural Rights, principles 19–35.

13 See: General Comment 12, UN Doc. E/C.12/1999/5,para 36. Concluding observations on Switzerland, UN. Doc. E/C.12/CHE/CO/2-3, para 24. Concluding Observations to Germany, E/C.12/DEU/CO/5, paras 10–11.

14 Report of the Special Rapporteur on the Right to Food, Olivier de Schutter: "Large-Scale Acquisitions and Leases: A Set of Core Principles and Measures to Address the Human Rights", UN Doc. A/HRC/13/33/Add.2, 28 December 2009, paras. 5 and 15.The Principles are considered to be an interpretive instrument reflecting existing law setting criteria for land grabbing, see Golay, Christophe, Mahon, Clair and Cismas, Ioana, "The impact of the UN special Procedures on the development and implementation of economic, social and cultural rights", *The International Journal of Human Rights*, 12(2): 304 (2011).Guiding principles on human rights impact assessments of trade and investment agreements, UN Doc.A/HRC/19/59 Add.5, para. 2.6.

15 For more information, see http://www.oas.org/en/iachr/ and http://www.corteidh.or.cr/

286 Land Grabbing in South America

are the American Declaration of the Rights and Duties of Man (1948), the American Convention on Human Rights (1969) and the Additional Protocol to the American Convention on Human Rights in the Area of Economic, Social and Cultural Rights (Protocol of San Salvador) (1988). The Commission can receive petitions from alleged victims of human rights violations regarding human rights enshrined in the Inter-American Convention and the right to education and trade unions rights as stipulated in the San Salvador Protocol providing they have exhausted the national remedies. Following a quasi-judicial procedure, the Commission issues a merits decision containing a decision that includes recommendations to the State concerned. If the State is party to the American Convention, the Commission must attempt to formulate a friendly settlement. If the State is party to the American Convention and has accepted the Court's optional jurisdiction, the Commission or the State may refer the petition to the Court for a judicial review culminating in a binding judgment.

The Inter-American human rights system has issued several decisions recognizing State obligations to respect and ensure human rights.[16] Nonetheless, for the specific case of land grabbing, two questions must be analyzed: the justiciability of economic, social and cultural rights and the justiciability of extraterritorial human rights obligations.

The first issue, which is not the primary focus of this chapter, elicited an extensive discussion during the 1990s and 2000s.[17] Several decisions have been handed down by the Inter-American Commission and the

---

16 Although this is the terminology derived from Article 1.1 of the American Convention and used in the jurisprudence, it has to be clarified that Inter-American human rights bodies have adopted a number of decisions corresponding to what in the UN human rights system is defined as the obligation to protect. Cases recognizing the obligation to protect include: *Ximenes Lopes v Brazil*, Serie C- 149, 4 July 2006, Inter-American Human Rights Court, *Case Masacre de Mapiripan v Colombia*, Serie C-134, 15 September 2005; Inter-American Human Rights Court, *Pueblo Saramaka v Surinam*, Serie C-172, 28 November 2007; *Pediatric Clinic in the Region of Los Lagos v Brazil*, IHRC, N. 70/08, Admissibility petition 12.242, 16 July 2008.

17 Melish, Tara, *La Protección de los Derechos Económicos, Sociales y Culturales en el Sistema Interamericano de Derechos Humanos: Manual para la Presentación de Casos* (Quito 2003), p. 335; Rossi, Julieta, Abramovich Victor, "La Tutela de los Derechos Económicos, Sociales y Culturales en el Artículo 26 de la Convención Americana sobre Derechos Humanos", in Claudia Martin, Diego Rodríguez Pinzón, José Antonio Guevara (eds), *Manual de Derecho Internacional de los Derechos Humanos* (Mexico City 2003), S. 457–80; Caravallo, James, Schaffer, Emily, "Less as More, Rethinking Supranational Litigation of Economic, Social and Cultural Rights in the Americas", 56 *Hastings L.J.* S. 217–81; Melish, Tara, "Rethinking the 'Less as More' Thesis: Supranational Litigation of Economic, Social and Cultural Rights in the Americas", 39 *N.Y.U.J Int'l L. & Pol* 171–343; Suárez Franco, Ana María, *Die Justiziabilität wirtschaftlicher, sozialer und Kultureller Menschenrechte* (Frankfurt 2010), pp. 165–6.

Litigating Transnational Human Rights Obligations 287

Inter-American Court on ESCR in connection with violations of CPR.[18] These decisions, recognizing the property rights of indigenous communities over their traditional lands and other related rights, are important precedents for the interdependency of ESCR and CPR and also show how ESCR can be protected in the context of land conflicts. Though there is no decision specifically mentioning the phenomenon of land grabbing, such precedents can provide a basis for judgments protecting victims of violations of large scale land acquisitions.[19]

In the field of Extraterritorial Obligations of States, most of the decisions thus far in the Inter-American human rights system relate to the extraterritorial application of the American Declaration on the Rights and Duties of Man[20] (American Declaration) in cases occurring outside the Americas. Although these cases are not identical to many of those examined in this volume, this jurisprudence serves to make clear the criteria adopted by the Commission to determine its competency to adjudicate ETO cases.

In the Inter-American system, jurisdiction has generally been defined territorially. However, as Cerna[21] explains, under the American Declaration there are three groups of cases in which jurisdiction is defined extraterritorially (similar to the jurisprudence under the European Convention): cases in which lawful acts committed within the territory of a State are likely to

---

18 See, e.g. *Villagrán Morales et al (Street children case) v Guatemala*, judgment of 19. 11. 1999, Reihe C, Nr. 63, Abs. 237. IAMRG, Fall *""Instituto de Reeducación del Menor"" v Paraguay*, judgment of 2.09.2004, Serie C, No. 112. *Case Indigenous Community Yakye Axa v Paraguay*, judgment of 17. 06. 2005, Reihe C, Nr. 125, *Case Indigenous Community Sawhoyamaxa v Paraguay*, judgment of 29.03.06, Serie C, No. 146, case *Loayza Tamayo v Peru*, reparation judgment, judgment of 27. 11. 1998, *Case Masacre Plan de Sánchez v Guatemala*, reparation judgment of 19.11.2004, Serie C No. 116, para. 105, *Case Masacre Pueblo Bello v Colombia*, judgment 31.01. 2006, Serie C No. 140, *Case Masacre de la Rochela v Colombia*, merits and reparations judgment of 11. 05. 2007, Serie C, No. 163. Advisory Opinion 17/02 Legal condition and rights of the child of 28.08.2002, Serie A No. 17, Advisory Opinion18/0, legal condition and rights of undocumented migrants of 17. 07. 2003, Serie A, No. 18. IAHR Court merits and reparations judgment, *Indigenous Community Kichwa de Sarayaku v Ecuador*, 27 June 2012.

19 See the following judgments: *Case Community Mayagna (Sumo) Awas Tigni v Nicaragua*, judgment of 31.08.01. Serie C, No. 79 *Indigenous Community Yakye Axa v Paraguay*, judgment of 17. 06. 2005, Reihe C, Nr. 125; *Case Indigenous Community Sawhoyamaxa v Paraguay*, judgment of 29.03.06, Serie C, No. 146, Corte IDH; *Case Indigenous Community Xákmok Kásek v Paraguay*, merits, reparations and costs judgment 24.08.2010 Serie C No. 214. IAHR Court, merits and reparations, *Indigenous Community Kichwa de Sarayaku v Ecuador*, 27 June 2012.

20 Applicable to States Parties of the OEA which are not parties to the American Convention on Human Rights. Statute of the IACHR, Adopted by the OAS General Assembly, 9th Regular Session, La Paz, Bolivia, October 1979, Res. No. 448 Article 1.2.b.

21 Cerna, Christina M. "Out of Bounds? The Approach of the Inter-American System for the Promotion and protection of Human Rights to the Extraterritorial Application of Human Rights Law", Centre for Human Rights and Global Justice Working Paper Number 4, 2006, pp. 2, 3, 14.

288   *Land Grabbing in South America*

give rise to actual violations outside the State's territory;[22] cases in which States are considered responsible for human rights violations in territories that are under their *effective control or authority*, even if the territories are outside the State;[23] and cases where extraterritorial responsibility is recognized by the mere fact of the violation, without any specific criteria for the extraterritorial application of the applicable human rights instrument.[24]

Recently, the Commission has applied the American Convention extraterritorially between two States in the Americas following an inter-State petition (similar to the hypothetical case below). In this case, Ecuador accused Colombia of the extrajudicial killing of an Ecuadorian citizen while members of the Colombian armed forces entered Ecuador's territory. The decision to hold Colombia responsible for the violations was based on the arguments of control and authority described in the second group of cases above.[25]

The existing case-law shows that the Inter-American Commission has admitted cases on violations of ETOs, although most of the cases regard a narrow concept of extraterritorial jurisdiction linked to situations of control and authority. However, the rationales used by the Commission open a window for a broader concept of jurisdiction, which gives access to justice to victims of violations of land grabbing. The application of the Maastricht Principles on Extraterritorial Obligations of States in the Area of ESCR, when applied with other international law principles such as the *pro personae* principle,[26] the effectiveness principle,[27] and the *bona fides* principle,[28]

---

22 Cases in line with the *Soering v The United Kingdom* case, ECHR, 7 July 1989. An inter-American case in this line is: IAHRC, Case 10.675 United States March 13, 1997, REPORT N° 51/96 on US Interdiction of Haitians on the High Seas, see para. 167.

23 Cases in line with the *Cyprus v Turkey* case, Application No. 25781/94, ECHR 10 May 2001, para.77; *Loizidou v Turkey* (Preliminary Objections), ECHR 23 March 1995, para. 62. Inter-American cases in this line are: IAHRC, *Case Victor Saldaño v Argentina*, 11 March 1999, Report No. 38/99, para. 17–20; Case 10.951 *Coard et al. v United States*, 29 September 1999 Report N° 109/99, Military Occupation – US Intervention in Grenada, see para. 37 and footnote 6. Case 11.589, *Armando Alejandre Jr., Carlos Costa, Mario De La Peña, and Pablo Morales v Cuba*, 29 September 1999, Report N° 86/99Military Control – Cuban Military Intervention in International Airspace, see para. 23. Case 9903, *Rafael Ferrer-Mazorra et al.v United States*, 4 April 2001 Report N° 51/01, Detention – Indefinite Detention of Aliens in Guantanamo (case of "Marielito" Cubans), see para. 183. Precautionary Measures in Guantanamo Bay, Cuba, Inter-American Commission on Human Rights, 13 March 2002.

24 In line with the *Issa v Turkey* case, Application No. 31821/96, ECHR, 16 November 2004. An IAHRC decision in this line is case 10.573 United States, 14 October 1993, Report No 31/93US Military Intervention in Panama.

25 IAHRC, Inter-state petition IP-02, admissibility Franklin Guillermo Aisalla Molina, Ecuador – Colombia, Report No. 112/10, see para. 98, 102, 103.

26 See i.a. Pinto, Mónica, "El principio pro homine, criterios de hermenéutica y pautas para la regulación", in M. Abregú and C. Courtis (eds) *La Aplicación de los Tratados sobre Derechos Humanos por los Tribunales Locales* (Buenos Aires 2004), S. 163.

27 See i.a., Magdalena Sepulveda, *The Nature Obligations under the International Covenant on Economic, Social and Cultural Rights* (Antwerp, Oxford and New York 2003), S. 636; De Schutter Olivier, *International Human Rights Law*, Cambridge, 2010, p. 127 on *Loizidou v. Turkey*, judgment of 18 of December (preliminary objection and merits, paras 49–57.

28 Vienna Convention on the Law of Treaties, Vienna on 23 May 1969, Articles 26 and 31.

Litigating Transnational Human Rights Obligations 289

should close gaps in human rights protection in the context of globalization and the crises that arise thereunder.

Facts of the case

In 2011, the government of State A adopted the national policy "PRO-
AGRO" to promote the production of "flex" crops by companies based in A
willing to invest in other Latin American countries. The strategy included
financial support by the National Investment Bank, tax benefits, technical
advice and diplomatic support.

In the framework of a bilateral investment treaty concluded between
States A and B, in 2009, MIAPALMA & Co., a company with headquarters
in State A, received a land concession of 3000 hectares in State B. MIAPALMA
was awarded the concession with the support of A's Embassy in State B. The
project, under A's PRO-AGRO policy, initiated cultivation of palm oil.

After three months of discussions and hostilities between company
employees and community members, representatives of MIAPALMA and
the judicial authority of State B forcibly evicted 500 families of La Esperanza
indigenous community, and in the process destroyed their houses and cul-
tivations, killed their animals and retained their food stocks. Later, two children died from under-nutrition and health problems caused by the
displacements. Many other people also suffered various health problems.

After this forcible eviction, a group of community members settled on
small plots of land. However, not only were the resources insufficient, but
the pollution from the MIAPALMA plant contaminated their scarce food
and water. Since food production decreased substantially, the communities
were forced to depend on MIAPALMA for food. However, food prices
increased markedly and many traditional food products disappeared.
MIAPALMA's private security forces prevented community members from
entering other lands, and threatened community leaders and, at times,
physically injured them. Some community members began working in the
plantation, but labour contracts were limited to three months, and salaries
were below the national minimum wage. Many were forced to acquire
credit to be able to cover subsistence costs. These debts increased their
dependency on their employers. Due to food scarcity, other victims were
forced to migrate to the capital city, where most ended up living in extreme
poverty.

La Esperanza members organized themselves and initiated a political
and legal advocacy movement to work towards restitution of the grabbed
lands and being awarded compensation. They interposed a constitutional
writ against State B, claiming the denial of their constitutional and human
rights. Lacking access to other mechanisms to seek remedies from State A,
they addressed political claims to A's embassy, providing evidence of human
rights breaches by the company and asking for protection. However, there
was never any response to these claims. Although B's Constitutional Court
ultimately decided in favour of the communities, the pressure and influence of State A guaranteed that the ruling would not be implemented. In

290 *Land Grabbing in South America*

March 2019, community representatives submitted a petition to the Inter-American Human Rights Commission.

LEGAL OPINION[29]

REPORT N° 95/14
  CASE 56.789
  MERITS (PUBLICATION)
  Indigenous Community La Esperanza
  States A and B
  December, 2021

I. SUMMARY

1. On May 15, 2019, the Inter-American Commission on Human Rights ("the Commission") received a petition submitted by the non-governmental organization ETO Now, ("the petitioners") in representation of La Esperanza Indigenous Community (or the Indigenous Community") against Republic A ("State A") and Republic B ("State B"). The petition alleged that States A and B have violated various provisions in the American Convention on Human Rights (hereinafter "the Convention"): Article 1 (obligations to respect and ensure the rights); Article 2 (duty to adopt provisions of domestic law); Article 4 (right to life) in interconnection with Article 26 (progressive realization of ESCR); Article 5 (right to personal integrity); Article 21 (right to private property); and Article 25 (judicial protection), to the detriment of the indigenous community and its members.

2. The petitioners argue that more than five years have elapsed since the available procedures in State B were first set in motion to recover part of the ancestral lands of the La Esperanza Indigenous Community, which was negatively affected by large-scale acquisitions by foreign investors from State A. Yet, the situation has not been favourably resolved. Even though legislation in States A and B recognizes the right of indigenous peoples to develop their ways of life in their own habitat as constitutional rights, neither State has offered sufficient protection. In addition, the members of the community are living in sub-human conditions with people suffering from hunger, malnutrition and health problems. Two children have died due to lack of adequate food, water and medical care. Furthermore community leaders have been attacked and have also faced criminal prosecution.

---

29 Compared to the original structure of an IAHRC merits report, the present decision is much more succinct on procedural formalities, position of the petitioners and the state, and territorial responsibility. Moreover, the issue of admissibility, and in particular of jurisdiction, is included in the part preceding the merits.

Litigating Transnational Human Rights Obligations 291

3. The petitioners alleged that their petition regarding State A is admissible by virtue of the exceptions to the requirement of prior exhaustion of domestic remedies set out at Article 46(2) of the Convention. Regarding the Commission's competence to examine the claims against State A, the petitioners argued that the Commission is competent because the violations were carried out under its jurisdiction.

4. On the merits, the petitioners request the IACHR to find State A responsible for the violation of the rights mentioned in para. 1. Since an amicable solution was reached with State B, no petition is submitted against that State. State A argues that the events in question were not carried out under its jurisdiction and do not constitute violations of the Convention, therefore it owes no reparations.

5. After examining the positions of the parties, the Commission concluded that State A is responsible for the violation of Articles 1, 2, 4 (in interconnection with Article 26 and the Protocol of San Salvador), 21, and 25 of the Convention.

II. PROCESSING BEFORE THE COMMISSION

6. On 11 February 2021, the Commission issued its decision on admissibility. The legal debate around admissibility is summarized in the following paragraphs.

7. With regard to the territorial application of the American Convention, Article 1.1 of the Convention establishes that:

> The States Parties to this Convention undertake to respect the rights and freedoms recognized herein and to ensure to all persons subject to their jurisdiction the free and full exercise of those rights and freedoms, without any discrimination... (emphasis added)

8. The terms of a treaty are to be interpreted in good faith and in accordance with the ordinary meaning in their context and in the light of the object and purpose of the treaty (Vienna Convention Article 31.1). Unless it is established that the parties intend that a special meaning be given to a term, any relevant rules of international law applicable in the relations between the parties shall be taken into account.[30] Therefore, the word "jurisdiction" in Article 1.1 of the American Convention must be understood and applied in its ordinary meaning as a term of international law, unless it is clear that the parties intended otherwise.

---

30 Vienna Convention on the Law of Treaties, Article 31.3.(c)

292 *Land Grabbing in South America*

9. The drafting history of the Convention does not indicate that the parties intended to give a special meaning to the term "jurisdiction". The *travaux préparatoires* of the American Convention reveal that the initial text of Article 1.1 provided that:

> [t]he States Parties undertake to respect the rights and freedoms recognized in this Convention and to ensure to all persons within their territory *and subject to their jurisdiction* the free and full exercise of those rights and freedoms, without any discrimination...[31] (emphasis added)

10. At the time of adopting the American Convention, the Inter-American Specialized Conference on Human Rights omitted the reference to "territory" and established the obligation of the State parties to the Convention to respect and guarantee the rights recognized therein to all persons subject to their jurisdiction. In this way, the scope of protection was widened to the extent that the States not only may be held internationally responsible for the acts and omissions imputable to them within their territory, but also for those acts and omissions committed wherever they exercise jurisdiction.

12. In line with international jurisprudence,[32] the Commission also has considered in the past that the bases of jurisdiction are not exclusively territorial. The IACHR has applied the concept of jurisdiction extraterritorially, arguing that "under certain circumstances, the exercise of its jurisdiction over acts with an extraterritorial locus will not only be consistent with but

---

31 Inter-American Specialized Conference on Human Rights, San José, Costa Rica, November 7–22, 1969, Acts and Documents, OEA/Ser.K/XVI/1.2, Washington, DC, 1973, p. 14.

32 For its part, the International Court of Justice, in analyzing the scope of the International Covenant on Civil and Political Rights in its Advisory Opinion on the legal consequences of the construction of a wall on occupied Palestinian territory, stated that: "while the jurisdiction of States is primarily territorial, it may sometimes be exercised outside the national territory" and that "[c]onsidering the object and purpose of the [ICCPR], it would seem natural that, even when such is the case, States parties to the Covenant should be bound to comply with its provisions", (emphasis added). It ruled in the same sense in deciding the case *Democratic Republic of the Congo v Uganda*, when it stated that international human rights law is applicable in respect of acts carried out by a State in the exercise of its jurisdiction outside its own territory. CIJ, *Case concerning Armed Activities on the Territory of the Congo (Democratic Republic of Congo v Uganda)*, 19 December 2005, para. 216. The European Court of Human Rights has also concluded that the term "jurisdiction" is not limited to the national territory of a State party, as it may incur responsibility for acts of its authorities which produce an effect outside its territory, Eur. Ct. HR, *Drozd and Janousek v France and Spain*, judgment of 26 June 1992, para. 91. ECHR, 1611/62, *X v Federal Republic of Germany*, 25 September 1965; Petition no. 6231/73, *Hess v United Kingdom*, 28 May 1975; petitions 6780/74 and 6950/75, *Cyprus v Turkey*, 26 May 1975; petitions 7289/75 and 7349/76, *X and Y v Switzerland*, 14 July 1977; Petition 9348/81, *W. v United Kingdom*, 28 February 1983.

Litigating Transnational Human Rights Obligations 293

required by the norms which pertain".[33] Thus, although jurisdiction usually refers to authority over persons within the territory of a State, human rights are inherent in all human beings and are not based on their citizenship or location. Under Inter-American human rights law, each State is therefore obligated to respect and ensure the rights of all persons within its territory and of those present in the territory of another State *but subject to the control of its agents.*[34]

13. While the extraterritorial application of the Convention has been based on a broader interpretation of the term jurisdiction, mainly in the application of the concepts of *control and authority* in protecting victims of violations in situations of occupation, military intervention or peace-keeping operations, limiting the application of jurisdiction to the exercise of *control and authority* may be too restrictive for the effective protection of human rights in other instances. In fact, a State may affect the enjoyment of human rights outside of its territory through its *influence*, even in the absence of effective control or authority over a situation or a person.[35] Aware of this need for protection, the Commission has also applied inter-American human rights law in cases involving lawful acts committed within the territory of a State that give rise to human rights violations outside that state's territory.[36] Furthermore, in the case of the military intervention in Panama, extraterritorial jurisdiction was recognized even without any specific reference to control, authority or other criteria. The Commission focused on the occurrence of the extraterritorial violations and the obligation to guarantee judicial protection to the victims.[37]

14. As stated in the preamble of the Maastricht Principles on Extraterritorial Obligations of States, "...*The advent of economic globalization in particular, has meant that States and other global actors exert considerable influence on the realization of economic, social and cultural rights across the world.*" Both the Inter-American

---

33 IAHRC, Report N° 109/99 Case 10.951 *Coard et al. v United States*, 29 September 1999, Military Occupation – US Intervention in Grenada, see para. 37.

34 IACHR Report No. 38/99 *Case Victor Saldaño v Argentina*, 11 March 1999, para. 17–20; Report No. 86/99, Case 11.589, Armando Alejandre Jr. et al. (Cuba), 13 April 1999; Report N° 51/01, Case 9903, *Rafael Ferrer-Mazorra et al. v United States*, 4 April 2001, Detention – Indefinite Detention of Aliens in Guantanamo (case of "Marielito" Cubans), see para. 183; Precautionary Measures in Guantanamo Bay, Cuba, Inter-American Commission on Human Rights, 13 March 2002.

35 See Maastricht Principles on the Extraterritorial State Obligations in the Area of Economic, Social and Cultural Rights, Principle 9 (b).

36 IAHRC, Report N° 51/96 Case 10.675 United States 13 March 1997, on US Interdiction of Haitians on the High Seas, see para. 167; with similar argumentation as ECHR *Soering v. United Kingdom*, 161 Eur.Ct.HR (ser.A) (1989).

37 IAHRC case 10.573 United States, 14 October 1993, Report N° 31/93US Military Intervention in Panama.

294 *Land Grabbing in South America*

Declaration[38] and Convention[39] as well as the San Salvador Protocol (ratified by the States involved in the case *sub judice*) have recognized ESCR. Experience shows that violations committed within the current economic and political context frequently involve violations of both CPR and ESCR, showing the interdependency of human rights.[40]

15. Interpreting the term jurisdiction under the effectiveness principle,[41] the Convention and the San Salvador Protocol, the Commission shall analyse and apply the term in its context and taking into account new relevant rules of international law applicable in the relations between the parties.[42] The Commission considers that the term jurisdiction shall be interpreted in a way that enables the effective protection of all human beings and all categories of human rights, in accordance with the newly developed Maastricht Principles on Extraterritorial Obligations.

16. The following is essential for the Commission in determining jurisdiction: a) the exercise of authority or effective control over persons or situations – by agents of a State or non-State actors acting on the instructions or under the direction or control of the State, or empowered by the state to exercise elements of governmental authority – even if not acting within their territory; and/or b) the existence of State acts or omissions which bring about foreseeable effects on the enjoyment human rights, whether within or outside its territory; and/or c) the situation in which a State is in the position to exercise decisive influence or take measures to realize economic, social and cultural rights extraterritorially, which are in accordance with international law, acting separately or jointly, whether through its executive, legislative or judicial branches.[43]

19. The exercise of jurisdiction should not be confused with the limits imposed under international law on the ability of a State to exercise

---

38 ArticlesVI, VII, XI, XII, XIII, XIV, XV, XVI.

39 Article 26.

40 e.g. Colombian fumigations affecting Ecuadorian population IACHR related documents at: http://search.oas.org/es/cidh/default.aspx?k=fumigaciones&s=CIDH; Text of the Ecuadorian Claim against Colombia at the ICJ (2008) http://www.ecuadorinmediato.com/index.php?module=Noticias&func=news_user_view&id=74862&umt=texto_demanda_ecuador_contra_colombia_ante_corte_internacional_justicia, on the Pulp Mill on the River Uruguay:CIJ, *Argentina v Uruguay*, April 2010.

41 On the effectiveness principle see: Magdalena Sepúlveda, *The Nature of the Obligations under the International Covenant of Economic, Social and Cultural rights*, p. 79 ss. "Due to the fact that the overriding function of human rights treaties is the protection of individuals' rights, it seems clear that their interpretation should make that protection effective". See also, Ian Brownlie, *Principles of Public International Law*, 5th edn (Oxford 1998), S. 636 and Art. 31.1 Vienna Convention.

42 Art. 31.3. (c) Vienna Convention.

43 Commentary to the Maastricht Principles on Extraterritorial Obligations in the area of Economic, Social and Cultural Rights, *Human Rights Quarterly* 34:1084–1169 (2012).

Litigating Transnational Human Rights Obligations 295

prescriptive or legislative and enforcement "jurisdiction".[44] Moreover, jurisdiction can be exercised without necessarily requiring the existence of a formal, structured and prolonged legal relation.[45]

17. As the evidence shows, alleged violations occurring in the territory of State B have a causal nexus with acts or omissions of State A, thereby affecting the enjoyment of ESCR and CPR of people living in State B. In addition, operating within the framework of bilateral and economic relations, the acts or omissions of A's agents have had a decisive influence on human rights protection in State B.

18. Although the attribution of the alleged violations to State A and its ultimate responsibility are to be decided in the decision of the merits, as a result of the foregoing analysis, the Commission concludes that it has competence *ratione loci* to examine this individual petition.

19. State A submitted its arguments on the merits.

III. ANALYSIS OF THE MERITS: CONSIDERATIONS IN FACT AND IN LAW

20. In the following, the Commission will analyze the possible non-compliance with the obligations to protect and respect in order to determine whether CPR, in interconnection with ESCR, were violated in the context of the large-scale land acquisition by the MIAPALMA enterprise, which resulted in widespread evictions, destruction of livelihoods, criminalization and attacks on community leaders, and finally, lack of effective judicial protection. Regarding the right to property of indigenous peoples, the Commission will analyze the alleged breaches of human rights of the community in line with relevant existing inter-American jurisprudence.[46]

21. The initial question relates to the possibility of attributing legal responsibility to State A for the alleged violations that were all directly carried out by MIAPALMA, a non-State actor. The Commission observes that from the outset, the adoption of PRO-AGRO Investment Policy – a policy financially supporting production of agro-fuels by companies based in State A, in other Latin-American countries – represented a real risk to the enjoyment of human rights in other countries of the region, and especially increased the likelihood of retrogression in ESCR.[47]

---

44 See Maastricht Principles, commentary to Article 12, (3).
45 Report No. 112/10 Inter-state petition ip-02, admissibility, Franklin Guillermo Aisalla Molina, Ecuador – Colombia, para. 99.
46 Ibidem.
47 ETO Maastricht Principle 13 and its commentary.

296   *Land Grabbing in South America*

23. Under the obligation to avoid causing harm, States must desist from acts and omissions that create a real risk of nullifying or impairing the enjoyment of economic, social and cultural rights extraterritorially, and the responsibility of States is engaged where such nullification or impairment is a *foreseeable* result of their conduct.[48]

24. This risk of impairment was, or at least should have been, foreseeable for State A when the policy was adopted in 2011, especially regarding vulnerable rural communities in countries where PRO-AGRO projects would be implemented. First, the expansion of flex crops production for agro fuels had similarly undermined the ESCR of rural communities in the territory of State A when it began in 2000. Second, scholars, UN experts and NGOs had registered similar impacts in diverse regions of the world. Both the Special Rapporteur on the Right to Food and the High Level Task Force to the Committee on World Food Security issued reports calling attention to the impact of large-scale land acquisitions for the production of flex crops. Also, specialized NGOs have well documented the impact of agro-fuels production in low and middle income countries.

25. Although State A argues that when this policy was adopted it was not aware of these studies and that the effect of flex-crop monocultures on human rights was not scientifically proven, such lack of awareness does not justify the adoption of PRO-AGRO policy and its implementation since *State A should have foreseen the risk.*[49]

26. According to various human rights standards,[50] States should conduct prior human rights impact assessments with full public participation and results must be made public. Every effort should also be made to identify the necessary measures needing to be taken to prevent violations or ensure their cessation as well as measures to ensure an effective remedy should violations occur.[51] If State authorities are aware, or should be aware, of the risk of impairing or nullifying human rights and they have not exercised due diligence in taking all steps to avoid such, State responsibility may be engaged.

27. State A was aware of the risk caused by the adoption of its PRO-AGRO policy, yet it proceeded to finance MIAPALMA for this operation. Although

---

48 Ibidem.

49 *Articles on Responsibility of States for Internationally Wrongful Acts, with Commentaries adopted by International Law Commission*, Report of the International Law Commission on the work of its 53rd session (23 April to 1 June and 2 July to 10 August 2001) UN Doc. A/56/10 (at 76, Article 23, common para 2.

50 Including the Guiding principles on human rights impact assessments of trade and investment agreements (A/HRC/19/59 Add.5, Principle 1) and the principles for land acquisitions (UN Doc.A/HRC/13/ 33/Add.2, Principle 9).

51 ETO Maastricht Principle 14.

the petitioners and diverse NGO and UN authorities demanded otherwise, State A did not adopt corrective measures to stop the harm its policies and practices were causing. These facts allow the Commission to attribute to State A the responsibility for the violation of the rights of La Esperanza Community, on the basis of the existence of reasonably imputable damage.[52]

28. Regarding the investment treaty between State A and State B, which frames the concession of land, State A's arguments in favour of continuing with its application without considering its human rights impacts is contrary to international law. According to the Court,[53] States must interpret and apply relevant international agreements and standards in a manner consistent with their human rights obligations. Therefore, State A should adopt measures to ensure that application of an investment treaty is consistent with its own and State B's human rights obligations.

29. The American Convention recognizes that States have two kinds of obligations, the obligation to respect and the obligation to ensure.[54] States acting extraterritorially have obligations to respect and ensure as well. The extraterritorial obligation to protect requires all States to refrain from conduct nullifying or impairing the enjoyment and exercise of ESCR of persons outside their territories.[55] There is indirect interference when a State impairs the ability of another State to comply with its obligations or coerces another State to breach that State's human rights obligations where the former State does so with knowledge of the circumstances of the act.[56]

31. In this case, at least two measures violate the obligation to respect. First, executive and diplomatic officers of State A exercised political and economic influence for a large-scale concession of land, which then impaired the protection of property and other human rights of the affected community by State B. Second, they exercised influence to impede the implementation of the decision of B's Constitutional Court, which protected the rights of La Esperanza community. The damages caused by this conduct are attributable to State A.

32. States also have an obligation to protect human rights extraterritorially. To comply with this obligation, States must take necessary measures to

---

52 On reasonably imputable damage see: Text adopted by the International Law Commission at its fifty-eight session, in 2006 and submitted to the General Assembly as part of the Commissions' report covering the work of that session (A/61/10). See also commentary to Maastricht ETO Principle 13.

53 Inter-American Human Rights Court, case *Indigenous Community Sawhoyamaxa v Paraguay*; judgment of 29.03.06, Serie C, No. 146, para 140, see also ETO Principle 17.

54 The obligation to ensure corresponds to the obligations to protect and to fulfil in the language of the UN Committee on ESCR.

55 ETO Maastricht Principle 20.

56 ETO Maastricht Principle 21.

298 *Land Grabbing in South America*

ensure that non-State actors *which they are in a position to regulate* do not nullify or impair the enjoyment of ESCR. These include administrative, legislative, investigative, adjudicatory and other measures.[57] Moreover, States must adopt and enforce measures to protect ESCR through legal and other means, including diplomatic, as regards business enterprises where the corporation or its parent or controlling company are domiciled in the State concerned and where there is a reasonable link between the State concerned and the conduct it seeks to regulate.[58] "*Particularly where the investor is a private entity and the host State is unable or unwilling to act in accordance with its obligations, the home State of the investor must ensure that these obligations are complied with [referring to obligations to respect, protect and fulfil]. The minimum principles listed in the annex seek to ensure that these responsibilities are met.*"[59] The aforementioned principles include: transparency; participation; free, prior and informed consent of the local communities; compliance of international standards with regard to forced evictions; adoption of legislation to protect local communities; cooperation in identifying ways to ensure that the modes of agricultural production respect the environment, and do not accelerate climate change, soil depletion, and the exhaustion of freshwater reserves; a clear definition of investors' obligations; implementation of sanction mechanisms for cases of non compliance; realization of *ex ante* and *ex post* impact assessments; and adequate protection for agricultural workers.

33. In this case, State A was in a position to regulate and influence companies implementing projects under PRO-AGRO and managed by the National Development Bank. The direct link between MIAPALMA and the National Development Bank gave the State the opportunity to regulate specific human rights conditions of the project, to monitor implementation of these measures, and the ability to sanction and prevent any impairment or nullification of human rights. Nonetheless, this obligation to protect was not complied with, and therefore the consequences of this failure are attributable to State A.

34. In line with Articles 55 and 56 of the UN Charter and Article 26 of the Convention, States must cooperate in working toward the universal fulfilment of ESCR, including regarding bilateral and multilateral trade, investment and environmental protection, and which should be implemented through elaboration, interpretation, application and regular review of multilateral and bilateral agreements as well as international standards. Toward this end, States should adopt measures and policies in respect of its foreign relations, including actions within international

---

57 ETO Maastricht Principle 24.
58 ETO Maastricht Principle 25 c) and d.
59 Principles for Land Acquisitions, UN Doc.A/HRC/13/ 33/Add.2, 28 December 2009, Principle 15.

Litigating Transnational Human Rights Obligations 299

organizations, and domestic measures and policies that can contribute to the fulfilment of ESCR extraterritorially.[60]

35. State A was not complying with this obligation since instead of enabling ESCR implementation, through agreements or through diplomatic relations, it impaired the realization of ESCR. The State should adopt all corrective measures to change this position and revise its international trade agreements and policies, as well as carry out its diplomatic activities in a way that ensures that these are in line with its obligation to cooperate towards ESCR implementation.

36. The petitioner alleged the lack of judicial mechanisms in State A to complain about violations of their human rights committed in State B, and complained about the influence of the diplomatic services of State A in impeding the implementation of the decision of the Constitutional Court.

37. On the existence of complaints mechanisms for violations, Article 25 of the American Convention, stipulates that: "*Everyone has the right to simple and prompt recourse, or any other effective recourse, to a competent court or tribunal for protection against acts that violate his fundamental rights recognized by the constitution or laws of the state concerned or by this Convention*" and thus, States should provide judicial or other mechanisms to protect the rights of affected right holders. Furthermore, Article 25.2 prescribes that States Parties undertake, "b) to develop the possibilities of judicial remedy". The Inter-American Convention does not differentiate between recourse mechanisms for territorial or extraterritorial obligations, but due to the nature of the usually claimed cases, it has been understood as relating to mechanisms for territorial obligations. Nonetheless, given the ETO Principles, this understanding should be expanded to include extraterritorial obligations. In fact, according to the ETO Principles States must ensure the enjoyment of the right to a prompt, accessible and effective remedy before an independent authority, including, where necessary, recourse to a judicial authority, for violations of ESCR. Where the harm resulting from an alleged violation has occurred on the territory of a State other than a State in which the harmful conduct took place, any State concerned must provide remedies to the victim.[61]

39. In the case of La Esperanza, no effective mechanisms were available for the victims to claim against State A. Therefore, the State did not comply with its obligation of effective judicial protection under Article 25 of the Convention.

40. The Commission also declares that State A violated Article 25.2.c. which requires States "*to ensure that the competent authorities shall enforce such remedies*

---

60 ETO Maastricht Principle 29.
61 ETO Maastricht Principle 37.

300 *Land Grabbing in South America*

when granted". In fact, official agents of State A hindered the implementation of the decision adopted by State B's Constitutional Court in favour of the victims, and State A thereby violated its obligation to respect human rights and to cooperate towards effective judicial protection of human rights.

41. On the distribution of responsibility among State A and State B, although State B accepted its responsibility during the amicable settlement, the Commission reiterates that extraterritorial obligations of States do not exclude the territorial responsibility of the state of the victims. Both States are co-responsible for the violations and for the reparations to the victims.

IV. CONCLUSIONS

42. In light of the foregoing analysis, the Commission reiterates its conclusions to the effect that State A is co-responsible for the violation of La Esperanza indigenous communities' right to life (Article 1) in connection with the rights to food, water, housing and health (Article 26 and Protocol of San Salvador), right to personal integrity (Article 5), right to property (Article 23), right to judicial protection (Article 25) of the American Convention on Human Rights, and of the general obligations to respect and ensure rights (Article 1(1)) and to adopt domestic measures (Article 2) of said treaty.

V. RECOMMENDATION

43. Based on the arguments of fact and in law expressed above the Inter-American Human Rights Commission recommends to State A:

a) To promptly adopt all necessary measures to support State B in the implementation of the Constitutional Court's judgment in the case of La Esperanza community, including cooperation in protecting the ancestral territory of the La Esperanza community, and demarcating and conveying title to their lands pursuant to their customary law, values, usage and customs, and to guarantee the members of the community the exercise of their traditional subsistence activities.

b) To adopt international assistance measures as necessary to assist State B to meet the nutritional, water, medical and health emergency needs of the La Esperanza Community.

c) To carry out an ex-post impact assessment of the PRO-AGRO policy and the specific project of the National Development Bank with MIAPALMA to determine the corrective measures needed to halt violations of the rights of La Esperanza community and to implement measures guaranteeing the principles of participation, information and transparency to the Community.

Litigating Transnational Human Rights Obligations 301

d) To regulate the activities of enterprises based in A that *implement* projects in the framework of the PRO-AGRO policy in other States of the region including: safeguarding measures to protect the CPR and ESCR of local rural communities; establishing specific rules prohibiting the direct participation or complicity of the company in forced evictions; regulating the use of private forces and establishing sanctions for attacks and threats to the local communities by such forces; establishing a monitoring system for the activities of the enterprises as well as sanctions for breaches of human rights committed by the enterprises in development of projects in the frame of PRO-AGRO.

e) To revise the respective investment treaty and include necessary amendments in order to ensure the compliance with its human rights obligations.

f) To establish all adequate judicial and other accountability mechanisms to ensure effective judicial protection to victims of violations of the extraterritorial obligations of State A.

g) To publicly acknowledge international responsibility for the human rights violations determined by the Commission in this report. In particular, to conduct a public ceremony with the members of La Esperanza Community and its representatives to acknowledge the State's international responsibility for the events in this case, and to publish, within two months from notification of this decision, at least once, in the Official Gazette.

h) To make individual and communal reparations. The reparations to be paid by State A must be calculated pursuant to international standards and be adequate to compensate pecuniary and non-pecuniary damages caused by the human rights violations addressed by this report. The manner and amount of the reparation must be agreed upon with the affected community members pursuant to customary law, values, usage and customs of the indigenous community, State A and State B.

i) To adopt any measures necessary to prevent similar events from happening in the future, in accordance with the duty to prevent and safeguard the fundamental rights recognized in the Convention.

18 Enforcing Extraterritorial Social Rights in the Eurozone Crisis (European Committee of Social Rights)

Matthias Sant'Ana

Abstract

The present hypothetical case explores the possibility of implementing extraterritorial obligations through the European Social Charter in the context of the Eurozone crisis. As a condition for receiving financial assistance, Greece has been tasked by the EU and the IMF with implementing an extremely ambitious, far-reaching structural adjustment programme. The national measures of implementation adopted by Greece have led to a severe deterioration in the provision of social services, and have decreased the protection of socioeconomic rights for vast portions of Greek society. This hypothetical admissibility decision illustrates the use of the collective complaints mechanism of the Charter as a means for the European Committee of Social Rights to reaffirm the central place of social rights in the broader European constitutional order. Going beyond the raft of collective complaints presently pending before the Committee relating to the austerity measures in Greece, the complainant organization in this fictional case addresses its legal challenge to all Eurozone member States that have accepted the jurisdiction of the Committee to receive collective complaints. It is argued that all nine States share responsibility for the violation of social rights in Greece on the grounds that by negotiating, designing, implementing and funding the 'Greek bail-out' these States have jointly produced the conditions for the violation of the Charter on an unprecedented scale. The case discusses issues of responsibility – both in attribution and in allocation between States and international organization – tackles the question of implicit jurisdictional limits in international law, and illustrates the complex interactions between human rights law, EU law, and the extraterritorial dimensions of social rights within the European project.

Introductory note

Collective complaints within the European Social Charter[1] system are the first claims mechanism established for a treaty protecting economic, social

---

1 The ESC was signed by 13 member States of the Council of Europe in Turin on 18 October 1961 (CETS No. 35; 529 UNTS 89). It entered into force on 26 February 1965. A Revised Social Charter was opened for signature in Strasbourg on 3 May 1996 (CETS No. 163). The Revised ESC entered into force on 1 July 1999.

Litigating Transnational Human Rights Obligations 303

and cultural rights. Before the adoption of the 1995 *Additional Protocol to the European Social Charter providing for a system of collective complaints,*[2] the European Social Rights Committee had been interpreting the Charter's provisions through a national reports mechanism, not unlike the procedures existing under the UN Covenant on Economic, Social and Cultural Rights.[3]

The special features of the Charter and of its two-pronged enforcement mechanisms are too many to be productively summarized in this chapter. However, it is important to highlight the incredibly innovative nature of the mechanism, which allows a select number of international non-governmental organizations to present collective complaints with respect to the situation of socioeconomic rights on the territory of any contracting party, without identifying individual victims, without exhausting domestic remedies, and – subject to the proviso that complainant organizations must have competence in the subject-matter of the complaint – without proving any interest to act. The complaint must not concern an individual situation so that the mere existence of a law or practice may suffice to establish a violation of the Charter.

The collective complaint presented here concerns the situation of social rights in one contracting party, but attempts to engage the responsibility of the territorial State and of eight other States. What these States have in common is that they are all contracting parties to the Charter and to its Additional Protocol; that they are all EU member States that share the common currency; and that in one capacity or another, they are all involved in the European economic assistance programme for Greece. This programme has required that Greece deeply restructure its economy and the social and labour relations that underpin it in order to satisfy conditions that, according to the International Monetary Fund (IMF), the European Central Bank (ECB) and the European Commission (EC), will lead, in time, to a sustained economic recovery. After three years of strong austerity measures, a second economic assistance programme was adopted in March 2012. As of this writing (March 2013), Greece is still struggling to satisfy the ever-evolving list of requirements of the Troika, and recovery, sustainable or otherwise, is seemingly nowhere in sight. For those used to studying the structural adjustment programmes carried out by the IMF and the World Bank across the developing world, this is nothing new. However, besides the fact that this is happening closer to the core of the global economy, the other remarkable feature of the crisis is that the actors involved have embarked on a long and deep process of integration, and have entrusted the progressive development of this project to a number of international institutions with partially conflicting, partially overlapping competences.

2 Adopted in Strasbourg on 9 November 1995, ETS No. 158.
3 *International Covenant on Economic Social and Cultural Rights,* adopted by General Assembly resolution 2200A (XXI), 993 UNTS 3.

304   *Enforcing Extraterritorial Social Rights in the Eurozone Crisis*

For all its potential to be a constitutional instrument of the (broad) European space in the field of social rights, the Charter has suffered from a number of deficits. A remarkable gap relates to the fact that, unlike the ICESCR, the Social Charter does not refer to obligations of international cooperation explicitly. At first sight, this would seem to reduce the scope for arguments based on extraterritorial obligations. Because of this, the complainant organization in the present hypothetical case mobilizes different grounds for attributing responsibility to the eight other respondent States. It first attempts to find a textual basis in the Charter itself, through a purposive and progressive interpretation of the instrument. Despite the limited nature of such textual focus, there is a plausible argument that the Charter does indeed contain extraterritorial obligations. A second line of argument seeks, within the general rules of State responsibility, a reading of the Charter that allows for derived forms of responsibility, such as 'aid and assistance' or 'direction and control' in the commission of a wrongful act.

Collective Complaint No. 93/2013 – *Social Justice International (SJI) v Belgium, Cyprus, Finland, France, Greece, Italy, Ireland, The Netherlands, and Portugal* **(Admissibility decision)**

The complaint

Social Justice International presented a collective complaint against Greece, as the territorially competent state, on the one hand, and against Belgium, Cyprus, Finland, France, Italy, Ireland, The Netherlands, and Portugal, on the other hand. It is the first time that a single collective complaint is presented against multiple States.

In its complaint, SJI alleges that the following rights have been breached through the implementation, in Greece, of the structural adjustment policies agreed to in the Memorandum of Understanding between Greece and the European Commission (acting on behalf of the Eurogroup):

- The right to fair remuneration (Article 4)
- The right to health (Article 11)
- The right to social security (Article 12)
- The right to social and medical assistance (Article 13)
- The right to benefit from social welfare services (Article 14)

Moreover, in respect of the eight other respondent States, it is further alleged that they have failed to comply with the right to protection against poverty and social exclusion (Article 30 of the Revised Social Charter) with respect to Greece.

SJI alleges that Greece accepted and implemented economic policy measures required of it by the European Union economic assistance programme and that it knew, or should have known, would produce multiple, distinct violations of economic and social rights within its own territory. It is further adduced that no circumstances precluding wrongfulness were present that might have diminished or eliminated Greece's responsibility. According to the complainant organization, the eight other respondent States violated extraterritorial obligations arising from the European Social Charter with regard to the same provisions binding upon Greece, as they have accepted to 'pursue [these rights] by all means both national and international in character' (Charter Part I), which must be interpreted in accordance with other relevant international treaty obligations including the UN Charter, the ICESCR, and EU Law instruments. Additionally, the complainant alleges that even if Charter rights had limited or no extraterritorial application, the eight States would incur derived responsibility on the ground that they either assisted, aided or compelled Greece to adopt the first and second economic adjustment programmes, and therefore contributed foreseeably and with clear intent to the underlying violations of social rights in Greece.

Observations on admissibility – Greece

Greece, as the principal respondent State, acknowledged the deterioration of its socioeconomic situation – attributed by the defendant to the global financial crisis and of the European-wide sovereign debt crisis – but contested SJI's characterization of the facts and its interpretation of the Charter. On preliminary grounds, Greece objected to the admissibility of the complainant with respect to the eight other respondents, denying that it had been compelled or assisted in the commission of alleged wrongful acts. Greece reserved its arguments on the merits, and in particular issues of necessity and *force majeure*, for a latter phase in the proceedings.

Observations on admissibility – eight other respondent States

(joint written submission by Belgium, Cyprus, Finland, France, Italy, Ireland, The Netherlands, and Portugal)

The eight other respondents objected to the admissibility of the complaint in their regard. Recalling that complaints must refer 'to a provision of the Charter accepted by the Contracting Party concerned', the defendant States alleged that SJI had *prima facie* failed to indicate in what respect each of them had 'not ensured the satisfactory application of [the Charter] provision[s]', as required by Article 4 of the Additional Protocol providing for a System of Collective Complaints. The eight defendant states argued that if issues of compliance with Charter rights could arguably have been raised with respect to Greece, none of the

306 *Enforcing Extraterritorial Social Rights in the Eurozone Crisis*

other respondents had any binding Charter obligation towards persons in the territory and under the exclusive jurisdiction of Greece. According to these States, the European Social Charter of 1961, applicable to Greece, as well as the Revised European Social Charter of 1996, applicable to all other respondents, imposed no extra-territorial obligations of any kind.

The other respondent States grouped seven different preliminary objections to jurisdiction and to admissibility under three categories, as will be discussed in detail in Sections A–G below. Having made a full report of the proceedings before the Committee, and of the arguments presented by the parties in paragraphs 1 through 44 of the decision, the ECSR began the analysis of the admissibility of the complaint.

The law

As to the admissibility conditions set out in the Protocol and the Committee's Rules of Procedure

45. Due to the number of parties and the unusual characteristics of the complaint, the Committee has found it necessary to discuss the issue of admissibility by clearly distinguishing the position of Greece and that of the other eight respondent States (Belgium, Cyprus, Finland, France, Italy, Ireland, The Netherlands, and Portugal). Facts and policies that relate to the enjoyment of Charter rights by persons in the territory of Greece constitute the cause of action for the complainant organization. However, SJI also argues that the other eight respondent States have engaged their international responsibility through their actions and omissions with respect to Greece.

46. The different roles of Greece and of the other respondent States in the realization of economic and social rights in Greece explain that the Committee must ascertain not only how the responsibility of the different defendants may vary, but also on which grounds the Committee might establish its own jurisdiction to entertain the complaint. In light of these considerations, the Committee will analyze whether the requirements of admissibility are satisfied in the present complaint with respect to Greece (Section I, below), and whether they are also met with respect to the eight other respondent States (Section II, below).

I. On the admissibility of the complaint with respect to Greece

In paragraphs 47–8 the Committee notes that the complaint alleges that the implementation of the economic adjustment programme by Greece has led to multiple violations of social rights within its territory. Therefore, the complaint indicates in what respect Greece is alleged to have failed to ensure the satisfactory application of the Charter's provisions, as required by Article 4 of the Additional Protocol. Greece acknowledges that the

Litigating Transnational Human Rights Obligations 307

alleged violations fall within the competence of the Committee, but denies that other States have any obligations with respect to the enjoyment of social rights within its territory, and therefore rejects the Committee's jurisdiction with respect to the eight other respondent States. Having satisfied itself in paragraphs 49–52 that the formal requirements of admissibility have been met with respect to Greece, the Committee declares the complaint admissible with respect to Greece.

II. On the admissibility of the complaint with respect to the eight other respondent States (Belgium, Cyprus, Finland, France, Italy, Ireland, The Netherlands, and Portugal)

53. As all other admissibility requirements have been found to be present in the present complaint, the admissibility of the complaint with respect to the eight other respondents hinges on the findings that the Committee is required to make regarding the preliminary objections raised by them. These have been grouped into three general objections, under which different arguments have been advanced.

54. Firstly, the Committee must determine whether the respondent States have obligations towards persons under the jurisdiction and within the territory of Greece, in order to satisfy the requirements of Article 4 of the Protocol. This provision has two material requirements.

55. On the one hand, the complaint must deal with an obligation that has been accepted by the respondent party. In this case, Cyprus has not accepted the entirety of Article 4, as well as paragraphs 1 and 4 of Article 13. Finland has not accepted paragraph 1 of Article 4. All other respondent States accepted all of the provisions under review.

56. On the other hand, and more crucially, a complaint must indicate in what respect the respondent party has not ensured the satisfactory application of the Charter. All nine respondent States assert that the Charter does not contain obligations of an extraterritorial character imposing that they fulfill positive obligations – of due diligence, or of any other sort – towards persons under the jurisdiction and in the territory of other States. On this issue the respondent States have advanced four distinct objections to jurisdiction *ratione materiae* (Sections A–D).

57. Secondly, in order to declare the Complaint admissible, the respondent States have argued that the Committee must determine whether conditions of admissibility applicable under general international law obtain in the present case. In particular, the respondents argued that since any finding of violation that the Committee might make would also determine the wrongfulness of the conduct of States that have not accepted its jurisdiction under the collective complaints procedure – namely Germany, Denmark, Spain, Luxembourg, Malta, Austria, and Slovenia – the Committee must

308   *Enforcing Extraterritorial Social Rights in the Eurozone Crisis*

decline jurisdiction based on the *Monetary Gold* principle upheld by the ICJ (Section E).[4]

58.   Thirdly, the allegedly wrongful conduct giving rise to the complaint must be attributable to the respondent States. On this issue, all respondent States agree that the acts complained of are imputable to Greece alone: the acts were negotiated by international organizations with autonomous legal personalities (Section F) and there is no ground to apply the doctrines of 'derived responsibility' – assistance, direction or control – to any of the respondents (Section G).

First Objection: Absence of extraterritorial obligations under the Social Charter

A. Charter obligations have a narrow territorial scope

59.   The respondent States have argued that the Committee must interpret the territorial scope of the Charter narrowly, focusing on the textual limitations set in Article 34/L of the Charter, according to which the Charter 'shall apply to the metropolitan territory of each Party', and on the presumption, codified in Article 29 of the Vienna Convention on the Law of Treaties, according to which '[u]nless a different intention appears from the treaty or is otherwise established, a treaty is binding upon each party in respect of its entire territory'.

60.   The complainant organization, in its response on admissibility, argued that the issue of territorial applicability of a treaty is not to be confused with the question of whether a given treaty obligation imposes on the State the duty to adopt internal measures – legislative, administrative, diplomatic or economic – that might impact on situations or persons abroad. In this sense, positive human rights obligations might require that the State act, or abstain from acting, in a certain manner in its international relations so as

---

4 Editorial note: paragraphs 89–99 discussing this question are not reproduced below, as they do not directly concern the question of the extraterritorial scope of Charter obligations. The Committee dismissed this objection by drawing attention to the fact that the 1995 Protocol on collective complaints instituted a *sui generis* mechanism for the protection of human rights, subject to admissibility criteria quite distinct from those of general international jurisdictions such as the ICJ. Most notably, the complaints mechanism dispensed with such typical requirements as the exhaustion of local remedies, the identification of victims and the quantification of damages. Furthermore, in line with its conclusion in paragraph 88, the Committee argued that its assessment of the wrongfulness of conduct was to be carried out separately for each defendant state in the present complaint. *A fortiori*, the same principle held with respect to states not having accepted the jurisdiction of the Committee: the wrongfulness of their acts could not be presumed on the basis of any findings in the present complaint, and would only be discussed – if at all – through the general national report monitoring procedure established under Part IV of the Social Charter.

Litigating Transnational Human Rights Obligations 309

to comply with its own Charter obligations. Relying *inter alia* on the European Court of Human Rights (ECHR) decision in *Matthews v the United Kingdom* (Grand Chamber Judgment of 18 February 1999 [no. 24833/94], ECHR 1999-I, §34) SJI argued that obligations under Part I of the Charter require that States adopt measures (internal and external) that facilitate, or at least do not unduly restrict, another State's capacity to fulfill its own obligations.

61.   The Committee notes that a strict reading of Article 34/L of the Charter indicates that this provision was meant to allow States that had overseas or colonial territories to decide whether, and to what extent, Charter provisions would apply to them. It is not a provision that determines the extent of the metropolitan territory, nor does it provide that the Charter can have no effects over situations or persons under the jurisdiction of other States. On the latter questions this provision is silent.

62.   It is notable, in this respect, that when the drafters of the European Social Charter decided to limit the scope of its provisions with respect to territories or persons, they took care to do so explicitly (Section C, below). Provisions such as Article 34, or the interpretative declaration on the personal scope of the Charter, address clearly circumscribed issues – the applicability of the Charter to overseas territories or the situation of immigrants under the Charter, for instance – and cannot be construed as limiting the possibility that Charter obligations might have extraterritorial dimensions.

63.   The same can be said with respect to Article 29 VCLT: that a treaty is binding on the entire territory of a State does not imply that it *only* creates obligations with respect to events or situations arising on that territory. Whether or not the treaty will oblige States to act in specific ways in their cross-border relations will depend on the nature of the obligations contained in the treaty and on the goal and objective of the treaty.

64.   In light of these considerations, the Committee is not persuaded by the respondent States' argument according to which the territorial scope of a treaty provides definitive evidence that the contracting parties did not envisage extra-territorial obligations emerging from the implementation of the Charter's provisions. This part of the preliminary exception must therefore be rejected.

B. The Social Charter does not contain general duties of cooperation

65.   The Complaint relied on the Preamble, provisions of Part I of the Charter, and on Article 33/I to argue for the existence of extraterritorial obligations under the Charter. In raising their second set of objections, the respondent States attributed great weight to the fact that the Social Charter could be distinguished from other conventions for the promotion of economic and social rights, and in particular the International Covenant on

310   *Enforcing Extraterritorial Social Rights in the Eurozone Crisis*

Economic, Social and Cultural Rights (ICESCR), in that it contained very few references to a duty of international cooperation between contracting parties.

66.   According to the respondent States, the commitment to pursue the realization of all Charter rights, made in Part I of the Charter, 'by all appropriate means both national and international in character' is non-binding, and a mere statement of policy aims agreed by the contracting parties. This position is textually supported by Article 20/A of the Charter, which States that '[e]ach of the Contracting Parties undertakes (...) to consider Part I of this Charter as a declaration of the aims which it will pursue by all appropriate means'. In particular, the respondent States argue that nothing in the Charter allows for the Committee to review the implementation of this political agreement.

67.   Furthermore, Article I/33 on the means of implementation of the Charter contains no reference to the conclusion of international agreements as a means to realize Charter rights. Respondent States note that, despite the Complaint's reliance on this provision in order to found alleged extraterritorial obligations, the reference to 'other means' – in Article I(3)(d) – merely suggests that the adoption of legislation and collective agreements are not the only *domestic* measures of implementation available. For reasons made clear under Section C, below, respondent States further argued that when international cooperation was necessary for the implementation of Charter rights, treaty provisions would reflect this requirement explicitly.

68.   In its response on admissibility, the complainant organization affirmed that this particular objection could not be analyzed without reference to the principle of systemic integration (see Section D, below) by which the interpretation of the Charter must be carried out in conformity with the other agreements to which the respondent States are parties and in which the extraterritorial character of these obligations is clearly stated. SJI further argued that the Charter is a 'living instrument' that must be interpreted in light of the current conditions, including the context of greater awareness of the interdependence of economic and social systems.

69.   The Committee considers that the Charter contains obligations the implementation of which may require international cooperation, and has affirmed this throughout its practice under the reporting mechanism. The present complaint is the opportunity for the Committee to clarify its understanding of the question of extraterritorial obligations arising from the Charter.

70.   There is no doubt that under the Charter, as is the case with the European Convention on Human rights, it falls *primarily* on the territorial State to implement Charter obligations as, by definition, it has the broadest set of tools and the greatest degree of control over its own territory.

Litigating Transnational Human Rights Obligations 311

71.   However, this does not imply that other States have no obligations of cooperation towards the territorial State. As rightly noted by the respondent States, the Charter clearly requires certain rights – for instance, the right to benefit from social security in a country other than the country of work – be implemented through international agreements. That the Charter refers to these situations explicitly does not imply *a contrario* that there are no other obligations the implementation of which will be made possible, or more effective, through international cooperation.

72.   The Committee acknowledges that Part I as well as Parts III–V of the Charter do not establish undertakings of a legal nature equivalent to those Articles and paragraphs contained in Part II. This, however, does not imply that the Parts and Articles that are not subject to acceptance by States under Article A/20 of Part III produce no legal effects (*Collective Complaint No. 52/2008 Centre on Housing Rights and Evictions (COHRE) v Croatia*, decision on admissibility of 30 March 2009, §17). To the contrary, both Part I and the other provisions of the Charter contain obligations of a legal nature that are binding on all parties (*Collective Complaint No. 30/2004, MFHR v Greece*, Decision of 6 December 2006, §229).

73.   It results clearly from the head paragraph of Part I that all contracting parties have accepted, as a goal of their policy, the objective of the attainment of conditions for the full realization of all Charter rights, and not simply those rights to which they expressly accepted under Article A/20. This provision resembles Article 2(1) of the ICESCR to a remarkable degree: without specifying the forms that cooperation must take, it acknowledges the interconnected nature of social and economic systems through space and over time. By ratifying the Charter each of the Contracting Parties has undertaken to pursue the policy aims of Part I by all appropriate means, both national and international in character. Although this provision was not designed as an individual substantive right subject to specific, independent review through the Charter monitoring procedures, it can and should influence the interpretation of Charter provision over which the Committee has jurisdiction under the complaints procedure.

74.   The Committee therefore rejects the respondent States' argument that no obligations of the Charter have extraterritorial implications. It remains to be seen, however, to what extent specific Charter provisions might, in the specific situation raised by the present complaint, imply duties of an extraterritorial character. While admitting their possible existence, the Committee will operate from a strong, rebuttable presumption that no such obligation exists insofar as the territorial State preserves its capacity to ensure the enjoyment of rights through ordinary means. In principle it is only when the State's capacity to pursue policies consistent with the Charter is impaired that the question of extraterritorial obligations may arise.

312 *Enforcing Extraterritorial Social Rights in the Eurozone Crisis*

75. For the above reasons, the Committee rejects the second branch of the first objection by the respondent states.

C. Situations involving cross-border aspects of rights are dealt with explicitly in the Charter

76. Respondent States adduced the existence of specific Charter provisions on cross-border implications of the protection of social rights as evidence that, in their absence, no obligation of international cooperation ought to be presumed. In this respect, respondent States referred in particular to Article 12(4) and 19(3) of the Charter, which explicitly require States to adopt international agreements. The respondent States further observed that the Committee's own practice shows scarcely any references to extraterritorial obligations, and that questions were never raised by the Committee, under the reporting procedure, in regard to such obligations.

77. SJI argued that the Charter imposed obligations that could be implemented by various means, depending on the circumstances. In its view, the fact that the drafters had envisaged certain forms of international cooperation could not be taken as incontrovertible evidence that cooperation was never required outside those explicit references. As to the alleged scarcity of references to extraterritorial obligations in the practice of the Committee, the complainant organization referred to specific cases and practice in which the Committee had, in effect, required States to adopt measures that were to benefit persons under the jurisdiction of other States (see, *Collective Complaint No. 52/2008 COHRE v Croatia*, decision on the merits of 7 July 2010, §62 '...the Government of Croatia is under a positive obligation by virtue of Article 16 to take appropriate steps to provide housing and security of tenure, to displaced families who lost housing rights and have expressed a clear desire to return to Croatia, or who have been discouraged from returning due to a lack of housing and other forms of protection').

78. On this preliminary objection, the Committee must first recall that from its practice under Articles 12(4) and 19(3) it is clear that States must adopt measures that allow foreign workers protected by the Charter to enjoy the benefits of social security and social services to which they have contributed in whichever state they reside. In its review of the implementation measures adopted by States, the Committee has consistently sustained the view that where no international agreement has been adopted, or when the agreements adopted do not benefit workers from non-EU States, the State has failed to comply with Article 12(4) (see *Conclusions 2009 (Ireland) – Article 12-4* adopted 1 February 2010). However, in such cases, the State can bring its legislation into conformity with the Charter even without adopting an international agreement, by

Litigating Transnational Human Rights Obligations 313

simply extending under national law the benefits that it already allows to EU-member State nationals, or other nationals covered by bilateral agreements. The same reasoning applies, *mutatis mutandis*, to the interpretation of Article 19(3) (*Conclusions XIV-1 Volume 2 (Norway)*, adopted 30 March 1998).

79.   The Committee considers that the existence of provisions in which the Charter explicitly calls for international cooperation for the realization of a specific right does not foreclose the possibility that international cooperation might be required when it is the most efficient, or the only, means to protect a given right in exceptional circumstances. Whether this is the case with respect to any of the provisions relied upon by the complainant will depend on a careful assessment of the policies implemented by Greece, on the availability of alternative policies and on the reasons that are adduced by Greece in order to justify its policy choices.

80.   Should it be clearly established that international cooperation with the other respondent States or with States and organizations not taking part in the proceedings was required in order to meet a satisfactory level of rights protection in the present case, then it would follow that the Committee ought to assess whether, and to what extent, efforts were realized by each respondent in order to cooperate to that end. In this sense, a finding by the Committee that obligations of cooperation might be implicitly required by certain binding provisions of the Charter would in no manner prejudge the question of whether a given respondent took the required steps, in good faith, to discharge said obligations.

81.   Therefore, whether or not in the present complaint the presumption against extraterritoriality that governs most cases may be rebutted is a question that can only be answered during the examination of the merits of the complaint. The Committee cannot, therefore, refuse to review the precise circumstances of the situation of social rights in Greece prior to deciding whether or not, under these circumstances, international cooperation – sought by Greece, and afforded by the other respondent States – might have been the proper means for the realization of Charter rights.

82.   For these reasons, the Committee rejects the respondent States' objection based on the alleged inexistence of extraterritorial obligations under the Charter.

D. Systemic integration does not allow the ECSR to extend or create rights

83.   In the last branch of the first preliminary objection, the respondent States have argued that the principle of systemic integration is being improperly relied on by the complainant organization in the present complaint. In particular, the respondent States sustain that neither Charter

Article 32/H),[5] nor general international law as expressed in Article 31(3) (c) of the VCLT,[6] would empower the Committee to extend its jurisdiction to situations that were not envisaged in the Charter. In their view, interpreting the Charter in light of other treaties such as the ICESCR, the UN Charter and EU Law must not lead the Committee to accept a broadening of the scope of Charter obligations. The respondent states have also argued that such other international obligations cannot confer jurisdiction on the Committee on their own. Although the respondent States acknowledge that these provisions taken together do exclude any interpretation that would afford a lower level of protection than the level afforded by another treaty, for an equivalent human right, it does not allow for the wholesale introduction of new rights into the Charter.

84. The complainant organization insisted that systemic integration, well understood, involves neither the unwarranted introduction of new rights into the Charter system, nor the undue extension of the Committee's jurisdiction. To the contrary, the principle only requires that the Committee interpret the Charter's provisions with a strong presumption in favor of the concurrent and full applicability of all obligations binding on the parties to the dispute. All respondent States are simultaneously parties to the Social Charter, the UN Charter, the ICESCR, and to the EU Charter of Fundamental Rights. According to the complainant, the task of the Committee is that of interpreting the Social Charter so as to give the fullest possible effect to all these norms.

85. The Committee notes that it is bound, by virtue of Article H/32 of the Charter, to interpret its provisions in a manner that does not reduce the protections offered by any other norm of domestic or international origin. The Committee agrees with the respondent States insofar as this obligation does not empower it to introduce new obligations in to the Charter, by an expansive and unbounded interpretation of other treaties. It does, however, oblige the Committee to make sure that its interpretation of any provision that has a counterpart in another treaty affords a standard equal to or higher than the standard of protection contained in any other applicable source.

86. Although various Charter provisions relied on by the complainant organization do indeed have counterparts in both UN and EU treaty law,

---

5 '[t]he provisions of this Charter shall not prejudice the provisions of domestic law or of any bilateral or multilateral treaties, conventions or agreements which are already in force, or may come into force, under which more favourable treatment would be accorded to the persons protected.'

6 'A treaty shall be interpreted in good faith in accordance with the ordinary meaning to be given to the terms of the treaty in their context and in the light of its object and purpose. (...)3. There shall be taken into account, together with the context: (...) (c) any relevant rules of international law applicable in the relations between the parties.'

the substantive protection offered by these instruments is roughly equivalent. As to the issue of whether certain provisions of the Charter impose extraterritorial obligations, this question cannot, and need not, be addressed by reference to other international law sources. It is only if the Charter requires that States adopt measures of an extraterritorial nature that the provisions of other human rights agreements might be used to interpret the scope and extent of this obligation.

87.   Given these considerations, the Committee considers that this final branch of the objection to its jurisdiction is equally unpersuasive and must therefore be rejected.

*
* *

88.   For all the above reasons, the Committee rejects the first objection by the respondent States to its jurisdiction *ratione materiae.* It reaffirms its view that Charter obligations are to be implemented principally by the territorial State. This rebuttable presumption against extraterritoriality can be set aside in those situations where a given provision may only be effectively implemented by concerted action by multiple States. When such is the case, the Committee will assess the responsibility of each respondent State separately. For States the extraterritorial conduct of which might have influenced the realization of social and economic rights in the territory of other states, the Committee will assess responsibility on the basis of the non-territorial State's influence over the circumstances, and when necessary, its intentions in so acting, as required under general international law (see Section G, below).

Second Objection: General rules of international law exclude jurisdiction on the ground of the absence of interested parties

E. The Monetary Gold principle requires the Committee to decline jurisdiction

[Omitted. See note 4, above]

Third Objection: Rules of attribution exclude the respondent States from any responsibility

100.   A final set of objections raised by the eight other respondent States, with which Greece concurred, asserts that the allegedly unlawful conducts presented by the complainant organization are not attributable to them. They sustain that the grounds for attribution relied on by SJI are improper because the economic adjustment programme complained of is an agreement concluded between the 'Troika' – composed of the IMF, the ECB and the European Commission – and Greece, and not an agreement between the latter and the other respondent States. The acts of these international

316   *Enforcing Extraterritorial Social Rights in the Eurozone Crisis*

organizations are not attributable to the eight other respondent States (Section F). Moreover, SJI's second grounds for asserting responsibility is equally unpersuasive: criteria for attribution based on aid and assistance in the commission of a wrongful act, as codified in Article 16 of the *Articles on State Responsibility for Internationally Wrongful Acts* ('ASR', reproduced in UN General Assembly resolution 56/83 of 12 December 2001), are not met in the present complaint (Section G).

F. Acts attributed to the respondent States were adopted by international organizations to which the respondent States transferred the relevant competences

101.   The Committee is asked, firstly, to declare that the impugned acts must be considered acts of the Troika, composed of the EC, the ECB and the IMF. In the respondent States' views, their role was limited to providing funding to the programme, to be disbursed following the satisfaction, by Greece, of conditions agreed to with the Troika.

102.   The respondent States argued that the negotiations for the adoption of the economic assistance programme were undertaken within, and by, three autonomous international organizations, on the one hand, and Greece, on the other hand. The three organizations in question had a distinct legal personality from that of their members. In effect, the defendant States had transferred some of their competence in monetary and financial matters to the European Union, under Article 3 of the Treaty on the Functioning of the European Union (TFEU). This implied that, within the scope of these matters, it was the EC and the ECB, and not the individual States, that had conditioned economic assistance to Greece to the satisfaction of the programme's objectives. Since none of these international organizations is a party to the Charter, the complaint did not fall within the jurisdiction of the Committee.

103.   States further argued that even with respect to national measures adopted in view of the conclusion and implementation of the Greek economic assistance programme, the duty to comply with other international obligations emanating from international organizations should be considered a legitimate aim justifying limitations to Charter rights, as long as the organization issuing such obligations afforded an 'equivalent' level of protection for human rights. In this matter, respondents relied on the criteria established in the ECHR's *Bosphorus* decision (case of *Bosphorus Hava Yolları Turizm ve Ticaret Anonim Şirketi v Ireland* [45036/98], Grand Chamber judgment of 30 June 2005). In line with this precedent, respondents argued that when States are required by EU Law to adopt national measures, had no discretion in the manner of implementing its obligations, and to the extent that the EU afforded 'protection equivalent' to that of the Charter, the Committee should consider that such acts are not attributable to them:

If such equivalent protection is considered to be provided by the organisation, the presumption will be that a State has not departed from the requirements of the Convention when it does no more than implement legal obligations flowing from its membership of the organisation.

However, any such presumption can be rebutted if, in the circumstances of a particular case, it is considered that the protection of Convention rights was manifestly deficient. In such cases, the interest of international cooperation would be outweighed by the Convention's role as a 'constitutional instrument of European public order' in the field of human rights. (§157, references omitted)

104. Acknowledging that the *Bosphorus* presumption of conformity between EU Law and European human rights law had been rejected by the Committee on the grounds expressed in *CGT v France* (Collective Complaint No. 55/2009, *Confédération générale du travail (CGT) v France*, decision on the merits of 23 June 2010, §§31–8), the respondent States affirmed that the Committee should reconsider the reasoning behind that decision. They argued, in particular, that the protection of 'solidarity rights' in Chapter IV of the *Charter of Fundamental Rights of the European Union* (adopted 7 December 2000, Official Journal of the European Communities, 18 December 2000 [OJ C 364/01]) provided sufficient guarantees of the respect, within the European Union and its institutions, of the social rights embodied in the European Social Charter. Moreover the respondents recalled that 'the Treaty established a complete system of legal remedies and procedures designed to permit the Court of Justice to review the legality of measures adopted' (Court of Justice of the EU, *Case 294/83 [Les Verts v Parliament]*, judgment of 23 April 1986).

Assessment of the Committee

105. The Committee recalls that in *CGT v France* it clarified the relationship between European Union law and the European Social Charter and reiterated that provisions of national law that are adopted in the implementation of European Union law are not excluded from the ambit of the Charter (see also, *CFE-CGC v France*, Collective Complaint No. 16/2003, decision on the merits of 12 October 2004, §30–5):

[the Committee] is neither competent to assess the conformity of national situations with a directive of the European Union nor to assess compliance of a directive with the European Social Charter. However, when member states of the European Union agree on binding measures in the form of directives which relate to matters within the remit of the European Social Charter, they should – *both when preparing the text in question and when transposing it into national law* – take full account of the commitments they have taken upon ratifying the European Social

318 *Enforcing Extraterritorial Social Rights in the Eurozone Crisis*

Charter. It is ultimately for the Committee to assess compliance of a national situation with the Charter, including when the transposition of a European Union directive into domestic law may affect the proper implementation of the Charter. (§33, emphasis added)

The Committee then concluded that, with respect to the protection of social rights under the European Treaties,

neither the situation of social rights in the European Union legal order nor the process of elaboration of secondary legislation would justify a similar presumption – even rebuttable – of conformity of legal texts of the European Union with the European Social Charter.

Furthermore, the lack of political will of the European Union and its member states to consider at this stage acceding to the European Social Charter at the same time as to the European Convention on Human Rights reinforces the Committee's assessment. (*ibid.*,§§35–6)

106.   The Committee must now consider whether the circumstances of the present complaint require it to reconsider the reasoning of *CGT v France*. After carefully considering the arguments put forth by the parties, the Committee is of the opinion that the respondent States failed to indicate which facts of the present complaint can be distinguished from those of the earlier case: no indication has been made of developments in EU law, or in the jurisprudence of the CJEU that suggest that the Committee's original assessment was unfounded or ought to be modified in the present com- plaint. But even if the Committee were to accept the respondent States' argument concerning the validity of the *Bosphorus* presumption in the pre- sent complaint, their preliminary objection would still fail. In effect, the criteria set forth in *Bosphorus* are not met in this complaint.

107.   If the Committee were willing to accept the presumption, the respondent States would have had to prove the following facts: firstly, that the legal acts underpinning the two Greek economic adjustment pro- grammes are acts of the EU; secondly, that the respondent States' acts of implementation of these EU measures allowed them no margin of apprecia- tion, and that in fact they were acting as organs of the EU; and thirdly, that in transferring sovereign powers to an international organization, that the latter 'is considered to protect fundamental rights, as regards both the *sub- stantive guarantees* offered and the *mechanisms controlling their observance*, in a manner which can be considered at least equivalent to that for which the [Charter] provides' (case of *Bosphorus v Ireland*, §155, emphasis added). The respondent States have failed to provide evidence of any of the three points.

108.   The Committee observes, on the first criterion, that it does not result clearly from the arguments presented by the respondent States whether the impugned act – the economic assistance programme for Greece – is a

Litigating Transnational Human Rights Obligations 319

normative act of the EU. However, this question is crucial at two distinct levels. First, it determines whether the act is attributable to the EU *under general rules of international law* (see Article 6 of the ILC's *Draft articles on the responsibility of international organizations* [DARIO], Report of the International Law Commission Sixty-third session, Supplement No. 10 (A/66/10), p. 82), or whether, to the contrary, the act is an independent international agreement. Secondly, it determines whether *under EU law* individuals, institutions or member States have judicial remedies to challenge such acts.

109.   From the information submitted by the parties, financial support to Greece was structured through two mechanisms: the *Greek Loan Facility* (GLF), used during the first economic adjustment programme and based on the pooling of bilateral loans totalling roughly 80 billion Euros for years 2010–12, and the *European Financial Stability Facility*, established by an intergovernmental framework agreement, expected to disburse up to 144.7 billion Euros from 2012–14. With respect to Greece, these mechanisms are founded on three main legal instruments: a *Memorandum of Understanding* between Greece and the European Commission (acting on behalf of the Member States which belong to the Euro Group) of 3 May 2010 (MoU); the *Council Decision of 10 May 2010* adopted under the excessive deficit procedure and addressed to Greece with a view to reinforcing and deepening fiscal surveillance and giving notice to Greece to take measures for the deficit reduction judged necessary to remedy the situation of excessive deficit (2010/320/EU, OJ L 145/6, 11 June 2010); and the 7 June 2010 Intergovernmental Agreement creating the *European Financial Stability Facility* (EFSF framework agreement). Of these, only the Council Decision of 10 May 2010, based on the excessive deficit procedure (Article 126§9 of the TFUE), is formally an act of the EU. However, recital [8] of the Decision conditions economic support by EU member States – and not the EU – to compliance by Greece with its MoU commitments. This aspect of the Decision is a *sui generis* provision that had no precedent in EU practice in the field of monetary policy. The exceptional nature of the measures adopted have, it must be stressed, been acknowledged by the respondent states, and justified in terms of the urgency and gravity of the Greek situation. It must be noted that in a recent challenge to the validity of the ESM Treaty, the successor to the EFSM (CJEU, *Case C-370/12 [Thomas Pringle v Ireland]*, referral for a preliminary ruling, Judgment of the full court of 27 November 2012, §105) the CJEU has clearly stated that the EU lacks competence to establish a permanent stability mechanism, which indicates that the bail-out of Euro member States must be accomplished outside the EU institutional framework.

110.   The Committee concludes that the first Greek economic adjustment programme resulted from the multilateral negotiation of terms and conditions for loans (via the Greece-Troika negotiations leading to the MoU and

320   *Enforcing Extraterritorial Social Rights in the Eurozone Crisis*

to the Council Decision of 10 May 2010), the establishment of a novel form of multilateral financial cooperation (in the form of the pooling of bilateral pools through the GLF), and a further international agreement between Greece and the IMF (through the Exchange of Letters that granted access to that organization's funds on the same terms as those set out in the MoU). The second adjustment programme was negotiated by the Troika, and implemented by an agreement between Greece and the EFSF, a *société anonyme* of which EU member States are parties, and in which the EU commission has a coordinating role. It is understood that the complexity and impromptu nature of these institutional arrangements result from the need to comply with EU law restrictions on bail-outs to member States (Article 125§1 of the TFUE), and the limited grounds under which economic assistance may be granted to member States facing severe difficulties arising from exceptional occurrences beyond their control (Article 122§2 TFUE). It is therefore clear that these programmes are not carried out by the EU, or within its competences. The programmes represent a novel form of cooperation between the EU and its member States, but EU institutions are limited to a coordination role, and the organization's own funds are not used in the economic assistance. This point has been made clearly by the CJEU in its *Pringle v Ireland* referral for a preliminary ruling decision.

111.   As to the second condition for the invocation of the *Bosphorus* presumption, the Committee notes that even if the impugned acts were attributable to international organizations, there is scant evidence that participation in the stability mechanism left little or no discretion to States. EU member states not only *could do* but actually *did* choose not to participate in the GLF, as illustrated by Slovakia's decision to opt out of these arrangements. States were not reduced to a mere implementation role, and retained a certain margin of discretion. In particular, States were under no extraordinary constraints with regard to the design of the economic adjustment programmes or the conditions imposed for making disbursements: States retained the capacity to influence the terms and conditions being offered to Greece and could presumably have opted out of any schemes they considered incompatible with their other international obligations. At no point could EU Institutions have determined, against the will of any individual State, the amounts of financial resources that they should make available or the conditions for their disbursement, as implied in the recent decision by the German Federal Constitutional Court's decision declaring the permanent European Stability Mechanism compatible with the German Basic Law (Bundesverfassungsgericht, 2 BvR 1390/12 vom 12.9.2012, Absatz-Nr. (1–248)).

112.   As to the third and final requirement for the validity of the *Bosphorus* presumption in the present complaint, States provided no evidence that in transferring powers to the EU, or to an *ad hoc* financial stability mechanism external to the EU, they ensured a level of protection 'equivalent to' the

Litigating Transnational Human Rights Obligations 321

substantive guarantees of the Charter, or of the supervisory mechanisms it established. There is no doubt that the EU Charter of Fundamental Rights enshrines some of the same rights protected by the Charter. However, judicial review on the basis of the Charter is only available where the act attacked is adopted to implement a normative act of the EU: only acts adopted by member States 'as members of the Council' are subject to judicial review (CJEU, *Joined Cases C-181/91 and C-248/91 (Parliament v Council and Commission)*, Judgment of the Court of 30 June 1993, §12). As mentioned above, the acts setting the adjustment programme in action are not acts of the EU, according to the CJEU: in its recent validation of the ESM Treaty (*Case C-370/12(Thomas Pringle v Ireland)*, §§178ff), the Court clearly stated that the right to effective judicial protection embodied in Article 47 of the EU Charter of Fundamental Rights is not available to disputes arising out of the interpretation of the ESM Treaty, as said treaty is not an act adopted in the implementation of EU Law. Even when the CJEU is given the opportunity to disapply national legislation on the grounds that it violates social rights protected by the EU Charter of Fundamental Rights, it does so in ways that disregard other social rights norms such as non-discrimination under the ECHR or the Social Charter, and authorizes States to adopt laws that have been repeatedly declared incompatible with the Social Charter (compare CJEU,*Case C-571/10 [Servet Kamberaj v Istituto per l'Edilizia sociale della Provincia autonoma di Bolzano (IPES), Giunta della Provincia autonoma di Bolzano, Provinciaautonoma di Bolzano]*, Grand Chamber Judgment of 24 April 2012 [authorizing Italy to adopt laws distinguishing EU citizens from third State nationals from Social Charter contracting parties in the field of housing benefits] with ECSR, *Conclusions 2011 [Italy] – Article 31§3*, p. 47). These cases provide clear evidence that EU law does not afford a *substantial* or *procedural* level of protection of social rights equivalent to that afforded by the Social Charter.

113.   For all the above reasons, the sixth objection raised by the respondent States must be rejected.

G. Derived responsibility not a ground for attribution: Absence of foreknowledge and intent to commit a wrongful act

114.   Finally, all eight other respondent States argued that responsibility for breaches of the Social Charter could not be attributed to them under the doctrine of derived responsibility, as argued by SJI. According to the respondent States, the provisions of the Articles on State Responsibility referring to aid and assistance in the commission of a wrongful act were not applicable to this case because assistance of a financial character cannot generally be considered to ground responsibility, and because, in the present case, the requirements of *knowledge* and that of *intent* were lacking. The same reasoning applied, *mutatis mutandis*, to claims made by SJI to the effect

322   *Enforcing Extraterritorial Social Rights in the Eurozone Crisis*

that Greece had been directed, controlled or coerced into accepting and implementing the economic adjustment programme.

115.   Article 16 of the International Law Commission's *Articles on State Responsibility for Internationally Wrongful Acts* ('ASR', reproduced in UN General Assembly resolution 56/83 of 12 December 2001), relied on by the Complainant, reads:

> A State which aids or assists another State in the commission of an internationally wrongful act by the latter is internationally responsible for doing so if:
> (*a*) That State does so with knowledge of the circumstances of the internationally wrongful act; and
> (*b*) The act would be internationally wrongful if committed by that State.

This provision, accepted as reflecting international custom (ICJ, *Application of the Convention on the Prevention and Punishment of the Crime of Genocide [Bosnia and Herzegovina v Serbia and Montenegro]*, Judgment of 26 February 2007, ICJ Reports 2007, §420), recognizes that a State is only responsible if it has knowledge of the circumstances and if the act would be wrongful if committed by the aiding State. SJI has asserted that even if the Charter does not contain extraterritorial obligations, the eight other respondent States have been complicit in the violation, by Greece, of its Charter obligations. As these obligations are shared by all nine respondent States, and as it is implausible that the respondents were unaware that violations could arise from the implementation of the economic assistance programme, all eight other respondent States share responsibility for the violation of social rights in Greece.

116.   As an auxiliary argument, SJI alleges that the economic assistance programme conditions could also be qualified as 'direction and control exercised over the commission of an internationally wrongful act' (ASR, Article 17) given the extreme financial duress affecting Greece, and its lack of capacity to refuse the conditions imposed to its loans.

117.   All respondent States reject the complainant's argument. Greece insists that it was acting under no compulsion from the other Euro member States, and that all assistance given to it was in order to avoid violations of Charter rights. Moreover, Greece argues that the extreme duress under which it operated must be considered as grounds to *preclude* the wrongfulness of its own acts, rather than a reason to *extend* responsibility to other States. The eight other respondent States agree that any financial assistance given to Greece aimed at stabilizing the economy of that country, thereby ensuring the protection of social rights in Greece to a far greater extent than would be the case if no assistance were forthcoming. Additionally, it

Litigating Transnational Human Rights Obligations 323

was argued that their assistance was not given with knowledge of the circumstances of a wrongful act, much less with the intent of breaching any international obligations of Greece, or of their own. They allege that conditions attached to the assistance programme were carefully tailored to protect the most vulnerable, and are therefore compatible with Charter obligations. Where any breach of the Charter might otherwise have emerged, responsibility ought to be precluded on the ground that the measures adopted were necessary and pursued a legitimate and crucial goal in a democratic society.

118.   The Committee observes that in order to determine whether the implementation of the MoU might raise questions of 'derived responsibility' it must satisfy itself that the assisting States knew that their financial aid to Greece might assist in the commission of wrongful acts. The ILC's commentaries to the ASR underline that 'a State providing material or financial assistance or aid to another State does not normally assume the risk that its assistance or aid may be used to carry out an internationally wrongful act' (ILC, *Report of the International Law Commission on the work of its fifty-third session* [A/56/10], p. 66, §4). It further clarifies that 'aid or assistance must be given with a view to facilitating the commission of the wrongful act, *and must actually do so*' (emphasis added). Consequently, an element of *intent* must be present for derived responsibility to take place. Although the contribution must be 'significant' it must not necessarily be 'essential' for the commission of the act (*ibid.*, §5).

119.   The assessment of whether these different criteria are met in the present complaint depends on a detailed analysis of what the States negotiating the economic assistance programme knew, or should have known, about the impacts of the policies prescribed and what measures were taken in order to ensure that no *additional harm* was caused by the adoption of these policies as compared to what would have been the case if (i) no assistance had been given, or if (ii) the assistance had been offered on different terms, or subject to different conditions.

120.   If the Committee were to find that any of the eight other respondent States provided assistance to Greece in a manner that had foreseeable negative impacts on social rights, and that said States did not exercise sufficient care to design their economic assistance in a manner to minimize, as far as possible, such negative impacts, then this State would be considered to have knowingly facilitated the commission, by Greece, of a wrongful act consisting in a violation of its Charter obligations.

121.   A different reading of the Charter, whereby States could only have their derived responsibility engaged on the condition that they pursue the violation of social rights in another contracting party with deliberate intent, would be patently contrary to Charter Article 1, which requires that all contracting parties 'accept as the aim of their policy, to be pursued by all

324   *Enforcing Extraterritorial Social Rights in the Eurozone Crisis*

appropriate means both national and international in character, the attainment of conditions in which [Charter] rights and principles may be effectively realised'. Part I, although not subject to monitoring by the Committee, clearly requires that States not only abstain from doing harm *directly*, but that they ensure the establishment of conditions whereby all Charter rights can be realized in the territories of all contracting parties (see, *mutatis mutandis*, §66ff, above). This international obligation cannot be construed as allowing States to condition economic assistance to policies that amount to a foreseeable breach of Charter obligations by another contracting party, regardless of what other intentions the assisting State might have.

122.   The Committee concludes, therefore, that it cannot exclude on preliminary grounds that the eight other respondent States might have had knowledge that the assistance they were making conditionally available to Greece might lead to the commission of wrongful acts, and that they deliberately assumed the risk of facilitating said acts. However, deciding this matter cannot be done in the abstract, and certainly cannot be decided at the admissibility phase. Therefore, the Committee joins this preliminary objection to the merits of the complaint. It clarifies that in assessing the matter of derived responsibility during the merits phase, it will examine in particular to what extent the eight other respondent States abided by their positive obligation to ensure, through their joint action, the respect by Greece of its Charter obligations, particularly in the design of the economic assistance programme, and in the selection of policy conditions attached to said programme.

*
* *

For these reasons, the Committee, on the basis of the report presented by _____ and without prejudice to its decision on the merits of the complaint,

DECLARES THE COMPLAINT ADMISSIBLE.

19 Military Interventions in Non-European States (European Court of Human Rights)

Nico Moons

Abstract

Since Banković, the European Court of Human Rights has considered jurisdiction, the prerequisite for having obligations under the European Convention on Human Rights (Article 1), as a primarily territorial concept. The limited "exceptional circumstances" that trigger extraterritorial jurisdiction have been incoherently applied throughout the case law and tailored to the facts of each specific case, the outcome often depending on the suitability of a certain interpretation. This has drawn an arbitrary line between situations that in regard to the question of jurisdiction should be treated in the same way, but are not. In the Al-Skeini judgment, a case regarding the deaths of six Iraqi civilians killed by British soldiers during the occupation of Iraq, the Court seems to have made another distinction. By deliberately focusing mainly on the fact of occupation and the exercise of public powers for establishing UK jurisdiction, the decision raised the following question: what if the facts had taken place after the end of the formal occupation of Iraq and the accession of the Iraqi interim government? In a way, this hypothetical judgment is a reply to Al-Skeini. It tries to harmonize, and where necessary repudiate, the many inconsistencies of the relevant case law on extraterritorial jurisdiction in general. On a broader note, it proposes a single new jurisdiction test based on the universal nature of human rights, which should be able to eliminate the imperfections of the current interpretation(s) by the ECtHR.

Introductory note

The European Court of Human Rights is an international court set up in 1959 in the context of the Council of Europe and based in Strasbourg, France. It is competent to rule on both individual as well as State applications alleging violations of the civil and political rights set out in the European Convention on Human Rights (and its protocols), which had already entered into force six years earlier. In order to lodge a complaint, the applicant needs to be the personal and direct victim of a Convention rights violation by one of the States bound by the Convention, has to have suffered a significant disadvantage and must have exhausted all the domestic remedies in the State concerned that could have provided redress for the relevant situation, up to the highest possible level of jurisdiction. The Court is comprised of

326　*Military Interventions in Non-European States*

47 judges, equal to the number of member States of the Council of Europe that have ratified the Convention, and delivers binding judgments, rendering the countries concerned under an obligation to comply with them.

A highly awaited judgment was delivered on July 7, 2011, when the Grand Chamber decided on the case of *Al-Skeini and others against the United Kingdom.* The facts underlying the case took place in occupied Iraq, in and around the city of Basrah, between May and November of 2003. Five Iraqi civilians were shot dead by British soldiers during security operations, while the sixth victim had first been arrested, brought to a British military facility and tortured before dying of his injuries. The applicants complained that the UK government had violated Article 2 of the European Convention on Human Rights by failing to carry out an effective investigation into the killings. The more important question for the subject of this article was whether the deceased fell within the jurisdiction of the United Kingdom for the purposes of Article 1 of the Convention. Of course, it is only then that the respondent state had Convention rights obligations.

Regardless of the outcome, the judgment in *Al-Skeini* was bound to become a landmark decision in the Court's case law given the unprecedented and sensitive character of the case. The Court basically had to make a statement on the place of human rights in the war on terror. A very narrow judgment would have endangered the universal principle of human rights, while an overly broad judgment would have threatened the effectiveness of future military operations. This tension is of course not new. In its jurisprudence, the Court has repeatedly tried and failed to balance the universality of human rights and political reality in a satisfying way, with *Bankovi* as the ultimate low point. Unfortunately, one cannot dismiss the feeling that in *Al-Skeini*, the Grand Chamber has once again struggled with this difficult balance.

Over the years, this exercise has led to a strict and incoherent approach to the concept of "jurisdiction".[1] Even though the *Al-Skeini* judgment

---

1　For a discussion of the case-law of the Court, see inter alia Altiparmak, K., "Banković: an obstacle to the application of the European Convention on Human Rights in Iraq?", *J.Conflict & Sec.L.* 2004, 213–51; Gondek, M., *The reach of human rights in a globalising world: extraterritorial application of human rights treaties*, Antwerp, Intersentia, 2009, 442; King, H., "The extraterritorial human rights obligations of states", *HRLR* 2009, 521–56; Lawson, R., "Life after Banković: on the extraterritorial application of the European Convention on Human rights", in F. Coomans and M. Kamminga (eds), *Extraterritorial application of human rights treaties*, Antwerp, Intersentia, 2004, 83–123; Milanovic, M., "Al-Skeini and Al-Jedda in Strasbourg", *EJIL* 2012, 121–39; Miller, S., "Revisiting extraterritorial jurisdiction: a territorial justification for extraterritorial jurisdiction under the ECHR", *EJIL* 2009, 1223–46; Roxstrom, E., Gibney, M. and Einarsen, T., "The NATO bombing case (Banković et al. v. Belgium et al.) and the limits of Western human rights protection", *B.U. Int'l.L.J.* 2005, 56–136; Scheinin, M., "Extraterritorial effect of the International Covenant on Civil and Political Rights", in F. Coomans and M. Kamminga (eds), *Extraterritorial application of human rights treaties*, Antwerp, Intersentia, 2004, 73–81; Williams, J. "Al-Skeini: a flawed interpretation of Banković", *Wisconsin Int'l.L.J.* 2005, 687–729.

Litigating Transnational Human Rights Obligations 327

succeeded in solving some of the questions that earlier case law had raised, it created new ones at the same time. In *Al-Skeini*, the Court decided that the United Kingdom had exercised jurisdiction and that it had violated Article 2 ECHR in regard to the first five victims. Although the result might have been satisfying for this particular case, the reasoning behind the decision, which will be focused on more in the hypothetical judgment itself, leaves a lot to be desired. In short, the Court attached great importance to the fact that the events took place during the occupation of Iraq, which was considered to have ended on 30th June 2004 with the accession of the Iraqi interim government.

One of the questions that arises is this: what if the deaths had occurred a couple of days after the occupation had finished? Would the Court then have kept to the same line of arguments as it has done in *Al-Skeini*? Or would it perhaps have made the case law even more inconsistent by relying on a different test? I will aim to improve the deficiencies from *Al-Skeini* and more generally the European Court's case law on this topic and present a different interpretation of "jurisdiction" and the extraterritorial application of the ECHR. Although the hypothetical judgment has been inspired by *Al-Skeini* and therefore takes place in Iraq, the reasoning should be able to be applied whenever contracting states act extraterritorially.

Against this background, I have chosen the completely fictitious facts of my case to take place on 3 July 2004, in other words a couple of days after the formal end of the British occupation of Iraq. The first applicant's son died by a stray bullet during an exchange of fire between British military forces and a small group of militants. The second applicant's husband had been killed during a missile attack from a British unmanned aerial vehicle (UAV), also known as a drone. For the record, I would like to stress that in reality, although the British army has conducted drone attacks in other countries, the United States has been the only country thus far to have done so in Iraq. This second set of facts has been added to also include the specific situation of an air strike. Both applicants argue that the United Kingdom has violated both the substantive obligation of Article 2 not to arbitrarily deprive someone of his life as well as the procedural obligation to carry out an effective investigation into the deaths of the victims. However, in this contribution I will confine myself to the question of jurisdiction. It would thus be more correct to speak of a hypothetical admissibility decision.

In order to draft a decision that is legally sound, credible, justifiable and in a way usable from the European Court's point of view, I believe I cannot simply neglect the Court's jurisprudence and start from scratch without further explanation. That does not mean that my judicial opinion does not aim to improve the concept of jurisdiction. I will just use the case law as a basis to invalidate the direction the Court has taken over the last couple of decades. Therefore, the decision begins with a short reprise of the existing principles developed by the Court. In that regard, the style of my judicial

328 *Military Interventions in Non-European States*

opinion will differ slightly from those of the other authors, who often do not have such a relatively large amount of case law similar to their hypothetical facts to use, criticize and improve.

Case

DECISION AS TO THE ADMISSIBILITY OF
Application no. 12345/08
by X and Y against The United Kingdom

1. Summary of the case law

1. Article 1 of the Convention reads as follows:
> "The High Contracting Parties shall secure to everyone within their jurisdiction the rights and freedoms defined in Section I of the Convention."

The exercise of jurisdiction is a necessary condition for a Contracting State to be able to be held responsible for acts or omissions imputable to it which give rise to an allegation of the infringement of rights and freedoms set forth in the Convention (see *Ilascu and Others v Moldova and Russia,* 8 July 2004, no. 48787/99, § 311).

2. The Court has stated in earlier jurisprudence that a State's jurisdictional competence under Article 1 is primarily territorial (*Soering v United Kingdom,*7 July 1989, no. 14038/88, § 86; *Banković and Others v Belgium and Others* (dec.),12 December 2001, no. 52207/99, § 61; *Ilascu,* § 312). Throughout its case law, the Court has recognized a number of exceptional circumstances, divided under two main strands of principles, which it considered able to give rise to the exercise of jurisdiction by a contracting State acting outside its own territorial borders. The *Al-Skeini* judgment, which is the most recent significant link in the chain of development of the case law on extraterritorial jurisdiction, provided an overview of these exceptions developed over the years (*Al-Skeini and Others v the United Kingdom,* 7 July 2011, §§ 133–40). In the light of this decision, the Court finds it necessary to summarize these principles.

3. In *Al-Skeini,* the Court recognized that jurisdiction is established and the responsibility of a contracting party may arise when as a consequence of military action – whether lawful or unlawful – it exercised effective control of an area outside its national territory. The obligation to secure, in such an area, the rights and freedoms set out in the Convention, derived from the fact of such control whether it be exercised directly, through its own armed forces, or through a subordinate local administration (*Loizidou v Turkey,* 23 March 1995, no. 15318/89, § 62; *Banković ,* § 70; *Al-Skeini,* § 138). It sufficed that the local authorities had survived by virtue of the contracting State's military or other support. Consequently, there

Litigating Transnational Human Rights Obligations 329

was no need for the exercise of detailed control over the policies and actions of this local administration (*Loizidou v Turkey*, 18 December 1996, no. 15318/89, § 56; *Cyprus v Turkey*, 10 May 2001, no. 25781/94, §§ 76–77; *Ilascu*, §§ 388–394).

4. The second extraterritorial exception mentioned in *Al-Skeini* was based on a personal notion of jurisdiction. A contracting State may be held accountable for violations of the Convention rights and freedoms of persons who are found to be under the former State's authority and control through its State agents (*Issa and Others v Turkey*, 16 November 2004, no. 31821/96, § 71). Firstly, this can be the case with regard to acts of diplomatic and consular agents (*Banković*, § 73). Secondly, the Court noted that the use of force by State agents operating outside its territory may bring the person within the State's jurisdiction in certain circumstances (*Al-Skeini*, § 136). This has been applied when an individual is taken into custody abroad (*inter alia Öcalan v Turkey*, § 91; *Medvedyev and Others v France*, 29 March 2010, no. 3394/03, § 67). Thirdly, jurisdiction could also be established if a contracting State exercised all or some of the public powers normally to be exercised by a sovereign government through the consent, invitation or acquiescence of the government of that territory. Therefore, a contracting State may be responsible for violations of the rights set forth in the Convention when it carried out executive or judicial functions on foreign territory in accordance with custom, treaty or other agreement (*Al-Skeini*, § 135).

2. Whether there is a need for a development of the case law

5. In *Al-Skeini*, the Court held that the victims fell within the UK jurisdiction because the respondent State had exercised some of the public powers normally to be exercised by a sovereign government (*Al-Skeini*, § 149). In the domestic proceedings, the House of Lords rightly stated that although there is a significant resemblance between the facts in *Al-Skeini* and those in this case (in particular regarding the first applicant's son), the facts currently before the Court took place when the United Kingdom was no longer an occupying State. Indeed, UN Security Council Resolution 1546, adopted on 8 June 2004, endorsed the formation of a sovereign Iraqi interim government, which replaced the Coalition Provisional Authority (CPA) and took over the legally obtained temporary powers of the latter on 28 June 2004. Consequently, the House of Lords concluded that, by the time the events under scrutiny took place, the United Kingdom no longer exercised some of the aforementioned public powers and did thereby no longer have formal authority and responsibility for the maintenance of security in the relevant region. It therefore decided that the jurisdictional link between the deceased and the United Kingdom for the purposes of Article 1 of the Convention was not established.

330 *Military Interventions in Non-European States*

6. However, the Court considers that the present case, as will be further clarified, highlights the unsatisfying limits of the principles applied in *Al-Skeini* and other cases and shows that it can lead to anomalous and unjust results, in particular in regard to the universal character of the Convention and the clarity of the jurisprudence (see below). Therefore, in the Court's view, a change of direction on the concept of jurisdiction is an absolute necessity. Since the Convention is first and foremost a system for the protection of human rights, it is of crucial importance that it is interpreted and applied in a manner which renders its rights practical and effective, not theoretical and illusory. A failure by the Court to maintain a dynamic and evolutive approach would risk rendering it a bar to reform or improvement (*Stafford v the United Kingdom*, 28 May 2002, no. 46295/99, § 68; *Goodwin v the United Kingdom*, 11 July 2002, no. 28957/95, § 74).

7. The Court is of the opinion that the legal status of a State's conduct according to international law cannot be decisive for the purposes of the Convention. It considers it unacceptable that the first applicant's son, killed by a bullet from a British soldier's gun, as well as the second applicant's husband, killed by a missile from a British controlled drone, would have to be considered unlucky not to have been shot dead a couple of days earlier. The question of jurisdiction is primarily a factual question and should not only depend on a formal document that dates the official exercise of public powers. The Court therefore rejects the possibility that the respondent government could be excused from any human rights obligations purely based on this distinction. The United Kingdom could just as much have been in a position to exercise authority and control in this case as in *Al-Skeini*, certainly given the fact that the situation on the ground had not changed in any significant way since the transfer of power from the CPA to the Iraqi interim government. The transfer was not accompanied by a significant number of British troops leaving the country. According to figures by the British Ministry of Defence, the number of British troops decreased by only a hundred between the end of May 2004 (8600) and that same period in 2005 (8500). The coalition partners, led by the US, continued to factually maintain security and control and to fight insurgencies, albeit with the help of the new Iraqi army.

8. Although those facts only concern the war in Iraq and the need for a development might be triggered by this specific case, the Court emphasizes that these remarks cover a broader issue. In that regard, the Court considers that not adapting the case law to these vital concerns would create a dangerous precedent for future military interventions by contracting States. Whenever State parties engage in military interventions, there would be no legal incentive to take human rights into consideration as long as these contracting States do not exercise public powers normally exercised by the sovereign government. Following that logic, a contracting State would thus prefer not to be officially recognized as an occupier in future military interventions.

Litigating Transnational Human Rights Obligations 331

9. Nevertheless, the Court is aware that a small addition to the interpretation of the existing tests laid out in *Al-Skeini* would only harm the coherency and clarity of the case law. Firstly, with regard to coherency, the Court refuses to add any further exceptions to the current territorial concept of jurisdiction in order to prevent the exceptions from becoming case-to-case adjustments to specific circumstances. The Court expresses the need to return back to basics and create a simple and clear test applicable to all cases. This test must avoid the possible desire to artificially shape the judgment one way or another whenever the normal outcome of the test would feel unsuitable or could burden State parties amidst an already complicated situation with onerous obligations. The Court considers this development vital for the coherent application of Convention rights obligations.

10. Secondly, regarding clarity of the case law, the Court recalls that the first real test regarding Article 1 of the Convention was built on the personal notion of jurisdiction (*Cyprus v Turkey*, Commission decision of 26 May 1975, § 8 and 10). The second exception to the territorial principle of Article 1, effective control over an area, was only established later on (*Loizidou v Turkey*, 8 July 1993, no. 15318/89, § 62). Regardless of the purpose behind this spatial test, the Court admits that by extending the "exceptional circumstances" to two strands of principles, it has overly complicated the concept of extraterritorial jurisdiction for national courts. The development of the case law through subtests has further contributed to the impression that the Court "does not speak in one voice" (House of Lords, *Al-Skeini*, § 67 (Lord Rodger)). Since it is in the interest of the protection of human rights that national courts have a good understanding of the extraterritorial application of the Convention, it is also in the interest of the Court to make sure its judgments are easily interpretable and void of ambiguities.

11. The Court considers that these qualities of clarity and coherence are also of importance for the foreign policies of contracting States. A clear view of when an individual falls within the jurisdiction of a contracting State and consequently triggers its human rights obligations could affect a contracting State's behaviour outside of its borders. By adopting a simple and straightforward test which enables contracting States to predict the outcome of the jurisdictional question with a considerable degree of certainty and to know in advance whether or not it has human rights obligations, these States would also be able to take measures to prevent violations of these rights. In that regard, the Court wishes to stress that it does not interfere with the foreign policies of the contracting States or more particularly with military interventions of any kind. The Convention does not prevent states from taking reasonable and proportionate actions to defend democracy and the rule of law (former president of the Court Luzius Wildhaber, opening speech of the judicial year 2002), since it does not have the desire nor the competence to play such a role. It merely holds States accountable for violations of their human rights obligations.

332 *Military Interventions in Non-European States*

12. It is against this background and for these reasons that the Court wishes to review, rewrite and simplify the established principles by confirming the basic functions of the Convention. The Court aims to adopt one test to decide whether extraterritorial jurisdiction must be established, a test applicable to all relevant cases. While it is normally in the interests of legal certainty, foreseeability and equality before the law that the Court should not depart, without good reason, from precedents laid down in previous cases, it is not formally bound to follow its previous judgments (*Mamatkulov and Askarov v Turkey*, § 121; *Vilho Eskelinen v Finland*, § 55). Given the circumstances as described above, the Court notes that there is good reason to depart from its earlier case law. Moreover, the Court believes that a deviation of earlier jurisprudence on this subject would enhance the legal certainty in the long run rather than threaten it. The Court hereby also recalls that the Convention is a living instrument which must be interpreted in the light of present-day conditions (*Tyrer*, § 31; *Mamatkulov and Askarov*, § 121).

3. The scope of the Convention

13. The Court observes that the first draft of the Convention prepared by the Committee of the Consultative Assembly of the Council of Europe stated that its member States must ensure the rights of "all persons residing within their territories". This was changed to its present form in order to "widen as far as possible the categories of persons who are to benefit by the guarantees contained in the Convention" (*Travaux Préparatoires of the European Convention on Human Rights*, 5 February 1950). The object of this different wording of Article 1, as emerges from the *travaux préparatoires*, was to ensure the inclusion of persons who were not residents but were nevertheless present in the territory of a member State. In that regard, when drafting Article 1 of the Convention, extraterritorial acts by contracting States were simply not taken into account.

14. However, this does not mean that the Convention rights and freedoms do not apply throughout the world (compare *Banković*, § 80) and that human rights, universal by their nature, should not be secured by States nor protected by the Court outside a State's borders or outside the Convention's legal space (*espace juridique*). Human rights are applicable to all persons for the one and only reason that they are human beings. The preamble of the Convention clearly reflects this idea by stating that the aim of the text is to secure the universal and effective recognition and observance of the Convention rights. The Oxford English Dictionary describes the adjective "universal" as follows: "relating to or done by all people or things in the world or in a particular group; applicable to all cases". "Universal" thus hardly suggests an observance parcelled off by territory on the checkerboard of geography (*Al-Skeini*, concurring opinion Judge Bonello, § 9).

Litigating Transnational Human Rights Obligations 333

15.   In other words, a State party to the Convention is not able to escape its human rights obligations on a solely geographical basis. If this were the case, a State would have Convention rights obligations for acts of its State agents just inside its own territory, while the same acts conducted a couple of steps across the border would release this State from these obligations and leave the concerned person outside the Convention protection. In regard to the Convention rights and freedoms, the Court stresses that there is no predetermined area of impunity anywhere in the world.

16.   Therefore, the Court emphasizes that the legal space is no require- ment for the establishment of jurisdiction and that the Court has never had the intention to limit the scope of the Convention as such (*Al-Skeini*, § 142; *Pad and Others v Turkey*, 28 June 2007, no. 60167/00, § 53). In its case law, the Court has repeatedly established jurisdiction in States outside the Convention legal space (*Öcalan v Turkey; Xhavara and Others v Italy; Issa v Turkey; Al-Saadoon and Mufdhi v the United Kingdom; Medvedyev and Others v France*).

17.   Since most cases before the Court involve member States simply exer- cising jurisdiction on their own territory, the Court confirms that factually the exercise of jurisdiction is primarily territorial. As a concept, however, jurisdiction is neither territorial nor extraterritorial. In other words, juris- diction can be perceived as primarily territorial because contracting States are not brought before the Court that often in regard to their extraterritorial acts, but not because such acts can constitute the exercise of jurisdiction only in exceptional circumstances.

18.   In addition, the Court clarifies that Article 56 of the Convention, which allows contracting States to "extend the Convention to all or any territories for whose international relations it is responsible", cannot be inter- preted in present day conditions as limiting the scope of the term jurisdiction in Article 1 (*Al-Skeini*, § 140). With regard to the actual rationale behind this provision, it is clear that Article 56 was included for historical reasons on the grounds that the responsibility of State parties for their colonies could only be established with a special notification by these States, as a way to respect the autonomy of local culture. The Court therefore considers that the provision does not relate to the concept of jurisdiction and that relying on Article 56 to support a narrow interpretation of Article 1 ignores its character as a colonial clause.

4. Interpretation of extraterritorial jurisdiction

19.   In the Court's view, considering the universal meaning of the Convention, Article 1 cannot be interpreted so as to allow a State party to perpetrate violations of the Convention on the territory of another State, which it could not perpetrate on its own territory (*Issa*, § 71; see also Human

334 *Military Interventions in Non-European States*

Rights Committee, *Lopez Burgos v Uruguay*, 29 July 1981, no. 52/1979, § 12.3). In that regard, the preliminary question of jurisdiction must not overshadow the substantive extraterritorial application of the Convention rights.

20.   By ratifying the Convention, a State shows its unconditional commitment to human rights and its universal and effective recognition and observance of the Convention rights. Upholding human rights can be called neither universal nor effective when a State party can easily abdicate all responsibility for acts of its State agents abroad. The Court considers it fundamentally wrong and contradictory to the supremacy of the Convention rights that a State would assume that the protection of an individual's most fundamental rights does not weigh up against the effectiveness of its extraterritorial acts. The Court is of the opinion that a State party cannot treasure and promote human rights on its own territory, and at the same time defend the legality of a human rights vacuum on foreign territory, certainly when given regard to the fact that these extraterritorial acts are regularly carried out in the name of human rights. The Court therefore distances itself from the use of human rights as a rhetorical vehicle to invade other countries or to act out military operations when the contracting States deem themselves not to be bound by these same values abroad.

21.   Jurisdiction as inscribed in Article 1 of the Convention is not a question of normativity. It means simply actual authority and control over an individual by a State, most of the time through its own agents (*Assanidze v Georgia*, concurring opinion Judge Loucaides). Every form of a contracting State's authority which directly affects an individual establishes jurisdiction. The applicability of the Convention does not depend on the existence of a formal legal relationship between the contracting State and the concerned person. In fact, whether the conduct or act by the State was legal or illegal according to public international law is irrelevant for the application of the Convention. Since jurisdiction is conceptually neither territorial nor extraterritorial (see above, § 17), the Court notes that jurisdiction functions in the same way inside as outside a contracting State's territory. When, hypothetically, a State party has lost its actual control and authority over the individuals within the borders of its own territory, this State cannot be expected to secure all human rights of the concerned individuals (compare *Ilaşcu*, § 333). The Court summarizes that an individual falls within the jurisdiction of a State party when the alleged violation in question was the direct result of the exercise of authority and control by the concerned contracting State.

22.   By defining the scope of the term jurisdiction, the Court emphasizes that it does not tend to give an exhaustive list of the circumstances in which a State can exercise authority and control over persons. In any case, for the purposes of Article 1, authority and control must be interpreted in a broad

Litigating Transnational Human Rights Obligations 335

sense. Otherwise, there would be an arbitrary and artificial distinction between different forms of authority which would lead to absurd results. Control is not only limited to occupied territories or acts by diplomatic and consular agents, nor is the existence of some kind of physical component necessary to establish jurisdiction. Although the arrest and detention of an individual might be the most obvious case of personal control, it is only one instance when the Convention becomes applicable abroad (compare *Al-Skeini*, § 136). Limiting the application of the jurisdiction test to such circumstances would exclude a lot of other cases where, for example, the most basic human right of all, the right to life (Article 2), has allegedly been violated. While a State agent killing an individual from a distance does not physically control this person in a way that would have been the case if he had been apprehended, the Court considers that the agent's use of lethal force is the ultimate act of authority over a person and thus brings this individual into the State's Article 1 jurisdiction. Finally, the Court also emphasizes that the exercise of authority and control over a person does not depend *in se* on the choice of weapons used.

23. The Court has already recognized jurisdiction of a contracting State in a couple of cases where an individual has been killed on the territory of another State outside the context of occupation or custody. For example, in *Pad v Turkey*, § 54, the Court held that seven Iranian men were subject to the authority and therefore jurisdiction of Turkey on the basis that "the fire discharged from the (Turkish) helicopters had caused the killing of the (applicants)", irrespective of the questions raised in that case as to whether the deceased had first been arrested and whether the events had taken place on the Turkish or on the Iranian side of the border. The Court took the same approach in three separate cases involving violence by Turkish forces in the UN buffer zone in Northern Cyprus. In *Isaak v Turkey*, § 21, the Court held that the deceased, who had been beaten to death by members of the TRNC police while demonstrating against the Turkish occupation, fell under the Turkish jurisdiction. In *Solomou v Turkey*, §§ 50–1, the Court established jurisdiction on the basis that "the bullets (...) had been fired by the members of the Turkish-Cypriot forces". Finally, in *Andreou v Turkey*, the Court held that the applicant was within Turkish jurisdiction because "the opening of fire on the crowd from close range (...) was the direct and immediate cause of her injuries".

24. The Court considers it helpful for the interpretation of Article 1 of the Convention to pronounce on the specific meaning attributed to jurisdiction in other international monitoring bodies (compare *Banković*, § 78). Although the American Declaration on the Rights and Duties of Man contains no explicit limitation of jurisdiction, the Inter-American Commission on Human Rights has used the term as the basis for considering the scope of the contracting State's obligations. It has adopted a similar broad personal notion of jurisdiction by examining "whether the state observed the

336 *Military Interventions in Non-European States*

rights of a person subject to its authority and control" (Inter-American Commission on Human Rights, *Coard et al. v the United States*, 29 September 1999, Report No. 109/99, Case No. 10.951, § 37). In *Alejandre Jr. v Cuba*, the Commission held that the pilots of two small and unarmed civilian airplanes which were brought down by a Cuban military aircraft in international airspace were subject to Cuban authority because the victims had died as a consequence of direct actions taken by the concerned State agents (IACHR, *Alejandre Jr. v Cuba*, 29 September 1999, Report No. 86/99, Case No. 11.589, § 25). In *DRC v Uganda*, the International Court of Justice found human rights treaties to be applicable in case of military activities outside the context of occupation and considered lethal force to be an exercise of authority (ICJ, *DRC v Uganda*, 19 December 2005, §§ 219–20). Finally, the Human Rights Committee has expressed in its General Comment No. 31 on Article 2 of the International Covenant on Civil and Political Rights that a State party "must respect and ensure the Covenant rights to anyone within the power or effective control of their forces acting outside its territory, (...) regardless of the circumstances in which such power was obtained, such as constituting a national contingent of a State Party assigned to an international peace-keeping or peace-enforcement operation" (HRC, General Comment No. 31, 29 March 2004, §10).

25. The Court summarizes that a State party is accountable under the Convention to an individual directly affected by any exercise of authority and control by a State party, regardless of whether the concerned individual had been taken into custody and irrespective of the method of warfare used.

26. The obligation of contracting States under Article 1 to secure the Convention rights is not based on an all-or-nothing concept where, in case of jurisdiction, the whole package of rights must automatically be applied. The Court considers that such a concept tends to ignore the reality of the situation and to forget the different possible graduations of control over individuals, both outside as inside the context of occupation. When there is an immediate link between the alleged human rights violation and the extraterritorial exercise of authority and control by a contracting State, this State cannot avoid having any human rights obligations at all only because of a lack of authority and control to secure *all* rights and freedoms as mentioned under Section I of the Convention. The same applies in the other direction. A State cannot be expected to secure, for example, the right to marry when exercising only a limited amount of authority. The Court therefore holds that Convention rights can be divided and tailored and must be secured by a contracting State in so far as it is capable of doing so, or in other words, to the extent that it exercises *de facto* authority and control (*inter alia Al-Skeini*, § 137; *X v the United Kingdom*, Commission decision of 15 December 1977; *Cyprus v Turkey*, Commission decision of 26 May 1975, § 8; ICJ, *DRC v Uganda*, 19 December 2005, § 219). The degree of responsibility by a State party is thus proportional to the degree of jurisdiction. In that

Litigating Transnational Human Rights Obligations 337

regard, a State party will only have positive human rights obligations when it has the authority and control to secure these kinds of obligations.

5. Application of these principles to the facts of the case

27.   The Court notes that it is undisputed between the parties that the first applicant's son was killed by a gun shot fired by a British soldier and that the second applicant's husband was killed by a missile fired from an armed unmanned aerial vehicle (UAV), controlled by a British state agent via satellite communication from a military base outside of Iraq. The applicants complain about violations of Article 2 of the Convention regarding the obligation not to arbitrarily deprive someone from his life and to carry out a full and independent investigation into the circumstances of both killings. In the light of these facts and the above principles, the Court must ascertain whether the applicants' relatives were under the authority and control, and therefore within the jurisdiction of the respondent State.

28.   Regarding the first applicant's son, the Court considers that the British soldier, by pointing and subsequently firing his gun in the direction of the individual, has exercised authority and control over the latter. The alleged human rights violation by the United Kingdom is the direct result of the exercise of authority and control by its State agent. It follows that there was a jurisdictional link for the purposes of Article 1 of the Convention between the respondent State and the deceased.

29.   Regarding the second applicant's husband, the Court considers that the British State agent operating the UAV exercised authority and control at the time that he followed, locked on and aimed at the intended target and pressed the fire button. The Court rejects the argument by the respondent government that a drone attack by a contracting State cannot establish jurisdiction. The pilot of an armed aircraft, regardless of whether he mans the plane or operates it from the ground from thousands of kilometers away, exercises the ultimate act of authority over an individual's life when he fires a missile in this person's direction.

30.   Moreover, the Court takes note of the significant technological advancements in weaponry made over the last couple of decades. UAVs, including the one used during the concerned drone attack, are equipped with high-resolution cameras and accurate sensors which should allow States to follow and hit targets with greater accuracy and fewer collateral civilian casualties and injuries. However, the Court notes that UN Special Rapporteur Philip Alston in his Report on extrajudicial, summary or arbitrary executions nuances this presupposition by stating that the precision and accuracy of a drone strike still depends on human intelligence. While drones provide the capability to conduct useful aerial surveillance which enhances the ability of a State's forces to undertake precautions in attack,

338   *Military Interventions in Non-European States*

the report States that "these optimal conditions may not exist in every case". As a result, a drone operation team might be at an even greater human intelligence gathering disadvantage than ground forces (§ 81–2).

31.   Nevertheless, this detailed vision of the events on the ground is one of the main arguments for its increased popularity among States. Due to this feature, States argue that pilots are able to strike with pin-point precision. The Court therefore finds it irreconcilable with the characteristics and the respondent State's perception of drone attacks that the United Kingdom denies any form of authority and control over the concerned individual and consequently abdicates all possible responsibility under the Convention. Due to its cost-efficiency and low risk factor to a State's forces, the production and use of drones is increasing significantly. However, the aforementioned report by UN Special Rapporteur Philip Alston has mentioned that policymakers and commanders could be tempted by these drone characteristics to interpret the possible use of drone attacks too expansively (§ 80). The Court also considers that the display of human beings as small dots on a computer screen and the geographical and psychological distance between the UAV operator and the target could lower the threshold to launch a missile or a bomb from a drone and develop "a playstation mentality of killing" (Report UN Special Rapporteur Alston, § 84). In the light of future military interventions, the Court therefore confirms the importance of establishing jurisdiction as a consequence of authority and control irrespective of the weapons used.

32.   The Court holds that at the time of the events, the United Kingdom did not exercise this authority and control to the extent that the respondent state could be expected to secure all rights and freedoms as defined in Section I of the Convention. However, the United Kingdom did exercise authority and control over the right to life of the concerned individuals. Considering the respondent State maintained its strong presence in the area (see above, § 7), the Court does consider that in both cases the United Kingdom was in a position not only to respect the substantive obligation of Article 2 not to arbitrarily deprive anyone of his life, but also to fulfil the procedural obligation to carry out a full and independent investigation into the circumstances of the killings. Against this background, it follows that in both cases the deceased fell within the British jurisdiction with regard to Article 2 of the Convention.

33.   The Court concludes that the United Kingdom has exercised jurisdiction over the concerned individuals with regard to the rights and obligations brought forward by the applicants.

For these reasons, the Court, unanimously,

DECLARES THE APPLICATION ADMISSIBLE, without prejudging the merits of this case.

Part IV

Domestic Courts

20 Extraordinary Rendition (U.S. Supreme Court)

Mark Gibney

Abstract

The following hypothetical ruling is based on a real-world scenario: the extraordinary rendition of Maher Arar, a Canadian-Syrian national who was subjected to months of torture in a Syrian prison. In the actual case, Mr. Arar's lawsuit against a group of federal (U.S.) agents was dismissed by the Second Circuit Court of Appeals, and this ruling was upheld when the U.S. Supreme Court declined to grant Mr. Arar's appeal. In that way, there was no effective remedy – no measure of justice – for Maher Arar in an American court. This, however, has been the rule in extraordinary rendition proceedings, although most of these cases have been dismissed based on what is known as the "States secrets" doctrine, which, as its name would indicate, seeks to prevent the disclosure of government secrets. The present case takes certain liberties by extending Arar's cause of action to include suits against three States – Jordan, Syria and the United States – thereby invoking sovereign immunity and State responsibility. In this alternative ruling, Mr. Arar is successful, with the reconstituted Supreme Court relying heavily on the human rights obligations of the United States – a subject that was strikingly absent in the real-world proceedings.

Introductory note

All of the "opinions" in this book are from regional and international adjudicatory bodies. However, it would be a mistake to overlook the important role that domestic courts can (and should) play in the protection of human rights. The present "opinion" is by the United States Supreme Court. As Louis Henkin[1] and Harold Koh[2] have shown though historical analysis, the Court has purposely removed itself from matters thought to involve "foreign affairs".

---

1 Louis Henkin, *Foreign Affairs and the Constitution* (1972)
2 Harold Hongju Koh, *The National Security Constitution: Sharing Power After the Iran-Contra Affair* (1990).

342   *Extraordinary Rendition*

In the *Curtiss-Wright* case,[3] the Court justified this deference on the basis that the constitutional scheme of checks and balances only applied within the domestic realm, but that the President's foreign affairs powers came directly from the (unchecked) power of the King of England. According to the Court, in foreign affairs the President serves as the nation's "sole organ". One of the uglier episodes in U.S. history – the internment of Japanese-Americans during World War II – was stark evidence of this lowered judicial role.[4]

With this as background, one of the more surprising aspects of the "war on terror" has been the manner in which the Supreme Court has been engaged, particularly with respect to the rights of Guantánamo Bay detainees. In *Rasul v Bush* (2004), the Court rejected the entreaties of the Bush administration that the conduct of the "war on terror" was a political matter beyond the scope of judicial review, as well as the substantive argument that foreign nationals held in a detention facility outside the territorial borders of the United States could not invoke a federal (U.S.) *habeas corpus* statute. In quick response, the political branches passed the Detainee Treatment Act, which (seemingly) removed the jurisdiction of the courts to hear such cases. However, in *Hamdan v Rumsfeld* (2006), the Court countered by holding that the act only applied to prospective *habeas* petitions, but not those that had already been filed. Once again, the Congress and the President responded quickly, this time by passing the Military Commissions Act, which included the following provision:

> No court, justice or judge shall have jurisdiction to hear or consider an application for a writ of *habeas corpus* filed by or on behalf of an alien detained by the United States who has been determined by the United States to have been properly detained as an enemy combatant or is awaiting such determination.

Notwithstanding this clear directive, the Supreme Court ruled in *Boumediene v Bush* (2008) that the military commissions created by the act were not an adequate substitute for *habeas corpus* proceedings. Perhaps even more importantly, the Court held, for the first time, that nonresident foreign nationals have certain rights under the U.S. Constitution.

Given this saga, it is difficult to square these Supreme Court's decisions with its refusal to address extraordinary rendition, or other aspects of the "war on terror". Of course, the Court was deeply cognizant of the judiciary's longstanding reticence to confront the political branches in this realm. Yet, as the world's lone superpower continues to exert its military,

---

3 *United States v Curtiss-Wright Export Corp.*, 299 U.S. 304 (1936). But see, *Youngstown Sheet & Tool Co. v Sawyer*, 343 U.S. 579 (1952) (commander in chief powers do not extend so far as to allow the president to order federal personnel to take over striking steel plant).

4 *Korematsu v United States*, 323 U.S. 214 (1944).

Litigating Transnational Human Rights Obligations 343

political and economic power over the four corners of the globe, with enormous human consequences for the people living in those countries, these rather quaint notions of judicial review need to be seriously questioned. The following "opinion" provides one manifestation of how this might happen – and why it must happen.

Case

SUPREME COURT OF THE UNITED STATES

Maher Arar v John Ashcroft (Attorney General of the United States) et al.

Justice Gibney Delivered the Opinion of the Court

On September 11, 2001, the United States was attacked by Al Qaeda operatives, a day that will never be forgotten by people in this country, and elsewhere, who lived through these horrible events. The response of the Executive department was swift. Virtually overnight, hundreds of Muslim immigrants who were suspected of having terrorist sympathies were rounded up and flown to various unknown destinations, and many of these men were eventually deported. Certainly, the central component of what has come to be called the "war on terror" was the U.S.-led invasion of Afghanistan, which sought to remove from power the Taliban government that had provided sanctuary to the Al Qaeda forces behind the September 11 attacks. A less visible tactic in this fight has been the practice of extraordinary rendition, which involves the case before us.[5]

Under governing federal law, in any motion to dismiss all factual declarations made by the complaining party are assumed to be true. Maher Arar is a native of Syria whose family moved to Canada when he was a teenager and who is a dual national of these two countries. In September 2002, while vacationing with his family in Tunisia, Arar was called back to Canada by his employer to consult with a prospective client. He purchased a ticket to Montreal with stops in Zurich and New York. On September 26, 2002, Arar arrived from Switzerland at John F. Kennedy airport in New York expecting to catch his connecting flight to Montreal. However, after presenting his passport to U.S. immigration officials he was identified as being on the government's terrorist watch list. Arar was interrogated for a number of days, after which he was flown to Washington D.C. and then sent to Amman, Jordan, where he was delivered to Syrian authorities.

Arar alleges that during his subsequent ten month detention in Syria he was placed in a "grave cell" measuring six feet long, seven feet high and

---

5 It should be pointed out that extraordinary rendition did not begin with the 9/11 attacks. Former CIA Director George Tenet estimates that approximately 80 renditions had been carried out before September 11, 2001.

344 *Extraordinary Rendition*

three feet wide. He claims that he was repeatedly tortured by Syrian officials, and he also claims that his interrogation sessions were coordinated with U.S. officials who he believes sent the Syrians a dossier containing specific questions, and that Syrian officials reciprocated by supplying information extracted from him to U.S. officials. Arar was eventually released to Canadian authorities and brought home. A Canadian commission cleared Mr. Arar of any connection with terrorism and he was awarded $10.5 million in compensation,[6] which was accompanied by a State apology issued by Prime Minister Stephen Harper.[7] However, Arar's suit against the Syrian government was dismissed on the basis of Canada's law on sovereign immunity.[8]

Arar also brought an action in federal district court in New York. His complaint against several U.S. government officials alleges violations of the Torture Victim Protection Act and the Fifth Amendment of the U.S. Constitution. The TVPA creates a cause of action for damages against "any individual who, under actual or apparent authority, or color of law, of any foreign nation... subjects an individual to torture", 28 U.S.C. § 1350. In terms of the constitutional claim, Arar sought a *"Bivens"* style remedy, named as such from our ruling in *Bivens v Six Unknown Named Agents of Federal Bureau of Narcotics*, 403 U.S. 388 (1971), where this court held that victims of particularly egregious constitutional violations could receive monetary damages in suits against federal officials.

The District Court dismissed Arar's complaint, *Arar v Ashcroft*, 414 F. Supp. 2d 250 (E.D.N.Y. 2006), and in a 2–1 vote this ruling was upheld by a Second Circuit appeals panel, *Arar v Ashcroft*, 532 F. 3d 157 (2d Cir. 2008). After a *de novo* hearing, the Second Circuit issued an *en banc* ruling upholding the dismissal of Arar's complaint, *Arar v Ashcroft*, 585 F. 3d 559 (2d Cir. 2009). In terms of the TVPA claim, the court held that the act requires a demonstration that these officers were acting under color or the authority of foreign law, and it concluded that there was no evidence that federal (U.S.) officials had in any way acted under Syrian law. In dealing with Arar's *Bivens* claim, the court noted that there has been great hesitancy to extend this remedy to "new contexts". However, the gist of its holding was based on separation of powers principles, most notably, that judicial bodies should be hesitant to provide a remedy in any matters affecting national security without prior Congressional approval and guidance, which the court believed was absent in this case. Arar subsequently sought to appeal to this court and we granted *certiorari* on this matter. We also address Mr. Arar's claims against Syria, Jordan and the United States.

---

6 Arar Commission, *Report of the Events Relating to Maher Arar* (2006).
7 The state apology was issued on January 26, 2007, at which time the Prime Minister also promised to carry out all of the recommendations made by the Arar Commission.
8 *Arar v Syrian Arab Republic* (2005), 127 C.R.R.2d 252 (Can. Ont. Sup. Ct. J.).

Litigating Transnational Human Rights Obligations 345

I.

Torture violates both international and domestic law, and as pointed out by the Second Circuit in its landmark decision in *Filartiga v Pena-Irala*, 630 F. 2d 876 (2d Cir. 1980), those who carry out this barbarous practice are like the pirate and the slave trader before them: *hostis humanis generis* – the enemy of all mankind. Following the *Filartiga* precedent, the Alien Tort Statute, 28 U.S.C. § 1350, has provided an essential avenue of redress for a number of foreign nationals who had been subjected to torture in other lands and who have located in this country those who either directed or carried out this torture.[9] In that way, if Arar's Syrian torturers could somehow be found in the United States (and properly served) he would have grounds for a civil suit against those individuals under the ATS.[10] Furthermore, as a state party to the Torture Convention,[11] the U.S. government would have a legal obligation to criminally prosecute any of Arar's Syrian torturers who are within this country's territorial jurisdiction – or else, extradite these individuals to another state where such prosecution would take place.[12]

Of course, all of this is speculative because there is no indication that any of the relevant Syrian operatives involved in this case are in the United

---

9 In *Sosa v Alvarez-Machain*, 542 U.S. 692 (2004), this court held that federal courts are authorized to recognize a common law cause of action for violations of clearly defined and widely accepted human rights norms. Torture, which constitutes a *jus cogens* norm under international law, would certainly meet the *Sosa* standard.

10 Nothing in our recent ruling in *Kiobel v Royal Dutch Petroleum*, 569 U.S. ____ (2013) would dictate a contrary result. On the basis of the presumption against extraterritoriality in Kiobel we ruled that a suit brought by foreign plaintiffs (Nigerian) against a foreign corporation (Dutch) for human rights in a foreign state (Nigeria) could not proceed under the Alien Tort Statute. Our reasoning was that the connection to the United States was limited, at best. However, in the present case suit is being brought against federal (U.S.) officials and against the United States for human rights violations that were set in motion by actions of the U.S. government.

11 United Nations Convention Against Torture and Other Cruel, Inhuman or Degrading Treatment or Punishment, opened for signature December 10, 1948, G.A. Res. 39/46, 39 UN GAOR Supp. No. 51 at 197, UN Doc. A/RES/39/708 (1984), entered into force June 26, 1987, 1465 U.N.T.S. 85, 23 I.L.M. 1027 (1984).The United States ratified CAT in October 1994 and CAT entered into force with respect to the United States on November 20, 1994. In its instrument of ratification there were a number of declarations, reservations and understandings relevant to the United States. One of these was the declaration that Articles 1–16 were not self-executing – which is to say that there must be implementing legislation to have any domestic effect. In addition, the United States ratified the CAT subject to an understanding that it would interpret Article 3 "where there are substantial grounds for believing that he would be in danger of being subjected to torture" to mean "if it is more likely than not he would be tortured". Finally, the U.S. government issued an understanding that Article 14, which provides that each state party "shall ensure in its legal system that the victim of an act of torture obtains redress and has an enforceable right to fair and adequate compensation ..." only applies to torture committed within a state's own territorial boundaries.

12 CAT, Article 5.

346 *Extraordinary Rendition*

States. However, what Arar does allege is that federal (U.S.) officials played a central role in his torture by purposely sending him to a country with full knowledge that he would be tortured, and perhaps for this very purpose. Unfortunately, each of the lower courts that have heard this case has grossly minimized the involvement of U.S. officials in Arar's ordeal, tending to see the legal wrong as something that is only attributable to Syrian officials. This exhibits an extraordinarily rigid view of both international and domestic law.

Admittedly, the greatest wrong in this case has been carried by Syrian officials working as agents of the Syrian State. But there are other legal wrongs committed by other parties as well. As the European Court of Human Rights ruled in *Soering v United Kingdom*,[13] a country that sends a detainee to a State where there is a substantial likelihood that this person will be subjected to torture has itself violated the prohibition against torture. According to *Soering*, what does not matter is that the torture will be carried out in another land and at the hands of agents of a foreign State. Rather, there is a separate legal wrong for sending a person to a country where there is a good chance that he will be tortured. And what this case also stands for is the proposition that this wrong occurs the moment the individual is extradited – or in the present case the moment the rendition takes place. Thus, what is immaterial is whether the detainee is subsequently subjected to torture or not. However, for purposes of this motion to dismiss we are required to assume that Arar's horrifying account of his own torture is true.

In this case, it is quite clear that federal agents violated the prohibition against *refoulement* by sending Mr. Arar to a country (Syria) where there were certainly more than "substantial grounds" for believing that he would be in danger of being subjected to torture. The Foreign Affairs Reform and Restructuring Act of 1988 (FARRA), Pub. L. 105–277, div. G, Title XXII, § 2242, federal legislation that implements the Torture Convention, addresses transfers from the United States either by extradition or removal and it provides that the "United States [shall] not... expel, extradite, or otherwise effect the involuntary return of any person to a country in which there are substantial grounds for believing the person would be in danger of being subjected to torture, regardless of whether the person is physically present in the United States", *Id.* at § 1242 (a). We conclude on the evidence before us that if Mr. Arar's claims are believed to be true, federal agents violated the *nonrefoulement* provisions of CAT and FARRA.

Yet, Mr. Arar is claiming even greater wrongs. He alleges that federal agencies worked alongside Syrian officials in what amounted to a conspiracy to torture him. On the basis of his ten-month nightmare in Syria, he claims that his interrogation sessions were coordinated by U.S. government

---

13 11 Eur. Ct. H.R. (ser. A) (1989).

Litigating Transnational Human Rights Obligations 347

officials, and that Syrian authorities regularly provided information regarding his repeated "interrogations" to their American counterparts.

Later we will address the issue of the legal responsibility of the United States. Here, our concern is only with the responsibility of federal authorities for purposes of a *Bivens* remedy. Assuming Mr. Arar's claims are true, as we must in any motion for summary judgment, American officials were engaged in a conspiracy to see to it that the claimant was subjected to torture.

The lower courts that have heard this case have all shown some degree of sympathy for Mr. Arar, but each has ultimately dismissed his claim. One repeated rationale has been that courts should be wary of extending *Bivens* to a "new context". But the real issue is what this "new context" happens to be, namely, U.S. involvement in the "war on terrorism". This hesitancy is best summed by Chief Judge Jacobs, writing for the *en banc* majority:

> We recognize our limited competence, authority, and jurisdiction to make rules or set parameters to govern the practice called rendition. By the same token, we can easily locate that competence, expertise, and responsibility elsewhere: in Congress. Congress may be content for the Executive Branch to exercise these powers without judicial check. But if Congress wishes to create a remedy for individuals like Arar, it can enact legislation that includes enumerated eligibility parameters, delineated safe harbors, defined review processes, and specific relief to be accorded. Once Congress has performed this task, *then* the courts in a proper case will be able to review the statute and provide judicial oversight… (585 F. 3d at 581 (emphasis in original))

This court is cognizant of its limited role in the realm of national security, and it will certainly not deny the enormous national security implications of this case. On the other hand, judicial deference need not – and should not – lead to judicial abdication. One of the most distressing aspects of this case is that if one were to adopt Judge Jacobs' approach concerning the need for judicial deference to Congress, Mr. Arar would still be denied a *Bivens* remedy *even if* federal agents purposely sent him to Syria in order to be tortured – and *even if* federal agents themselves carried out the torture, whether in Syria or even in the United States – so long as Congress had not provided a remedy.

We simply cannot countenance such a result. This court must be mindful of our nation's national security goals but it must also be protective of the constitutional rights and the human rights of all individuals. This balance has not been sufficiently achieved in this case. Through its Alien Tort Statute litigation in particular, the American judiciary has been at the forefront of combating the practice of torture. In addition, the United States has become a party to both the Torture Convention and the International

348 *Extraordinary Rendition*

Covenant on Civil and Political Rights,[14] and through FARRA it has passed implementing domestic legislation. In order to meet its obligations under international law, *Murray v The Charming Betsey*, 6 U.S. 64 (1804), the U.S. must not only outlaw the practice of torture (which it has done), but it must investigate[15] all instances of torture and it must also provide an effective remedy for those who have been tortured.[16] By dismissing his case, Mr. Arar has been denied any form of remedy against U.S. officials.

Thus, we overturn the Second Circuit's *en banc* ruling and remand the case to the trial court to allow Mr. Arar to proceed with his *Bivens* claim against federal agents. Admittedly, what will make his task that much more difficult is the so-called Westall Act, Federal Employees Liability Reform and Tort Compensation Act, Pub. L. No. 100-94, 102 Stat. 4563 (1988) (codified in 28 U.S.C. § 2679 (2000)), which converts suits against individual officials into suits against the United States if these agents are acting within the scope of their employment and if they are not alleged to have violated any statutory or constitutional norm. In most cases what this act has done is to effectively immunize not only federal officials, but the U.S. government as well.[17] However, we are confident that the district court will ensure that Mr. Arar will be provided with the effective remedy that is required of the United States by both domestic and international law.[18]

II.

In addition to his suit against federal officials, Mr. Arar is also bringing suit against three states: Syria, Jordan and the United States, which we will take up in that order. We begin this analysis by pointing out that unlike the universal proscription against torture, there is no single governing standard under international law regarding sovereign immunity. One commentator (Mathias Reimann) has described the law on sovereign immunity as being

---

14 International Covenant on Civil and Political Rights, adopted and opened for signature, ratification and accession by General Assembly resolution 2200A (XXI) of 16 December 1966, entry into force 23 March 1976.

15 CAT, Article 12.

16 The right of an effective remedy can be found in both Article 13 and Article 14 of CAT. Article 13 provides:

> Each State Party shall ensure that any individual who alleges he has been subjected to torture in any territory under its jurisdiction has the right to complain to, and to have his case promptly and impartially examined by, its competent authorities ...

Article 14 (1) reads:

> Each State Party shall ensure in its legal system that the victim of an act of torture obtains redress and has an enforceable right to fair and adequate compensation, including the means for as full rehabilitation as possible ...

17 *See generally*, Elizabeth A. Wilson, "Is Torture All in a Day's Work? Scope of Employment, The Absolute Immunity Doctrine, and Human Rights Litigation Against U.S. Federal Officials", 6 *Rutgers Journal of Law and Public Policy* 175 (2008).

18 *See generally*, Francesco Francioni (ed.) *Access to Justice as a Human Right* (2007).

in flux, nuanced and contested.[19] Another leading authority (Alexander Orakhelashvili) has argued that no rule of international law presently exists to delineate the scope of sovereign immunity, but rather, states act on the basis of considerations such as "interest, comity and reciprocity".[20]

Throughout much of its history the United States recognized the principle of absolute sovereign immunity, best articulated by Chief Justice Marshall in *The Schooner Exchange v M'Faddon & Others*, 11 U.S. (7 Cranch) 116 (1812).

> One sovereign being in no respect amenable to another; and being bound by obligations of the highest character not to degrade the dignity of his nation, by placing himself or its sovereign rights within the jurisdiction of another, can be supposed to enter a foreign territory only under an express license, or in the confidence that the immunities belong to his independent sovereign station, though not expressly situated, are reserved by implication, and will be extended to him. (*Id.* at 137)

Notwithstanding the absolute nature of this language, Marshall's ruling also acknowledged that sovereign immunity was not something that the forum state is bound to grant, but rather, it has refrained from exercising jurisdiction because of its explicit or implicit consent, always retaining the ability to withdraw that consent if circumstances demanded it.[21]

The law on sovereign immunity began to be transformed in the middle of the previous century, especially as an increasing number of States began to engage in proprietary matters. In 1952 the United States adopted the "restrictive theory" of sovereign immunity. As a general rule, states continued to enjoy an absolute immunity in our courts when they engaged in "governmental practices", but were denied such immunity in the commercial realm. In terms of how this came to be operationalized, the judiciary was to make the determination of whether sovereign immunity was to be granted – unless and until the Executive branch interceded in a particular case and provided "direction" to the courts. This approach not only caused problems in terms of separation of powers principles, with the judiciary nearly always following the lead of the Executive branch, but it also made for great uncertainty in the law itself.[22]

---

19 Mathias Reimann, "A Human Rights Exception to Sovereign Immunity: Some Thoughts on *Prinz v. Federal Republic of Germany*", 16 *Michigan Journal of International Law* 403 (1994–1995).

20 Alexander Orakhelashvili, "State Immunity and International Public Order", 45 *German Yearbook of International Law* 227 (2002).

21 Beth Stephens, "The Modern Common Law of Foreign Official Immunity," 79 *Fordham Law Review* 2669 (2011).

22 *See generally*, Sean Hennessy, "In Re The Foreign Sovereign Immunities Act: How the 9/11 Litigation Shows the Shortcomings of FSIA as a Tool In the Name of the War on Global Terrorism", 42 *Georgetown Journal of International Law* 855 (2011).

350   *Extraordinary Rendition*

Partly in response to these problems, in 1976 Congress passed the Foreign Sovereign Immunity Act, 28 U.S.C. § 1330, 1602–1611 (2006), which remains the governing law today. Under the FSIA, all states enjoy sovereign immunity protection in U.S. courts, subject to the exceptions set forth in the act.[23] In *Argentine Republic v Amerada Hess Shipping Corp.*, 488 U.S. 428 (1989), this court refused to recognize an additional international law exception, and there is nothing in our holding today that directly challenges this ruling. Still, we hold that neither Syria nor Jordan is exempt from Mr. Arar's suit against them.

The FSIA has been amended several times since its enactment. However, the most significant change occurred in 1996 with the passage of the Antiterrorism and Effective Death Penalty Act (AEDPA), which created a new sovereign immunity exception for states that engaged in terrorism themselves or else provided material support to entities that did. This exception provides that:

> A foreign State shall not be immune from the jurisdiction of courts of the United States or of the States in any case not otherwise covered by this chapter in which money damages are sought against a foreign State for personal injury or death that was caused by an act of torture, extra-judicial killing, aircraft sabotage, hostage taking, or the provision of material support or resources for such an act if such act or provision of material support or resources is engaged in by an official, employee, or agent of such foreign state while acting within the scope of his or her office, employment, or agency. (28 U.S.C. § 1605A (2008))

Although this exception speaks in broad terms, there are two important restrictions to it. The first is that it is limited to U.S. citizens; the second is that the sovereign immunity exception only applies to states that have been designated as "State sponsors of terrorism" under the National Defense Authorization Act. The original list of States consisted of: Iraq, Libya, North Korea, Cuba, Iran, Sudan and Syria. However, as of this writing this list has been winnowed down to: Cuba, Iran, Sudan and Syria.[24]

Syria is presently on the NDAA list of "state sponsors of terrorism". However, as a Canadian-Syrian national Mr. Arar cannot invoke this exception. Just the opposite was true in *Saudi Arabia v Nelson*, 507 U.S. 349 (1993), where Scott Nelson met the nationality requirement, but his suit against

---

23 These exceptions can be categorized as follows: 1) an explicit or implied waiver of immunity by a foreign state; 2) commercial activity of the foreign state in or directly affecting the United States, 3) non-commercial torts committed by a foreign state (including by its officials and employees), and 4) disputes involving real estate and real property.

24 As Hennessy points out, *supra* note 22 at 862, the State Department has complete authority over which countries are (or are not) on the state sponsors of terrorism list.

Litigating Transnational Human Rights Obligations 351

Saudi Arabia for acts of torture carried out against him in that country was dismissed on the basis that Saudi Arabia was not listed as being a "State sponsor of terrorism", nor was Nelson able to fit his claim under any of the other exceptions in the act.

In our constitutional schema, Congress makes law. Our own role is merely to interpret and apply this law. However, this court would be amiss if it did not at least point out some of the glaring inconsistencies that presently exist. For one thing, the "State sponsors of terrorism" exception smacks of the same kind of Executive domination that existed before the passage of the Foreign Sovereign Immunity Act in the sense that the courts remain dependent on the Executive branch in terms of making determinations with regard to sovereign immunity.

Perhaps a more serious problem is that acts of terrorism, including torture, will be treated completely differently depending on where these cruelties took place. If a U.S. national is tortured in one of the countries now designated as a "State sponsor of terror" – Cuba, Iran, Sudan and Syria[25] – this individual will be able to invoke this exception and bring suit against the offending State. However, if this person is brutally tortured in some country that is not on the list, as was the case in *Nelson*, this individual will be denied any chance of recovery against the offending State.

Torture is a universal wrong. What does not matter – or at least what should not matter – is where it takes place.[26] Thus, one of the more troubling aspects under present law is the manner in which different locations will lead to completely different results. We are confident that Congress did not intend for such inconsistent practices to exist.

However, we need not pursue this line of argument any further because we believe that Mr. Arar can rely on the exception for non-commercial torts committed in the United States.[27] To be clear, there is no evidence that Mr. Arar was ever physically tortured while he was within the territorial boundaries of the United States.[28] But what is clear, at least to this court, is that his

---

25 What also needs to be said is that there is little evidence that two of these four countries – Cuba and Sudan – engage in terrorism or provide "material support" to entities that do.

26 Given the fact that the Alien Tort Statute provides a cause of action specifically to foreign nationals, we also take this opportunity to question the restriction to American nationals.

27 28 U.S.C. § 1605 (a) (5) provides:
     (a) A foreign state shall not be immune from the jurisdiction of courts of the United States or of the States in any case—
     (5) not otherwise encompassed in paragraph (2) above, in which money damages are sought against a foreign state for personal injury or death, or damage to or loss of property, occurring in the United States and caused by the tortious act or omission of that foreign state or of any official or employee of that foreign state while acting within the scope of his office or employment;

28 An interesting situation would arise if Mr. Arar had been handed to Syrian or Jordanian officials in the United States, as opposed to federal agents flying across the ocean and delivering him over there themselves.

352   *Extraordinary Rendition*

gross treatment in Syria was part of a much larger project that began at JFK airport in New York and which was then moved to the Middle East, initially to Jordan and then to a filthy grave cell in Syria where Mr. Arar was subjected to months and months of torture.[29]

Form should never be allowed to take precedence over substance, especially in a case such as this. Likewise, territorial borders should not be used as a means to exonerate barbaric behavior. Syria (and Jordan to a lesser extent) has committed a "tortious act", which began in the United States.[30] For these reasons, Syria (and Jordan) should be denied sovereign immunity protection. Any other result leads to impunity.

III.

The final issue relates to the legal responsibility of the U.S. government. Although agent immunity and State sovereign immunity are not the same, they do share a common basis. Intuitively this makes a lot of sense. State agents work for the State, and it would indeed be odd if State agents enjoyed immunity while the State did not – or *vice versa*.[31]

However, what makes the present situation more complicated is Mr. Arar's claim, assumed to be true, that U.S. officials played an essential role in his torture in Syria, and that because of this the United States should bear at least some (legal) responsibility for his torture. We first address the issue of responsibility before turning to whether Mr. Arar has a cause of action under the Federal Tort Claims Act.

---

29 In *Letelier v Chile*, 488 F.Supp. 665 (1980), the "tortious act" in the United States exemption was used to sue the Chilean government for a bombing attack that took place in DuPont Circle in our nation's capital. One thing that is interesting about the *Letelier* case is that although the Chilean government apparently hatched the idea, it hired a group of Cuban exiles to carry out the bombing. Thus, technically, it could be argued that the Chilean state itself had not committed a "tortious act" in the United States. To its credit, the district court did not address this issue.

30 Admittedly, the present case is not as clear cut as *Doe v Bin Laden*, 663 F. 3d 64 (2011), where the Second Circuit Court of Appeals allowed a suit brought by survivors of the 9/11 attacks on the United States to proceed against Afghanistan. The Afghan government had argued that the claim should have been limited to the "terrorism" exception – and dismissed on the basis that Afghanistan was never on the state sponsors of terrorism list. The court rejected this claim and allowed the claimants to proceed on the basis of the noncommercial tort exception, noting that the tortious act – the destruction of the two World Trade Center buildings and the killings and injuries that ensued from this – most decidedly occurred "within" the United States.

31 For a analysis of the relationship between individual and state responsibility see Andre Nollkaemper, "Concurrence Between Individual Responsibility and State Responsibility in International Law", 52 *International and Comparative Law Quarterly* 615 (2003).

Litigating Transnational Human Rights Obligations 353

This issue of transnational responsibility has been raised in international fora before. In *Nicaragua v United States*[32] the International Court of Justice ruled that while the U.S. government was responsible for its direct wrongful acts in Nicaragua, such as the CIA's mining of the country's harbors, it was not responsible for acts carried out by its *contra* allies. In arriving at this conclusion, the ICJ developed an "effective control" test, and it held that the U.S. had not exercised the requisite level of effective control in order to be responsible for human rights violations committed by the *contras*. At one point in its ruling the ICJ held:

> [I]n light of the evidence and material available to it, the Court is not satisfied that all the operations launched by the *contra* force, at every stage of the conflict, reflected strategy and tactics wholly devised by the United States.[33]

The *Nicaragua* decision has been subject to much criticism,[34] not only for the degree of control required by the ICJ in order to establish legal responsibility, but also for the either-or nature of State responsibility in the sense that a State that provides aid and assistance to an entity that commits an internationally wrongful act is either fully responsible (assuming the requisite "effective control" standard is met), or else it is not responsible at all. Subsequent to this, the International Criminal Tribunal for the (former) Yugoslavia (ICTY) rejected the *Nicaragua* test and employed a much broader "overall control" standard.[35]

However, in *Bosnia v Serbia*,[36] the ICJ applied various provisions of the International Law Commission's Draft Articles on State Responsibility[37] and essentially reaffirmed *Nicaragua*, declining to hold Serbia responsible for acts of genocide carried out by its Bosnian Serb allies notwithstanding the extraordinarily close relationship between the two. The key issue was whether Serbia had "aided and assisted" in the genocidal acts carried out by the Bosnian Serbs. In addressing this issue, the Court first referred back to the Genocide Convention and noted that under Article III not only is genocide itself a punishable crime, but so is *conspiracy* to commit genocide, *directing and inciting* genocide, *attempts* to commit genocide, and finally, *complicity*

---

32 *Case Concerning Military and Paramilitary Activities in and against Nicaragua (Nicaragua v United States), 1986 ICJ Reports.*

33 *Id.* par. 106.

34 *See,* e.g., Mark Gibney, Katarina Tomasevski and Jens Vedsted-Hansen, "Transnational State Responsibility for Violations of Human Rights", 12 *Harvard Human Rights Journal* 267 (1999).

35 *Prosecutor v Tadic,* Appeals Chamber Judgment, IT-94-1-A (2001).

36 ICJ Reports (2007).

37 Draft Articles on Responsibility of States for Internationally Wrongful Acts, 2001, UN Doc. A/56/10 at 43.

354 *Extraordinary Rendition*

in genocide. The Court then proceeded to equate "complicity" in Article III of the Genocide Convention with "aiding and assisting" under Article 16 of the Draft Articles on State Responsibility.[38] After this, it ruled that in order to be responsible for aiding and assisting in genocide, the sending State had to have full knowledge of the genocidal intent of the receiving entity and, presumably, take measures in furtherance of this genocidal goal. According to the Court's interpretation of events, this had not been established "beyond any doubt".

In sum, although the ICJ readily recognized the near-symbiotic relationship between Serbia and its Bosnian Serb allies, it ultimately rejected the notion that Serbia was to bear any legal responsibility for the acts of genocide that had been carried out by paramilitary forces that it was deeply associated with. Turning to the case before us, it is clear that under the *Bosnia v Serbia* standard, the United States would not be responsible for acts of torture carried out by Syrian agents – and apparently what would not matter is if federal (U.S.) agents not only coordinated the torture, as Mr. Arar claims, but such agents were actually present in the torture chamber.

This, however, does not settle this issue. Although we must respect and honor the views and the opinion of this sister judicial institution, ICJ rulings have no bearing and influence on this court. In our view, rather than relying exclusively on the Draft Articles on State Responsibility, as the ICJ did in its *Bosnia* ruling, a much sounder way of determining State responsibility is by first turning to the law itself – the Torture Convention in particular. The real question is whether the United States acted in a way that was consonant with its obligation under this international treaty. The clear answer is that it did not. The whole point of the Torture Convention is to prevent torture. With regard to Mr. Arar at least, the policy and practice of the United States appeared to be just the opposite.

Yet, even if the United States is "responsible", for its complicity in Mr. Arar's torture, a separate issue is whether he can pursue a claim against the United States under the Federal Tort Claims Act, 28 U.S.C. § 1346 (b), 2671–2680, which is the statute through which the United States authorizes tort suits be brought against it. The FTCA makes the U.S. liable for:

> injury, loss of property or personal injury or death caused by the negligent or wrongful at or omission of any employee of the government while acting within the scope of his office or employment, under

---

38 Article 16 provides:

> A State which aids or assists another State in the commission of an internationally wrongful act by the latter is internationally responsible for doing so if:
> (a) That State does so with knowledge of the circumstances of the internationally wrongful act; and
> (b) The act would be internationally wrongful if committed by that State.

Litigating Transnational Human Rights Obligations 355

circumstances where the United States, if a private person would be liable to the claimant in accordance with the law of the place where the act or omission occurred.

The goal of the FTCA is to make the United States liable for the torts of its employees to the extent to which private employers would be liable under State law for the torts of their employees.[39] However, the FTCA contains a number of exceptions under which the U.S. may not be liable even though a private employer would otherwise be. Four of these exceptions are pertinent to the matter at hand.

The first and most widely used is the "discretionary function" exception.[40] The issue here is whether sending Mr. Arar out of the United States and conspiring with Jordanian and Syrian officials to torture him would fit into the category of being a "discretionary act". We believe that it is not. As a general rule, the discretionary function exception seeks to protect the United States for decisions based on policy decisions, broadly defined. Yet, there is no "policy" that we can conjure up – or at least none that would be legal – that would result in purposely sending a person to another country in order to be tortured.[41]

The second possible exception relates to combat operations: "Any claim arising out of the combatant activities of the military or naval forces, or the Coast Guard, during time of war", 28 U.S.C. § 2680 (j). Although there is much talk involving the "war on terror", it is important to note that neither Mr. Arar nor the federal officials involved in this case were involved in combat operations as such.

The third possible exception that might bar suit involves torts "arising in a foreign country", 28 U.S.C. § 2680 (k). This court recently addressed this provision in our ruling in *Sosa v Alvarez-Machain*, 542 U.S. 692 (2004). In that case we dismissed a suit brought against the United States by Humberto Alvarez-Machain, a Mexican physician thought to be in league with drug dealers who had tortured and murdered an agent of the Drug Enforcement Agency (DEA). After a federal grand jury indicted Alvarez, the DEA sought the assistance of the Mexican government for help in

---

39 Congressional Research Service, *Federal Tort Claims Act* 1 (2007).

40 28 U.S.C. § 2680 (a) provides:

> Any claim based upon an act or omission of an employee of the Government, exercising due care, in the execution of a statute or regulation, whether or not such statute or regulation be valid, or based upon the exercise or performance or the failure to exercise or perform a discretionary function or duty on the part of a federal agency or an employee of the Government, whether or not the discretion involved be abused.

41 For an excellent discussion of how the "discretionary function" exception has been used – and quite often misused – see William G. Weaver and Thomas Longoria, "Bureaucracy that Kills: Federal Sovereign Immunity and the Discretionary Function Exception", 96 *American Political Science Review* 335–49 (2002).

356 *Extraordinary Rendition*

getting him to the United States. However, when negotiations between the two governments proved fruitless, the DEA approved a plan to hire Mexican nationals to seize Alvarez and bring him to the United States for trial. As planned, a group of Mexicans, including Jose Francisco Sosa, abducted Alvarez from his house, held him overnight in a motel, and then flew him by private plane to El Paso, Texas, where he was arrested by federal (U.S.) agents. Once in U.S. custody, Alvarez moved to dismiss his indictment on the ground that his seizure constituted "outrageous government conduct", and violated the extradition treaty between the United States and Mexico. This motion was denied and Alvarez was brought to trial. However, the District Court did grant Alvarez's motion for a judgment of acquittal.

After returning to Mexico, Alvarez filed a civil suit against U.S. and Mexican agents under the Alien Tort Statute, and a claim for false arrest against the United States under the FTCA. Applying what is commonly referred to as the "headquarters doctrine", the Ninth Circuit ruled in favor of Alvarez's FTCA claim. However, this court reversed on the basis that the foreign country exception "bars all claims based on any injury suffered in a foreign country, regardless of where the tortious act or omission occurred", 542 U.S. at 712. One important difference between these two situations is that in Alvarez's case the tortious act (unlawful arrest) had already been effectuated by the time he was taken to the United States, while in the present case the tortious conduct (unlawful arrest) was initiated within the territorial boundaries of the United States, although it later continued in a foreign state. Thus, we hold that the tort suffered by Mr. Arar did not "arise" in a foreign country as such, but in the United States.

However, we have a much deeper concern and it is that all this is nothing more than a matter of semantics. We also fear that territorial boundaries are being used as a way of avoiding State responsibility. Why, after all, was Mr. Arar sent to Syria for interrogation? It seems eminently clear to this court that the U.S. government did not feel comfortable in having its own agents torture him themselves. Therefore, they found agents of another country that would torture him, and serve as a further buffer against its own responsibility Our point is that if the "foreign country" exception is being relied upon for these kinds of purposes – as a way of exonerating the United States for torture that it is decidedly complicit in – then there is good reason why this exception should be given serious reconsideration by Congress.

The fourth and final exception is for intentional torts. The FTCA does not apply to claims:

> arising out of assault, battery, false imprisonment, false arrest, malicious prosecution, abuse of process, libel, slander, misrepresentation, deceit, or interference with contract rights. (28 U.S.C. § 2680 (h)).

Litigating Transnational Human Rights Obligations 357

Note, however, that the United States might be liable for any of the first six torts in this list if committed by an "investigative or law enforcement officer of the United States government", 28 U.S.C. § 2680 (h). In our view, although not listed by name, torture is merely an aggravated example of assault and battery. In addition, the named defendants in this case, including Attorney General Ashcroft, are all investigative officers of the United States – actually the highest ranking law enforcement agents in the entire country.

In conclusion, we hold that the U.S. government has committed a wrongful act and that it can be held legally responsible under the Federal Tort Claims Act in this case for carrying out what amounts to little more than "torture by proxy".[42]

---

42 The Committee on International Human Rights of the Association of the Bar of the City of New York and The Center for Human Rights and Global Justice, New York University School of Law, *Torture By Proxy: International and Domestic Law Applicable to "Extraordinary Renditions"* (2004).

Index

Abuja target 87–8
accountability: human rights and development 188; taxation and 117–18, 129–30
Additional Protocol to the American Convention on Human Rights in the Area of Economic, Social and Cultural Rights (Protocol of San Salvador) 286
Additional Protocol to the European Social Charter providing for a system of collective complaints 303, 305
admissibility: European Court of Human Rights 325–38; Eurozone crisis case 302–24
African Charter on Human and Peoples' Rights 190, 241, 261–82; Article 4 279; Article 7(1) 280–1; Article 12(2) 247; Article 14 275–7, 278, 282; Article 16 278, 279; Article 18(1) 278; Article 21 277–8, 282; Article 22 279, 282; Article 23 247; Article 56(5) 243–5; Articles 60 and 61 247–8; no territorial limit 270; no territoriality or jurisdiction clause 247
African Commission on Human and Peoples' Rights 190, 240–1; Zimbabwe forced evictions 261–82
African Development Bank 49
African Overview Report 101
Agreement on Subsidies and Countervailing Measures 39
agro-fuel production 283–301 *see also* biofuels
AIDS *see* HIV/AIDS
Al-Skeini judgment 326–7
Alien Tort Statute (US) 345
Alma-Ata Declaration 80

American Convention on Human Rights 41; complaints mechanisms for violations 299
American Declaration of the Rights and Duties of Man 286, 287; three groups of extraterritorial cases 287–8
anti-retroviral (ARV), access to 80, 83
Antiterrorism and Effective Death Penalty Act (US) 350
apportioning of responsibility 174–5
Arar, Maher 341, 343–57
Asian Development Bank 49

Bank Information Centre 50
bank secrecy laws 123, 128–31, 133
Bankovic case 220, 325, 326, 328, 329, 332, 335
BankWatch.org 50
Bassiouni, M. Cherif 230
Belgium: arguments submitted to CESCR 141; locus standi to submit complaint 142–4; non-injured State party 140, 141, 142–3
Benin 35, 36, 46
Beyond Territoriality – Globalisation and Transnational Human Rights Obligations (GLOTHRO) 4
bilateral investment treaties 264, 265, 281, 297, 298
biodiesel 36, 46
biofuels 31–48 *see also* agro-fuel production
"*Bivens*" style remedy 344–8
Bosnia 353–4
Bosnian Genocide case (ICJ) 108
Botswana 190–1
Bretton Woods Project 50
Burmese Freedom and Democracy Act (BFDA) 14

Canada 156–7, 343, 344
Centre on Housing Rights and Evictions (COHRE) v Sudan 281
Cerna, Christina M. 287
Chad 251–2
child abuse images 63–4; case background and facts 66–7; simple possession of 68, 74–5
Child Exploitation and Online Protection Centre (UK) 64
child mortality 80
child pornography 63–78; case background and facts 68–9; complaint 67–8; consideration of admissibility 69–71; consideration of the merits 71–6; remedy 76–8; state parties' submissions on the admissibility and merits of communication 67–8
children with disabilities 172–85
China, People's Republic of: arguments submitted to CESCR 140–1; jurisdiction of 145–6; responsibility for labour rights violations 150–4
climate change case 155–71; alleged breaches of Covenant obligations 171; applicability of Covenant articles 168–9; attribution of acts 166–7; complaint 165; facts 162–5; issues and proceedings before Commission 166; jurisdiction 167–8; relevance of international climate change law 168; Respondent State's observations 165–6; state's obligations under Covenant 170–1
clothing, right to 113
cloud computing 64
collective complaints mechanism, European Social Charter 302–3
collective interest 143–4
Colombia 288
Committee on Economic, Social and Cultural Rights (CESCR) 84, 99–115, 203, 269, 272; Competence of the Committee 84–5; General Comments 136; General Comment 2 95; General Comment 3 86, 87, 90, 94; General Comment 12 110, 212; General Comment 14 85, 88, 89, 90, 93, 94; General Comment 15 85, 90, 110, 263, 273; General Comment 19 152; labour rights case 135–54; reports by State parties 135–6; Statement on the

obligation of States Parties regarding the corporate sector and economic, social, and cultural rights 148; tax evasion 116–34
Committee on the Rights of Persons with Disabilities 172–85
Committee on the Rights of the Child 63–78, 127
compensation 114, 115, 243; for loss of assets and amenities 54, 57, 58; forced evictions 189, 198; Maher Arar 344; tax evasion 134
Compliance Advisor Ombudsman (CAO), World Bank 49–60; Compliance Audit background 54–5; constraint of audit 51; three roles 50
concurrent human rights responsibilities, State parties 73–4
control and authority 109, 288, 293
Convention Against Torture and Other Cruel, Inhuman or Degrading Treatment or Punishment 345–57
Convention Concerning Indigenous and Tribal Peoples in Independent Countries (ILO) 100, 101
Convention on the Elimination of all Forms of Discrimination against Women (CEDW) 40, 263, 273–4
Convention on the Prevention and Punishment of the Crime of Genocide 353–4
Convention on the Protection of Children against Sexual Exploitation and Sexual Abuse 73, 74–5
Convention on the Rights of Persons with Disabilities (CRPD) 1; Article 16 176, 181–2; Article 24 176, 181–2; Article 32 176, 179–85; international co-operation scope 173–4
Convention on the Rights of the Child (CRC) 1, 40, 63, 65, 66, 67, 68, 69, 70, 71, 78, 182, 183; international co-operation scope 173–4, 180
Corfu Channel case 232
corporations *see* multinational corporations
corruption 221–36
Council of Europe 64, 325, 326, 332
crimes against humanity 221–36

De Schutter, O. 156
defence spending, human rights commitments and 86–7

360 Index

Democratic Republic of Congo v Burundi, Rwanda and Uganda 270–1
derived responsibility 305, 321–4
Detainee Treatment Act (US) 342
development: human rights and 212; rights-based approach to 187–8
development aid, tax evasion and 131, 132–3
development assistance children with disabilities case 172–85; admissibility 177–9; complaint 176; facts 175–6; issues and proceedings before Committee 177–85; observations on admissibility and merits 176–7
diamond mining 261–82
disability mainstreaming 175, 180–1
disguised restriction on international trade 29–30
domestic remedies, exhaustion of 69–70, 105, 121–2, 125, 142, 162, 197–8, 245, 291, 303, 325
domestic versus external obligations 131
drone attacks 327, 337–8
due diligence 296; IFC investment 55–6; states over corporations 111
'duty' to co-operate 42

economic crime against humanity case 221–36; conclusion 236; cross-cutting issues 233–6; definition of crimes against humanity 227–32; legal issues on merits 226–36; parties and facts 223–4; specific complaints 225–6; specific criminal charges 224–5; state/individual responsibility 232–3; submissions of parties 226
economic growth, tax havens and 130–1
Ecuador 288
education: children with disabilities 172–85; right to 113
environmental and social impact assessments 55–6
equality 254–6
Equator Principles 52
European Bank for Reconstruction and Development 49
European Central Bank 303, 315, 316
European Commission 303, 315, 316
European Committee of Social Rights 302–24
European Consensus on Development 175

European Convention for the Protection of Human Rights and Fundamental Freedoms 214, 325; Article 1 328, 332; Article 2 338; Article 56 333; drafting of 332; limited by jurisdiction 262; living instrument 332
European Court of Human Rights (ECtHR) 173, 190, 214, 280; military interventions case 325–38; torture 346
European human rights system, extraterritorial elements in 248–9
European Investment Bank 49
European Social Charter 302–24; Article 4 304; Article 11 304; Article 12 304; Article 13 304; Article 14 304; collective complaints mechanism 302–3; number of deficits 304; Revised Charter 304, 306
European Union 38, 41, 43; European Ombudsman 49; Renewable Energy Directive 35, 36
Eurozone crisis case 302–24; absence of extraterritorial obligations 308–15; absence of interested parties 315; admissibility (Greece) 305, 306–7; admissibility (other respondents) 307–17; assessment of committee 317–24; complaint 304–5; derived responsibility 305, 321–4; international co-operation 309–13; rules of attribution 315–17; systemic integration 313–15
extradition 68, 75–6
extraordinary rendition case 341–57; 'Bivens' style remedy 344–8; sovereign immunity 348–52; state responsibility 352–7
Extraterritorial Obligations (ETO) Consortium 4

famine crime 229
farmers in India case 206–20; applicable law 206–7; extraterritorial obligations of States 211–15; human rights obligations 207–9; loan conditionalities 217–20; nature of right to life 209–11; obligations of States as members of World Bank and IMF 215–16
Federal Tort Claims Act (US) 352, 354–7

Feminist Judgments: From Theory to Practice 52
food, right to 113, 279–80
food security 31, 59
forced evictions 242, 283–301; Zimbabwe 261–82
forced evictions case 187–201; application of ETO principles 198–201; conclusion and orders 201; facts 192–5; justice denied 197–8; land laws 195–7
forced labour 28
Forced Labour Convention 28
Foreign Affairs Reform and Restructuring Act (US) 346
Foreign Sovereign Immunity Act (US) 350, 351
foreseeability 46–8, 155–71, 172–85, 219–20, 296
free prior informed consent 52, 58
fulfil, duty to 269, 272

GATT 1994: Article XX(a) 16, 18–21, 30; Chapeau of Article XX 25–6, 28; preamble 32, 35, 37–8, 39, 41, 43, 44; violation of Article XI:1 16, 17–18, 30
gemstones trade 13–30
gender analysis, IFC investment 58–9
Gender Justice: a Citizen's Guide to Gender Accountability at International Financial Institutions 51
Germany, forced evictions case 198–201
global financial crisis 81
good faith, principle of 37, 44
Greece 302–24
greenhouse gas emissions 45, 164, 165–6, 166–7
Guantanamo Bay 342
Guiding Principles for the Implementation of the United Nations 'Protect, Respect, and Remedy Framework' 140, 151

health, multinational corporations and 90, 259–60 *see also* right to health case study
health and safety, Zambian Mines 139
Henkin, Louis 341
High Level Panel of Experts of the Committee on World Food Security 284

HIV/AIDS 8, 80, 81–2, 83, 87, 91, 92, 94, 110
housing, right to 113 *see also* forced evictions
human rights: balance in ECtHR 326; extraterritorial obligations of States 211–15; financial sustainability and 92, 93, 94
Human Rights Committee 203; extraterritorial obligations of States 212, 214
Human Rights Council 140, 203; climate change 157–8
human rights impact assessments 296
human rights review procedure 95

ifiwatchnet.org 50
import restrictions 13–30
India 190, 202–20 *see also* farmers in India case
indigenous land rights 99–115
indigenous peoples 99–115, 242–60, 261–82, 283–301
information, access to 121–2, 123, 129–30, 133
Inter-American Commission on Human Rights 106, 112, 156–7, 215, 286; Article 1.1 291–2; Article 25 299
Inter-American Development Bank 49
Inter-American Human Rights Commission 250; jurisdiction 291–5; three categories of case 248
Inter-American Human Rights Court 285
Inter-American human rights system 285–9; jurisdiction generally defined territorially 287
interdependency of ESCR and CPR 287, 29
Intergovernmental Panel on Climate Change (IPCC) 163, 167, 171
International Association of Internet Hotlines (INHOPE) 64
International Bank for Reconstruction and Development *see* World Bank
International Centre for Missing & Exploited Children (ICMEC) 63
International Centre for the Settlement of Investment Disputes (ICSID) 265, 266, 281
international co-operation 309–13; in CRPD 173–4, 179–85; Switzerland 125, 127, 132–3, 134

362 *Index*

International Court of Justice 159, 192; Bosnia case 353–4; farmers in India advisory opinion 206–20; Nicaragua case 353

International Covenant on Civil and Political Rights (ICCPR) 106, 191, 206, 209, 347–8; Article 1 165, 167, 168–9; Article 2(1) 211, 213–14; Article 6(1) 165, 169; Article 17(1) 165; ad-hoc Conciliation Commission 155-71; Human Rights Committee 158, 166, 167; inter-State complaint procedure 158–9

International Covenant on Economic, Social and Cultural Rights (ICESCR) 1, 31, 37, 41, 112, 113, 206, 209, 303, 304, 305, 309–10, 311, 314; Article 2(1) 84, 86, 88, 89, 114, 121, 126, 132, 147; Article 7 125, 147, 150, 151, 152–3; Article 8 147, 150, 151, 152–3; Article 9 122; Article 11 104, 113, 115, 122, 126; Article 11(1) 211–12; Article 12 86, 88, 104, 113, 115, 122; Article 13 104, 113, 115, 122; Article 28 126; drafters of 80; international co-operation scope 173–4, 180; national obligations 85–6; no territorial restrictions 145, 273; retrogressive measures 182–5; right to water 263

International Criminal Court 191, 221–36; complementary jurisdiction 222; economic crimes against humanity 226–36

International Criminal Tribunal for Rwanda 228

International Criminal Tribunal for the Former Yugoslavia 230–1

International Finance Corporation (IFC): Compliance Advisor Ombudsman (CAO) 49–60; gen-dered impacts of investment 58–60; performance standards 49, 52, 54, 59; processing of investment 55–6

International Financial Institutions (IFIs) 82; Independent Accountability Mechanisms (IAMs) 49

International Labour Organization 28–9

international law, forced evictions and 187

International Law Commission (ILC): Articles on Responsibility of States

for Internationally Wrongful Acts 42, 44, 94, 96, 107, 108, 137, 140, 142, 144, 146, 160, 316, 322, 323, 353–4; Draft Articles on the Responsibility of International Organizations 82, 94, 319

International Monetary Fund (IMF) 83, 303, 315, 316; human rights obligations 207–9; loan conditionalities 217–20; obligations of States as members 215–16; structural adjustment programme in India 203

internet: absence of borders 72–3; increase in child abuse images 64

Interpol 64, 66, 67, 75

inter-state complaints: abuse of procedure 141; labour rights 135–54; tax evasion 116–34

Inuit communities 156–7

Iraq 325–37

JADE Act 13, 17–18

Japan Bank for Regional Co-operation 49

Japan – Film case 33

Joint Action and Learning Initiative on National and Global Responsibilities for Health 81

Jordan 344, 348–52

jurisdiction *see also* admissibility: European Court of Human Rights (ECtHR) 173; Inter-American Human Rights Commission 291–5; military interventions case 325–38; notion of in Maastricht Principles 177–8

'justiciability' of economic, social and cultural rights 100

Kenya 190

Koh, Harold 341

Korea – Government Procurement case 37

Korea – Various Measures on Beef case 21

Kyoto Protocol to the United Nations Framework Convention on Climate Change 159, 164, 167, 168, 171

Laban, David 222

labour rights 33–4, 242

labour rights case 135–54; admissibility 142–6; arguments submitted to

Committee 139–41; facts 138–9; views of committee 146–54
land eviction *see* forced evictions
land grabbing 49–60, 187–201; definition 51; gendered impacts of 58–60
land grabbing South America case: admissibility 291–5; analysis of the merits 295–300; conclusions 300; facts 289–90; legal questions on ETOs 285–9; processing before the Commission 291–5; recommendation 300–1; summary 290–1
land laws, Uganda 195–7
land titles 52, 56, 57, 59–60
legal capacity, children and CRPD 179
life, right to 165, 169, 170, 171; extraterritorial obligations 211–15; general principle of international law 209–11; Indian farmers and 202–20
Limberg Principles for the Implementation of the International Covenant on Economic, Social and Cultural Rights 199
local remedies test 243–5

Maastricht Guidelines on Violations of Economic, Social and Cultural Rights 199
Maastricht Principles on the Extraterritorial Obligations of States in the area of Economic, Social and Cultural Rights 5, 9, 51, 53, 82, 85, 90, 91, 92, 93, 94, 95, 126, 127, 132, 137, 145, 152, 173, 174, 177–8, 184, 185, 186–7, 198–201, 213, 219, 251, 253, 260, 263–4, 275, 276, 285, 288, 293, 294; Article 31 122; Principle 9 108–9; Principle 24 112; Principle 32 113; Principle 37 114; tripartite typology framework 90
Maputo Protocol to the African Union's Charter on Human and People's Rights 52, 53, 58–9, 60
market access benefits 33–4
maximum of available resources 86–8, 126–7, 132, 183; Zambian government and 139–40, 147–50
Military and Paramilitary Activities case (ICJ) 108
Military Commissions Act (US) 342

military foreign occupation 145
military interventions case 325–38; application of principles 337–8; development of case law 329–32; interpretation of extraterritorial jurisdiction 333–7; scope of Convention 332–3; summary of case law 328–9
Monterrey Conference Financing for Development 175
Multilateral Investment Guarantee Agency (MIGA) 50
multinational corporations 188, 199–201; direct human rights obligations 280; South Africa mining 261–82
multinational corporations (African Charter) case 239–60 *see also* Purak peoples case; admissibility 243–5; Article 1 violation 253–4; findings 260; private acts/public responsibility 251–3; quartet layers of state obligations 249–51; right to equality and work 254–6; right to food 258; right to health 259–60; right to water 256–8; spatial scope of obligations 246–9
multiple attribution of responsibility 96
murder, economic crime and 224–5
Myanmar 13–30

National Defense Authorization Act (US) 350
Neumann Kaffee Gruppe 187–201
Nigeria 190, 249, 251, 253, 259
Nippon Export and Investment Insurance 49
non-attainment complaints 35
non-injured State party 140, 141, 142–3
non-intervention, principle of 274
non-repetition remedy 115
Norms on the Responsibilities of Transnational Corporations and Other Business Enterprises with regard to Human Rights 5
Norwegian Government Commission on Capital Flight from Poor Countries 128, 129, 133
Nowak, Manfred 192

OECD Risk Awareness Tool for Multinational Enterprises in Weak Governance Zones 102

364 Index

Office of the High Commissioner for Human Rights (OHCHR) 155–6
Operation Carousel 65
Optional Protocol on the Sale of Children, Child Prostitution and Child Pornography (OPSC) 65–78
Optional Protocol to the International Covenant on Civil and Political Rights 159
Optional Protocol to the International Covenant on Economic, Social and Cultural Rights (OP–ICESCR) 84, 102, 103, 109, 178–9; article 2 115; Article 10 136, 141, 142, 144; Article 10(1) 119, 121, 125; Purak peoples case 99–115; three complaint procedures 136
Optional Protocol to the Convention on the Rights of Persons with Disabilities (OP CRPD) 177
Optional Protocol to the Convention on the Rights of the Child on a communications procedure (OPIC) 63–78, 178–9
Optional Protocol to the Convention on the Rights of the Child on the involvement of children in armed conflict 181
Optional Protocol to the Convention on the Rights of the Child on the sale of children, child prostitution and child pornography 264
Organization of American States 40–1
Organization for Economic Co-operation and Development (OECD) Guidelines for Multinational Enterprises 197
Outcome Statement of the 2005 World Summit 111

palm oil 36, 45
parallel responsibility 150–1
Paris Declaration on Aid Effectiveness 176, 185
Poverty Eradication Action Plan 194
precautionary principle 170
Proclamation of Tehran 212
promote, duty to 269
protect, duty to 268–9, 272, 297–8
protected values, importance of 22–3
Protocol on Rights of Women in Africa *see* Maputo Protocol

public apology remedy 115
public interest, bank secrecy laws and 129–30
public morals exception 13, 15; meaning of 'public morals' 19–20
Purak peoples case: admissibility (jurisdiction) 105–9; background and facts 102–4; complaint 104–5; consideration of merits 109–14; remedy 114–15; state party's observations on admissibility and merits 105

recipient country ownership 172–3, 176, 184–5
remedy, basic right 114–15
Renewable Energy Directive 35, 36, 43, 45
respect, duty to 268, 271–2, 297
retrogressive measures 174, 182–5
right to health case 83–98; accountability and remedy 97; core obligations 90–1; direct interference 90; extraterritorial obligations 89–90; factual summary 83; indirect interference 91–2; international enabling environment 93; legislative measures including co-operation agreements 88–9; maximum of available resources 86–8; minimum essential levels of economic, social and cultural rights 86; non-discrimination 91; obligation to fulfil 93; principles and priorities in co-operation 94; recommendations 97–8; states as members of international organizations 95–7; transnational obligations of bank members 94
right to property 130
Rights Group International on behalf of Endorois Welfare Council v Kenya 268
Rome Statute of the International Criminal Court 221–2; cross-cutting issues 233–6; definition of crimes against humanity 227–8
Ruggie Guiding Principles 138

Sainath, P. 205
Saldano v Argentina 106
Salomon, Margot 81

Index 365

San Salvador Protocol *see* Additional Protocol to the American Convention on Human Rights in the Area of Economic, Social and Cultural Rights
Schabas, William 230
Scheinin, Martin 101
self-determination, right to 167, 168–9, 170, 171
Serbia 353–4
Shell 190, 251, 253
situation complaint 32
social and environmental sustainability, IFC performance standard 56–7
soft law instruments: General Comment 14 on the right to health 80; Independent Accountability Mechanisms (IAMs) 49
South Africa 190, 261–82; Bill of Rights territorially limited 265; Constitutional Court 266
sovereign immunity 348–52; Canada law on 344
standard of living 31; right to adequate 113
standard of 'necessity' 20–2
standards of environmental protection 33–4
State-owned Assets Supervision and Administration Commission (SASAC) 146
State Peace and Development Council' (SPDC) (Myanmar) 13
state responsibility 43, 160, 166, 167, 173, 262–3, 352–7, 296–7; distribution of responsibility 300; United Kingdom 224, 232–3
state sovereignty 246, 274; bank secrecy laws and 128–9; overriding principle of 124; principle of non-intervention 140–1, 153
structural adjustment programme: Greece 302–24; India 202–20
subsidies 33, 35, 39
Sudan 259
suicide, not violation of right to life 217
Suriname case 110
Switzerland: bank secrecy laws 123, 128–31; human rights impact assessment 133; international co-operation 125, 127
Syria 344, 348–52
systemic integration 313–15

tax evasion 116–34; scale of 117
tax havens: definition 118; remedy for monies lost over time 133; unequal impact of 119
Thailand 13–30
The Gender Implications of Large-Scale Land Deals 51
The Social and Economic Rights Action Centre and the Centre for Economic and Social Rights v Nigeria (SERAC case) 249, 251, 253, 257, 258, 268, 269, 278, 279–80
Tilburg Guiding Principles on the World Bank, IMF and Human Rights 5, 95
torture, Maher Arar 343–4, 345–57
Torture Victim Protection Act 344
trade liberalization 43, 47, 218
trades unions 139, 150
trans-boundary harm, principle of 126
Treaty on the Functioning of the European Union (TFEU) 316
tripartite obligations of states 111–14

Uganda: delays in justice system 198; forced evictions *see* forced evictions case
Uganda Participatory Poverty Assessment Process (UPPAP) 193–4
United Nations: Commission on Human Rights 191; Committee on Economic, Social and Cultural Rights (UNCESCR) 189; Committee on the Elimination of Racial Discrimination (CERD) 110–11; Declaration on the Rights of Indigenous Peoples 101; Declaration on the Right to Development 89, 212; Economic and Social Council 203, 206; Environment Program (UNEP) 163; Framework Convention on Climate Change (UNFCCC) 158, 163–4, 165, 167, 168, 171; human rights record of Myanmar 29; Millennium Declaration 89
United Nations Charter 42, 80, 110, 141, 143, 153, 203, 207, 305, 314; Article 55 298; Article 56 84, 89, 298; Article 103 215–16
United Nations Guiding Principles on Business and Human Rights: Implementating the United Nations

366 *Index*

"Protect, Respect and Remedy"
Framework 274, 275
United Nations Human Rights
Committee (HRC) 192; General
Comment 31 106, 112, 114, 144
United States 13–30, 40, 41, 156–7;
Burmese Freedom and Democracy
Act (BFDA) 14; JADE Act 13, 17–18;
non-resident foreign nationals under
Constitution 342
United States Overseas Private
Investment Corporation 49
United States Supreme Court
341–57
Universal Declaration of Human Rights
(UDHR) 40, 143; Article 28 212;
effective remedy right 282; no
jurisdictional limitation 262
unjustifiable discrimination 27–8

Value-Added Taxes 119
Velasquez case 112
Vienna Convention on the Law of
Treaties (VCLT) 39, 40, 160, 166,
291, 308, 309, 314
Vienna Declaration and Programme of
Action 213

war on terror 326, 342, 343, 347, 355
water, right to 256–8
weak governance zone 102
websites: abuse images on 67–8;
remedy for dissemination and
distribution 77–8
women, rights to ownership and access
to land 52, 56–7, 58–9
work, right to in Switzerland 125 *see also*
labour rights
World Bank 83; Compliance Advisor
Ombudsman (CAO) 49–60; human
rights obligations 207–9; Inspection

Panel 49; loan conditionalities
217–20; maco-level goals 208–9;
obligations of States as members
215–16; structural adjustment
programme in India 202–20
World Court of Human Rights
(hypothetical) 191–2; draft statute
192; three models for 191–2
World Health Organisation (WHO) 163
World Trade Organization: disciplines
33; Dispute Settlement Body 13–30;
dispute settlement mechanism
219; non-violation remedy 31, 37, 47;
nullification and impairment of
benefits remedy 35

Zaire 259
Zambia, labour rights: arguments
submitted to CESCR 139–40;
jurisdiction of 144–5; obligations
under Covenant 147–50
Zambia-Switzerland case 116–34;
admissibility 121–2, 125; facts 120–1;
holdings and recommendations
132–4; merits 122–3, 126–31;
respondent state party's observations
123–5
Zimbabwe forced evictions case
261–82; duty to fulfil 269; duty to
promote 269; duty to protect 268–9;
duty to respect 268; extraterritorial
rights obligations 270–5; facts 264–6;
legal issues 267–75; merits 267;
obligations imposed by African
Charter 268–9; recommendations
282; right to food 279–80; right to
freely dispose of wealth 277–8; right
to housing 278–9; right to property
275–7; right to remedy 280–2
*Zimbabwe Human Rights NGO Forum v
Zimbabwe* 281

CPSIA information can be obtained
at www.ICGtesting.com
Printed in the USA
JSHW021512211219
3107JS00008B/46